ML

C F A VOYSEY

WENDY HITCHMOUGH

C F A VOYSEY

Opposite: 'The Huntsman' design for
machine-woven textile, c.1919.
This page: portrait of Voysey by Harold
Speed, 1896.

CONTENTS

Design for wallpaper or textile, 1918.

At the turn of the last century C. F. A. Voysey was the most influential designer in Britain, with a reputation that spread across Europe and as far afield as the United States of America. He is important to today's designers and architectural historians because he can be seen as a vital link between the Arts and Crafts and Modern movements. To his contemporaries his significance lay in the fact that he took up the complex critical philosophies of John Ruskin and A. W. N. Pugin and translated them into simple and practical statements in his writings and his work. He resolved the Victorian dilemma of reconciling craftsmanship and mass-production, he extended the architect's influence to the design of every element in the make-up of a house, and he invented a housing type which was fashionable, founded on tradition, and at the same time at the cutting edge of progressive architectural design.

Voysey was brought up in an extraordinary family to believe that ideological certainties surpassed all other considerations. He probably learnt the teachings of Ruskin and Pugin at his father's knee and once he had decided to become an architect the qualities which were to distinguish every aspect of his work and make him an innovator amongst his contemporaries: his clarity of vision; his refined sense of simplicity; the insistence on harmony and balance in his work and an uncompromising scrutiny of every detail, could all be described as consciously developed family traits.

Though I set out to write a survey of Voysey's life and work and to consider his architecture in detail, Voysey was also a complex designer of all things domestic. He explored the same ideals and motifs in his domestic objects, decorative designs and furniture as in his architecture, without any hierarchical distinctions between media. This versatility was difficult to convey within the structure of the book, so here the decorative and furniture designs have been separated out, and comparisons made between similar buildings without a catalogue of furniture and fabrics obscuring the picture. To keep the text to a workable length some excellent buildings and unexecuted designs by Voysey have had to be omitted, and his decorative designs, his furniture and metalwork have been given less attention than they deserve. A book that covered every aspect of Voysey's career would be so large that it would need wheels to transport it.

INTRODUCTION

The entrance front of Holly Mount, near Beaconsfield, Buckinghamshire, 1905.

The events of Voysey's childhood and the formative influence of his father had a profound and seemingly irreversible effect on his character, and on the shape of his adult architectural philosophy. In 1927 *The Architect and Building News* said of Voysey: 'His sense of the matter is that he owes everything to his father; that all his beliefs and convictions are part and parcel of the fabric of his father's thought and teaching';[1] later, John Betjeman wrote, 'What his father preached to thousands in London, Mr Voysey has interpreted in stone and colour.'[2] To understand the life and work of C. F. A. Voysey, therefore, it is first of all necessary to know about his upbringing, his father and the circumstances of the Healaugh trials.

Charles Francis Annesley Voysey was born on 28 May 1857, at Kingston College in Hessle, Yorkshire, to Charles Voysey a young curate, responsible for running the local school and Frances Maria, the daughter of a banker.[3] Voysey's early childhood was disrupted by the frequent moves that his father made with his clerical career – to Jamaica, Great Yarmouth, London and finally to Healaugh in Yorkshire. Shortly after the family had settled, when Voysey was twelve years old, his father became the subject of a national controversy, culminating in his expulsion from the Church of England and the family's removal to London.

The Reverend Charles Voysey was an extraordinary, outspoken man with a strong religious vocation and a resolute faith in his own vision. His attributes were celebrated as hereditary characteristics by the Voysey family: his great-great-grandmother, Susanna Wesley, was the sister of the religious reformer, John Wesley, who had founded the Methodist Church in England. The names Annesley and Charles were passed down through the family from John Wesley's brother Charles, and his mother, Susanna Annesley, who was the great-granddaughter of Viscount Valentia, first Earl of Anglesea.

Reverend Charles Voysey was born in London in 1828, the son of an architect, Annesley Voysey, and educated at Stockwell Grammar School and St Edmund Hall, Oxford. When he graduated in 1851, he was ordained and appointed to the Curacy of Hessle, and the following year, at the age of twenty-three, he married his cousin Frances Maria

FOUNDATIONS: CHILDHOOD
AND FORMATIVE INFLUENCES

Edlin. C. F. A. Voysey was the third of ten children and the eldest son.[4] His elder sisters, Frances and Mary, were both born at Hessle in 1853 and 1855, and Voysey was later to describe these sisters as having a 'salutary and humbling effect upon their brother'.[5]

In 1859, the family moved to Craigton, Jamaica, where Charles Voysey became incumbent of St Andrew's Church. His father, Annesley Voysey, had designed the parish church of Port Antonio, Jamaica, nearly twenty years earlier and died there after a sudden illness at the age of forty-six while overseeing its construction. But whatever personal motivation there might have been for the family's expedition, after eighteen months, when C. F. A. Voysey was only three years old, they returned to England and Charles Voysey became Curate of Great Yarmouth, before being transferred to St Mark's Church, Whitechapel.

Soon after his arrival in London, Charles Voysey demonstrated the family trait for religious reform; in one of his sermons he denied the doctrine of eternal punishment, causing such offence among the congregation that he was dismissed from St Mark's. However, Charles Voysey was by no means isolated in his challenge to the testaments of the Church of England, nor was he chastened by his dismissal. His questioning of the infallibility of the Church's doctrines reflected a growing concern in Victorian England that a reconciliation between scientific discovery, social reform and the position of the Church of England would have to be resolved.

Charles Voysey's controversial beliefs were championed by the Bishop of London, who appointed him to the Curacy of North Woolwich, where he was visited by the Vicar of Healaugh who invited him to become his curate. In 1864, he was promoted to Vicar of Healaugh and within months of his promotion, and presumably with the support of his predecessor, he published the sermon 'Is every statement in the Bible about our Heavenly Father strictly true?' This was swiftly followed by his most famous and reputedly his most blasphemous work 'The Sling and the Stone', which was first published in monthly instalments, and then in a ten volume collection.

In 'The Sling and the Stone' Charles Voysey challenged the very foundations of the Church of England. He denied the divinity of Christ and the miracles recounted in the Bible on rational grounds, and he preached of a loving Father, in direct communion with his subjects through their innate ideas: 'This sense of God's presence, and this entire confidence in it, is … the supreme ideal in religion. It is of course, pure faith, originated in the heart of man by God, independent of books, churches, priests, and is the only real revelation possible by God to man.'[6] Voysey's preaching accommodated the scientific and philosophical developments of the age, but coming in the wake of Darwin's *Origin of Species*, at a time when the Church could countenance no dissent from within its ranks, it exacerbated a division between the ultra-orthodox party of the Anglican Church and the more progressive elements, and it became the focus of a national controversy.

In 1869, Charles Voysey was charged with heresy and ordered to appear before the Chancellor's Court of the Diocese of York, where he was tried and found guilty. He appealed to the Privy Council, conducting his own defence both in the ecclesiastical court and in the public arena: his trial notes were published in London in 1869 and according to a contemporary, Voysey, 'for some days virtually edited the London papers, and turned *The Times* into a rationalist tract'.[7] *The Times* obligingly announced that, 'A fund is being raised for the purpose of enabling the Rev. C. Voysey, vicar of Healaugh, to defend himself',[8] and the Dean of Westminster was listed as one of the most eminent subscribers.

Voysey's trial became, 'a cause célèbre of its day … It was the old fight, staged in mediaeval form, of religion versus dogma; and, as usual, dogma ceremoniously claimed the victory and religion won the entire field and more than it ever sought or fought for.'[9] On 11 February 1871 the Privy Council confirmed the ruling of the Chancellor's Court, finding Voysey guilty of maintaining doctrines 'contrary and repugnant' to the Church of England, and it was ordered that he should be deprived of his living, and that costs should be awarded against him unless he retracted his heretical preaching within a week. Voysey's response was a written re-affirmation of his beliefs, published in *The Times*, and on 20 April 1871 the notice of his deprivation was pinned to the door of St John's Church, Healaugh, and the Voysey family was moved to London.

2

3

2 *The Rectory, Healaugh, Yorkshire, built in the 1860s for the Voysey family.*

3 *The Norman church of St John the Baptist, Healaugh.*

The effect of these prolonged and dramatic proceedings on C. F. A. Voysey's childhood are worth evaluating in detail because they had such a profound, and in some respects disastrous, effect on his adult character and behaviour. Voysey watched his father take on the full force of the Church of England, and although he lost his case, he won the support of some of the nation's most respected figures – Darwin, Ruskin, Huxley, Stanley, Hines and Tyndal were listed amongst his personal friends[10] – and he went on to found, in the Wesley tradition, a new church in London, 'perfectly independent of every other religious communion'.[11] Charles Voysey became the founder of the Theistic Church, and for forty years he was regarded as a pioneering preacher whose sermons were published and widely distributed every week.

Much later, in the early 1900s, C. F. A. Voysey challenged the architectural establishment by resolutely defending the Gothic tradition in the face of a sweeping classical revival. He supported it on spiritual, national, rational, and artistic grounds by propounding its merits in letters, in lectures, in his book *Individuality* and in his buildings, which became more overtly Gothic as the fashion for the Classical Revival took hold than they had ever been before. But Voysey's moral defence did not lead to influential friendships (he had these already) or to the establishment of a new and independent movement; it led instead to the terminal decline of his practice.

There are no references to Voysey's boyhood in Yorkshire in any of his interviews or published writings. His own early history is always overshadowed by accounts of his father's moral fortitude in the Healaugh trials, but in his very brief autobiographical notes he recalled that he had been thrown very much into his father's company, partly because of the difference in ages between himself and his younger brothers, and partly because it wasn't considered proper for a minister's son to play with the other children of the village.[12] Whatever lessons he had been given, he wrote, had been taught by his father and he often accompanied him on visits to his parishioners, or helped him in the garden. It is perhaps not surprising that Voysey's description of his childhood years was succinct. However, he was painfully exacting in his description of the line of descent from John Wesley, 'From which family he gratefully acknowledges

what little moral courage and independent spirit he happily inherits. This independence has crushed out the love of limelight and thirst for worldly gain or social advancement. Pioneer work & poverty are more attractive to his nature.'[13] Poverty was never attractive to Voysey, although he suffered it with stoicism in later life, and the pious formality of some of his writing only partially disguised a vulnerable sensitivity.

It would be wrong to imagine the Healaugh years as entirely bleak for the young Voysey. He was six years old when the family moved there and almost, if not quite, fourteen when they returned to London. It was a remote and beautiful parish in the heart of Yorkshire, midway between the industrial centre of Leeds and the historic town of York. At first, the advantages of a more settled life in the country and the prospect of a secure ecclesiastical position for Charles Voysey must have established a period of optimism and stability in the life of the family. However, the Reverend must also have undergone some disappointment at the remoteness of the parish from the centre of progressive ecclesiastical thinking, and some sense of social isolation.

Healaugh was a small farming community of around two hundred and thirty inhabitants, of whom all but a handful had lived and worked in Yorkshire for all their lives. They were mostly tenant farmers, farm labourers and estate workers, who farmed the land that their parents and grandparents had worked before them. The single village street, which has hardly altered in the last hundred and thirty or so years, reflects the structure of the Victorian community: at its top on a hill, set back from the road, is the fine Norman church of St John the Baptist and towards its base is the seventeenth-century manor house, Healaugh Old Hall, which was the home of Reverend Edward Brooksbank, Charles Voysey's predecessor and effective lord of the manor. Next to the Old Hall, at the top of a village street made up of picturesque red brick cottages, stands a substantial rectory building, constructed by the Reverend Brooksbank for the Voysey family. The rectory is one of the largest buildings in the village, second only to the Old Hall and Healaugh Hill Farm, and it was strategically positioned next door to the village school and opposite the post office – the only two gathering points for gossip apart from the church.

4

5

4 *Portrait of Reverend Voysey, drawn and etched by Voysey in 1884.*

5 *Voysey as a small child on his father's knee.*

6

The church day school, which had less than thirty pupils, was run by William and Lydia Stead, and although it was next door to the rectory, Voysey was educated at home. His father's individual tuition would certainly have helped establish the singular quality of Voysey's moral fibre and philosophy, but it must have done so at the expense of friendships and affinities with boys of his own age in the village, none of whom would have been considered suitable friends in terms of their social background. One senses too, that Voysey was perhaps always a little old fashioned in his mannerisms, a little too earnest and precise, as a child brought up too much in the company of adults can sometimes be.

Voysey's position within the family would have strengthened his relationship with his father. He was one of ten children with two elder sisters and four younger ones separating him from his three younger brothers. His elder sisters, Frances and Mary, were ten and eight when the family moved to Healaugh, and his four younger sisters, Margaret, Emily, Alice and Cicely, were five, three, two and a baby of less than a year old, respec-

tively.[14] The younger brothers, Arthur, Herbert, and Ellison, were all born at Healaugh: Arthur on the family's first New Years Eve there, and Herbert and Ellison at two year intervals thereafter; the age difference between them and C. F. A. was too great for them to have been playmates, and as the eldest boy he turned to his father for company.

The young Voysey would have spent a good deal of time at the church of St John's, over which Reverend Voysey presided, and it is tempting to see this simple stone church as an early architectural influence. It is a fine Norman church with a square tower and an impressive south doorway, elaborately carved with kneeling figures and with tiny beasts half hidden in intertwining foliage. The oak doors are grey and weathered with age, and the priest's door has wrought-iron strap-hinges similar to the type that Voysey was to adopt. Inside St John's, a narrow window set into an arched niche is stone dressed, in what was to become the Voysey style. In his own buildings, Voysey also sometimes half concealed a carved caricature of himself or his patron in a fireplace or a sundial, perhaps recalling the carvings and beak-heads at St John's. However, potential influences as early as this can only be ascribed with the greatest caution. Voysey's regard for simplicity and craftsmanship, and for an inherently British architectural tradition might have originated, in part, from St John's, but by this same strain of logic he could as easily have adopted the picturesque qualities of the red brick village cottages, in much the same way as M. H. Baillie Scott (1865–1945) was to do, and these do not appear to have impinged on his embryonic architectural consciousness at all.

Only one building from Voysey's early years is known to have influenced his architectural career and this was a house facing the west front of Salisbury Cathedral, described by Voysey as 'The King's House Close'. His grandfather, Annesley Voysey had been born there, and C. F. A. Voysey retained a photograph of it with a handwritten inscription on the back listing the monarchs from Richard III onwards who had lived in, or visited, the house, and ending, 'The fine proportions and sturdy treatment of the architecture of this house deserve study. In this house Annesley Voysey, the father of the Reverend Charles Voysey, was born and lived with his immediate family.'[15]

6 *The King's House Close, Salisbury,*
Wiltshire. Photograph from Voysey's
collection.

12   CHAPTER I

No boyhood drawings or sketch-books have survived to present the historian with irrefutable evidence that other buildings or details were observed and absorbed by the young Voysey; and to frustrate matters still further, he decided as a young architect that sketching was a form of theft, 'What you can remember is your own, what you sketch you steal.'[16] He did occasionally make sketches of buildings, but advised the designer to take inspiration directly from nature.[17] His reverence for nature, together with his analytical observation of its details must have begun during the Healaugh years in the fields, which stretched as far as the eye could see all around the village.

Voysey was twelve years old when his father was first tried for heresy, and even though the trials and controversy appear to have been the consequence of a calculated and sustained provocation on the part of Reverend Voysey, they must have created a considerable amount of stress and uncertainty in the Voysey household. Coming from an intellectual middle-class family whose origins were firmly rooted in the south of England (both Charles and Frances Voysey were born in London), C. F. A. Voysey would have grown up in Yorkshire with the concept that he was different from other children. The Healaugh trials, however, made him into a martyr's son.

The reaction of the people of Healaugh to the case against their vicar is not recorded, and we do not know whether Charles Voysey had the support of his congregation in his battle against the Church of England, or whether he was ostracized by the local community. Popular opinion may well have swung dramatically during the trials, and to a large extent it would have been carried by Charles Voysey's predecessor, the Reverend Edward Brooksbank. Brooksbank was a magistrate, a Yorkshireman, and the major landowner and employer in the area, responsible for rebuilding a substantial part of the village as well as restoring the Norman church. Most of the people in the village depended on him for their livelihood. Though in the first instance he may have supported Voysey, there is a story that much later when C. F. A. Voysey fell ill during a trip to Windermere, at the height of his architectural career, he sent for a doctor and Brooksbank's son in local practice there arrived at his bedside; on realizing the relationship between Dr Brooksbank and his father, Voysey is reputed to have shouted, 'Then do you know your father turned my father out of his living, and now you come to doctor me. *I won't have you!*'[18]

Whichever of its vicars the village supported, C. F. A. Voysey must have been isolated by the trials. Their emotional repercussions were to remain with him all his life. He saw his father's philosophy challenged and criticized in the national press – the Reverend was condemned for his crude and extravagant expressions in *The Times* – at a critical time in his adolescence; as an adult, Voysey still remembered the humiliation of the family being turned out of their lodgings by a landlady when they first moved to London because the case had caused so great a sensation.[19] By the time he went to school in London he had become a resolute and stubborn child and there is a story that while he was at Dulwich he hurt himself badly during a game of fives, 'I think he even fractured his hand – he did not stop but played on, pale and determined.'[20]

Much of the intractability of C. F. A. Voysey's adult character and his obstinate refusal to revise a principle, even in the face of substantial personal loss, must be attributed to the Healaugh trials. Voysey and his father were to remain close until Reverend Voysey's death in 1912 and the tone and philosophy of Voysey's writings on architecture echoed his father's published sermons. The continuing effect of Reverend Voysey's doctrine and personality on C. F. A. Voysey's work cannot be measured, but the decline of his practice may have been exacerbated by a personal crisis after the death of his father. To some extent the evangelical quality in Voysey's writing and his architectural stance became more entrenched after 1912.

The final outcome of Reverend Voysey's trials was a just one. Although he was expelled from the Church of England, the public support generated by his very public trials was channelled into the foundation of the Theistic Church. A religion based on reason, it addressed many of the controversial issues of the day presenting a doctrine that was compatible with the theory of evolution and the changing assumptions of the Victorian age. Charles Voysey benefited from an educated and affluent congregation, many of whom were men of business and science, who provided him with a spiritual outlet and an income for the rest of his life.

7

7 *Decorative design, undated.*

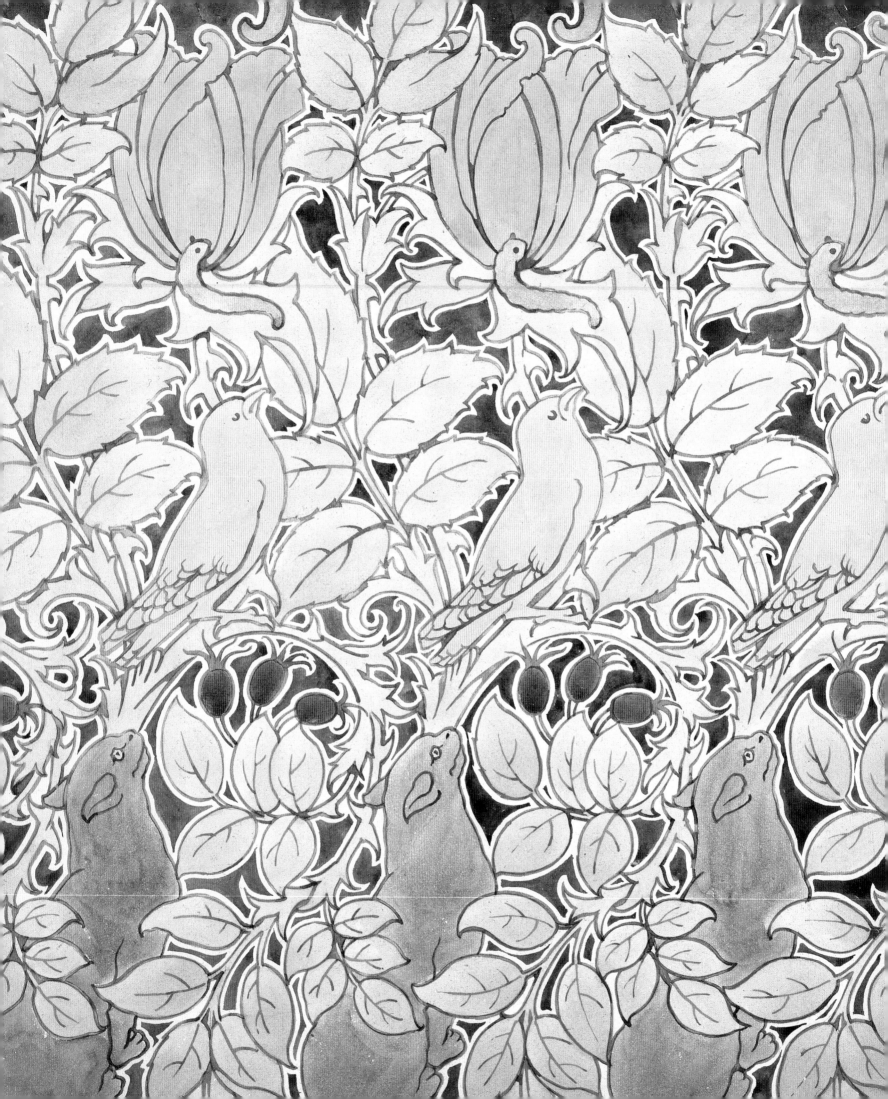

After the expulsion of Reverend Voysey from the Church of England in April 1871 the family moved to Dulwich in London, to a fine Georgian house in College Road.[1] C. F. A. Voysey was sent to Dulwich College, and his father, who had already begun to hold services in London at St George's Hall, Langham Place, before the family's removal from Yorkshire, founded the Theistic Church.

Dulwich College and its surrounding buildings can hardly have failed to have made an impact on the architectural sensibility of the young C. F. A. Voysey. The new school buildings had recently been completed in a florid North Italian style by the younger Charles Barry (1823–1900). They were painted by the French Impressionist Camille Pissarro in the year that Voysey arrived, and cited as amongst Barry's best work when he was awarded the RIBA Gold Medal in 1877.[2] As a qualified architect, C. F. A. Voysey would have found them damnable, and they were criticized in *Building News* for the proportions of their cloisters and the 'fussy erections' set around the roof, 'like bottles in a cruet stand'.[3] However, as an impressionable schoolboy he might well have been seduced by their elaborate blue and buff ter-racotta decorations, by the Venetian-style campanile and the centre block with its triangular gable and great arched window, and by the resplendent wrought-iron entrance gates.

Voysey was already interested in art when he arrived in London. In February 1870, his father had given him a book on the Elgin Marbles, which he kept for the rest of his life.[4] Every morning he would have passed Sir John Soane's Dulwich Picture Gallery, set back from College Road, on the short walk to school; and the Crystal Palace, resited at Sydenham Hill, was only a few minutes walk from the school. Perhaps it was one of these buildings, or a combination of all three, that turned Voysey's attention to architecture, or perhaps, more prosaically, the truth was closer to his own declaration, 'I determined to become an architect because it was the only profession I could take up without passing any examinations'; his grandfather before him had also been an architect.[5]

Though Dulwich College had a strong academic reputation by the early 1870s, Voysey failed to settle there. Throughout his life his spelling and grammar

EDUCATION: DULWICH COLLEGE AND ARCHITECTURAL TRAINING

1 *'Let Us Prey' textile design.*

2

were so erratic that whenever he wrote anything for publication he would send it first to be checked by his younger brother Ellison, before submitting it to an editor. He may have suffered from what would be described today as dyslexia, or the Healaugh years might have taken their toll on his early education. Dulwich College was not held responsible for Voysey's lack of academic success because all three of his brothers were sent there after him, and when they were successful at school, where he had failed, he developed an idea of himself as the dunce of the family.[6]

Voysey left school in July 1873 at the age of sixteen.[7] Whatever the reasons for his departure, he would have benefited from the artistic tuition of the Royal Academician J. L. C. Sparkes, who was Drawing Master at Dulwich during the 1870s. His fellow pupils included the Victorian painters H. H. La Thangue and Stanhope Forbes, who went on to found the 'Newlyn School', but it was unlikely to have been Sparkes who encouraged Voysey to make his career in architecture: in later years he delighted in the recollection that Sparkes had condemned him as 'quite unfit for an artistic

profession'.[8] A private tutor was employed to educate Voysey at home until the following May when, just a few weeks before his seventeenth birthday, he was articled to John Pollard Seddon and his training as an architect began.

Reverend Voysey, as an architect's son with extensive connections through his preaching, would have selected his son's first master with careful consideration. John Ruskin himself was listed as one of Reverend Voysey's supporters during the Healaugh trials; and further family links are suggested by the fact that he had also been a patron and frequent visitor to the school that C. F. A. Voysey's sisters attended. C. F. A. Voysey acknowledged the influence of Ruskin in his later writings, and his own written philosophy reiterated many of Ruskin's aphorisms. His interpretation of Ruskin was simple and direct, almost intuitive, and often in his later writings Ruskinian theories are expressed using the language of Reverend Voysey's religious teaching, suggesting that C. F. A. Voysey had been introduced to Ruskin's work at a relatively early age through his father. If this was the case, then Ruskin's influence would have been assimilated with a certain bias, and his lasting influence on Voysey's own design philosophy must be linked with that of the Reverend Voysey.

The family's connections with architecture, and in particular with the roots of the Gothic Revival went even further back. Throughout his life Voysey was a vehement defender of A. W. N. Pugin (1812–52): 'No living architect of his time could compare with him for intimate knowledge of that (Tudor) style. You may search the Houses of Parliament from top to bottom, and you will not find one superficial yard that is copied from any pre-existing building.'[9] He claimed that when the Government insisted on the Gothic style for the Houses of Parliament, Sir Charles Barry (1795–1860) laid out the plan, 'knowing nothing about Gothic, and caring less, employed Pugin for the work',[10] and, more significantly, that 'Augustus Welby Pugin … showed my grandfather his designs for the Houses of Parliament, in the presence of my father, the Reverend C. Voysey, who is still alive.'[11] This must have been shortly before Annesley Voysey's sudden death in 1839, when C. F. A. Voysey's father was only eleven years old. Annesley Voysey had been an engineer/architect responsible for the design of lighthouses, churches, and credited with the design of the first purpose built office block in London in 1823.[12] He was not a strong exponent of the Gothic, but evidently an admiration for Gothic design, and in particular for Pugin, was passed from Annesley to Reverend Charles Voysey, and Reverend Voysey ensured that it was passed on to his son by selecting one of the most highly regarded Gothic Revivalists of the day, J. P. Seddon, as Voysey's first master. It is hardly surprising, therefore, that C. F. A. Voysey became such a staunch defender of Pugin and the English Gothic tradition; he must have accepted it, together with the pioneering determination of John Wesley, as a hereditary obligation.

J. P. Seddon (1827–1906) specialized in the design and restoration of churches. He had a strong practical as well as theoretical understanding of English Gothic architecture, and, like G. E. Street, he was interested in developing a 'Modern Gothic' capable of adapting ancient Gothic principles to the design of new secular building types. Like Pugin, he had absorbed the essential principles of Gothic and his practice of interpreting Gothic traditions rather than producing copies in a Gothic style was to have a lasting influence on Voysey:

He was, in fact, far the most original of the Gothic revivalists; for though among the strongest in his love for and belief in the revival, he was always a modern rather than a mediaevalist … and in his work almost alone among the early revivalists was it impossible to trace the origin of the detail to any particular mediaeval style or building. In this respect he was certainly before his time. While others were content to produce copies more or less of ancient detail, he went deeper and sought to look behind at the reasons that prompted mediaeval form, and to produce what a mediaeval designer would have done.[13]

In 1867 he had been invited, along with William Burges, Alfred Waterhouse, Sir George Gilbert Scott and others, to submit designs for the controversial law courts competition. It was won by G. E. Street, but when Voysey joined Seddon's practice, in May 1874, work was under way on his most famous building, the University College of Wales in Aberystwyth.

Voysey's pupillage was a happy and productive one. Young architects were trained during the 1870s, as in any other craft, by being articled to an established master for a set period of time paid for by their parents. Voysey was articled for five years from 11 May, when his father paid Seddon two hundred guineas, out of which Seddon agreed to provide his young clerk with 'lodging and necessary and proper food clothing and medical attendance', in addition to his training.[14] He would have learnt first to copy Seddon's drawings by pricking them through and then to detail, to draw and to go on site. In the evenings articled pupils could attend classes at the South Kensington Schools, the Royal Academy or at the Architectural Association, where they could meet other pupils from the big London practices and exchange ideas. The Royal Academy, where E. M. Barry was Professor of Architecture, has no record of Voysey as a student, but he is included on the membership roles for the Architectural Association, from the 1873–4 session onwards, with formal election as a member on 20 December 1878.[15] Seddon was an early member of the Architectural Association, and he may have introduced his young pupil to their lively informal meetings and their occasional visits to buildings of interest.

During his years in training, Voysey began to develop his own drawing style, which was undoubtedly influenced by the clarity of Seddon's style: the strikingly coloured, watercolour washes contained within the strongly defined lines of drawings and the distinctively mannered captions, with each sheet headed with childlike lettering. On a less superficial level, Seddon's architectural philosophy and his quest for simplicity and individuality were to make an indelible impression on his pupil; he lectured to the Architectural Association:

We want neither a new nor a universal style, we should know nothing about styles; the very name is a hindrance to architects, however useful to the antiquary … Let us leave to posterity our productions and be sure that if we work simply, neither copying nor striving for singularity, we cannot so far emancipate ourselves from the feelings of our own age and country but that they will give an impress to our work, though we may not discern it for ourselves.

Seddon was rigorous in his attention to detail and progressive in his extension of Gothic to meet modern requirements. He was friendly with some of the most influential architects of the period, including William Burges and E. W. Godwin, and he had been involved in the founding years of Morris, Marshall, Faulkner & Company. He designed furniture as well as buildings, and he was an accomplished decorative designer. In 1862, an elaborate inlaid desk designed by him was exhibited on the Morris stand at the International Exhibition at South Kensington, and one of his early cabinets, entitled 'King Rene's Honeymoon', was decorated with panels painted by Edward Burne-Jones, Ford Madox Brown and Dante Gabriel Rossetti. Rossetti painted an important reredos for his restoration of Llandaff Cathedral, and Seddon's designs for floor tiles, stained glass, and ecclesiastical embroideries demonstrate a practical application of Arts and Crafts principles.[16]

It may well have been in Seddon's office that Voysey first picked up the rudiments of decorative design and grasped the concept of a broader design discipline, which brought the furniture, fittings, and even the fabrics of a building's interior into the architect's realm. Pugin, too, would have been an important early influence in this respect, and Voysey was aware of his fabrics and wallpapers and of the detailing of the Houses of Parliament down to the design of the doorhandles. The practical and theoretical skills that Voysey learnt during his pupillage can be demonstrated, but Seddon's office might well have been equally influential on a much more direct and emotional level, in a way that cannot be proved by historical documentation. His house and office were frequented by some of the most colourful and influential artists of the day. E. W. Godwin, Dante Gabriel Rossetti, Edward Burne-Jones and William Morris must have made a strong impression on Voysey, not only as practitioners who were shaping a new direction for art and design, but also as passionate and extravagant individuals who set their own rules for life as well as for art. Voysey was to continue to seek out and enjoy the company and friendship of painters, sculptors, illustrators and writers through his friendship with A. H. Mackmurdo, and then through the Art Workers' Guild and the Arts Club. J. M. Barrie and Arthur Rackham became life-long friends, and he could cut the figure of a dandy. However, when in later life he recalled the influential figures of the day it was almost exclusively a list of architects.

As an elderly man, Voysey said that it was William Burges, E. W. Godwin, A. H. Mackmurdo and G. F. Bodley who took up the principle that, 'All that was necessary for daily life could be, and ought to be, made beautiful' and that these men 'regarded nothing in or outside a home as too small to deserve their careful consideration.' Why did he not include William Morris and Philip Webb? Indeed, this statement is more telling in its omissions than as a piece of historical documentation. It says nothing of the sense of vitality and excitement that Voysey must surely have felt on finding himself, before he was even twenty, in the company of an artistic élite. What is even more surprising is that it pointedly gives Morris and Webb no part in an impetus in which history has accorded them two of the principal roles. Later in the same speech, Voysey described Morris's position rather derisively as 'working for crafts as handmaids to architecture'.[17]

Voysey's pupillage with Seddon coincided with the opening of Morris's London showroom in 1877. He once confessed to having been so overwhelmed with admiration for Morris's work on visiting the shop that he vowed never to go there again, 'lest his own designs should degenerate into copies of Morris!'[18] There are clear affinities between the design, although not the political ideologies and practice of Voysey and Morris; Voysey recognized that without the pioneering work of Morris and Godwin, and the retail marketing of Morris's own shop and that of Liberty, the market for his wallpaper, fabric and furniture designs would not have existed. He told *The Builder's Journal & Architectural Record* in September 1896: 'It is he [Morris] who prepared the public mind and educated it, and who has done for me what I might not have been able to do for myself, made it possible for me to live.' Voysey had copies of Morris's books in his library: *Art and the Beauty of the Earth*, and an 1894 lecture delivered to the Birmingham School of Art, which were both printed by the Chiswick Press in 1898.[19] However, he later famously declined John Betjeman's offer of the loan of some of Morris's other books, inferring that he disapproved of his politics.

Perhaps in later life Voysey was irritated by the insistent attempts of historians and critics to compare his work and influence with that of Morris, or

3 *William Morris, 'The Trellis' textile design, 1863.*

perhaps more simply he disliked Morris as a man and most of what he stood for. He once told Nikolaus Pevsner that he disliked Morris's atheism, and he criticized his lack of spatial feeling: 'Only in the flat, he said to me, could Morris work at ease.'[20]

Voysey's exclusion of Philip Webb (1831–1915) from the list of influences on his own work and on the course of architecture in general is more difficult to interpret because it was absolute. Webb's profound sense of architectural integrity, his philosophy of rooting the building in its landscape, and his rigorous attention to detail cannot have escaped Voysey's attention and nor can it have failed to influence him. He would have known Webb and his work through the Architectural Association meetings, he might well have visited Webb's buildings with some of his contemporaries, and he must surely have listened to Lethaby's enthusiastic accounts of Webb's work.[21] W. R. Lethaby (1857–1931) was Voysey's exact contemporary and one of Webb's closest followers.[22] Webb's principle that the design of a building should be a direct response to the vernacular building techniques and materials of its locality, and in consequence his deliberate avoidance of an individual and clearly recognizable architectural style were diametrically opposed to Voysey's mature architectural practice. However, Voysey would have learnt a great deal from Webb's considered, rational interpretation of the vernacular, and his refusal to acknowledge Webb's importance may have been the result of a self-conscious denial of an influence that was, if anything, too pervasive for Voysey's refined sense of individuality.

Richard Norman Shaw (1831–1912) by comparison was a less complex master to follow. Voysey described him as a 'leading rebel'.[23] Shaw's ability to reinvent an old English architecture out of a random collection of architectural elements: the tile hanging of a Sussex farm house; the towering chimneys and mullioned windows of a Tudor mansion; and the half-timbered bays corbelled out at first-floor level of a medieval street, all reassembled in a modern country house, evidently impressed the young Voysey. He would have known 'Leyswood' in Sussex, designed by Shaw in 1866 and some of his own early design experiments attempted to draw together a similar concoction of old English ingredients, with less aesthetic results.

Shaw's influence as an urban architect was at its height during the period of Voysey's training. Bedford Park was being built in the late 1870s and early 1880s and the freshness and decorative eloquence of Shaw's houses, tavern and church there, together with the enlightened ideology of a 'garden village', were artistically and intellectually experimental while at the same time being extremely fashionable. In his mature work, Voysey achieved the same extraordinary balance between serious intentions and fashionable desirability, and his urban buildings owe a debt to Shaw. However, it is interesting that when, in 1891, he designed an artist's house in Bedford Park, he rejected the red brick, Queen Anne type championed by Shaw, and others, and built a white tower house instead.

In 1884 Shaw encouraged five of his pupils to found the Art Workers' Guild, in order to unite the arts of architecture, painting, sculpture and craftsmanship. It was an organization of which Voysey was to become one of the first members. By this time he was a young designer in independent practice, and he was able to bring practical experience as well as idealism to the Guild, not least because during his training, 'Seddon entrusted him alone with paint-pots in a Church'[24] to paint life-size figures of angels, and later Voysey was given the design for a large mosaic mural at Aberystwyth University College.[25] This mural design is important, not for its artistic merit, but as the earliest expression of Voysey's disregard for authority, his wry sense of humour, and of a still sharp indignation at the religious dogma that had persecuted his father. It represented, through studied symbolism, 'Science tearing down Sacredotalism' and Voysey is reported as having recalled the episode with mischievous relish in later years:

I observed that this early exploit is a happy memory for the designer, not because it was his first executed design of the kind, but because two years after it was put up it was hurriedly pulled down by indignant authority which then for the first time discerned the true meaning of the symbolism employed in it … it's triumph for him is that it published to those who had eyes to see a denunciation of an opprobrious dogma the University espoused, and the glee with which Voysey recalls this exploit ignores the discomfiture of the learned dons on finding the decoration they had bought and paid for had been grimacing at them behind their backs for two years.[26]

4

4 *William Morris, 'Strawberry Thief' design, 1883.*

Voysey, according to this writer, paid dogma, 'the unusual respect of being enraged by it, instead of laughing at it as he does at most other stupid things'.

Voysey remained in Seddon's office for an additional year as an assistant after the completion of his pupillage, before going to a similar post in the office of Saxon Snell. But whatever might have drawn Voysey to Snell's office, and the two men would have known one another through the Architectural Association, the attraction was short-lived. Snell (1830–1904) specialized in hospital and workhouse building, and Voysey's meticulous attention to ventilation is often credited to his time with Snell. Clearly the experience gave him a good grounding in hospital design because one of his first designs in independent practice was for a sanatorium at Teignmouth in Devon (unexecuted), but after a matter of months Voysey was offered a position in the office of George Devey, and he left Snell to learn the finer points of country house design.

George Devey (1820–1886) was one of the first Victorian architects to combine a successful commercial practice with a detailed exploration of English vernacular architecture. He specialized in the design of substantial country houses for the aristocracy and the wealthy landed gentry, and his prestigious client list included Princess Louise and the Duke of Argyll (he was once summoned to Osborne to discuss his drawings with Queen Victoria, but she was 'a little indisposed' on the day),[27] several members of the Rothschild family, the Duke and Duchess of Sutherland, and Lord Spencer. While his country houses were designed in a variety of styles to accommodate the preferences of his clients, often contrived to give the impression of several centuries of additions, his estate cottages, stables, and lodges always adhered to the vernacular. Devey was one of the first architects to make a detailed study of vernacular cottages, barns, and lodge buildings in the 1840s.

Devey was a member of Reverend Voysey's congregation, and C. F. A. Voysey's position as 'an improver' was undoubtedly procured, albeit passively perhaps, through his father. On his death, in 1886, Devey left £2,000 each to the Reverend Voysey and to the Trustees of the Theistic Church, and Reverend Voysey wrote of his unfailing generosity towards the church, 'Two or three times

when funds were well nigh exhausted, he would send his £100 at once to relieve the anxieties of the Hon. Treasurer; and I must add that but for his personal bounty to myself, and the yearly supply to me of alms-money for cases of necessity, I should often have been sorely embarrassed and utterly unable to relieve the poor who came to me ...'[28]

Devey was 'an able and accomplished architect, and a chivalrous high-minded gentleman'.[29] His manner and professional success made him an ideal master for the completion of C. F. A. Voysey's architectural training, and he must have set an example for the young Voysey in character as well as in his practice: 'his extremely sensitive and kindly nature … and his old-fashioned courtesy exercised a kind of fascination over all whom it was his lot to meet, either in business or society',[30] and he was considerate towards clients and workmen alike. James Williams's description of his character and professional principles, given in a lecture to the AA in 1909, might almost in part have been a description of Voysey himself:

Quiet, modest, somewhat reserved at first, at times vivacious, alert, full of humour, of deep feeling and genuine sympathy, considerate, thoughtful, kind and generous, showing great indignation against all injustice, and the warmest approval of everything noble and good. With large and expressive eyes, he saw very much more than most people, and he had the keenest pleasure in using them.[31]

The period in Devey's office gave Voysey invaluable practical experience in designing and supervising construction with increasing independence. Although the office was considerably quieter in the 1880s than during its heyday a decade earlier (a decline directly related to the effect of the agricultural depression, which began in 1879 on country estates), Voysey became familiar with many of the great country estates and with the manner in which their owners should be treated – an experience which was to stand him in good stead in his own practice. In later life Voysey described Devey as the most extensive practitioner of a dying picturesque, claiming that 'there was no man alive at that time with a bigger domestic practice'. He joked about Devey's facility for captivating clients rather than following his designs through to working drawings:

When asked by his client to join a house-party, he would make the most fascinating, catch-penny sketches while dressing for dinner and present them during dessert, charming everyone, but getting them worked out by clerks who had to make all detail on the traditional lines of a bastard Jacobean period.[32]

As Devey preferred to illustrate the details of a design through models, rather than by having presentation drawings made for his clients, this anecdote was probably recounted for its capacity to amuse rather than as a more sceptical observation. Nevertheless, the details of a bastard Jacobean period were adeptly integrated into Voysey's own early style; his first designs in independent practice bear more than a passing resemblance, in drawing as well as architectural style, to the Devey office drawings. His knowledge of simple local building traditions, of rustic cottages and half-timbered gables would have been informed by Devey, and if there were fewer country houses to be designed as a result of the agricultural depression, then this was to work in Voysey's favour: he was given far more freedom in the design of smaller estate buildings – all in the vernacular – than an improver could have hoped for in more imposing buildings, and the ability to plan efficiently and economically on the domestic scale necessitated by these smaller buildings established the basis for Voysey's later practice.

In one of Voysey's early independent designs, for 'a house with an octagonal hall', published in *The British Architect* in 1889, he demonstrated the extent of his early dependence on Devey's style; Dutch gables, diapered brickwork, half-timbering and a steeply pitched tile roof – broken by tall chimneys, dormer windows, and even a cupola – all made specific references to Devey's work; although Voysey's interest in incorporating octagonal elements into a plan must stem from his time in Seddon's office.[33] Devey was credited with first introducing the Dutch gable to English country house architecture, at Betteshanger in 1856, but by the 1880s the pages of *The Architect* and of *Building News* were full of comparable designs and the 'House with an octagonal hall' complies with a very general vogue for 'Olde English' rusticity.

Voysey's lasting affection for white roughcast might have owed at least a little to Devey's designs for cottages at Penshurst in Kent.[34] Devey had started work at Penshurst almost at the outset of

5

6

21   C F A VOYSEY

5 *Fulham pottery capital,*
   undated watercolour, drawn by
   Voysey and signed by J. P. Seddon.

6 *George Devey, contract drawing*
   for Penshurst, 1850.

his career, on restorations to the castle for Lord De L'Isle in about 1850, and over the years he had added new cottages and lodges to the estate, some of which were so convincingly vernacular that they were photographed as old buildings.[35] His contract drawing for cottages at Penshurst of 1850 must certainly be considered as a potential influence on Voysey, with its first floor jettied out and roughcast exterior, and a note insisting that, 'The Workmanship etc. of this Front in no aspect different from any other part.'

Devey regularly took his pupils with him on site visits and perhaps he took Voysey to Penshurst. Another of his pupils recalled:

The journeys with Mr Devey were always delightful. Often when the day's work was over we would saunter round an old town or village, finding features, examining old buildings, making sketches, or hunting up old furniture shops. He had a keen sense of humour, and the sparkling sallies of wit, cheery banter, and quiet sarcasm always turned business into pleasure.[36]

Trips such as this, and weekend scrambles with colleagues to the rural depths of Surrey, Sussex and Kent were common practice among the young Arts and Crafts architects, and although the evidence for Voysey's scrambles is sparse (there is a sketch by him of an old house in Tenterden, Kent of 1884), there is no reason to suppose that he did not make any.[37]

Devey had plans and elevations made for his lodges and estate cottages, but the details of construction were left to a local builder who could be relied upon for his practical understanding of local building techniques. At Penshurst:

The greater part of the work was done by an interesting and independent old character – an excellent type of the yeoman farmer and builder combined, who used to talk to his Lordship and Mr. Devey just as he talked to his men. He was well versed in the old methods, and did good work.[38]

Elsewhere he used the builder George Myers, who had worked for Pugin, preferring to deal regularly with one set of men who knew his ways.

Voysey was to follow Devey in this traditional relationship between architect and craftsman or builder up to a point, entrusting the business of construction to a good builder, although,

with the exception of Muntzer, he did not favour any particular building firm, preferring to use a local firm for each house. Voysey's drawings and specifications demonstrate that he was exacting in his attention to detail, insisting upon a disciplined and rational structure for all his work. However, he does not appear to have been interested in construction as a craft in its own right in the way that Webb and Lethaby were: Webb would have discussed local building techniques and materials with his builder, and then made drawings to rationalize and revitalize these vernacular traditions; Lethaby used unreinforced concrete in the roofs of his chapel at Melsetter, Orkney (1898) and at All Saints' Church, Brockhampton, Herefordshire (1901–2), but his experimental use of materials and his practical involvement in the process of construction was founded on a desire to reconcile tradition and innovation, and for both men design and construction were inextricably linked.

For Voysey, design and structure were interdependent, but the manner in which the structure was constructed was less critical. He was one of the first architects to use steel beams in a domestic context, concealing the steels within oak casing in a manner that broke irrevocably with tradition and craftsmanship, and it seems probable that in his discussions with builders he was as likely to consider building technology, as craftsmanship. Voysey utilized tradition. He did not share the profound respect for historic buildings or the nostalgia for a bygone age that many of his contemporaries felt, and it is significant that, as far as we know, he played no part in the Society for the Protection of Ancient Buildings founded by Morris and Webb in 1877. The difference between Voysey's attitude to construction and that of Lethaby can be summarized, to some extent, by a comparison between the sheer volume of drawings made for two projects. There are 225 surviving sheets of drawings for W. R. Lethaby's Avon Tyrrell (1891–3), while there are less than thirty surviving sheets for the design of Voysey's Broadleys (1898). The comparison is flawed by the fact that Voysey selected a few key drawings to be retained for each house, and the remainder have been lost: there are only a dozen sheets of drawings for Broadleys in the RIBA and V&A collections, whereas the specification was to be read in conjunction with twenty-three contract drawings.[39] Even allowing for losses, however, Voysey clearly left a great deal more to the builder's discretion than Lethaby did. Having said this, twenty-three contract drawings would have been seen as a very detailed visual specification at the time. Any reliance on the separate expertise of the builder did not imply sloppiness on the part of either Voysey or Devey:

He [Devey] would never hurry over inspections and instructions to foremen, and many were the hairbeadth escapes in catching the last train, and there were times when clerks of works and foremen wished that he had not been so devoted to his work.[40]

On discovering poor construction work, which was excused on the grounds that it could not be seen, Devey is reported to have blasted a foreman: 'What, not seen? I should be ashamed for the birds to see it';[41] the same importance of craftsmanship in every detail became seminal to Voysey's work.

Voysey might also have been impressed by his master's informal style of dress: Devey chose to wear home spuns and coloured shirts to work rather than the black dress-coat of the business-man. Later on in life Voysey was to design his own clothes.

There are no records to tell us exactly which projects Voysey was engaged upon during his two years with Devey. Around 1876, before Voysey's arrival at the office, Devey had made a number of drawings for buildings for Lord Spencer's estate in Northamptonshire, including designs for five different types of house to be made available with 'Plots of various sizes' and 'Houses built to suit requirements'. These drawings can be cited as an early influence on Voysey, both for the variety of architectural styles that they presented for smaller houses, and as a rudimentary example of the speculative development of a tract of land within a major estate.[42] The houses were never executed, but in 1880, around the time that Voysey joined the office, Devey was commissioned to design additions to the mansion house at Brampton Ash for Lord Spencer and to make drawings for new barns and sheds on the estate. The mansion house was not extended, but there are plans and an elevation for a simple barn in a different hand to that of the mansion drawings, and the date of 4 May 1880, the

SPENCER ESTATE NORTHAMPTON.

Plots of various sizes.

Houses built to suit requirements.

Plans and full particulars of Mess[rs] Becke and Green, Solicitors, Northampton. M[r] J.N.Beasley, Chapel Brampton, and Northampton. M[r] George Devey, Architect, 123. Bond Street. London. W.

7

handwriting, and the tentative drawing style may suggest that this barn was one of Voysey's first designs under Devey.[43]

In 1881, Devey purchased some land adjoining the Spencer estate and gave Voysey the job of designing a pair of small cottages for the plot and of overseeing their construction. It was his first autonomous job of any consequence. He made the working drawings, ordered the materials, and lived on site where he carried out the duties of a project architect. The building was by direct labour, to be hired by Voysey, and he was responsible for, 'not only the manner of construction, but the organization of the works and the keeping of accounts'.[44] All that was required of him by the Devey office was that he send in a weekly time-sheet, and the only design stipulation was that the two cottages should not exceed a budget of five hundred pounds for the pair.

The Northamptonshire cottages have never been located, but the experience of their design and construction gave Voysey the confidence to take an office in Queen Anne's Gate, Westminster, and set up his own practice.

7 George Devey, five designs for housing on the Spencer Estate, Northampton, c.1876.

There is some confusion over the exact date and circumstances of the setting up of Voysey's first practice: the series of anonymous biographical articles in *The Architect and Building News,* based on interviews with Voysey, initially gives the address for his first practice as Broadway Chambers, Westminster, and his age as twenty-six; then dates the practice from 1884, 'he being then – to be exact – in his twenty-fifth year'; and finally, links the early practice to Voysey's marriage. In fact, Voysey was twenty-six turning twenty-seven in 1884, and twenty-eight when he married Mary Maria Evans on 30 July 1885; his first practice was not at Broadway Chambers, but at 8 Queen Anne's Gate. In spite of the caution that must be attached to relying on journalism for a historical chronology, *The Architect and Building News* article still creates an evocative picture of the establishment of Voysey's practice:

When Voysey in 1884 set up in practice on his own account, he being then – to be exact – in his twenty-fifth year, he did so in the blind faith that has justified many others in taking that step, bolstered by one small commission. This was for a little house. It was never built, because the builder's estimate was too high, or, possibly, because the architect's was too low. At any rate, the proposal fell to the ground, and I have to exhibit a young architect, newly married, with no work nor any prospect of work to come, who, according to his own accounts, had no definite architectural ideas to market, no sense of any individual point of view or of anything within him which clamoured, or even reached out, to express itself.[1]

Voysey was twenty-four when he set up in practice at 8 Queen Anne's Gate, near Seddon's home and office at 1 Queen Anne's Gate. The practice was established by the autumn of 1881, but on 25 March 1882 it moved around the corner to Broadway Chambers in Westminster.[2] A proof for a change of address card was 'Olde English' in style, with a Medieval herald gesturing towards the announcement that:

Unto alle and sondrie. Know ye hereby yt ye Architect Master C F A Voysey heretofore of Queen Anne's Gate hath now removed unto ye more commodious premises situate at ye Broadway Chambers Westminster. Where from henceforth all ye craft of ye master architect will be exercised.[3]

AN INDEPENDENT PRACTICE, IMAGINARY CLIENTS & WALLPAPER DESIGNS

1   *Textile design, c.1888.*

2   *Voysey designed graphics, as well as wallpapers, for Essex & Co. throughout his career. This trademark was published in* Dekorative Kunst, *1897.*

It was not unusual in the 1880s for a young architect to establish a practice on the strength of one commission. Richard Norman Shaw launched his former pupils with a good job to get them started as a matter of course, and Voysey's own record of work, written in chronological order in a small black book, suggests that even while he was articled to J. P. Seddon he was taking on some independent commissions.[4] There were two entries in the 'black book' for 1881, the year that Voysey established his practice. The first was for the Northamptonshire cottages, 'Built cottages at Northampton and made drawings', for Devey, and the second, very probably representing Voysey's first abortive commission, was for Octavius Deacon Esquire, 'Plans, details and specification for new house at Epping Forest.'

Voysey might have looked to his father for useful contacts when his first commission fell through. The romantic story of Devey's introduction to aristocratic clients through a connection of his father's is well known,[5] but here *The Architect and Building News* article was emphatic:

One active step only did he take to establish himself in practice and I mention it because, so far as my knowledge or imagination can inform me, no other architect in the history of the world has even [sic] taken that particular step: he intervened to restrain his father from writing to family friends and well-wishers in the interests of his newly-constituted architect son. This is exactly the kind of tangential action his friends are never surprised at in Voysey; but there was nothing Quixotic in the step he took: he had his usual logical reason for what he did informed by a deeper wisdom than directs the conduct of most young men, or of old ones either, for that matter. Voysey's sense of the position would be that it is the Almighty who rules, and not Man, and that it was his part, as an architect, to take his chance, perform to the best of his ability what he was called on to do, and abide by the good or bad fortune which came to him. That would be his wisdom; his logic would show him that a client chooses his architect because he likes the man and his work, and has confidence in his taste and discretion, and that being so, he will be likely to accept the advice given him and be satisfied with the results; but if he has his architect thrust upon him, or employs him to favour a friend or as an act of patronage, he will be likely to challenge his opinion on all points, and view the finished work only as a store-house of regrets.[6]

This was not entirely true and it smacks of Voysey cant. Either the anonymous journalist was heavily under the influence of Voysey mythology when he wrote the article, or more probably, large chunks of copy were taken verbatim from the mouth of a sixty-nine-year-old Voysey with a highly selective memory. The client for Voysey's first house, the Cottage at Bishop's Itchington, was certainly known to his father, and although Voysey, even at twenty-four, was undoubtedly a man of the highest moral fibre, he was surely not quite as formidable a character, then, as the picture that has been handed down to us would suggest.

Voysey's training had focused on domestic architecture, and so it is all the more surprising that, between 1882 and 1884, with staunch determination and no small measure of ambition he entered a competition for the Admiralty Offices in Whitehall. According to John Brandon-Jones the effort of preparing a complete set of competition drawings for such a large and complex building exhausted him. He took a holiday in the country to stay with a friend who was a master at a preparatory school for boys, and there he met his future wife, Mary Maria Evans, who was on the school staff. His submission for the Admiralty Offices was unplaced and no record of it has survived. However, undeterred and drawing on his experience in the Snell office, Voysey designed a sanatorium for the South Devon Sanatorium Company in Teignmouth. Plans, details, and a specification for the building and its furnishings and decoration were drawn up, but again the design was never built. It is known to us only through a drawing of the main elevation with which Voysey chose to illustrate his early work for an article in *Dekorative Kunst* in 1897.[7]

The proximity of Voysey's first offices to those of Seddon and the date of his designs for the Aberystwyth mosaic (c.1885) suggest that Seddon may have given him work from time to time – possibly small alterations and survey work – and the black book lists various small projects: a brick and stone summer house and the decoration of a library for L. B. Knight Bruce in Sunbury-on-Thames; alterations to a shop at Notting Hill; and the ventilation of offices for G. W. Digby. There were various surveys and reports on drainage and plumbing, but quite early in his years of independent practice Voysey embarked upon a line of work, almost if not quite completely apart from his

3

architecture, which was to provide him with a financial life-line for the rest of his working life: he began to produce wallpaper and textile designs.

Voysey was to become almost as celebrated for his decorative designs as for his architecture. Henry Van de Velde described his wallpapers in the fashionable magazine *Emulation*, and his designs were illustrated regularly in *The Studio*. However, the two lines of work – architecture and decorative design – remained quite separate throughout Voysey's career. He seldom used patterned wall papers or fabrics in the buildings that he designed and he was quoted in an interview in *The Studio* as having advised, rather pointedly:

If you have really beautiful furniture, and only fine pictures, and such pieces of bric-a-brac as are entitled to be called works of art, then he counsels exquisite reticence in internal decoration. But if you must needs use unlovely ornate furniture, and fabrics with patterns, then he would have you unafraid to welcome pattern everywhere; so that in its very abundance you may escape the contours of badly shaped furniture sharply defined against a plain wall, or some one dominant pattern thrusting itself on you without any rivals to modify its insistent claim to be noticed.[8]

Voysey pleaded for restraint and simplicity in the overall design of interiors:

We cannot be too simple. A true desire to be simple strengthens our sense of fitness, and tends to the perfecting of proportion and workmanship, and a more reverent regard for the natural qualities of material … We are too apt to furnish our rooms as if we regarded our wallpapers, furniture and fabrics as far more attractive than our friends.[9]

But he stated, 'When pattern is required for textiles, papers, or what not, the same artist who is unflinching in repressing it when he believes it will be superfluous, revels in the beauty of intricate line and complex colour when the occasion justifies it.'[10]

Voysey is reputed to have been introduced to the advantages of decorative design by his friend Arthur Heygate Mackmurdo. Mackmurdo (1851–1942) was six years older than Voysey and considerably more experienced. After training as an architect in the methodical ecclesiastical practice of James Brooks, he had studied at Oxford where he came to know John Ruskin, 'the most powerful impulse of his life as an artist'.[11]

3 *South Devon Sanatorium,
Teignmouth, unexecuted design.*

4

Mackmurdo followed Ruskin's advice to the letter, studying 'buildings from barns to cathedrals'.[12] He made a systematic study of thirteenth-century cathedrals, first in England, then in France, and finally he travelled to Italy where the Renaissance buildings of Florence struck him as 'nothing less than a revelation'.

After two winters in Florence, spent making sketches and measured drawings, Mackmurdo was obliged to leave by the Italian authorities. He had intervened in the 'restoration' of the Duomo, pointing out to the Minister of Fine Arts of the Italian Government that the washing of its marble surfaces with acids was removing the protective surface of the marble. The restoration was stopped, but the local authorities 'bore a bitter grudge against the interfering stranger within their gates' and Mackmurdo's permits and privileges were peremptorily cancelled.

When Mackmurdo returned to England in 1875 and began a study of Wren's City churches, his concern for the protection of old buildings, and in particular for some of Wren's churches, brought him into contact with William Morris. Mackmurdo's study of the Italian Renaissance:

forcibly brought home to him how vast a difference subsists between the artist of the present and the artist of the past. In former days there was, for all intents, no demarcation between the artist and the craftsman. Most of them were proficient in several arts; whereas, unlike them, the man who in modern times practises one branch of art rarely turns his hand to any other.[13]

Mackmurdo and Morris had travelled separate routes to arrive at very similar destinations, and, like Morris, Mackmurdo wanted to put his theories to the test by setting up a small company which would unify the arts and infuse into them 'a renewed vital energy'. The firm of Morris & Co. was almost twenty years old when Mackmurdo founded the Century Guild, but its ambition, 'to render all branches of art the sphere no longer of the tradesman but of the artist', was essentially the same. In his autobiographical notes Mackmurdo wrote of himself, 'As Architect and Craftsman, Mackmurdo gathered round himself a band of Artists and Craftsmen enabling him to supply all those things that equip a home. These men became the nucleous [sic] of the Century Guild of Artists.'[14] Through the Century Guild, A. H. Mackmurdo and a small number of his designer friends set up workshops for the production of furniture and metalwork, and their designs for wallpapers, textiles and enamel work were executed through a network of specialist manufacturers. Voysey never joined the Century Guild, but Aymer Vallance noted in 1899 that:

There are other artists – Mr Voysey is a case in point – who, not formally members of the Guild, have been in close communication with it for years, and have known the benefit of resorting to it for advice, encouragement, and sympathy in their youthful days of struggle, while yet their success and fame had not been attained.[15]

We do not know exactly how or when Voysey first encountered Mackmurdo, but they were friends in the early 1880s, and after Seddon and Devey, Mackmurdo became one of the strongest influences on Voysey's developing style and design philosophy. The force of Mackmurdo's personality alone would have been influential, and his famously hospitable house at 20 Fitzroy Street must also have given Voysey the chance to meet a wide circle of fashionable artists and art lovers, including E. W. Godwin and James McNeil Whistler. Much later he wrote to Mackmurdo, 'I remember your own house and Thornicroft's. You were a great influence in those days and set me going on wallpaper and fabrics.'[16] Mackmurdo had an extensive collection of early embroideries and textiles, which might have influenced Voysey's decorative style, and his own pattern designs were prophetic in their use of graceful undulating lines and elongated forms.

Through his friendship with Mackmurdo, Voysey became increasingly caught up in what is now defined as the Arts and Crafts movement. Where Voysey had grown up with the teachings of Ruskin, Mackmurdo had been his devoted follower, learning from the master at first hand. Mackmurdo provided another link between Voysey and William Morris, and perhaps both men shared a sense of competition, of pitching their own designs against those of Morris & Co. Voysey's time with Seddon would already have instilled in him a commitment to the practice, as

well as the philosophy of 'unity of the arts', and a sense of belonging within an artistic élite. His membership of the Architectural Association had introduced him to the very different buildings and philosophies of Philip Webb and Richard Norman Shaw, and brought him into contact with a younger generation of architects who were to become his friends and colleagues in the Art Workers' Guild. Mackmurdo, much closer in age than his previous mentors, presented Voysey with a strikingly individual model of an architect, who was also a complex designer of all things, able to design graphics, furniture, lamp brackets and copper repoussé work with equal facility.

Unlike Morris, Mackmurdo designed for limited mass-production and Voysey later described the importance of this breakthrough, 'Mackmurdo's furniture, first exhibited in the Inventions Exhibition, showed how the machine should be recognized by the designer, and led many in his day to revolt from over-decoration and strive for the straight, simple, and plain.'[17] By 1895 Voysey was also designing metalwork and furniture, which could be described as 'straight, simple, and plain', for limited mass-production, but the influence of Mackmurdo's stand at the Liverpool International Exhibition of 1886 extended beyond the example of an artist designing for industry. The slender straight columns of the stand, elongated and capped with simple, square plates and the closely packed, straight balustrades between them were soon to be adopted by Voysey and adapted to his furniture designs, and to the rising newels and straight balustrades that were to characterize his staircases.

Voysey recalled Mackmurdo's importance, too, in founding *The Hobby Horse* magazine in 1884, almost a decade before *The Studio* was launched:

For those days it was beautifully got up and printed on good paper, before Morris came on the scene. The ordinary press was not accustomed to notice artists' work, so 'The Hobby-horse' was only ridden by its sympathetic professional brethren, and consequently short-lived as a publication. But the extent of its influence was impossible to measure.[18]

The Hobby Horse was not only a means of disseminating artistic ideas. It elevated the printed word to an art form:

5

5 *A. H. Mackmurdo, Century Guild Stand, Liverpool International Exhibition, 1886.*

Never before had modern printing been treated as a serious art, whose province was to embrace the whole process, from the selection and spacing of the type and the position of the printed matter on the page, to the embellishment of the book with appropriate initials and other decorative ornaments.[19]

Mackmurdo claimed that he took a number of *The Hobby Horse* to show William Morris and that, 'Morris was so filled with enthusiasm with what Mackmurdo was able to do that with the help of Emery Walker he started the Kelmscott Press.'[20] Allowances must be made, here, for Mackmurdo's exaggerated sense of his own importance. Earlier in the same notes he wrote:

At this time I became acquainted with William Morris and was frequently at his house. I kept off social questions as much as possible as I soon discovered William Morris had received no discipline in Science or Philosophy, and therefore had not been able to construct any plan for a new Social Structure. His Socialism had no philosophic basis.

The importance of *The Hobby Horse*, however, cannot be exaggerated. Contributors included Oscar Wilde, John Ruskin, Christina Rossetti, and William and May Morris, and although in later life Voysey could not remember the names of the contributors, he remembered the cover. The aesthetic distinction of the type-face and paper quality must have inspired and informed his own interest in calligraphy.

According to John Brandon-Jones, Voysey's introduction to pattern design was spontaneous: he visited Mackmurdo one day and found him designing wallpapers for Messrs Jeffrey & Co. When Mackmurdo encouraged him to have a go, explaining the technicalities of drawing up a motif and putting it into repeat, Voysey's natural talent for decorative design was immediately apparent. He sold his first design to Jeffrey & Co. in 1883, 'and the leading manufacturers of the period began to compete for his work'.[21] However, according to a Voysey interview: 'The manufacturers wanted the usual trade designs, Mr. Voysey would not consent to make them, and it took years before his work made its way.'[22] As an elderly man he insisted, perhaps a little petulantly, that 'my work was never popular' and that it was only through the friendship and 'characteristic courage' of Walter Essex of Essex & Co. that he was able to make a living.[23]

The clear, simple outlines and fresh colours of Voysey's early wallpapers were designed in reaction to the sepias and sludgy greens of the 1860s and 1870s, 'Let us do our utmost to raise the colour sense from morbid sickly despondency to bright and hopeful cheeriness, crudity if you will rather than mud and mourning.'[24] His designs were charged with a clarity of vision and a simplicity of form that were to carry through into his building design. They were fresh and original, and, as birds and animals were introduced from the late 1880s, they were touched with the same charm and naivety that had characterized the children's book illustrations of Walter Crane and Kate Greenaway – books that Voysey would have been familiar with. He worked with astonishing speed, normally producing a coloured design for wallpaper, fabric, or carpet in a day, and he seldom made sketches, 'in fact the idea of a sketch irritated him as something half-baked and sloppy'.[25]

In December 1884, Voysey was elected a member of the newly formed Art Workers' Guild. At its fortnightly meetings he was able to draw on the support of established designers like Walter Crane and John D. Sedding, and develop friendships that led to the exchange of information and ideas with fellow architects, artists and craftsmen.

The Art Workers' Guild was 'given its name, its first rules, and its first Members in the "Board Room" of the Charing Cross Hotel' on the evening of 11 March 1883.[26] It was founded in 1884 with Shaw's blessing by five of his pupils – Gerald Horsely, W. R. Lethaby, Ernest Newton, Mervyn Macartney and Edward Prior – in a determined attempt to unite the arts of architecture, painting, sculpture and craftsmanship; it was to become the nucleus of the Arts and Crafts movement in the 1880s and 1890s. Its masters included J. D. Sedding, Walter Crane, William Morris in 1892, C. Harrison Townsend, Edward Prior, Halsey Ricardo, Sir Edwin Lutyens, C. R. Ashbee, W. R. Lethaby and Voysey himself in 1924.

In 1886, Sedding defined the intentions of the Guild in a speech to its members:

The Art Workers' Guild is not a club for cronies. A mere club does not to my mind represent a force that communicates an electric shock to the thick hide of the Art Philistine of the present day ... If you find it, with me, helpful and inspiring ... If you find that it widens the outlook of your art, and brings fresh hope to you, in your lonely labours – if it gives you a sense of partnership in the toils, experiences and successes of your fellow guildsmen – if you feel that the Art Workers Guild has a real mission to fulfil to this Philistine world – you will not only yourselves be swift to help forward this work, but you will bring other trusty men to share the privileges that our fellowship ensures.[27]

Selwyn Image, four years later, was more candid, 'I confess now, as I have always felt, that the main value of our Guild – and it is a value that cannot be over-exaggerated – lies in bringing us all, various indeed in our characters, views and lines of work – into constant friendly intercourse with one another.'[28]

The Art Workers' Guild, and the Arts and Crafts Exhibition Society that developed out of it, pulled Voysey into the very hub of the Arts and Crafts movement. He benefited from the constant and friendly intercourse of the guild, particularly at the outset of his career and in the later fallow years. But he learnt, too, from the detailed and varied papers on which the guild's meetings were focused. When in October 1885, the subject of the meeting was 'Wallpapers and Paper-staining', a 'copiously illustrated' paper was read by Mr Metford Warner, and Voysey joined in the subsequent discussion. He must have spoken well because the following October he was invited to give a paper on pattern designing and wallpapers alongside papers by Lewis F. Day (1845–1910) and J. D. Sedding (1838–91).[29] In the event he was absent from the meeting and his paper had to be read by the Secretary, and although the contents of this paper are now lost, it is interesting to find that within a few years of the sale of his first decorative design Voysey was encouraged to offer his views alongside those of two of the most experienced designers of the day.

Voysey's decorative designs provided his young practice with an essential source of income and, 'kept him on his legs during the first few years'.[30] However, he was intent upon winning commissions and establishing his position as a practising architect. He may have joined the designing clubs of *Building News* or *The Architect,* which published the drawings of young unknown architects with brief critiques, but if he did, then the obligatory use of a nom de plume has concealed any early designs from the historian (and Voysey never owned

6

up to any in later years). Many young architects attracted attention to themselves through these clubs: Sir Edwin Lutyens was only seventeen when he was placed second in the *Building News* Designing Club competition for 'A Villa Residence' in 1886, and *The British Architect* Art Club, organized by Godwin, regularly invited designs for wallpapers, specific pieces of furniture and small buildings, such as a 'Bachelors' Chambers', or 'An Artist's House and Studio'.[31]

Whether or not Voysey submitted drawings to these clubs, the idea of designing for an imaginary client in order to catch a real one was current in the 1880s. In 1884, he became engaged to Mary Maria Evans and they were married on 30 July 1885. Around the time of the wedding he designed a cottage, ostensibly for himself and his bride, hoping to persuade a friend to make a loan of the necessary finances to build it.[32] The cottage was never built, and the couple lived briefly at 7 Blandford Road in Bedford Park before moving to 45 Tierney Road in Streatham Hill, but the design was published in *The Architect* in 1888, and it led to Voysey's first major commission.[33]

Voysey was fortunate that of all his early published designs it was the 'Design for a Cottage' of *c*.1885 that prompted his first commission.[1] Apart from the half-timbering of the first floor, this initial design incorporated many of the features that were to typify his mature style: the roughcast render; buttresses; a projecting first floor; windows arranged in horizontal bands and tucked under sheltering eaves; and the hallmark details of slender gutter brackets and a homely water-butt. The half-timbering, the jettied first floor, and the water-butt recalled George Devey's cottages. However, the buttresses, leading the eye up to simple straight chimneys, and the abrupt change in roof line, to the rear of the main elevation, which gave the barest suggestion of a white tower, were pure Voysey invention.

The plans were less adroit. A long 'picture gallery & lounge' linking the hall with the rest of the ground floor would inevitably have become a corridor, and the tower to the rear, which one might have expected from Voysey's later work to house and express the staircase, was to be used for stores below and a bathroom above. Nevertheless, the principle of providing, 'one or two large rooms – large, that is to say, in proportion to the dimensions of the whole building – instead of a lot of little rooms and narrow, unnecessary passages' was established, and *The Studio* applauded the generosity of the planning and even the provision of the long picture gallery:

Readers of THE STUDIO *will possibly remember a plan and elevation for an artist's cottage … where in a building estimated to cost between £700 and £800 there was a living room 28 ft. by 14 ft. This of course was in place of two so called drawing and dining-rooms, 14 ft. by 14 ft., which the average little villa would offer you; but although there was no other 'reception-room', a passage at the back was widened, and by the addition of a bay window figured as a smoking-room, or picture-gallery, some 20 ft. long, by 9 ft. wide in the bay and 6 ft. at either end. In short, the house was planned for people who prefer the easy, if unconventional menage, to the discomfort of the dull, ortho-dox routine. In place of a stuffy little parlour and an equally stuffy little feeding apartment, you had one spacious room and one handy lounge, avaible [sic] when domestic economy required the other to be given up to 'laying the cloth' or other household duties.*[2]

THE FIRST HOUSES:

BUILDING A REPUTATION

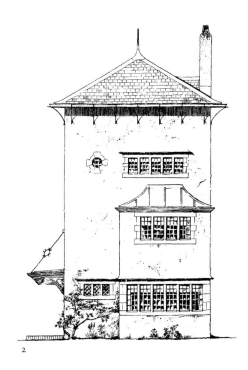

2

1 *Garden front, Walnut Tree Farm, Castlemorton, Worcestershire, 1890.*

2 *Front elevation, 14 South Parade, Bedford Park, Chiswick, London, 1891.*

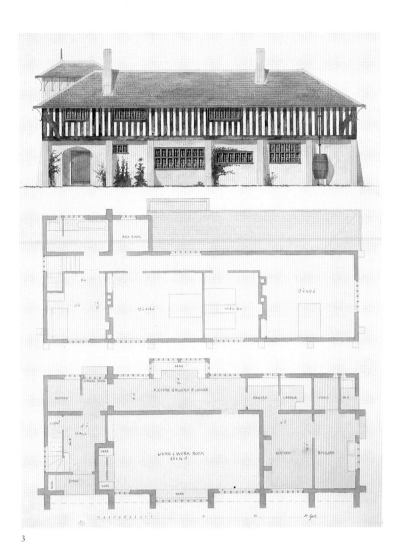

3

4

According to the Voysey legend, when The Cottage design was published in *The Architect* in 1888, it attracted the attention of Voysey's first client, Michael Lakin, and Voysey was invited to adapt his design for a site in Bishop's Itchington, Warwickshire.[3] However, Lakin was already known to the Voysey family. When his uncle, Richard Greaves (from whom he had inherited much of his estate), had bequeathed the sum of a hundred pounds to Reverend Voysey in 1870 with the 'express hope that the days of persecution for religious opinions will speedily close', he had been one of the executors of the will.[4]

THE COTTAGE, at Bishop's Itchington, was not to be Lakin's main residence. He was already established with his wife, three children, and five servants at his uncle's former home – The Cliff, in Coventry Road, Warwick – a fine Regency mansion house set in its own grounds, which Voysey was to butcher with startling insensitivity in 1890. Lakin was a cement manufacturer and The Cottage was more closely affiliated with his works, which later became known as Blue Circle Cement. It was designed for a site close to the cement works, about ten miles from Lakin's home and Voysey's specification of roughcast render for the walls and concrete tiles to cover the roof would almost certainly have been made in close collaboration with his client in a conscious attempt to exploit and develop the potential of cement in the building industry. The building is believed to have been constructed by the cement manufacturers. However, The Cottage was not a simple worker's cottage. Lakin used the house himself, and according to village reminiscences, when carriages bearing guests drew up in front of the house the servants were under strict instructions to keep out of sight – a feat made more difficult by the positioning of the kitchen and scullery adjacent to the living room at the front.

The design for a 'Cottage for M.H. Lakin. Esqre at Bishop's Itchington near Warwick' was published in *The British Architect* on 7 December 1888, within months of Voysey's earlier cottage, and it amplified the main elements of the 1885 design, while softening the starkness of its simplicity. Two elevations were prepared, one with half-timbering (which would have been infilled with concrete) and

3 'Design for a Cottage',
 unexecuted, 1885.

4 The Cottage, Bishop's Itchington,
 Warwickshire, 1888. Early photograph.

34   CHAPTER 4

one without, and Lakin chose the latter. On the ground floor the central bay stood flush with the projecting floor above, so that the original row of isolated buttresses became integrated into a series of shallow projections and recessions that enriched the elevation. Later, Voysey claimed that his buttresses and roughcast surfaces were introduced for the sake of economy:

Voysey used roughcast because he found that clients who came to him wanted inexpensive houses, and because an 11-in. hollow wall 'isn't a wall at all.' A 9-in. brick wall, rough cast, was the cheapest weathertight wall that could be built, and buttresses were introduced to restore to the wall the stiffness which it lacked. That stiffening by buttresses was probably not so much an actual constructive need, in an engineering sense, as an expression of the architect's aesthetic sense of a solid and adequate construction. The wall was reduced in thickness below what was the general practice, and the architect sought to correct the weakness this innovation caused.[5]

But Lakin's cement works must have played their part in impressing upon him the advantages of a roughcast-render finish and ten years later, when he was writing the specification for Broadleys at Windermere, Voysey still specified that all the cement for the works was to be procured from Messrs Graves, Bull and Lakin in Paddington, London.[6]

The front door of the Bishop's Itchington cottage was protected by a porch and moved to a more central position leading directly, if a little abruptly, into the living room, and the 'picture gallery and lounge' was more realistically labelled a hall. It was a hall with no direct access to the front door – Voysey and Lakin must have agreed that a side door would suffice for all practical purposes – and a small sitting room with a deep, square bay was gained in place of the original recessed porch and staircase area. The staircase itself was relocated in the rear corner of the plan, but the small square tower that might once have housed it was abandoned. At first-floor level, Voysey squeezed an extra two bedrooms into the plan, making a total of six, apparently at the expense of the bathroom. Additional windows were required in the front elevation to light these extra bedrooms and the roof line was broken by four shallow, hipped roofs, which sat like pointed hats over the windows below.

The rear elevation was broken into a series of sweeping roofs stepping down almost to the ground. The horizontal emphasis of this succession of roof lines and of the long bands of mullioned windows was to become as integral to Voysey's highly personal style as roughcast render. The roof was technically, as well as visually, innovative because of its use of very early concrete roof tiles, and the roughcast was not painted white, it was left a natural grey colour. It was not only on The Cottage's exterior that the hallmarks of Voysey's style were clearly emerging, but also in its interior details and in the salient features of its plan and elevation. The interior doors were in simple, cottage style – batten and ledge, painted white – with black tee hinges and distinctive (although not yet heart shaped) wrought-iron latches, and on each of the bedroom doors small metal grotesques, each to an individual design, bore the mark of Voysey's hand and humour. The fireplaces were simple and well proportioned, tiled in unglazed terracotta with a simple oak mantel. Even the staircase, although lacking in spatial drama and subtlety, carried the straight, closely packed balusters that were to characterize Voysey's mature work.

All of this would suggest that by 1888 Voysey had embarked upon the long straight path towards an individual architectural style, and that, although the details were to be honed and the vocabulary of form and planning were to be expanded and refined, the fundamental language was in place. Journalists and historians have corroborated in this neat, clearly defined retrospective view, choosing to illustrate the early buildings (and the later ones too) that best demonstrate tendencies towards the mature style. But a less selective study of Voysey's early designs reveals that right up to the end of the 1880s his style was a very fluid thing indeed.

In January 1889, within a month of the publication of The Cottage, *The British Architect* published designs for 'A Country Residence' by Voysey. Its half-timbered gables, diapered brickwork and evocation of old rural cottages owed more than a little to Devey. The following month, in February 1889, the publication of his 'Veranda House' in the same periodical was equally eclectic in composition and uninspired in plan. Voysey offered two alternative

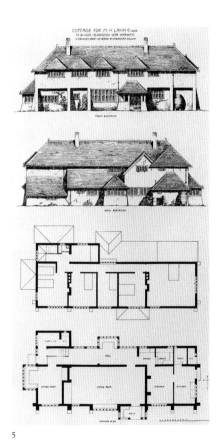

5

5 *The Cottage, Bishop's Itchington, 1888.*

6

7

deeply recessed within a Tudor arch; the steeply pitched, sweeping roof; fenestration arranged in horizontal bands; and an idiosyncratic affection for spiked finials. A few of the designs: The Cottage at Bishop's Itchington; the Tower House; and that of a house in Bedford Park for Mrs Forster, swept aside the trappings of old English vernacular architecture, and with them the pretence, social and architectural, of newly built tumble down cottages. It was these highly original designs that attracted clients and enabled them to be built. As Voysey's reputation and experience grew the old English excrescences fell away.

14 SOUTH PARADE: THE TOWER HOUSE. The modest simplicity of The Cottage at Bishop's Itchington was repeated in a design of the same period for a house to be built at Bedford Park, in Chiswick, London, for Mrs Forster, which was drawn on 19 August 1888. Like The Cottage, it was an inexpensive house for 'people who prefer the easy, if unconventional menage', with a large living room in place of the usual parlour and dining room, and the entire second floor given over to a studio. Five months later a design for 'A Tower House', published in *The British Architect*, took the hipped roof of Mrs Forster's house and pulled it upwards like one end of a piece of elastic. A couple of additional floors were slipped in between the Tudor front door and the half-timbered fourth floor, which remained open in plan as a studio, and the simple, splay-sided bay was lifted to form an oriel window. The oriel window and tall, corner buttresses would have established a three-dimensional relief to the flat simplicity of the 'yellow coloured cement' roughcast, and Voysey clearly intended colour to play an important part in the overall effect: the half-timber work was to have been tarred but the remaining external woodwork was to be 'painted bright blue' beneath a roof of 'green slate'.[10]

The main premise of the Tower House design was ostensibly one of economy, although Voysey fostered a lasting fascination for towers. It was to have cost only £850, and *The British Architect* described it as, 'an example of a very economical design. The building occupies an area of only 35 ft. frontage by 40 ft. depth, and it might be satisfactorily adapted even for a row of terrace houses …'[11] Particular attention was paid to the practicalities of

elevations and it was fortunate for his reputation that the stone version with its massive chimney, Dutch cross gable, and a few castellations thrown in for good measure was never built.

The 'Design for a house with an octagonal hall', published in the same year and still leaning heavily on J. P. Seddon and George Devey, was little better, but not all of Voysey's early designs were entirely speculative.[7] A bungalow in Bellagio appears to have been designed, although never built, for a W. Allport in 1889.[8] Voysey published designs for a drinking-fountain and a dovecot for named clients in the same year.[9] While the dovecot was reassuringly recognizable as a 'Voysey' design, with an incisive clarity of line and restrained use of a few, sharply defined horizontal mouldings to counter the verticality of the piece, the drinking-fountain would certainly be expunged from any selective view of Voysey's early work.

In spite of the uncertainty and eclectic quality of some of Voysey's early designs, there were familiar elements running through the 1880s designs that reappeared consistently and were refined in Voysey's mature style: the wide front door, often

6 *Alternative designs for a 'Veranda House', unexecuted, c.1888–9.*

7 *Design for a dovecot, 1889.*

the plan: 'A lift from the kitchen to the second floor would obviate a good deal of the difficulty and labour involved in a house of several floors … Hot and cold water are laid on to lavatory basins in all bedrooms and bathroom.'[12] The low ceilings that were to become a prerequisite for any Voysey house and the attendant insistence on adequate ventilation, presumably instilled in him by Snell,[13] were also specially mentioned: 'All the rooms are 8 ft. high, and are specially well ventilated.' Voysey believed that high rooms destroyed the effect of horizontality and repose in a room: 'An eight-foot room may be better ventilated and more comfortable to live in than a room twelve or fifteen feet high, and is certainly more easy to light and to warm. It is the modern craze for high rooms (originating in foreign travel) which has led to the destruction of all effects of repose.'[14]

The proportions and half-timbering of the Tower House had a bizarre quality, but the design appears to have revived Mrs Forster's interest in her architect because Voysey drew up a new set of plans and elevations for her house at 14 South Parade, Bedford Park, incorporating the elongated elegance of the Tower House. The wide bands of brick, roughcast and red-tiled roof of the first Forster house drawing (which give the design a distinctly suburban appearance today) were dropped, the half-timbering and oriel window of the Tower House were abandoned, and Voysey designed 'An Artist's House' for Mrs Forster that was extraordinary in its austere simplicity and elegant proportions. He borrowed from the 'Queen Anne' style made so popular by W. Eden Nesfield and Richard Norman Shaw in the provision of a side porch and bull's-eye window; the flat, rendered surfaces accentuating every nuance of form and shadow and of surface decoration are Regency in origin, along with the profiles and shallow pitch of the slate roofs. But the composition – the imposition of a stark white cube, sparsely detailed and emphatically vertical, into an area of refined red brick Queen Anne houses, which were designed with all the decorative variety that Shaw could muster – was overtly individual, if not a little shocking.

The residents of Bedford Park exercised considerable restraint in their public criticism of the house; they noted that the mullions and leaded lights of the windows were 'old fashioned'. The

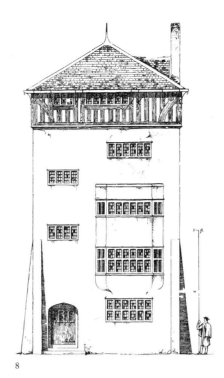

8

plans and elevations were published in *The British Architect* and in *The Builder's Journal & Architectural Record*, and a photograph of the house looking crisp and newly built appeared in *The Studio* in 1897.[15] Equally importantly to the scope of Voysey's reputation, the house was clearly visible to middle-class commuters travelling westwards out of London on the District Line.

The tall elegant arrangement of the Forster House and its adept planning can be likened to Regency houses. By placing the main entrance at the side of the house, opening into a hall and staircase vestibule, Voysey was able to put the parlour at the front of the ground floor, taking advantage of the full width of the house. John Brandon-Jones has pointed out that this aspect of the plan was probably influenced by a comparable layout at 11 Melina Place, St John's Wood, where Voysey moved with his wife, their son Charles, and a general servant in 1891.[16] It was one of a pair of white stuccoed Regency villas with a low pitch slate roof and wide eaves, and this move to St John's Wood may well have preceded the final set of plans for the Forster house.[17] The architect Edward Prior moved

9

8   *Tower House, design, 1889.*
9   *14 South Parade, Bedford Park, 1891. This photograph shows the addition of a new wing, designed by Voysey to extend the house in 1894.*

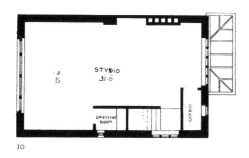

10

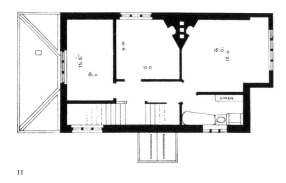

11

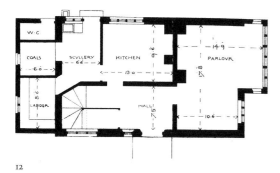

12

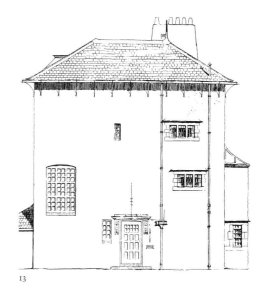

13

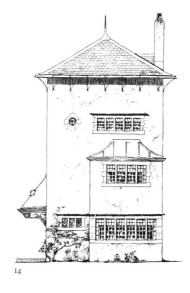

14

into the house next door at about the same time, but Voysey was by no means enamoured with Regency houses in general. When he was commissioned to extend Michael Lakin's Regency mansion in Warwick, in 1890, he stripped away the portico, substituted a window for the central front door, added an immense new wing in a style that was uncompromisingly his own, and replaced the original Regency fireplaces with Tudor.[18]

By locating the parlour on the ground floor of the Forster house, Voysey was able to devote the first floor to bedrooms and the top floor, as before, was left open as a studio. It was a compact plan with the first-floor walls sitting neatly and economically over the walls below; as *The Studio* pointed out, 'If you study the plans of his small houses, you will be amazed to find how liberal is the space compared with the cost of the building.'[19] The contract price was given as £494 10s., 'a price that takes one's breath away, and tempts one to believe that if the site were obtained it would be economic as well as delightful to quit one's present tenancy, and employ Mr. Voysey to design another for one's own needs.'[20] However, Voysey's insistence on simplicity

14 South Parade, Bedford Park.

10 *Second-floor plan.*
11 *First-floor plan.*
12 *Ground-floor plan.*
13 *Side elevation.*
14 *Front elevation.*

38 CHAPTER 4

15

and the absence of all decoration was not so enthusiastically accepted by the builders: 'so much has the architect studied to avoid elaboration that he has found it necessary to prepare 18 sheets of contract drawings so that the contractor may not put in the usual thing – "ovolo mouldings", "stop chamfers", "fillets", and (what without irreverence might be termed) "damnation" generally!'[21] Only the corbels to the original front porch were carved into decorative caricature profiles, and these were lost when Voysey extended the house in 1894.

In the rigorous simplicity of the Forster house, Voysey forged two of the most fundamental principles of his mature practice: 'The two great rules for design are these: 1st, that there should be no features about a building which are not necessary for convenience, construction or propriety; 2nd, that all ornament should consist of the essential construction of the building.'[22] The application of these principles, and the uncompromising consistency with which he administered them, directed him towards his own individual architectural style and philosophy. But the principles themselves were not his own and nor was he the first or the last to

adopt them. They were taken up and carried like a sacred torch from the writings of A. W. N. Pugin half a century earlier.

WALNUT TREE FARM. Between the first drawing for Mrs Forster's house of August 1888 and the completion of the final design by September 1891,[23] Voysey built another house which was to be equally important to the development of his 'reputation for producing effective and characteristic work in a simple, cheap, and unostentatious manner'.[24] Walnut Tree Farm at Castlemorton, in Worcestershire, was designed in the summer of 1890 for R. H. Cazalet and the plans and elevations for the stables and the main house were published in *The British Architect* in September and October of that year.

There was a clear progression from the design of The Cottage at Bishop's Itchington to that of Walnut Tree Farm, however the site and the budget for the house at Castlemorton were far more impressive; the house was designed with a youthful exuberance and an experimental quality that signified a growing sense of assurance in Voysey's work. In this way, Walnut Tree Farm was the testing

16

15 *Perspective of Walnut Tree Farm exhibited at the Royal Academy, 1895.*

16 *Model for Walnut Tree Farm, made by A. Creswick. This is the only model known to have been made for a Voysey house.*

ground for many of the compositional devices that were to preoccupy him in his later houses, and if the elevations were a little gauche, here and there, and the detailing a little crude then this was more than compensated for by their restless energy and innovation. Walnut Tree was a Voysey house in adolescence.

The plan was L shaped, wrapping around two sides of an entrance court with a succession of sweeping roofs cascading down around a simple porch in a manner that Voysey was to refine and perfect before the end of the decade at Broadleys. The gable ends to the service wing and above the porch were half-timbered, recalling Devey to some degree, but responding in equal measure to an existing old cottage on the site that was half-timbered beneath a red tile roof. Voysey used the half-timbering to give a sense of unity to his elevations. He studded the gables above the dormer windows breaking through the roof line on the garden front, and above the polygonal drawing-room bay, which created a sun-trap all day long, but he left one of the gables in the entrance court a plain white. There was balance and restraint, even in his youthful exuberance.

Where the half-timbering evoked a sense of unity through the elevations, Voysey used radical shifts in roof line to give contrast and character to the different aspects of the house. Walnut Tree Farm was not the first Voysey house to explore the aesthetic effect of a sequence of cascading roofs, but there was a sense of adventure, almost a cavalier boldness in the rhythm and sweep of its roofs that made The Cottage at Bishop's Itchington look fastidiously neat. In the short elevation, Voysey drew the disparity in roof line between the entrance and garden fronts into sharp focus. The deliberate asymmetry and considered arrangement of a few component parts in this end wall prefigures (a little awkwardly) some of the most dashing architectural quips of his mature work.

Again Voysey used a roughcast render finish – by now almost endemic to his style – and, as *The Studio* was later to note, buttresses were employed to full effect:

In Mr Voysey's designs for small houses buttresses frequently occur, but these are not used because mediaeval builders employed them, still less are they added to walls already strong enough to impart a 'quaint' or 'picturesque' effect. Mr. Voysey employs these buttresses to save the cost of thicker walls for the lower story of his buildings. That they chance to afford pleasant-looking shelters for a garden seat and break up the wall-surface happily, giving the facade a certain architectural pattern of shadows he realizes, and is, beyond doubt delighted by the picturesque qualities which happen to result from their use.[25]

However, Voysey was not (and the reader was admonished for even thinking it) 'purposely eccentric' in his use of buttresses. Nor was he deliberately straining after unusual effects: 'Mr Voysey would no more dream of adding a superfluous buttress than he would add an unnecessary panel of cheap ornament.'[26]

If Walnut Tree Farm was modelled on anything, then it was planned around the traditional English farmhouse, where The Cottage at Bishop's Itchington might be likened more to a simple estate worker's house. It was emphatically not, and here Voysey differed significantly from Devey and his generation, a substantial country seat, and nor was it a working-farm building designed to be used by estate workers. Voysey's smaller country houses were designed for a new breed of rural land owner, defined and identified by *Country Life* in 1899:

Prolonged town life is becoming more and more intolerable every year, and men of moderate means, who had long yearned for country houses on a small scale, are beginning to realise their desires. Sometimes they are men with families who are content to make the little country house their home, and to keep mere chambers in London for use when business calls them to London, or to some great provincial centre, for the working week. More often, perhaps, they are men who, after taking their families for years to poky and remote and expensive seaside lodgings, have discovered at last that it is cheaper healthier, and infinitely more enjoyable to possess themselves of an accessible house to which they may resort for holiday or semi-holiday purposes.[27]

Country Life brought suitable architects and their designs to the attention of these men who 'cannot all hit upon an old manor house, or find a farmhouse which will bear conversion', championing the designs of Voysey in general, and Walnut Tree Farm in particular as 'an accomplished, artistic, and thoroughly comfortable fact in Worcestershire', which potential clients might wave like a red flag at recalcitrant builders who made offers 'by the score' to build extravagant seats or unsuitable 'cottages'.

The red flag came with an appealing price tag and Voysey was particularly attractive to this new breed of potential clients because he 'eschewed materials which are expensive. But to anything in the nature of shoddy cheapness he is constitutionally opposed.'[28] There is a great temptation to add that Voysey, by his very nature, always stuck fast to his estimates, but in the case of Walnut Tree, for whatever reason, there was a discrepancy, albeit a small one: when the designs were published in *The British Architect* before construction, the cost was estimated to be £1,120 for the house, and £350 for the stable.[29] Nine years later, the building costs were applauded for having amounted to no more than £1,700.[30]

Walnut Tree Farm was to provide a model for the middle-class progressive country house. It was modest in price and character, but its cottage style was sharpened by a distinctly artistic edge. Voysey's flat white walls and deep sheltering roofs, the wide batten and ledged doors and carefully positioned green water butts were calculated to evoke a heritage of English vernacular building and a rural idyll of craftsmen and women gainfully employed in their cottages. And yet neither Walnut Tree Farm nor any other of Voysey's houses could be mistaken for a simple farmhouse as *The Studio* noted in 1897:

It is possible that Walnut Tree Farm, would not at once betray its author; but in the second from another point of view there would be little reason for doubt. But the garden front is entirely typical. The four gables breaking the long tile roof, the buttress to the lower storey, the simple yet novel treatment of the porch, and the placing of the chimney-stacks are entirely characteristic of their author.[31]

By commissioning a house that was easily identifiable as the work of an enlightened progressive, 'in every way suggestive of the clean, luxurious domesticity of an English homestead', patrons of Voysey houses declared their own wholesome regard for simplicity, repose, and fine materials and workmanship and, by extension, their rejection of artifice, shoddiness and superficial display.[32]

From the outset, Voysey's designs were championed by the influential magazines of the day: the drawings for Walnut Tree Farm were published not only in *The British Architect*, but in *The American Architect & Building News* in 1890 and in *The Studio* and *Country Life* magazines.[33] A perspective of the house was exhibited at the Royal Academy Summer Exhibition of 1895, and photographs of it were exhibited by the Arts and Crafts Exhibition Society and in the British section of the St Louis International Exhibition.[34] But this is jumping ahead, before the first volume of *The Studio* was launched in 1893, Voysey was to build three London houses – an artist's studio, in Hammersmith, and a pair of town houses in Hans Road, now facing the west elevation of Harrods – which were to consolidate his early reputation.

STUDIO HOUSE, ST DUNSTAN'S ROAD, Hammersmith, was closely related to a design for 'An Artist's Cottage – To Cost £500' published in *The British Architect* in December 1891.[35] It was built for the artist W. E. F. Britten; and in *The British Architect* design and the design as built, Voysey refined the artistic dwelling down to its minimum and most economic essentials. A large, double-height studio, 45 by 30 feet at the rear of the building with a 'hammered plate glass roof' dominated the plan.[36] Additional lighting was ensured through massive side windows and a glazed door, so that the studio had its own separate entry as well as a separate visual identity to the living quarters at the front of the house. These were very compact indeed, with a large kitchen and a 'living hall' (albeit a cold one because there was no fireplace) with a window seat enjoying the double aspect of the corner window. We must assume that Britten outlined the accommodation that he required, because no architect would impose so puritanical a balance of living to work space upon his client. But *The British Architect* design was praised for its economy and it was argued that the studio 'would make a very desirable living-room': 'Mr Voysey has here designed an artistic little house, and such a one as many who now live in a back street in town or doleful suburb might be both able and willing to buy outright, or in yearly instalments, to take the place of wasteful rent.'[37]

17

17 *Studio House, St Dunstan's Road, Hammersmith, London. Photograph, 1897 or earlier.*

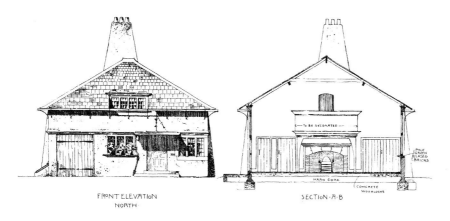

STVDIo·FoR·W·E·F·BRITTEN·ESQVIRE

FRONT·ELEVATIoN
NORTH

SECTIoN·A·B

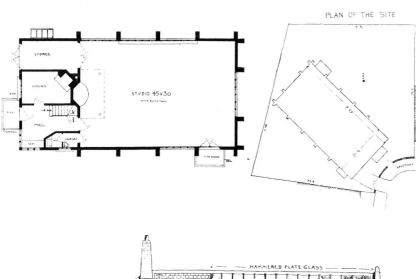

PLAN OF THE SITE

STORES

STVDIo 45×30

HAMMERED PLATE GLASS

WEST·ELEVATION

18

Voysey's address was given in full for the benefit of any potential clients. A large store room with double barn doors connected the front of the house with the studio and Voysey added a note of humour to the front porch: it was supported by two wooden corbels carved with the caricature of his own profile.[38] The wrought-iron stay supporting the porch from above, the stone window dressings and iron casements, and the shallow pitch, slate roof with its wide eaves and slender gutter brackets all link the Studio House with the Forster house in Bedford Park, with which it was almost contemporary. However, where the Forster house was artistic in temperament rather than in practice (the studio windows were too small), Britten's house was rigorously planned as a working studio, fronted by the barest essentials of living accommodation.

Voysey seldom marked his plans with a north point, but the positioning of the Studio House on a corner plot, tucked into the elbow of a conventional Victorian street was designed to maximize light rather than space. It was strikingly positioned at an angle behind a quadrant of elegant wrought and cast-iron railings and the urbane quality of these railings might be likened to Ashbee's work later in the decade at 38–9 Cheyne Walk. Voysey was employed to decorate the interiors of the relatively new number 7 Cheyne Walk, in 1891, for C. Stuart Wortley, MP and he narrowly missed the opportunity to build a complete terrace of houses in Chelsea in the same year. He was invited to design the terrace for Lord Wentworth's estate in Chelsea, just along the Embankment from Cheyne Walk overlooking the Apothecary's Garden in Swan Walk, but the circumstances of the commission were 'a little peculiar':

The vendor of the property, which overlooks the Apothecary's Garden, stipulated with the purchaser that Mr. Voysey should be allowed to design all the visible frontages of the four or five houses to be built on the land. So Mr. Voysey was verbally informed of the probable nature of the plans. In vain he pointed out the folly of designing the elevations before the plans were laid out and determined upon, no other course was left open to him but either to disoblige his patron or forego the work. Of course under such conditions as these it is not surprising to learn that other obstacles were placed in the architect's way, and the idea of using rough-cast, and various other notions Mr. Voysey had in view, had to be given up.[39]

18 *Plans and elevations, Studio House, St Dunstan's Road.*

In the event, the entire commission had to be given up, or else it was withdrawn. However, Voysey's elevation was published in January 1892, as 'a terrace of houses about to be erected' and he was praised for having 'managed to get very pleasantly out of the conventional architectural rut'.[40] Although he was 'thwarted and restricted to the use of red bricks and Portland stone' there were familiar motifs from Voysey's earlier houses, compressed and reorganized into an appropriately urban composition: the stone mullions and leaded lights; the profile of the lead bay roofs; and the emphatic horizontals of string courses above each line of windows were all recognizable Voysey features, but the Dutch gables punctuated by tall, straight chimneys represented a curious departure, suggesting that, when in doubt, Voysey still reflected back to his years with Devey.[41]

19

14 AND 16 HANS ROAD. The designs for 12, 14 and 16 Hans Road in Knightsbridge, London, must have been prepared at the same time as the Swan Walk terrace because a few months later, in March 1892, it was reported – again in *The British Architect* – that, 'some houses which in plan and exterior are an immense change from the usual type of dull terrace houses in London … are being built as Nos 12, 14, and 16, Hans Road, Kensington'.[42] The client was Archibold Grove, a Liberal MP who wanted one of the houses for himself and the remaining two to be built on a speculative basis. Voysey's black book records 'Plotting houses and arranging roads' for a Hans Court for him in 1891, in addition to the design of the three houses, and, two years later, 'Plans for house, and livery stables on N side of Hans Road'.

The elevation for Hans Road was clearly related to the Swan Walk terrace, but it owed at least a little to R. Norman Shaw's 'Swan House' on the Chelsea Embankment of 1876. Voysey's arrangement of three, wide oriel windows at first-floor level and, in particular, the use of high narrow oriels to arrest the composition and the steeply pitched roof, broken by dormers, all suggest that Voysey had considered Swan House in detail. However, these elements were already integrated into Voysey's own individual style: 'The two houses 14 and 16 Hans Road, Chelsea, do not amaze you by sheer novelty as Mr. Britten's studio surprises. Yet as you study

20

CFA VOYSEY

19 *Numbers 14 and 16 Hans Road, Knightsbridge, London, 1892. Detail of porches by T. Raffles Davison, c.1894.*

20 *The landing and nursery rail, 14 and 16 Hans Road.*

their simple but dignified facade, once again you recognise Mr. Voysey's handling as surely as if his name were written legibly across it.'[43]

In the Hans Road houses, Voysey successfully integrated his idiosyncratic handling of composition and detail into an existing terrace. Though, once again, Voysey was obliged to use the red brick of neighbouring buildings, the Ketton stone of the window dressings was continued in a pair of deep square porches raised above pavement level to give the houses an air of distinction and individuality. Initially the panels above the entrances were to have been carved by Conrad Dressler, but when the houses were built these carved panels were located within the porches, and the house numbers were incised within a heart shape over the entrances.

The proximity of a heart to a wide, oak front door, prominently decorated with tee hinges was soon to become a Voysey trademark, but at Hans Road the discreet use of carving (and the specification for the doors) denoted a more generous budget than Voysey had had at his disposal in the past, and, as a consequence, a determination to work with fine artists in accordance with the objectives of the Art Workers' Guild.[44]

The Studio described, 'the exquisite sense of proportion, and the reticent use of even purely architectural features' in the Hans Road elevation;[45] it was both extraordinary and absolutely typical of Voysey that the mouldings used in the exterior stonework were quietly repeated in the mantels and panelling of the interior. The corbels to the main oriels and the cornices above all conformed to standard Voysey patterns, as if there was a game by which you could take the smallest detail in a Voysey house and still find that it fitted perfectly into the grand design: 'It is rare to find personality revealed by simplicity; as a rule it is the flourishes or the eccentricity of the letters which betray handwriting. Here Mr. Voysey has no superfluous stroke, no affected detail, and yet his individuality stands clearly revealed.'[46] The interiors were generously lit and panelled with plain, square deal panelling, painted as Voysey's panelling always was unless it was oak. They were planned economically so that the main structural walls carried through from one floor to the next, and they were arranged around a square staircase vestibule, set to one side as at Melina Place so that the full width of the

house could be enjoyed in the drawing room and the front bedroom. Voysey obviously enjoyed the detailing and dramatic potential of a staircase rising through four floors. A photograph of the landing and staircase in the studio of 1893 was used to illustrate 'that fertility of invention and a curiously individual quality, at once simple and noble', and to highlight one of the details: a decorative panel, which could be fastened above the handrail to prevent small children from falling down the stairwell (the nursery was on the third floor). The panel was decorated with peasant figures: 'These figures in silhouette cut in fairly thick metal, not merely effectually prevent any daring youngster tumbling over a comparatively low baluster, but give a singularly individual touch to the work … this little jest detracts not from the dignity of its surroundings.'[47]

Not all the rooms in Hans Road conformed to Voysey's preference for a ceiling height of eight foot or less, but the insertion of a mezzanine ensured a variety of room heights, and the front rooms, at least, had low ceilings. Voysey was careful to maximize the use of natural light throughout the building. The wide bands of windows flooded the principal interiors with light but the staircase, too, was naturally lit by a lantern and a light well that ran the full height of the building. Even in the basement – the servants' quarters – the walls were lined with white glazed bricks to reflect light (a device that Voysey was to employ again at the Sanderson Factory) and outside the area walls were of pale, green glazed bricks with a stone coping.

Despite the success of the houses Voysey had a row with his client, which resulted in the loss of the commission to build 12 Hans Road. According to John Brandon-Jones, a disagreement over the fees – Grove claimed that Voysey's fees should be adjusted to take account of the fact that the three houses were identical – caused Voysey to sue his client, and 12 Hans Road was designed by Mackmurdo, who tipped his hat to Voysey's design in the adoption of a tall, narrow oriel window and the details of the front door and staircase. It is unlikely that Voysey would have appreciated the more classical number 12.[48] The dispute soured the friendship: one of Voysey's pupils recalled that when he praised a Mackmurdo building to Voysey the latter retorted, 'Oh he's a good architect but he's a very bad and unscrupulous man!'[49]

21

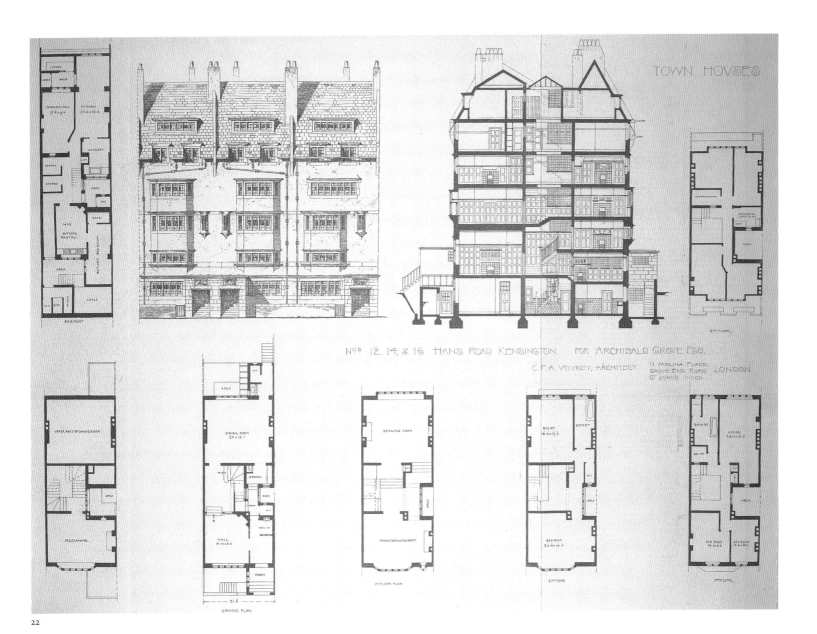

N.ᴼˢ 12. 14, & 16 HANS ROAD KENSINGTON.   FOR ARCHIBALD GROVE ESQ.

C. F. A. VOYSEY, ARCHITECT   11 MELINA PLACE
GROVE END ROAD LONDON
ST JOHNS WOOD.

45   C F A VOYSEY

22 *Plans, section and elevations,
numbers 14 and 16 Hans Road, 1891–2.
The elevation was originally to have
been roughcast with stone dressings.*

2

HANS ROAD

1892

Numbers 14 and 16 Hans Road, Knightsbridge, London, were designed for the Liberal MP Archibold Grove. Voysey adopted the materials – red brick and stone – of the existing terrace, but his own individual style is clearly defined in the detailing of oriel windows, crisp horizontal string-courses and shaped parapets. The building was recognized as exceptional when it was first completed for the quality of its stylish understated decoration.

3

47   C F A VOYSEY

1 *Ketton stone porches, decorated with graphic simplicity.*
2 *Front elevation.*

3 *Perspective by T. Raffles Davison, published in 1893, showing a more symmetrical composition with only two narrow oriels.*

1 Garden elevation and short service
  wing, arranged in an L-shaped plan.

2 Gable end showing change in roof
  line between garden front and
  entrance court.

3 Entrance court.

WALNUT TREE FARM

1890

Walnut Tree Farm,
Castlemoreton, Worcestershire,
was designed for R. H. Cazalet.
It was Voysey's second country
house and it has an exuberant,
experimental diversity,
which in its architectural motifs
and preoccupations hints at
those developed and refined
in his later buildings.

4 *Detail, garden elevation.*
5 *Polygonal 'morning-room'*
   bay and jettied first floor.

Voysey's work and his personality were inextricably linked. His artistic doctrine – his belief in honesty and simplicity and his painstaking attention to detail, insisting that the smallest element should be consistent with the overall intentions of the whole – was founded on his father's teaching. As such it was central to Voysey's sense of his own identity, to the belief in heredity that his family had instilled in him, and to the path which he believed his life, as well as his work should follow. His son wrote of him that, 'He must have known where he wanted to go and to have seen what he wanted to produce very clearly in his mind. He had none of our doubts and torments.'[1] Perhaps Voysey's doubts and torments were carefully concealed beneath a surface veneer of certainty, or maybe they were unleashed when events in his life or the products of his designs slipped out of his control. We shall never really know. However, we do know that between 1893 and 1896 Voysey emerged as an exceptionally versatile and confident young designer, who, by the application of a highly personal artistic doctrine, appeared to hold the answers to a wide range of questions that concerned designers and the design conscious public alike. Voysey was an astute self-publicist. He developed a relationship with *The British Architect* that ensured that his architectural drawings were published with remarkable regularity; the journal's coverage started with his early 'Design for a Cottage', published in 1888, and continued through to his late work. As a consequence he had a growing reputation as an architect amongst the profession, but it was not until *The Studio* magazine was launched in April 1893 that his position as a designer of all things domestic and his clear design philosophy – admitting to no doubts – came to be appreciated by a wider public in England and abroad.

The Studio represented a small revolution in magazine publication. It was beautifully illustrated, making full use of printing innovations to reproduce half-tone photographs of artists' and architects' work, and many issues featured a full colour illustration, protected by tissue paper. *The Studio* set out to bridge the gap between the traditional art journals and the specialist architectural press, and thus between an artistically inclined general public and professional designers working in

HEAD, HAND & HEART

5

2

1 *'The Demon' wallpaper design, 1889.*
2 *'Design for a Clock Case to be made in wood and painted in oil colour', January 1895.*

every field of the arts. Like the Art Workers' Guild it ignored the traditional divisions between art, design and craftsmanship. Its first issues included articles on 'Artistic gardens in Japan', the art of Aubrey Beardsley, the silk workers of Spitalfields by Lasenby Liberty and 'Designing for book-plates'. The writing style was lively and informative, often managing an easy balance between the technical detail required by professionals and the general explanations that a layman would need. It broke with the stuffy parochialism of earlier magazines by being assertively international in its content and in its appeal, covering the major art and trade exhibitions in Europe, and devoting articles to the work of architects, painters and sculptors as far afield as Vienna and America. As a magazine it was immensely important in disseminating artistic ideas internationally, and in bringing the work of the most innovative, as well as the most distinguished artists and designers of the period to the attention of an informed general public.

From the outset *The Studio* championed Voysey. It gave credence and exposure to his design philosophy and to his versatility as a complex designer of everything for the home. It made him famous and it made use of him as an articulate spokesman and an active practitioner of current design issues. Voysey designed the cover for its first issue. It was a symbolic and highly stylized composition, which summarized his own doctrine and that of *The Studio* with equal facility: two figures personifying Use and Beauty chastely hold hands and kiss beneath the boughs of a rose tree. Beauty bears a lily, symbolizing purity, while Use, rather curiously, holds the governor that controls the speed of a steam engine, presumably signifying scientific and technological advance and application. A circle of Voysey birds fly in pairs around the heads of the two figures (leaving insufficient space towards the base of the composition for their legs) and the design is crowned by *The Studio* banner, lettered with Voysey's distinctive calligraphy.

The first issue of *The Studio* gave coverage of Voysey's wallpapers and metalwork. This was followed up in the sixth issue with a leading 'Interview with CFA Voysey, Architect and Designer', which identified Voysey for the first time as a design personality whose work was inseparable from his character, and whose pioneering

3

attitudes and forceful arguments encompassed a complete design philosophy that would strike at the very heart of Victorian affectation and ostentatious vulgarity. *The Studio* interview is fascinating because it gives us the first detailed insight into Voysey as an individual. He was thirty-six when it was published in September 1893 and it is evident from the decisive, no-nonsense tone of his words that his opinions were clearly formulated. They were hardly to change over the remainder of his life and, according to his family, 'He had a lovely sense of humour but with very strong ideas ... whatever he said, this and this and this, I mean there wasn't any argument about it, or discussion, it was quite definite.'[2]

The interview is interesting too, because as a contemporary account of a young(ish) man it was distinctly deferential. Voysey was portrayed as a heroic figure, a modest and reluctant genius, and this set the tone for future appraisals of his life and work. It began with an observation that, 'the personality and opinions of a designer should be at least as interesting as those of a picture painter', bewailing the fact that, if anything, the lives and prejudices of contemporary painters were too well known. Voysey had been approached, it claimed, 'as a typical instance of an artist whose designs are better known than is their author,' and his refined sense of propriety was respectfully noted:

... it was a matter of doubt whether he would permit himself to be interviewed in popular fashion; indeed, his consent was only gained by representing to him that THE STUDIO *was especially anxious to raise the appreciation of design, and to that end the maker of patterns must sacrifice himself for the good of his art.*[3]

Given the frequency of Voysey's submissions to *The British Architect*, it is probable that he was more than willing to sacrifice himself in this way, but he may have had some reservations about the descriptions of his home and family that *The Studio* took as a necessary element in popularizing their subject. Eleven Melina Place was described as, 'the old-fashioned little house in one of the pleasant bye-roads of St. John's Wood ... exactly the right place for the abode of a creator of beautiful patterns'. The studio inside, only marginally more objectively, was, 'obviously not merely a work place but a living place, the reticence of its decoration, its furniture bearing the unmistakable impress of the owners hand' and the interviewer concluded (with a silent fanfare of trumpets), 'that the creed of the artist was the creed he lived'.[4]

This last statement is seminal to an understanding of Voysey, and so it is worth setting in the context of other sources of documentation on Voysey's family life and personality. Voysey drew a clear line between his professional and his private life, and insights into the latter are very rare indeed. The principal women in his life, his mother and his wife, have left only the slightest imprint on available records; and while it is not unusual for Victorian women to take on an almost translucent insubstantiality in historical documents, it does not dampen the historian's frustration. Mary Maria Voysey is described by one member of the family as a force to be reckoned with in her husband's life, and by others as a very sweet and forbearing woman. The early years of her marriage, as Voysey's career was beginning to gather momentum, must have been coloured by the death of their first two children. The first was a boy, still-born in October 1886, and the second, Sibyl Mary, was born in 1888 and died in the same year. Although infant deaths were relatively common at this time, no attempt was made to brush these two tragedies to one side and deny the brief existence of the babies. Many years later Voysey took pains to include them in his autobiographical notes, and they were entered with their two brothers and their sister in the family tree.

Charles Cowles Voysey was born on 24 June 1889. *The Studio* interview described him as 'a rosy-faced, flaxen-haired lad of four, clad in a blue smock', observing that he 'seemed the very spirit of design in its native simplicity'. When the interview was published, Mary Maria was six months pregnant with their third son, Annesley Voysey, who was born on 29 December 1893. They had a second daughter, Priscilla Mary Annesley Voysey, two years later in October 1895. These early years of marriage and managing three small children coincided with Voysey's rapid rise to architectural stardom. Apart from photographs of an immaculately tidy school room and children's bedroom, there are few tell-tale signs of Mary Maria or the three children in the published photographs of The Orchard. In addition to this, although Voysey's

architectural success necessitated frequent absences from home between 1897 and 1906, no letters between him and his wife are known to have survived.

Voysey was a short man with sandy hair, slightly receding even in his thirties, and very blue eyes. He prided himself on his physical resemblance to his ancestor John Wesley, who, 'was of short stature and his countenance fresh-coloured. His eye the brightest and most piercing that can be conceived'[5], and he once sat as a model for a portrait of him.[6] A profile by Harold Speed of 1896 confirms Robert Donat's much later description of Voysey as an elderly man, 'with features greatly distinguished by the cut of his nose and the arch of his brow', and photographs suggest that it was a perceptive depiction of an intelligent man, who presented his most determined expression to the portraitist, perhaps in an attempt to compensate for the gentleness of his eyes and mouth.

Throughout his career, Voysey maintained an austere public image. He made no concessions to the niceties of putting on a good face for the photographer and the fixed, unsmiling expression, staring into the middle distance with scraped back hair of some of the early published photographs would have done little to attract potential clients. The grim determination and down turned mouth of the later ones could hardly have failed to intimidate them. A profile of Voysey in *The Builder's Journal* of 1896 shows an idealistic young man whose smile might at any moment have got the better of him; in private photographs he was relaxed and at times almost dashing, but this private face known to his friends and colleagues, was seldom revealed to the general public. After Voysey's death Robert Donat, who had married his niece, described him in an affectionate radio broadcast, and although it is a description of an elderly Voysey, it gives an invaluable insight into aspects of Voysey's character that remained constant throughout his life:

... if you had wandered through various rooms of the Arts Club in Dover Street, London, any time after eleven o'clock in the morning until about the same hour at night, you would almost certainly have noticed an elderly gentleman with features greatly distinguished by the cut of his nose and the arch of his brow, the extraordinary sensitiveness and pugnacity of his mouth, and the distant, dreaming look of the visionary in his

4

eye. *Probably the first thing you would have noticed was the narrow immaculately clean starched collar, the colour of which was the brightest thing in the room. It was a beautiful blue… You would probably also have noticed that the collar of his jacket had no lapels. He designed all his clothing himself, and he had a rooted objection to anything that harboured dust or dirt of any description. Therefore there were no unnecessary nooks and crannies in his clothing, not even cuffs to his trouser bottoms. He was clean and prim and gentle, but of firm disposition.*

He was the sort of man you would never dream of taking any liberty with. You would probably have hesitated very much to introduce yourself. Automatically he commanded your respect. There was nothing forbidding about him and yet there was aloofness and distinction in abundance…

Of all his remarkable attributes, the most remarkable thing about him, I think, was his smile. It was a lovely smile. There was more kindness and more simple delight in humour and more sheer affection in that smile than in any smile I have every beheld.[7]

The description of a man, who on the one hand intimidated and 'commanded your respect' and on the other engendered trust and affection through the warmth of his smile and his 'simple delight in humour', was often repeated by Voysey's friends and family, and it was implied in *The Studio* interview. His apparent reluctance to be interviewed, the 'almost child-like rendering' of some of his decorative designs and the humourous expressions that animated the devils and birds in the designs, which *The Studio* reproduced, indicated the private face of Voysey, but *The Studio* interview was far more concerned with Voysey as a public figure.

Voysey would have been a gift to any magazine editor aiming to bring complex professional issues to a wider public. He was a colourful and distinctive character with an idiosyncratic line in metaphor, who could be depended upon to pack his punches in the name of honesty, 'Hoarding pretty things together is more often a sign of vanity and vain glory than good taste.'[8] His advice was practical and easy to follow:

Instead of painting boughs of apple-trees on our door panels and covering every shelf with petticoats of silk, let us begin by discarding the mass of useless ornaments and banishing the millinery that degrades our furniture and fittings. Reduce the variety of patterns and colour in a room. Eschew all imita-

tions, and have each thing the best of its sort, so that the decorative value of each will stand forth with increased power and charm, and concentrated richness will be more apparent with its simple neighbours.[9]

And his values appealed to a conservative regard for quality and craftsmanship, as well as incorporating the aesthete's dictum to, 'Have nothing in your house which you do not know to be useful or believe to be beautiful.'

By 1893, Voysey was establishing a reputation as a leading pattern designer, better known to the public for his decorative designs than for architecture. In the first exhibitions of the Arts and Crafts Exhibition Society, he had shown printed fabrics and wallpaper designs rather than furniture or architectural drawings, and *The Studio* interview focused on this area of his work.[10] Although Voysey made a good part of his living as a designer of wallpapers he was adamant that:

A wallpaper is of course only a background, and were your furniture good in form and colour a very simple or quite undecorated treatment of the walls would be preferable; … Do not think that I place wall-papers first. Wooden panelling, whether polished or hand-stained, is best of all; next to that comes painted panelling, but as papers wear better than the plain wall, we must permit them to exist on this ground.[11]

Seven years later he was photographed in his own study at The Orchard, surrounded by walls patterned with his own wallpapers; in fact, even within two years of this statement, the house that he designed for his father had been decorated with Voysey wallpaper.[12] Nevertheless, he was prepared to risk offending his readers in order to make his position unequivocal: 'as most modern furniture is vulgar or bad in every way, elaborate papers of many colours help to disguise its ugliness. Although elaboration makes confusion more confounded, yet if you have but enough confusion the ugliness of modern life becomes bearable.'[13]

Six of Voysey's pattern designs were used to illustrate the article, not the well-known papers in production by the company Essex & Co., but examples 'chosen specially to display the artist's most individual work from his unpublished drawings'. Of these, 'The Demon' (designed for wallpaper) and 'Three Men of Gotham' (for printed

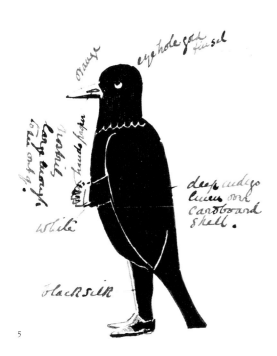

5

velvet) would have had a startlingly original effect in any room. Both designs are now in the Drawings Collection of the Royal Institute of British Architects, and it is interesting that Voysey included two such powerful (and unsaleable) designs to illustrate the article. They are full of drama and movement, strongly coloured, and, for all the humour of mustard-coloured demons licking at raging orange flames, they would have been difficult to place commercially.

The individual character of Voysey's patterns and the repetition of bird and tree motifs suggest that he designed at least in part for his own satisfaction, often taking risks with unusual characters. According to *The Studio*, the 'boldly presented repeats' and the introduction of animal life represented 'typical instances of his individual taste' and he broke away from the conventional floral and foliage designs, arguing:

I do not see why the forms of birds, for instance, may not be used, provided they are reduced to mere symbols. Decorators complain of small repeats and simple patterns, because they are apt to show the joints, and because the figures may be mutilated, in turning a corner for instance. If the form be sufficiently conventionalised the mutilation is not felt; a real bird with his head cut off is an unpleasant sight, so is a rose that has lost half an inch of its petals; but if the bird is a crude symbol and his facsimile occurs complete within ten and a half inches distance, although one may have lost a portion of his body, it does not violate my feelings.[14]

William Morris and Philip Webb had already incorporated birds into their decorative designs, but Voysey complained that the birds, figures and animals in his designs met with considerable opposition from many wallpaper manufacturers, who he publicly accused of a 'glutinous civility, which aims only at securing orders'. He railed against the 'unreasonable, unhealthy, and insane opposition to the conventional application of *animal* life to decoration . . . Perhaps when the public have given up telegraphing the rise and fall of railway shares, there will be left a little more sympathy for the poetic sense, and our playful delight in bird life and strong joyful colour will not meet with so much indifference and disdain.'[15] But the public as well as the wallpaper manufacturers were initially 'opposed to birds', and when Walter Essex of Essex

6

& Co. 'dared to deal' with Voysey's designs, 'All his friends told him he was a fool to do so.'[16]

Voysey recommended that the designer should take his inspiration directly from nature:

To go to Nature is, of course, to approach the fountain-head, but a literal transcript will not result in good ornament; before a living plant a man must go through an elaborate process of selection and analysis, and think of the balance, repetition, and many other qualities of his design, thereby calling his individual taste into play and adding a human interest to his work. If he does this, although he has gone directly to Nature, his work will not resemble any of his predecessors; he has become an inventor.[17]

In his determination to make an accurate and scientific appraisal of nature Voysey used what he called 'Hyslop's Prints', made by rolling oak, dandelion and acer leaves with ink and then pressing them to make a print of their outline and the delicate pattern of their veins.[18] These simple, flat outlines appear in his decorative designs precisely drawn and stylized into patterns. In addition, Voysey used photographs of details of flowers and

6 *'Three Men of Gotham' design for printed velvet, c.1889.*

7

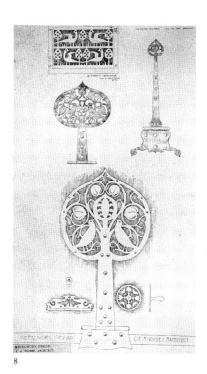

8

plete knowledge of our material, and be thorough masters of the craft to be employed in its production.' Furthermore, the flatness and the necessity of repeat in the pattern was to be honestly expressed: 'a wall-paper should be always essentially a pattern, the repeat of which is recognised as one of its chief characteristics, rather than a pattern disguising the repeat and presenting in detail interwoven pretty bits known to the trade as "all-over patterns"'.[21]

Large and bold patterns, limited to the 'simple expression of one or two ideas' were recommended in place of small and timid designs, even for smaller rooms and Morris was cited as an exemplar: 'Mr Morris is credited with the axiom "the smaller your room the larger the pattern you may put on your walls".'[22] If the design was thought to be too forceful for a small room, the effect could be modified in the colouring, but Voysey's preferred colouring was often as striking and original as his designs:

In 'The Demon,' a daring harmony in reds and yellows like a Gaillardia blossom is heightened by the cunning touches of dark green in the background, hardly noticeable without close study. ...The most sumptuous, 'Three Men of Gotham' recalls stained glass in its lustrous harmony: the sea is peacock green, the boats olive and sage green, the sails red and orange, the men a duller red, with the lightest touches in the yellow-green pennants, and white sea-birds like flashes of actual light in the sky between; it is not possible in words to convey the richness of the broken colour which ennobles this fine design.[23]

Voysey's affection for rich unusual colours was later to be expressed in his interiors, his furniture and in his own clothing: the clear 'butcher blue' colour of his shirts has already been noted; at The Orchard the hall walls were a deep purple colour, off-set by a rug 'in dead peacock blue' and the dining room was papered a plain dark green, with a blue and green carpet patterned with red and yellow flowers, a fireplace tiled 'green-grey of varying tones', and the 'turkey red' twill curtains that Voysey specified whenever he was given the chance.[24] In his later writings, he described the colours found in nature as a source of inspiration.

The Studio interview portrayed Voysey as an uncompromising idealist, but it suggested too that his ideals were founded on an inner strength, on

their leaves, which were evidently taken either by himself or a professional photographer for this kind of analytical study. Photographs of eryngeum, globe thistles, meadow cranesbil, nigella and of a kestrel were found among his collection of source materials, tied together with thin green ribbon; their forms were simplified and stylized in his patterns.

Not all of Voysey's source materials were of his own devising. He kept botanical drawings and line drawings of birds, cut out from magazines, and there were illustrated books in his collection like Edward Step's *Wayside and Woodland Trees. A pocket guide to the British Sylva*, which he used to identify and to press leaves and flowers that he had collected and brought home.[19]

He rejected 'those realistic flowery papers ... [which] we all know sell better than any others' because in order for a wall to remain 'subservient to pictures, furniture, and people ... the utmost flatness is essential'.[20] This insistence on flatness was essentially Puginian and Voysey followed Pugin's principle, too, that the designer should be truthful to his materials: 'We must acquire a com-

7 *Early botanical photographs from Voysey's collection of source material.*

8 *Metalwork designs published in* The British Architect, *January 1895.*

faith and humility. He was never very influenced by the work of his contemporaries and he urged designers that:

They should each use their God-given faculties, and if they have thoughts worth expressing, the means to express them sufficiently are, and always will be, at hand. Not that we need shut our eyes to all human efforts, but we should go to Nature direct for inspiration and guidance. Then we are at once relieved from restrictions of style or period, and can live and work in the present with laws revealing always fresh possibilities.

Voysey's relationship with God, in accordance with his father's teaching, was simple and direct, without the intervening rituals of, for example, the Catholic Church or the Church of England. He believed that nature was an expression of God's work, and that through thought and feeling man was in direct communication with God. The simplicity and depth of his faith were expressed in an undated piece in his collection:

Where there is trust there is love
Where there is love there is peace
Where there is peace there is God:
Where there is God there is No Need

His faith was fundamental to his life and work, as he wrote in the opening paragraph of *Individuality*:

Let us assume that there is a beneficent and omnipotent controlling power, that is perfectly good and perfectly loving; and that our existence here, is for the purpose of growing individual characters. These are the propositions upon which all the following conclusions are based, and the fertile soil out of which our thoughts must grow.[25]

Too often the rustic figures, the rounded trees, the birds and the heart motifs that recur again and again in Voysey's work are enjoyed for their quaint simplicity without any appreciation of their importance as symbolic figures of Voysey's profound faith. *The Studio* interview reproduced a design for an inlaid work-box, depicting two peasant figures, a man drawing and a woman who appears to be knitting, standing on either side of a tree and decorated with the words, 'Head Hand & Heart'. It gave no explanation for the design, however given the

9

10

9 *'Head Hand & Heart' design for an inlaid work-box, c.1893.*

10 *'Where There is Trust There is Love', drawing retained by Voysey in his private collection. The initials within the heart may have been those of his mother, Frances Maria Voysey.*

symbolism of Voysey's cover for *The Studio* a few months earlier and his urging to go to nature for inspiration, it is reasonable to suppose that the two figures with the tree between them were endowed with a symbolic significance, particularly if the design was for Voysey's own work-box.

The tree, the simple rural figures, the bird and the famous Voysey heart were all permanently ensconced in his design vocabulary by 1895. In January of that year *The British Architect* published a sheet of his metalwork designs ('Here are some instances of design in accessory art in which Mr Voysey never fails to interest'), which included an elaborate tee hinge terminating in two birds perched in the branches of a tree with heart-shaped leaves, whose outline formed the shape of an inverted heart. Other hinge designs on the same sheet incorporated pairs of birds within a heart-shaped outline; the decorative ventilator grille, the heart-shaped keyhole and the elongated door handle that were to be used as standard fittings in Voysey's houses also appeared.

Voysey seldom referred directly to his fondness for hearts in his writings, but he wrote of the impor-

tance of symbolism in art.[26] He might have recalled the symbolic use of the heart in the Dulwich College Crest, in which a hand emerging from flames of fire clasps a human heart, and he wrote repeatedly of the importance of heart felt emotion to all labour.[27] The heart was widely used as a symbol of love and affection, nevertheless, Voysey might have extended this symbolism to signify God's love. The expression of thought and feeling, of head, hand and heart, with or without his signature motifs, was apparent in all Voysey's work and to some extent his symbols had a general currency, as well as, a personal significance: in 1896, a Society of Designers was founded 'to support the dignity of the profession'; Voysey was a member alongside other designers like Walter Crane, William Butterfield, and C. J. Haité and manufacturers and retailers, including Arthur Lasenby Liberty and Alexander

Morton. They took as their motto the words on Voysey's work-box: 'Hand, Heart and Head.'

Voysey lectured that the designer must be 'allowed to exercise his God-given faculties; ... Free men from the bondage of imitation, and they *must* at once express living emotions' and he recalled Emerson's description of the solitary workshop of the ancient Greek sculptor:

who toiled, perhaps, in ignorance of the existence of other sculpture, created his work without other model save life, household life, and the sweet and smart of personal relations, of beating hearts and meeting eyes, of poverty and necessity, and hope and fear. These were his inspirations, and these are the effects he carries home to your heart and mind. In proportion to his force, the artist will find in his work an outlet for his proper character.[28]

Though Voysey was aware of other artists' and architects' work, design was a means for him to express his true character. Even when his decorative designs reflected the more flippant and fanciful aspects of his nature, a core element of completeness and integration was always present that ran through every aspect of his work. His niece recalled, 'One of the most exciting things was his feeling for proportion, and balance, and integration. Everything had to belong ... That was his life. Absolutely. He was all of a piece and extremely integrated.'[29]

The Studio interview was the first detailed exposition of Voysey's designs and doctrines, but it was not to be the last. If anything, it encouraged Voysey to be even more emphatic in his pronouncements on design. At the close of the interview the writer briefly described Voysey's house as a vessel for his philosophy:

Before leaving, my host took me through his house, and although it would be out of place to speak of the various pieces of furniture, the clever adaptation of use to beauty, one could not but feel that here was proof of comfort and entirely domestic requirements combined with art in a way that made it remarkable.[30]

Within a year Voysey had taken journalism into his own hands, publishing an article on 'Domestic Furniture' in the journal of the RIBA, and the following year his lecture on 'The aims and conditions of the modern decorator' was printed in *The*

12

13

Journal of Decorative Art. In both pieces he expanded upon the ideas that had already been in evidence in *The Studio* interview, adapting and developing his doctrine to address furniture and interior design. He condemned the decorator who tried 'to sneak up to a leading position without suffering for it' by pandering to 'any debased public taste that might happen to be in vogue' and he railed against:

the lazy and contemptible practise of relying upon precedent for justification of what is done. The revivalism of the present century, which is so analogous to this reliance on precedent, has done more to stamp out men's artistic common sense and understanding than any movement I know. The unintelligent, unappreciative use of the works of the past, which is the rule, has surrounded us at every turn with deadly dullness, that is dumb alike to the producer and the public.[31]

In place of imitation, Voysey argued for artistic reasoning and the honest expression of human emotion:

Turn a man on to any ordinary house to colour the wood and the walls without regard to tradition, and he will inevitably express, by his work and choice of colour, either unhealthiness or healthiness, sadness or joy. Some expression of thought and feeling there is sure to be, and thus may be imparted that human element which adds such immeasurable charm to all noble works of art.[32]

Voysey considered, 'everything inside the house [to be] within the Architect's province, from fittings and furniture to the very tooth brushes'.[33] And although no examples or even descriptions of a Voysey toothbrush have survived, by the mid 1890s he was publishing designs for carpets, tiles, embroidery, tapestry, metal screens, fireplaces, calligraphy and furniture.

Almost from the outset Voysey's furniture was distinguished by its simplicity and just as he had condemned the current trends in decorative and interior design, so too he pronounced that, 'the subject of "Furniture" is a most depressing one … Rich and poor alike are content to order their furniture from the upholsterer, as they do their funerals from the undertaker. The result is very similar, the bill being the most lasting impression made on their minds. What they have paid is the measure of

their greatness.'[34] He complained that the 'poor architect' was invariably, 'exposed to the insult and indignity of having all his work spoiled by the upholsterer. The client never dreams that his architect's province is beyond drain-pipes and drawings.'[35] But there were clients, even in the 1880s, who recognized the broad spread of Voysey's designing potential and who commissioned furniture, as well as interior designs from him. In 1889, he designed furniture for the showrooms of Essex and Co., the wallpaper manufacturers. The furniture and its designs are now lost, but an iron grille made to fill the space above a beam, in the form of a line of bird-inhabited trees with lead foliage, was described in *The Studio* as: 'the most noticeable feature in Messrs. Essex's show-rooms … they have a singularly light and graceful appearance.'[36]

Voysey's earliest surviving design for furniture is for 'an oak chair for reading room, writing room or hall' designed between 1882 and 1885.[37] No specific client was named, but the chair was later made for W. Ward Higgs and exhibited in the Arts and Crafts Exhibition of 1896. It was more curvaceous than Voysey's later designs with the uprights to the back ending in scrolls, carved into the shape of swans' heads. The structure of the piece was simple, with flat interlocking sections of oak pegged together. The form may have been influenced by Pugin's design for chairs for the House of Commons and by Seddon's furniture designs.[38] However, the curved legs and arm rests had a quirky springiness that Voysey did not repeat.

A second piece of furniture – a cabinet designed for Lady Wentworth in 1893 – showed Voysey still experimenting with furniture design. The following year, speaking to the RIBA, he confessed to a continuing struggle, 'I fear I am expected to say something much more practical about the design of furniture. I wish I could say something helpful; but I am myself groping in the dark, struggling to find out the true laws which govern fitness and beauty.'[39]

Even if the parameters of Voysey's style were still flexible, he was already formulating a set of principles and a series of ground rules that were to guide the design of his furniture for the rest of his career. The Wentworth Cabinet adhered to the ideals of 'simplicity, repose, harmony, dignity or breadth', which Voysey applied to all his work.

Mouldings were used to emphasize the strong horizontal lines in the same way that weathering and string courses, or a projecting upper floor were employed in Voysey's architecture, and the gently undulating line beneath the cornice and above the legs was to find its way into many of his later furniture designs (and a few of his buildings). However, the most radical aspect of the Wentworth Cabinet was its plainness. Voysey made reason the basis for all his art, and he made the inherent qualities of natural materials, sensitively and unobtrusively work, combined with the most exacting sense of proportion (although less exacting, perhaps, in the case of the Wentworth Cabinet) the pre-eminent factors in his designs. He anticipated the Modernists in his insistence that, 'moulding and carving figured marble, is a sacrilege not to be tolerated' and in his call to reason: 'Let every man judge furniture from the point of view of reason: Let us ask, Is it fit and thoroughly suited to the purpose for which it is intended? Is it as strong as, and no stronger than, it should be?'[40] In addition to reason, Voysey called on the moral and emotional faculties of conscience and love:

from the point of view of conscience ask, Is it true – is it all it pretends to be? Does it express qualities and feelings consistent with its owner and its surroundings? Is it faithful work? And for love's sake ask, Is it proportioned, coloured, and disposed as the natural beauties in creation? Are its lines and masses graceful and pleasing? Do any of its parts quarrel? Does it express sobriety, restraint, and purity?[41]

Where ornament was deemed appropriate it was concentrated and often credited with a functional relevance in the metalwork of the piece. The keyholes and hinges of the Wentworth Cabinet are the same as those illustrated in *The British Architect* sheet and Voysey clearly enjoyed designing for metalwork, complaining with typical directness that, 'Of the metal-work for furniture, saving the work of a few worthy men, to be numbered on the fingers of one hand, there is nothing done in this line that is not a disgrace. Depraved coarseness, brutality, and sickly elaboration characterise the metal-work on nearly all modern furniture.'[42]

Voysey's own furniture fittings, door furniture, bell-pulls, window fittings, ventilator grilles and letter-plates reappeared again and again like

14 *Keys and decorative metalwork, incorporating heart motifs.*

15

16

17

18

hallmarks in his houses and on his furniture, and it was characteristic that once satisfied with a design, he felt no compunction about reusing it whenever the opportunity arose. William Bainbridge Reynolds, a fellow member of the Art Workers' Guild, manufactured a range of Voysey hinges and many of the gate and furniture fittings that Voysey specified. In addition, Voysey made regular visits for each of his houses to the manufacturers of his metalwork, Thomas Elsley & Co., and Elsley's developed such a comprehensive range of Voysey designs that they were published in a special catalogue; Voysey fire grates, fenders, hinges, handles and even light fittings were specified by other architects of the period, and were installed in Arts and Crafts houses around the country.[43]

The clarity and progression towards professional maturity that Voysey demonstrated in his architectural designs were equally apparent in his decorative and furniture designs, and the growth of his architectural practice was not accompanied by any corresponding reduction in their diversity or quality. In the Arts and Crafts Exhibition of 1896 he exhibited an unprecedented number of textile,

wallpaper and furniture designs, which were applauded as '...at once the most restrained and the most novel in the Exhibition. It is especially good that his influence, which tends to simplicity and severity, should be made very prominent at a time that sees, especially in France and Germany, a tendency to be bizarre at any cost.'[44] A fireplace exhibited in the south gallery, immaculately proportioned and sparingly detailed was described as:

absolutely devoid of ornament. Excepting some relief decoration on the brass grate by T. Elsley, there is not an inch of pattern of any kind. The proportions of the white painted woodwork are exquisitely delicate, and with the eau-de-nil tiles which surround the grate itself, make up a most dainty harmony.[45]

Where Voysey did use ornament it was boldly expressed and strikingly original. The animals and birds that he had fought so hard to incorporate into his wallpaper and textile designs in the 1880s and early 1890s were by now predominant. A pair of crested birds prepared to kiss within an enclosure of delicate heart-shaped fronds in a tapestry design

C F A VOYSEY

15 *Fireplace, exhibited in the Arts and Crafts Exhibition, 1896.*
16 *'Green Pastures' carpet, c.1896*

17, 18 *Voysey rainwater-heads, manufactured and marketed by Thomas Elsley.*

19

per manufacturers, who were to continue to manufacture his designs for the remainder of his career.

One of the more unusual 1896 exhibits was a street lamp, which Voysey designed in 1894 as part of a 'Scheme for electric lighting narrow streets in the City' for his brother, Annesley, who was an electrical engineer.[47] It was manufactured by Aumonier, but not all of the exhibits were designed for mass production: a wooden clock, designed by Voysey the previous year and hand-painted by him for his own personal use was included in the exhibition. It was one of his most idiosyncratic designs, linking the architectural elements of domed roof and corner buttresses, which he was later to adapt to a full scale clock tower for Julian Sturgis, with the ornamental colours and motifs of birds and boats that he had explored in his decorative designs.

The Studio interview of 1893, an interview in *The Builder's Journal and Architectural Review* three years later and Voysey's own writings on 'Domestic Furniture' and 'The Aims of a Modern Decorator' of 1894 and 1895, respectively, all portrayed Voysey as a pioneering designer with 'a moral mission'[48] – a self-made man, 'who holds the loftiest views as to the dignity of the Profession'.[49] The vitriol with which he attacked public taste in general, and the lady client in particular, however, suggest that the struggle to build up his practice had, as he confessed to *The Builder's Journal*, 'been a hard one, that he almost starved when he first tried to make his living by Design' and that there were humiliations as well as disappointments along the way:

too often the decorator becomes a kind of head-foreman, whose opinion is not always asked, and indeed is often scornfully rejected. He is expected to carry out the ideas of others, although he has probably spent his life in the study and practice of his craft. His client – often the lady of the house – does not consider this, but will rather turn (fresh from the mysteries of millinery, and with a head full of notions begotten of Paris fashion-books) to her daughters for counsel and suggestion. And the decorator, with his years of experience, has to stand patiently by and listen to verbose feminine dogmatism upon a matter to which in many cases his client brings neither knowledge nor aptitude, but often, what is worse, will quote canting little catechisms and hand-books in defence of the views put forward.[50]

Voysey may not have been quite so personal in his criticisms if the hypothetical client had been male,

and a carpet with a 'quaint border of shepherds' was patterned with sheep grazing in pairs beneath stylized Voysey trees. *The Studio* pleaded a little prudishly that:

As a pattern, the shepherd and sheep is distinctly ingenious, and Mr. Voysey has enticed us to his point of view so often that possibly after more familiarity we could accept it as legitimate; but at present it seems as unorthodox as the use of perspective in wall-papers; and although it pleases you aesthetically, it would be too great a shock to one's theory to praise it unreservedly.[46]

Voysey's designs were often devastatingly simple. He was able to convey movement and character with the minimum use of colour and line, and yet, with the contour and position of an eye his birds were rendered tender or imperious, quizzical or irritable. The freshness and originality of his designs invariably succeeded in seducing public and manufacturers alike. By 1896 he had forged working relationships with many of the small specialist companies: Thomas Elsley, A. W. Simpson, Aumonier, Reynolds, and Tomkinson and Adam, as well as the larger wallpa-

20

but he repeatedly denounced clients who thought that they knew what they wanted:

who assume that they have a right to do what they like with their own money, and that, if they pay for anything, that fact gives them the right to determine exactly what that thing shall be.

Thus the labours of the decorator and designer are reduced to a commercial commodity, like so much butter or cheese, the flavour of which is to be regulated to suit the palate of the purchaser.[51]

According to Voysey, the notion that anyone but an expert could envisage a building or an interior from the presentation of drawings and an estimate was 'ridiculous' and the less a client understood of the work in hand the better: 'If a man goes to a doctor, he should have faith in that doctor. Similarly an Architect should be an autocrat, and lead his client along gently in the path he thinks to be best.'[52] Voysey had a tendency to preach in his published writings and even in magazine interviews he often railed against the iniquities of materialism and the revivalism of the age as though he were in the pulpit. He hated lecturing, describing it as 'an agony', and this goes some way towards explaining the stiffness of the publications that were adapted from his lectures.[53] He was a self-conscious writer and perhaps he tried to cover his academic difficulties by emulating the style of his father's published works, but he was not so sanctimonious in person, nor in his letters to his clients.

He was always frank. Perhaps this was the Yorkshireman in him, but there was an open honesty in his candour, which seldom caused serious offence, and that earned him the respect of builders and clients alike. The surviving client correspondence and drawings for many of his houses demonstrate a dialogue between architect and client;[54] it was not unusual for Voysey to produce several alternative elevations for a site incorporating changes requested by the client. Correspondence between Voysey and Cecil Fitch, the client for a house in Merton designed in 1899, shows that though Voysey was firm with his clients, he was quite prepared to explain his specifications and to accommodate his clients' requirements when his decisions were questioned or challenged. On artistic matters, however, there was to be no compromise:

My dear Fitch,
The detail drawings for your house are progressing and all will be finished by Xmas or end of the month. Certainly you had better not see the drawings until they are finished and coloured. They will not give you the slightest idea of what you are going to have. All artistic questions you must trust to me to decide. No two minds ever produced an artistic result.[55]

When Voysey was criticized in a letter to the RIBA journal for his arrogant attitude towards clients, he was at pains to defend himself and in his very brief autobiographical notes he stressed that, 'Fifty-three clients have commissioned him more than once.'[56] If, however, the level or direction of a client's involvement became too intrusive then he would throw the job up rather than compromise the integrity of his work. As early as 1896, Voysey made the public pronouncement that he: 'Never will design to please anybody but myself.'[57] But, as astutely pointed out, having 'struggled all his life against great odds … today he is able to feel – to use a famous phrase – that "the flowing tide is with him."'[58] By 1896, Voysey's reputation was established.

21–3 *Iron chimney-pieces and grates, and a lead flower vase, from Elsley's catalogue of Voysey designs.*

In Victorian England the country house was closely associated with the feudal past and the landed aristocracy. During the opening decades of the nineteenth century, when urban growth and industrialization created vast new fortunes among the middle classes, the ideal of owning a country house came to represent an opportunity to emulate the aristocracy. It was the ultimate social advancement (short of a knighthood) and if it was to be done properly it necessitated a massive new mansion set in a working estate of around one hundred acres. For the wealthy industrialist a country seat represented a tangible mark of social distinction. It was a means of buying into polite society, as a great deal of the social regime and exacting etiquette of the period revolved around country life. For the first seventy-five years of the century there was a steady increase in demand for substantial country houses, and architects like Sir Charles Barry (1795–1860) and Edward Blore (1787–1879) were employed on the remodelling of existing houses and the design of new ones, which were worthy of the ambitions of a newly rich and powerful clientele.

From the 1860s, overlapping with this boom in country-house building, the country house began to be identified with another set of social and aesthetic aspirations. It became associated with the writings of John Ruskin and William Morris, and with the ideals of a generation of 'artistic' designers and patrons who rejected the iniquities of industrialization and urban growth, and who celebrated rural life as a model for social reform. It became a symbol of harmony between man and nature. The old English buildings, indigenous to each county, were studied as models for a revival of English domestic architecture (and it is no coincidence that the series of articles in *The Studio* on modern architecture in the 1890s adopted this title), and idealized rural communities were invoked to inspire and inform collaboration between painters, architects, craftsmen and builders. The trend was launched with the youthful exuberance and optimism of Philip Webb's Red House in 1859, and it was developed in the 1860s, 1870s and early 1880s by architects like Richard Norman Shaw, William Eden Nesfield, Ernest George, William Burges and George Devey, all of whom influenced Voysey.

'6 THE IDEAL OF A MODEST COUNTRY HOUSE'

2

1 *Garden and west elevation, Perrycroft, Colwall, Herefordshire, 1893–4.*

2 *North elevation, Perrycroft.*

The agricultural slump of 1879–94, caused by the importation of cheap foreign beef, bacon and corn, and disastrous British harvests, brought about a substantial reduction in the demand for the sort of country house that was at the heart of a working estate, as it ceased to be financially desirable. The demand for modest country houses, however, which could be used as retreats from the rigours of urban life continued, and it was these smaller houses that Voysey was commissioned to design. Sometimes, as in the case of Norney, they were built on tracts of land that had formerly been part of a great estate, sold off as a consequence of the agricultural slump. Often they had extensive grounds of up to twenty acres, but these comprised gardens and woodland, and were seldom farmed.

The country houses of the first seventy years of the century were designed in every conceivable architectural style, and any summary treatment of their design must be superficial, but if they can be grouped together at all, then it must be for their determination to impress on a grand scale. Similarly, the more modest 'artistic' houses of the 1860s and 1870s are linked, however loosely, by a self-conscious preoccupation with the revival of vernacular traditions and materials. Some sort of marriage generally took place between the aspirations and intentions of the client and those of the architect, and if the marriage was a good one, the resultant house embodied an element of the status and sensibilities of both parties.

The status and sensibilities expressed in Voysey's country houses were exceptionally precise. They subsumed the nostalgia for old England, which his predecessors had openly expressed by combining the quintessential qualities of an old English cottage or farmhouse, with the tectonic considerations of an uncompromisingly functional modern building. They rejected ostentatious display, depending for their effect on sound proportions, fine materials and good workmanship, honestly expressed. It would be a fine thing to reason that whenever a patron commissioned a Voysey house he or she was openly expressing his or her affinity with Voysey's artistic doctrine, and given the publicity that this doctrine received, some credence could be attached to such an argument, but the status of a Voysey house in the 1890s was complicated by fashion.

In addition to his professional and artistic reputation, Voysey was one of the most fashionable architects in practice in the 1890s. The motivation to commission a Voysey house, therefore, might in some cases have been founded on little more than a glib desire to be in vogue. In addition, the success of one Voysey house often gave rise to a commission for another, simply because the clients knew one another socially. Today the historian has little chance of evaluating the sources of Voysey's commissions without a thorough knowledge of the membership of certain gentlemen's clubs, or a detailed appraisal of the subscribers to country hunts and other sporting activities. It is almost impossible to know who knew whom and how. Voysey's clients cannot be grouped together in any single social category. According to John Brandon-Jones his honest simplicity attracted commissions from Quakers, but his clients included industrialists and the aristocracy as well as artists and writers. Often, his houses were arranged in clusters in some of the most scenic parts of the country.

The houses were seldom visible from the roadside. They were secluded in several acres of grounds, often with a lodge-house and a distinctive gate offering the only clues to the passer by that a Voysey house lay beyond. Many were designed for 'men of moderate means' as weekend and summer retreats from the pressures and industrialization of town life, but they were entertaining retreats, in true country house tradition: Hermann Muthesius (1861–1927), the German architectural critic, noted that the English were far less prone to giving 'great feasts' than the Germans: 'The desire to impress his guests with special kinds of food and drink or to outdo, or even to try to rival, others is entirely alien to the Englishman and would be regarded as a mark of bad taste.'[1] Invitations to stay, on the other hand, particularly at one's country house, were 'far more highly evolved' in England than on the Continent:

The Englishman's highly developed sense of hospitality has evolved through living in the country, and still to this day it appears in its most striking form in country surroundings. Country houses are essentially planned with visitors in mind, and are equipped for entertaining them, not only in the provision of spare rooms, but also in domestic offices and outbuildings designed to cater for temporary large increases in numbers.[2]

PERRYCROFT, designed in 1893–4 as a country retreat for J. W. Wilson, MP, was set in a spectacular sloping site in the Malvern Hills, Herefordshire, within a few miles of Walnut Tree Farm;[3] and while we cannot know whether J. W. Wilson and R. H. Cazalet were acquainted or whether Wilson had been introduced to Voysey by his other client from Parliament, Archibold Grove, we do know that both houses were built by the same local contractor, W. Porter of Malvern, and it seems probable that Wilson and Voysey came to know one another through a mutual acquaintance.

Voysey must have seen the commission to design Perrycroft as a breakthrough. It was his most ambitious house to date, coming at the end of a year, which, in spite of *The Studio* interview, had been littered with 'alterations and additions' and suggestions for decorations without any new architectural work of substance.[4] The house alone was to cost £4,900 (compared with an estimate of £1,120 for Walnut Tree and £494 10s for the Forster House), and Voysey was to design stables, a lodge, and later a coachman's cottage and several pieces of furniture for the house.

At last Voysey had the chance to elaborate on the strict exercises in economy on which his young reputation was firmly grounded, and elaborate is exactly what he did. Some of the ideas that he had explored in his early published work – the spike at the apex of an ogee roof in the 'house with an octagonal hall' – and the successful and strongly individual elements in his early buildings were brought into play in a house that might be criticized for incorporating too many ideas all at once.

Perrycroft was approached from above so that it was first seen as a series of roofs and massive battered chimneys, with the Malvern hills beyond. It was unusual in being clearly visible from the road, 'so that most visitors to Malvern pass by it and are doubtless very much startled by it. (We won't repeat the remarks we heard.)'[5] The house wrapped around an entrance courtyard using an L-shaped plan with the barest suggestion of a third wing jutting out around the porch, and Voysey resisted the temptation to break the roofline with a collection of dormers and gables, or to send it sweeping down on one side as he had done at The Cottage and again two years later at Walnut Tree

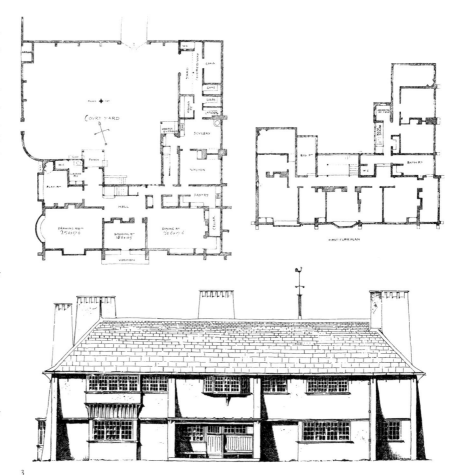

3

4

3 *South elevation and plans of Perrycroft.*

4 *Garden elevation, Perrycroft, showing complex arrangement of projecting planes.*

Farm. Instead he created a long, steady roof line, as a horizontal foil to the dramatic white chimneys, and a slender white stair tower to keep watch over the courtyard, reminding us of Voysey's romantic affection for towers. Porthole windows and a weathercock elevated high up above the main roof distinguished the romantic element of the tower, and endowed the front of the house with an air of assertive individuality that was reinforced by the wide front door.[6]

If Voysey had begun to understand the symbolic and emotive potential of a door during his boyhood in Healaugh (the great Norman door to St John's Church had been pinned with the public notice of his father's dismissal), then by the time he designed the Hans Road houses and Perrycroft this understanding was fully evolved: a simple porch supported by Doric columns framed the entrance to Perrycroft and the door itself was of oak, not machine finished, but planed by hand with, 'that thought and feeling which is the breath of life'.[7] It was heavy enough to withstand a Norman invasion and studded to recall the centuries of English (but never foreign) building tradition that Voysey regarded as his heritage. In its proportions it embodied Voysey's philosophy of 'hospitality and large-hearted generosity', later defined in his writings: 'The doors will be wide in proportion to height, to suggest welcome – not stand-offishly dignified, like the coffin lid, high and narrow for the entrance of one body only.'[8] John Betjeman suggested that Voysey's doors were low because he himself was a short man, but Voysey's doors were also unusually wide, and he was certainly not a fat man.[9] Among his collection of source material there was a sketch by him of a sixteenth-century door in a flint building in Norwich, in which the height of the door to the pinnacle of its pointed arch was measured as 5 ft 10 in high. It is therefore more likely that the dimensions of Voysey's doors were founded on Tudor proportions. As in his furniture, decoration was concentrated and confined to the metalwork, and the simple forms were loaded with symbolism. The image of the tree was potent amongst Voysey's contemporaries as an organic structure. The tree that decorated the massive wrought-iron hinges at Perrycroft might be taken as a symbol for domestic harmony, as Voysey was later to write:

5

We may learn something from the tree of the spirit of domestic happiness. We find the branches as they spring, radiating in rhythmic flow from the parent trunk, all harmoniously, not one on top of the other in confused angularity; each bough and each twig grows a little to one side of those above and below, so that all can enjoy the sun and shower. [10]

The garden elevation, facing south, was arranged to take maximum advantage of the sunlight and the views. Two of the bedroom windows were corbelled out into oriels, and on the ground floor the smoking room benefited from a door into the garden with a settle to either side, sheltered by a shallow veranda. The buttresses now reinforced the full height of the building and on the service-wing elevation they were dramatically replaced by chimneys projecting out from the plane of the wall and crashing up through the roof line.

Inside, Voysey arranged the principal rooms – drawing room, smoking room and dining room – in a line along the south side of the main wing, filling the rooms with light and taking full advantage of the views. The drawing room had bay windows in its south and west walls, and a window seat was provided in the south-east corner of the dining room so that the early morning sun could be enjoyed at breakfast. The position of the dining room in the south-east corner of the house, close to the service wing, conformed to a clearly thought through set of conventions, as did the arrangement of butler's pantry, kitchen, scullery, and stores in the service wing. Voysey was rigorous in his attention to every aspect of the plan, insisting in his later writing that:

In offices for servants' use, let them be cheerful, and not shabby and dark, as if it did not matter how you treated your servants because you were paying for their services. Some day men will be ashamed to do ugly things, and cheap and nasty treatment of servants will be regarded as dishonouring to the master. [11]

He was scrupulous too, about the provision of cloakroom and lavatory:

The delicacy in feelings with regard to lavatory and cloak-room arrangements is one of breeding, varying in the different classes, but one that is to be encouraged in all by careful planning. The builder who places his lavatory on the half-landing, in view of the main entrance or principal rooms, shows a want of delicate feeling. [12]

5 *South-east corner, Perrycroft.*

CHAPTER 6

At Perrycroft the cloakroom was situated just inside the hall and, conveniently, adjacent to the play room, in accordance with Voysey's carefully formulated and highly personal doctrine:

We like, on entering a house, to see our wants anticipated. A warm fire in the hall is akin to a warm welcome. You will provide a lavatory for coats and hats, boots etc., so that mud need not be taken upstairs – as we feel that coats and hats without a soul inside are distressful objects, so they should be stowed away out of sight.[13]

Perrycroft was fitted with extravagant marble fireplaces, cut simply to Voysey's designs. In the hall the fire surround was of blue marble beneath a white painted mantel, supported by tall slender columns, and it was illustrated in an article, 'Remarks on Domestic Entrance Halls' written by Voysey and published in *The Studio* in 1901. Voysey railed against, 'the modern craze for high rooms (originating in foreign travel) which has led to the destruction of all effects of repose. Doors, windows, and even furniture appear as if "stood on end". Verticality and unrest are our gods!'[14]

Taking his argument to its most extreme limits (and he was prone to do this), Voysey claimed that high ceilings necessitated huge windows '(to make up for the loss of reflection from the ceiling)' and that the combination of high rooms and enormous areas of glass necessitated 'hot-water pipes and various demoniacal contrivances for heating … like tombs to the memory of cremated air'. Voysey's sense of humour could be very dry indeed, but it was humour, rather than fanaticism, that took his lectures and writings off at such peculiar tangents. Many of his later houses were equipped with central heating and his own windows were often large. *The Studio* photograph shows that despite the generous budget, Voysey did not use his favoured oak panelling in the Perrycroft interiors. The staircase, mantel, picture-rail and architraves were painted white, and the walls were papered. (Was this a comment on the client's taste in furniture?) In addition, Voysey's ventilator grille, decorated with birds, appeared for the first time in an interior, 'to make rooms healthy, you need circulation of air, not space for foul air to collect in'.[15] On an equally practical note, he wrote: 'Let both hall and staircase be amply lighted. It is impossible to overrate the importance of light, especially on a staircase; and in cases where the hall cannot be carried up to include the first floor, let the ceiling be recognised as the most valuable reflector.'[16]

Although the hall at Perrycroft was on the north side of the house, it was lit from the first-floor landing by a long band of windows tucked up under the eaves. Voysey lit his staircases from above so that natural light was cast down on to the treads in most of his later houses. His staircases were seldom shut away in separate vestibules or along the side of a narrow hall. They were used instead to give a stylish rhythm and spatial charge to the interior. Often the staircase windows were the largest in the house, and the staircase was always clearly expressed in the elevation.

Perrycroft was applauded by *The British Architect* in 1894, which described it as a 'long, white-fronted cottage' that 'for comfort and simple artistic expression, it would be difficult to surpass'.[17] In an article devoted to the problems of elevating a house of limited size and cost into 'a work of art', they advised that the architect must:

… provide comfort, convenience, light, air, and sunshine, with nicely proportioned apartments, rich, 'elegant', picturesque or simple, yet cheerful withal, and avoid show or bombast like the plague. He must make the coming and entertaining of guests, as well as the private home life, equally pleasant, and aim to place the everyday life of father, mother, children, servants, and guests under the best conditions…

Mr Voysey's work in country house design has a great fascination, for his broad and telling manner with long, low proportions, seems singularly fitted for rural surroundings.[18]

6

However, Perrycroft was not without its faults. Despite its L-shaped plan, Voysey made no attempt to tuck the house into the hillside or, through craggy contours and local materials, to blend it into the landscape in true Arts and Crafts tradition. It stood apart from the Malvern hills, white and square on a levelled terrace, and yet the house was recommended because it did not have a strong sense of place in *The British Architect*: 'A long, white-fronted cottage, as shown in this south elevation, with grey stone flag roof, or green slates would lie most charmingly along a terrace out of the Surrey hills.'[19] No sooner was the article printed than Voysey was at work designing just such a house.

6 The hall, Perrycroft. Photograph published in 1901.

7

8

LOWICKS, near Frensham in Surrey, was a relatively small house on an estate of about twenty-nine acres. It was designed in 1894 as a country retreat for E. J. Horniman, again a Member of Parliament, who was related to the influential tea-importing family, and it was to be one of Voysey's most successful early houses. The long, low lines and the sweep of the Westmoreland green-slate roof, dipping down to either side of the first-floor windows, like snow weighing down the branches of a tree, gave the house an air of gentleness. It had what Voysey would describe as a 'spiritual quality', a fusion of 'love, reverence, humility, self-sacrifice, simplicity, truthfulness', which he pursued as 'a perpetual aim', and which he achieved, in one form or another, in his better houses.[20]

The plan was rectangular with the addition of a single-storey wing to accommodate a man servant's room, but each elevation was treated quite differently so that the house had a sculptural pull, drawing the viewer around the exterior in an attempt to understand it more fully; this element of intrigue was to recur in Voysey's work. The front elevation, featured in Voysey's watercolour perspective, gave the impression of an extraordinarily private house. It was almost devoid of windows below the roof line, with just two small lights flanking the simple front door, and a window in the man servant's wing, which Voysey used to give a semblance of enclosure to the entrance courtyard.

If E. J. Horniman had harboured hopes of an imposing front, then he must have been disappointed, but there was a clear indication that the front elevation was not the main elevation, and this was quite in keeping with Voysey's sense of modesty, and with the general philosophy of the period:

The Englishman builds his house for himself alone. He feels no urge to impress, has no thought of festive occasions or banquets and the idea of shining in the eyes of the world through lavishness in and out of his house simply does not occur to him. Indeed, he even avoids attracting attention to his house by means of striking design or architectonic extravagance, just as he would be loth to appear personally eccentric by wearing a fantastic suit.[21]

Nevertheless, the front of Lowicks was by no means austere. Voysey introduced a large half-timbered dormer that broke through the roof line in

7 *Perspectives with inset plans: Hill Close, Swanage, Dorset; Annesley Lodge, Hampstead, London; and Lowicks, Frensham, Surrey.*

8 *Lowicks, the south terrace. Photograph pre-1914.*

a picturesque, old English manner and this, together with the water-butts and the iron stay supporting the porch, gave an impression of simple, rural domesticity, which might almost have caused the visitor to wonder whether he had arrived at the wrong door.

The orientation of the house, with the principal rooms facing south-east and the front facing north-west, was in accordance with Voysey's ideal to enable, 'soul and body to capture the early morning sun, which is never too hot in England and is a great purifying influence'.[22]

In the short, south-west elevation, sharply defined by buttresses at either end, the sitting-room bay was decisively set to one side, positioned to take in the afternoon sun, and while the elevation was boldly asymmetrical and artistically balanced, the windows that broke through the smooth surfaces of roof and render as dormers and bays were dictated not only by Voysey's sense of composition, but also by the requirements of the plan. The sitting room was deliberately positioned at the corner of the plan, with its bay in the south-west elevation, so that it would enjoy sunshine throughout the day.

The plan of Lowicks was less adept than that of Perrycroft. Although the first floor was well laid out with 'five excellent bedrooms' and a dressing room, and the second floor was arranged as a servants' dormitory with 'Three Good Rooms accommodating five or six maids', the ground-floor plan was experimental, and not entirely satisfactory.[23] Voysey arranged the domestic offices in a line so that the pantry was pushed right up to the garden face of the house, where a reception room might more deservedly have benefited from the sunshine and views, undoubtedly resulting in an inconveniently hot pantry. Next to this, Voysey introduced a 'lounge hall', measuring 16 by 14 feet, with its own porch and bay looking over the garden. It was linked to the functional hall on its north side, which had the usual attributes of staircase, cloak-room and front door.

Voysey was to introduce the living hall with its attendant functional hall again, repeatedly and with more success, but at Lowicks the hall with its red-tiled floor and simple brick fireplace might have been a little Spartan for so small a house, and it was provided at the expense of a dining room.

The sitting room, however, was elegant and comfortable with white painted panelling and fitted bookcases and cupboards to either side of the fireplace. Voysey designed a built-in writing table to one side of the fireplace, and in the play room he carved his own profile (playfully) into the corbel supporting the mantel-shelf.

A visitor to Lowicks, William Plomer, describing the house in the early twentieth century, focused on the aspects of the house that were most strikingly modern, and in particular on the lowness of the house in contrast to the standard lofty Edwardian interior:

...everything was very high or very low. The roof, for instance, came down steeply almost to the ground; the casement windows were wide and low and the window seats very low; but the latches on the doors were very high and to open them one had to make a gesture like that of proposing a toast; straight and very high were the backs of the chairs which ... were pierced with heart-shaped openings; on high shelves near the ceiling stood vases of crafty green pottery filled with peacocks' feathers; and the hot water cans, coal-scuttles, electroliers and so on were made of beaten or hammered brass or copper. It was still, this house, the last word, or at any rate the last but one, in modern taste and comfort.[24]

Lowicks was one of the earliest houses for which Voysey is known to have designed furniture.[25] In August 1895 he designed an 'oak bedstead for E. J. Horniman' with four tall angle posts and slatted head and foot boards, each with its slats arranged in three groups of five. The design was later adapted for Moorcrag, and, apart from the foot board, it was similar to Voysey's own bed at The Orchard. A circular, draw-top oak table was also designed for Lowicks and the description of chairs with high backs, 'pierced with heart-shaped openings', suggests that Horniman bought some of Voysey's later furniture. Voysey often designed a piece of furniture for a particular house and then adapted the design, or had his cabinet-maker make up an identical piece for another client. He did the same with his metalwork designs, gradually building up a catalogue of standard components that could be drawn upon for any of his houses. There is no record of a client complaining that the unique quality of his furniture had been undermined in this way, just as there were no complaints when

9

9 *The tea lawn at Lowicks, with summer-house designed by Voysey in 1911.*

Voysey repeated a chimney-piece from one house to another, or an aspect of an elevation.

Voysey tied his elevations together with long horizontal lines. He wrapped them round with a thin, red string-course of tiles or a gutter picked out with delicate brackets. The lines flew proud of the building, where the deep overhanging eaves were cut away to accommodate a window, but were picked up again and carried through all the way round the building. The garden elevation of Lowicks, facing south-east, was delicately balanced and it was typical of Voysey that this most private face of the house, to be viewed by the family and its guests from the garden, should have been the most refined. It was dominated by the long sweep of green-slate roof, clipped around three first-floor windows and reaching almost to the flat roof of the veranda, which Voysey carried as a sleek horizontal the full width of the elevation. A rhythm of open and closed surfaces – of veranda and porch and loggia – enriched the ground floor, and, with the massive battered chimneys and the long low lines of the house running without interruption into high roughcast garden walls, the house was anchored to its surroundings and dove-tailed with its grounds.

For the first time Voysey was given the garden to design, as well as the house, and the two were inextricably linked.[26] He was no plants man. His garden designs were broadly defined with areas given over to 'turf', 'yew' and 'flowers'. The sweeping curves and abundant natural planting of Gertrude Jekyll's gardens, binding the gardener's art into a partnership with nature, had little influence on his designs. However, his gardens were typical of the Arts and Crafts movement in their combination of a strong sense of order and architectural structure with more natural planting, and often he worked in collaboration with a landscape gardener, or with the gardening expertise of his client. The order in his gardens, was a seamless continuation of the order in his houses, and although his paths were straight and his borders were rectangular, he brought the same exacting proportions and asymmetry into play, the same balance between the unadorned beauty of natural materials and the imposition of applied design that distinguished all his work.

A deep veranda with trellis sides extended the sitting room into the garden and from the sitting

room Voysey created a vista, aligning a simple roughcast sundial at the focus of the formal garden with steps down to a brick pergola:

from the Sundial Walk one descends by three steps to the Herbaceous Border Walk, thence across the delightful Lime Walk to a fine brick-built Pergola which leads to the ornamental Bridge crossing the Stream and terminates on the Island where there is a pretty sitting place protected by a clipped Thuja hedge.[27]

Two 'Fine Lawns' were set aside for tennis and croquet, and a yew hedge divided the main garden from a tea lawn with a charming summer-house designed by Voysey. Closer to the house, the high roughcast garden walls were pierced with massive, arched openings framed by capped pilasters, and imposing gates with heart-shaped strap-hinges that place the authorship of the garden design beyond any reasonable doubt. The gardens and the 'superb background of heather-clad Hills and Valleys, giving an endless succession of perfect Views' demonstrated that by 1894–5 Voysey had resolved his difficulty in integrating a house with its rural setting.[28] He had learnt to manage the succession of spaces from house, through formal gardens, to the meadows and woodland spaces of an estate, with a structured reduction in architectural intervention. If he defied the common ideology of his contemporaries by seldom using local materials to fix a house to its landscape he shared their intention, summarized by Muthesius: 'The aim is to adapt the house closely to its surroundings and to attempt to make house and garden into a unified, closely-knit whole.'[29] By 1895 he had acquired the insight and experience to carry it off.

Voysey designed extensions and additions to Lowicks, Perrycroft, the Forster House, Walnut Tree Farm and even The Cottage at Bishop's Itchington, quite soon after the houses were completed. At Lowicks, the house was altered in 1898 and extended in 1904, and again in 1907 and 1911, and Voysey went on to work on other projects for E. J. Horniman. He appears to have extended his buildings to accommodate the changing requirements of his clients without complaint. Provided that it was he, and not some other architect or builder, who was invited to ring the changes he saw nothing sacrosanct about his own finished work.[30]

10

It is worth noting that it generally was he to whom the clients returned for their extensions, reinforcing the idea that far too much credence has been given to the impression of Voysey as a difficult and intractable architect.

ANNESLEY LODGE. In 1895, before the construction of Lowicks was complete, Voysey began work on the design of a third important house. Annesley Lodge was designed for a small site in Hampstead, north London, which was then still partially surrounded by open fields, but with building lots already allocated for the development of the area. Voysey could have chosen to design a town house for the site, but instead he reflected on the rural qualities of the area in contrast to the densely populated inner-city. The client was a far more intimidating and dogmatic man than Voysey could ever have claimed to be.[31] It was designed for his father, the Reverend Charles Voysey.[32]

Where Lowicks settled into its site with long, low lines, Annesley Lodge adopted an upright disposition, much as Perrycroft had done, but without the romantic trappings of a slender, white stair-tower and oriel windows. It dominated its irregular, quadrant site with extraordinary openness and admirable simplicity. Two long arms reached out in an L-shaped plan and at their juncture a simple porch shaded the wide front door emblazoned with a heart. Annesley Lodge was much smaller than Perrycroft, however, and there were no private gardens sequestered away from public gaze. The house was set close to its boundaries on two sides, and the path to the front door cut across the courtyard in an arrow straight line to the very heart of the house. Voysey was unequivocal on the subject of paths: 'You will express decision and determination by forming a straight path or drive from the road to the house, making it wide to suggest hospitality and welcome, and avoiding any wobbling indecision which only suggests weakness.'[33]

No weakness was permitted either when the planning authorities insisted that the area between the house and its boundaries should be extended, and at one point Voysey and his father decided to abandon the site altogether rather than agree to compromise.[34]

The success of Annesley Lodge can be attributed to its honest simplicity and uncompromising unity.

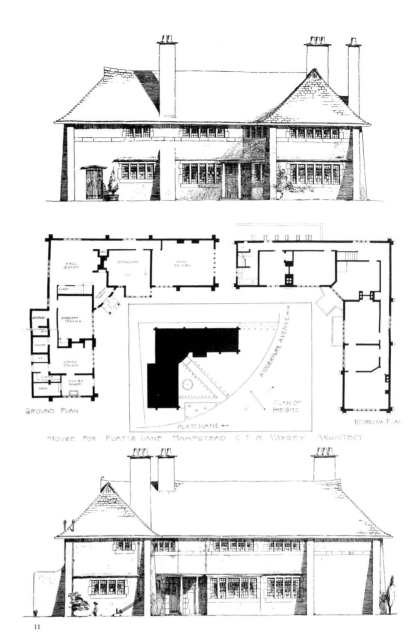

11

12

11 Elevations, plans and site plan of
    Annesley Lodge, 1895.
12 Photograph of Annesley Lodge, 1897.

13

The elevations were composed with absolute clarity. There were no superfluous frills and every detail of the building was crisp and clean, and fully integrated into the whole. Voysey used Broseley tiles to cover the roof, with a gablet light in each wing, and the same tiles were used on edge in a thin red line of weathering above the ground-floor windows. The Monk's Park stone window-dressings were extended to draw a long horizontal line right across the entrance elevations beneath the first-floor windows, repeating the emphatic horizontal of the eaves line and checking the vertical lines of buttresses and chimneys.

The windows, too, were arranged in horizontal bands, tucked up under the sheltering eaves on the first floor, and turning the corner of a square bay, or spaced between the buttresses on the ground floor – always varied to avoid monotony. Voysey was quite content to leave the south-east elevation, facing what was to become an adjacent building plot, almost blind of windows with an austere composition dominated by the vertical elements of buttresses and chimneys; he was careful not to illustrate this aspect of the building in the architectural press, although it was deliberately composed.[35]

Throughout the main elevations, and in the interiors of Annesley Lodge, Voysey took an ideological position on the importance of the horizontal as the governing factor determining every aspect of the design. His insistence upon the importance of the horizontal in the creation of an effect of calm and repose, and on the destructive effect of sharp angles was seminal to all his work:

The quickest thing in nature is a flash of lightning; it is made up of angles. So we find to give the effect of movement we require angularity of one kind or another. We call people crooked or cranky when they lack sweet reasonableness, and they show a want of stability that is disturbing. A stormy sea or sky is angular and cut up – the pained soul is said to be 'cut up'.

On the other hand, nature generally expresses the sweetest calm and repose. At sunset we see the horizontal lines as if all nature were reclining and preparing for rest, dim light drawing a veil over disturbing detail. Horizontalism thus suggests repose; it is the greatest contrast to angularity. These two opposite forms of angularity and horizontalism are the plainest statement of the opposite states of mind of disturbance and peace.[36]

13 *The hall, Annesley Lodge.*

Inside Annesley Lodge, horizontal lines predominated in the low ceilings and wide doorways, which by this time were an integral part of Voysey's style. Although they were often painted, Voysey invariably exposed the main beams to the ceilings of his ground-floor interiors, in order to reiterate the horizontal message, but also in a conscious attempt at an honest expression of structure.

There is a tendency always to associate Voysey interiors with white walls, hard floors, plain (originally pale) wood panelling and a stripped simplicity that would warm the heart of any Modernist. Many of the interiors did meet these conditions and it is certainly true that Voysey's sense of unity – of establishing a set of conditions that could be applied with equal validity to every part of the building from the smallest detail to the overall elevation – and his interest in designing every part of the house down to the teaspoons were fundamental to the development of the Modernist movement. But Voysey was quite capable of inconsistencies and contradictions.

Though the hall at Annesley Lodge was photographed to illustrate Voysey's article in *The Studio*, 'Remarks on domestic entrance halls', the walls were patterned with wallpaper, as they had been at Perrycroft, where Voysey had professed a preference for panelling or for a plain wall with a patterned frieze. In addition, although the chimney-piece was stretched out width-ways to emphasize the horizontal and to suggest welcome, 'Behold my wide, open mantelpiece, broad and simple as if to make room for many', the fireplace itself was narrow and mean in proportion to the room.[37] Voysey wrote of the fireplace as 'the heart of the room', insisting that: 'A warm fire in the hall is akin to a warm welcome. You will so proportion my fireplaces to their rooms that where I enjoy the company of my family and friends, there shall be ample room for all to gather round, and feel the moment they enter that there is room.'[38] There was room by Reverend Voysey's fireplace, but it would have been necessary to gather round in order to get warm because, although Voysey designed generous fireplaces with ingle-nooks for many of his living rooms, his hall fireplaces were often too small to warm the whole room and any heat would disappear up the staircase. They would draw the eye, but little more.

Annesley Lodge was the first house for which Voysey is known to have supplied carpets and curtains, as well as some of the furniture. The passage and stairs were carpeted, and the separate listing in Voysey's office accounts of curtain hooks and rods, as well as the curtains themselves suggest that by 1897, when the house was completed, he had already evolved an exacting specification for curtains.[39] Inevitably, almost all the illustrations of Voysey's original interiors were in black and white, and so we cannot know whether these were the turkey-red twill curtains, which he used in his later houses. But where Voysey's interiors were published in colour, they show that the rich tones and striking combinations of colours that he chose for his interiors could be as unconventional in some instances as the highly individual colouring of his decorative designs. The woodwork of Perrycroft and Lowicks is known to have been white, but in 1897 *The Studio* observed, 'That Mr. Voysey is fond of green painted wood-work, or of green coloured furniture',[40] and this may have been a reference to Annesley Lodge.

Voysey arranged to have his houses photographed soon after completion, often ordering a dozen or more prints. Sometimes they were shown in exhibitions, but more often they were used for publicity; Voysey commissioned and supervised many of the early photographs published in *The Studio* and in architectural journals.[41] In July 1897, he paid fourteen shillings for a dozen photographs of Annesley Lodge, and it was probably one of these photographs of the hall that was published in *The Studio* in 1901. Regrettably, no other photographs of the interiors have survived. Annesley Lodge, however, demonstrates a maturity in the handling of what were by now characteristic materials and motifs, which had still been relatively tentative in Perrycroft and Lowicks. Of the three, only Annesley Lodge was the client's main residence, and it is the only one for which we can be certain that the commission was motivated by an understanding for Voysey's architectural philosophy. The relationship between father and son would have been important in the design of the house, but Reverend Voysey did not attribute value to Annesley Lodge for its architect. In his will, written in 1912, he suggested that its value may have been enhanced by the eminence of its occupant.[42]

2

3

PERRYCROFT

1893–94

Perrycroft, Colwall,
Herefordshire, was designed
for the MP J. W. Wilson.
Presented with a spectacular
site in the Malvern Hills, and
with his most generous budget
to date, Voysey conceived
a substantial L-shaped house
that was both ambitious and
idiosyncratic in its detailing.

1 *Garden elevation viewed
   from the south.*
2 *Front door sheltered by a simple porch.*
3 *Veranda sheltered by buttresses
   in the garden elevation.*

4

4 *Courtyard viewed from the west,*
showing tower with ogee-profile roof.
The bay with porthole window is a
later addition by Voysey.

78   PERRYCROFT

5

6

7

8

5, 6 *Voysey's marble fireplaces were
      extraordinarily plain for their period.*

7 *Front-door hinge.*

8 *Wooden caricature profiles supporting
   one of the oriel windows in the garden
   elevation.*

Voysey's insistence on economy and simplicity, and the emphasis that *The Studio* and later, *Country Life* placed on these qualities in their coverage of his early houses, as we have seen, led him to specialize in the smaller country house. Annesley Lodge and Lowicks each had five bedrooms with a separate dressing room, and as such, they would have been considered small as country-house designs and of medium size for a town house. Any house with four reception rooms or less, excluding the hall, was considered small.[1] Voysey's reputation as a designer of modest and economical artistic houses, however, was not of his own choosing. He had no desire to be tied to any particular architectural type, and soon after the design of Annesley Lodge and the 1896 Arts and Crafts Exhibition he was able to expand his architectural vocabulary.

Between 1896 and 1898 Voysey designed a number of larger houses: Greyfriars, Norney, New Place and, to a lesser extent, Broadleys, which were not very much bigger than Annesley Lodge, but were all designed with an element of grandeur that was never so overt in his smaller houses. The reasons for this grandeur are easy to guess at but difficult to prove. Voysey was thirty-eight when he designed Greyfriars in 1896 and forty-one when the drawings were made for Broadleys. He was a successful and famous architect whose designs were acclaimed in the leading art and architecture magazines of the day. He had tested his artistic doctrine on every aspect of design that attracted his interest, from carpets to lamp posts, all with equal success, and he had the practical experience of a string of houses behind him. It was time to be adventurous again. In addition to this critical and material success there was something intangible, something in the air. Perhaps it was merely an unspoken friendly professional rivalry or perhaps there was a plethora of enlightened clients, but some of the finest houses of the Arts and Crafts movement were designed in the same period.

In 1896, Edward Prior designed The Barn, Charles Harrison Townsend produced plans for the Horniman Museum and Charles Rennie Mackintosh began his design for the Glasgow School of Art. A year later, C. R. Ashbee created 72–3 Cheyne Walk and Ernest Gimson designed the

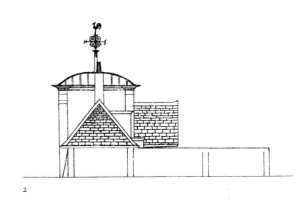

2

AMBITIOUS HOUSES
AND ELEMENTS OF GRANDEUR

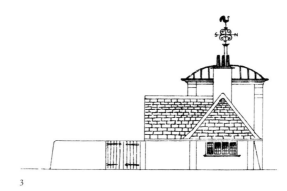

3

1   *Entrance front, Norney, near Shackleford, Surrey, 1897.*

2, 3   *Stable building for Greyfriars, The Hog's Back, near Puttenham, Surrey. Side elevations, c.1897.*

4

At Perrycroft Voysey had deliberately expanded his architectural vocabulary, mixing corbelled windows on one front with the thin white tower with its ogee roof on the other, in order to enrich his design. In the same way he introduced rogue architectural elements to these more ambitious commissions setting them in a quite separate category from the main body of his work.

GREYFRIARS was commissioned for a spectacular site on The Hog's Back, near Guildford in Surrey, by the novelist Julian Sturgis in 1896.[2] Sturgis had rented 16 Hans Road in Knightsbridge and so he had an intimate knowledge of Voysey's work, but where the Hans Road houses, as townhouses, had by necessity been tall and terraced, Greyfriars had its own site and could expand horizontally. In one of his most daring designs, Voysey drew the house out in a long extended line, and then, with effortless panache, terminated the line at one end with a cross gable, whose roof swept gracefully down, almost to the ground. It was the first time that Voysey used a cross gable to such dramatic effect, but it was not to be the last.

Voysey had understood the expressive potential of a roof from his earliest houses. Even in The Cottage and Walnut Tree Farm he had sent his roofs sailing down to the ground, to suggest shelter and intimacy, and to pay homage to the surrounding hills. On his London buildings, where the landscape and prevailing winds were less pertinent, the roofs were more aloof, but at Greyfriars every nuance of pitch and tone that could be culled from graduated Westmoreland slate was brought into play, and almost half the height of the building was taken up by the deep sweep of roof.

When the design for Greyfriars was first published in September 1896 Voysey was specific in his defence of white roughcast and green slates:

He finds that he can obtain effects more dignified and harmonious with white rough-cast and green slates. Slates, he says, have many advantages over tiles: they are more durable, are less liable to injury from hurricanes or storms, and make a better roofing; and these are points that true Craftsmen cannot afford to sacrifice for effect – especially effect that is not really either tasteful or desirable. Of course Mr Voysey does not employ the common Bangor slates, but the green slates, which are just as easy to obtain.[3]

White House, going on to work on Stoneywell Cottage in 1898–9. It was also in 1898 that W. R. Lethaby designed Melsetter House and M. H. Baillie Scott designed White Lodge. Sir Edwin Lutyens, always prolific, sustained a remarkable level of innovation throughout the period with Munstead Wood (1896), Orchards (1897), Goddards (1898) and 'Les Bois des Moutiers' (1898).

The wealth and expectations of Voysey's clients must have been a factor in the experimental designs of 1896–8. All four of the houses contrived to impress, and in this respect they must be likened to Voysey's design for Perrycroft, when he had first been given a generous budget and a large and very beautiful site. Voysey was never comfortable with the need to impress as an objective in its own right. He was too close a follower of A. W. N. Pugin to design anything that smacked of being a sham (although Pugin never had any difficulty in creating an impression), and his own natural language was restrained. Nevertheless, there seems to have been a clear desire to explore and express more ambitious aspirations for himself and for his clients in these houses, leading to a degree of eccentricity.

4 *Final design, Greyfriars, The Hog's
Back, near Puttenham, Surrey.
Executed March 1897.*

82 CHAPTER 7

Voysey flew in the face of accepted Arts and Crafts practice by repeatedly rejecting local-building materials and vernacular traditions in favour of roughcast and green slates, but he adhered to the general principle of rooting the building in its landscape and he was careful to justify his choice of materials:

Will you help me show my respect for local conditions of climate and soil, not ignoring altogether the modern facilities of transit, but as far as possible selecting your material to harmonise with local character in colour and texture. For instance, can there be any harm in using green slate from Wales or Cumberland in counties that produce no slate, considering that the green slate is far more harmonious with nature ...[4]

The first plan and elevation for Greyfriars was dated 26 July 1896, but the final design was not resolved until the following March, and Voysey produced twenty sheets of plans, sections, and drawings for the house, where only two sheets survive for Annesley Lodge.[5] The alterations to plan and elevation were relatively superficial, but the doors and windows, and the mouldings that Voysey used to emphasize the horizontals throughout his interiors, were specified with careful precision.

From his first 'Design for a Cottage' of *c*.1885 Voysey had developed the practice of arranging both plans and a perspective of his proposed house on a single sheet. Often these watercolour perspectives with plans inserted in the corners were drawn by H. Gaye; they were intended for exhibition in the Royal Academy's Summer Exhibition and would have been persuasive in presenting the design to the client. The coloured elevations and sections, however, were always drawn by Voysey and he appears to have been incapable of drawing even the most rudimentary sheet without an innate instinct for arranging pattern and colour on a flat sheet of paper. His detail drawings were intended neither for the client nor the public, but as a means of conveying technical information to the builder and yet they were exemplary graphic designs. The clarity of their information was irrefutable and the quality of their colour and composition places some of them among Voysey's most beautiful drawings. Perhaps this is not so surprising from a man for whom, 'Simplicity requires perfection in all its details'.[6]

5

Often Voysey was at his most adventurous in the design of lodge and stable buildings, where he was able to refine and even exaggerate the central idea behind the design of the main house, and there was always a clear relationship between house and outbuildings. The stable to Greyfriars explored the quintessential qualities of the house – it was long and sleek, and low and emphatically asymmetrical – but where Voysey had used the cross gable to anchor the main house, checking the runaway horizontals with buttresses, bays and chimney-stacks, the vertical element in the stable block was represented by a delicate, white clock-tower, and this clock-tower bore more than a passing resemblance to the small, hand-painted mantel-clock that Voysey had designed for himself in 1895.

He had nursed the idea of a long low stable with a domed clock-tower since 1894, when a very similar design was published for a lodge and stables for Perrycroft.[7] J. W. Wilson had required a different design for his stables and Voysey must have consoled himself with having the clock-tower made up in miniature, until, three years later, he was able to revive the design for Greyfriars. The tower had

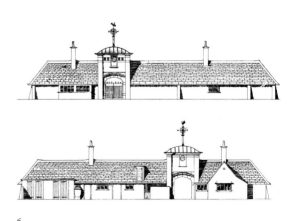

6

5 *Details of doors, Greyfriars, c.1897.*
6 *Design for stables and lodge, Greyfriars, c.1897.*

7

8

7, 8 *Entrance and side elevation of Norney.*

a functional as well as a romantic credibility. At both Greyfriars and Perrycroft the stable-block site was considerably higher than that of the house and Voysey housed the cisterns to hold 3,000 gallons of water for the main house within the clock-tower allowing the water to fall 'by gravitation'.[8]

NORNEY. Within months of the final design for Greyfriars, Voysey was at work on the design of a second important country house. Norney was designed for a country estate near Shackleford, in Surrey, less than five miles to the south-east of Greyfriars, for the Reverend Leighton Grane, but where Greyfriars had been slung across a terrace on the steeply sloping Hog's Back, Norney commanded a sheltered level site. Voysey still favoured a linear plan with the principal rooms at one end and the service wing, two rooms deep with a central corridor, at the other, but the elevations represented a startling departure in character and detail from Voysey's earlier work. Perhaps he believed that the dramatic impact of Greyfriars should be carried by the relationship between the house and its site, and at Norney, where the tension between nature and architecture was less acute, and the house could be enveloped within its estate as Lowicks had been, he saw an opportunity to expand his architectural vocabulary and elaborate on the long horizontals of Greyfriars.

Norney had a Baroque quality of grandeur and monumentality that owed more to Hawksmoor than to the idealized tumble-down cottages and Tudor architecture, which Voysey had taken as his starting point. The front elevation comprised a series of gables that gathered momentum towards two deep bays flanking the majestic stone porch. But where Voysey's porches generally gave a simple emphasis and protection to the front door, often suggesting domestic intimacy, at Norney the double-height stone porch dominated the elevation with sombre authority.

The stone arch of the porch and the circular window described within it have no precedent in the English Medieval architecture that inspired the series of gabled bays and mullioned windows. It is a classical composition, and Voysey would certainly have been aware of the geometric play of these elements in the churches of Sir Christopher Wren, and in the west towers of St Paul's Cathedral in particular. Much has been made of the introduction of classicizing elements into the design of Norney and New Place, when Voysey condemned the English Renaissance as, 'a style which was first introduced into this country at one of the most morally corrupt periods of the nations history'.[9] But the time span between Voysey first employing and then denouncing these elements, and the specific nature of his criticisms are worth exploring in detail. In his article of 1911, 'The English Home', Voysey condemned the English Renaissance as alien to the British temperament and climate:

The term English, as applied to Renaissance, is inaccurate, and a dishonest attempt to make an entirely foreign style appear national; ... Why, then, should England turn her back on her own country and pretend that as she is such a born mongrel she can have no truly national architecture? Has she no national climate? Are her geological and geographical conditions the same as all other countries? Is there no difference between English or Italian men? The absurdity of the suggestion is irritating. No one denies strong national character to the British people. Why, then, do we so persistently try to ape the manners of foreigners?[10]

More specifically, he claimed four years later that rustication was:

originally a deliberate attempt to deceive, it being adopted to make walls look more solid than they really were, a direct and immoral effort on the part of the originators...

It is inconceivable that so many of our leading architects at the present time should be reviving these samples of ancient sin, and, at the same time believe them to be evil.[11]

But he defended Wren as a great artist who was probably 'quite unconscious' of these underlying dishonesties.[12]

It was the 'clamouring for style' that raised Voysey's moral and professional indignation, and his writings and lectures became increasingly censorial in the first two decades of the twentieth century with the rising fashion for what Lutyens described as 'Wrenaissance'; directly related to this was the terminal decline of Voysey's increasingly Gothic practice. In September 1896, just a few months before the design of Norney, Voysey was a milder, less embittered man described as having neither Gothic or classicizing tendencies, and although his consideration for national requirements was already clearly established, his flirtation with classicizing elements the following year would not have seemed so very incongruous:

Formerly a man would either be all Gothic or all Classic, and could not be both; Mr Voysey ties himself to no Style. The first principles of Design, he holds, are the conditions and the requirements of the work to be executed – in England, the climatic conditions of the country and the national requirements of the home-life that is peculiar to it.[13]

Voysey was intrigued by the interplay of simple geometric forms through three dimensions in the same way that Wren and Hawksmoor had been before him, and at both Norney and New Place the theme of a circle rising out of (or contained within) a rectangular frame was explored through the elevations and the interior detailing. At Norney it was most prominent in the stone entrance porch and in the side elevation above a square bay, which housed an ingle-nook fireplace. However the same shape also recurred in the interiors above the hall fireplace, and even in the garden in the outline shape of the pond.

We are fortunate in knowing quite a lot about the client for Norney, the Reverend Leighton Grane, and the background to the commission through a collection of correspondence.[14] Grane was living at the Rectory in Bexhill, in Sussex, when he was first shown Norney's location at the beginning of January 1897, as a possible site 'for the erection of a thoroughly good private house for personal occupation'. The land formed part of Lord Middleton's estate and on 4 March 1897, Reverend Grane wrote to Lord Middleton, 'I am not a wealthy man and much wished to limit my expenditure upon site to £2,000: But I should be ready to offer your lordship £2,500 for this piece if that would meet your acceptance.' He was at pains to ingratiate himself with Lord Middleton, not least because he was offering a low price and they would become neighbours if the sale went through. He offered personal references and the assurance that:

As some evidence that I would not spoil the site by putting on it one of those atrocities in the way of house which are so common, I may mention that I have most reluctantly been forced to join the number of proverbial 'fools who buildse' [sic] after at least a year's fruitless search after a moderate sized house both convenient and picturesque, upon a site offering some interest, and in a habitable neighbourhood. In the course of this search one house designed by Mr Lutyens (who is, I think, known to you) has been almost the only one which has offered me any temptation. That reminds me that Mr L. showed me (quite in confidence) a possible site on a different part of your lordships Estate (near Borough Farm in fact) but this situation strikes us as being too isolated and rather low.

Lutyens was already employed on Lord Middleton's estates, but it is very interesting that Grane involved him in the search for a site, and then turned to Voysey for the design of his house. After some haggling over boundaries and acreage Lord Middleton reduced the site to twenty acres, keeping a slice of land between the site for Norney and his own Peper Harow for the sake of privacy and because, as his son pointed out: 'If ever we got a litigious neighbour he could feed every pheasant we have in the Balt.' Grane was a keen landscape gardener, and his letters suggest that he intended to retire to Norney. His plan was to initially get the grounds into shape and put up a gardener's cottage or lodge, before constructing the main house.[15]

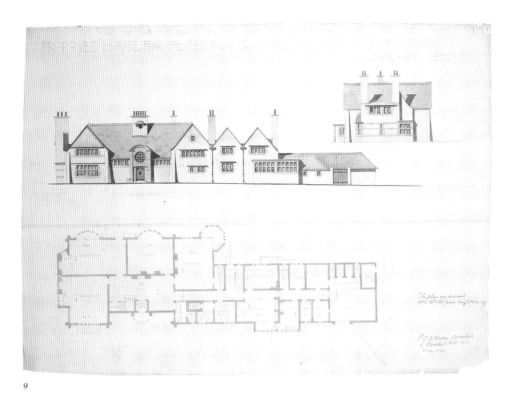

9

In June 1897, the design for one of these lodge-houses was drawn up. It was built the following year. On 29 May 1897 the preliminary designs for the house were made and discussed with Grane and his wife, and their suggested alterations were pencilled on to the plan.[16] The design for Norney went through a series of alterations and even when the building was almost complete the front porch was altered and partially rebuilt. Reverend Grane's letters suggest that he was a forthright and reasonable man, but, like Voysey, he had his own opinions.

The classicizing details became more prominent as the design progressed. The first plans and elevations drawn in May 1897 show a design firmly based in the English Medieval tradition, but with the imposition of an arched stone porch breaking through the sweeping roof line. Although the porch was incongruous in character, it represented only a shallow projection and the detailing of the heavy front door was consistent with Voysey's earlier work. The side elevation shown on the same sheet gives the impression of a startled bandit: arms straight up in two chimneys, hat pulled well down over the first-floor windows and a vertical slit

of ground-floor windows for the mouth. To one side of a chimney a parapet, sharply picked out in red tiles, swept down at a rakish angle; and in the revised perspective drawn in July, this eccentric arrangement remained unresolved. The bandit's hat became more prominently curved and his startled mouth was removed, but to either side of the upraised arms the ingle-nook bays were given curious ogee roofs.

The July perspective also gave more prominence to the entrance porch, increasing the curvature of the arch and projecting the curve outwards in a canopy over the front door. The earliest photographs of Norney, 'taken before the house was entirely completed', were touched up on either side of the front door, suggesting that the heavy stonework curving around the massive doors may have been an afterthought.[17] As the canopy was originally supported by a wrought-iron stay it could have been extended because this method of support proved to be visually or structurally inadequate.[18] The final design additionally differed from the July perspective in its arrangement of the end bay of the entrance front. Where Voysey had initially designed all the bays in the entrance front to be flat, in the final design he introduced a polygonal end bay beneath a flat gable, and this created a series of minor complications in an already complex roof: Voysey capped the buttresses to the bay with their own miniature hipped roofs, compounding the inconsistencies in the long front elevation as a whole.

The side elevation remained erratic in its finished form. The bandit's arms were replaced by a single chimney, but the stack was now enlarged and moulded to describe a circle rising out of a rectangular frame and the flanking ingle-nook bays were still capped by curious, ogee-profile roofs so that the elevation was dominated by an extraordinary juxtaposition of forms.[19] The garden front, by comparison, unencumbered by any self-conscious attempt to impress, was more cohesive in its composition and although the principal bays were again polygonal with flat gables, the strong coherent horizontals and the relative simplicity of the roof overwhelmed the fussy detailing of buttresses with their own hipped roofs.

In 1903, around three years after the completion of the house, Voysey's black book recorded, 'Additions to "Norney", Shackleford, for G. J. Wainwright.'

The house had a new owner and Voysey was required to add a new gable on to the service wing (the line of the original can still be traced in the roughcast), to design new stables (and perhaps one of the existing lodge houses) and to make some alterations to the interiors. The rounding out of the front porch may very well have dated from this period of alterations, and the windows to one side, which show in the 1899 photographs as a single line of lights, were deepened to admit more light into the hall. The reason for Reverend Grane's departure from Norney is not known, but in 1905 Voysey designed another house for him, a small house at Cobham in Surrey.[20]

It is easy enough to criticize the experimental qualities in the design of Norney, with the hindsight of Voysey's later more resolved houses, but at the time it was appraised as a 'charmingly characteristic example of Mr Voysey's work'.[21] Voysey chose the design as one of the illustrations to an article in the German magazine, *Dekorative Kunst*, devoted to his work in 1897, and the plans and elevations were published in *The British Architect* and *The Studio* and exhibited at the annual Arts and Crafts Exhibition Society show in 1899 and 1903. It is precisely because of its idiosyncrasies, its architectural impurities, that Norney must be credited as one of Voysey's most dramatic houses. It has a Romantic tension, which was to recur again and again in his better houses, and a sombre brooding quality, which, although it was never to be repeated, makes it one of Voysey's most memorable buildings.

The relationship between the house and its grounds was carefully planned, and Grane's letters suggest that it was he who laid out the gardens in a series of terraces, increasing in formality as they approached the house. When he was negotiating for the site, Grane described the timber on the land as 'probably of more account in the eye of a lover of the picturesque than in the estimation of the timber merchant'. Originally the site had been wooded with oaks and it is not altogether a coincidence that Norney was panelled and floored with the same wood (although Voysey used oak for many of his other houses where the wood was not indigenous, and at Norney he was obliged to use Austrian oak because it was cheaper than English). Grane was acutely aware of the importance of views and vistas from the house, and he com-

10

plained bitterly when Middleton's son insisted on replanting a screen of tall trees along the frontage to the common that would, in future years, rob him of the 'continual treat', 'of the view of the beautiful bank of forest trees on the far side of the Common, from the House windows'. He concluded that the Middletons wanted to punish him for the whiteness of his roughcast house.[22]

There were two lodge-houses at Norney, and one of these was almost as well publicized as the main house. Again Voysey focused on an aspect of the main elevation in the design of a succinct statement, which was clearly related to the main house, but more daringly exaggerated in character. The emphatic corner buttresses and the flat gable end above a polygonal bay of the main elevation were scrutinized in the design of the lodges, but in the first of these the bay itself was reduced to a small oriel window on the first floor and an asymmetrical bay below. It was the breaking back of the gable end and the balance between strong lines and cutaway voids that were explored. The massing of the gable end bears a striking resemblance to one of George Devey's cottages at Betteshanger. In plan,

the Norney lodge-house was admirably compact with two bedrooms on the first floor, a third on the ground floor and an octagonal bay in the corner of the living room, adapted from the first design for the main house.

The builder for Norney, Frederick Müntzer, was to become one of a number of contractors who Voysey called upon regularly and it was his photographs of the house, newly built, that were published in *The British Architect* in October 1899, almost two years after the working drawings for the house were made. Müntzer's was a small family firm, based in Farnborough. He worked for Lutyens, as well as Voysey, and he was a regular visitor to Gertrude Jekyll's house, Munstead Wood, designed by Lutyens the year before Norney.[23]

Although Voysey's plans were exceptionally economic in the alignment of first-floor walls directly over those of the ground floor, he gave precedence to the perfection of proportions over the advantages of structural economy, and there were occasions when a wall would be shifted out of alignment, even by a few inches, to achieve the optimum dimensions. On these occasions, Voysey was fully prepared to make use of the latest building technology and materials to achieve his ends; at Norney there was a thin concrete wall, supported below by a structural beam across the library, which divided one of the bedrooms from its dressing room.[24] This beam was almost certainly steel, and there was another like it in the billiard room that supported a bedroom wall above. Both were cased in oak in a rare concession to structural camouflage.

Inside Norney the drama and exploratory juxtapositions of the front porch were extended, quite logically, into the entrance hall, though the other principal rooms in the house were balanced and restrained in a manner that was typical of Voysey's mature work. Often an arch would be used to express the structural load of a wall above, for example, in the square bay of the billiard room (although not in the library), and the character of each room was subtly varied through the height and extent of the panelling. In the library, the panelling and oak bookshelves from floor to ceiling wrapped around and enclosed the space, whereas in the drawing room, the panelling was lower and the space was drawn out horizontally; it was gently compressed like brie between the simple oak floor and the low ceiling with its single structural beam. Where the library was intimate, the drawing-room space was expansive, swelling out into two bays and allied to the gardens through long formal vistas and a door on to the veranda. There was a deliberate pull between interior and exterior, but Voysey's rooms never tumbled out into the garden. The dividing line was always clearly defined.

Voysey disliked cornices, and generally abolished them from his interiors; yet in the drawing room and dining room at Norney there are cornices, which are consistent with other Voysey mouldings, and the window and door architraves are unusually elaborate. Did he originally include them as a gesture towards grandeur or to placate an insistent client? Or were they added later, when a window was substituted for the door into the garden, or when the chimney-piece was replaced?

Throughout his interiors, Voysey presented fine materials in an almost naked state. In the billiard room, the entire chimney breast up to the picture-rail – part of the interior rejoinder to the dramatic chimney, which dominated the side elevation

– was faced with blue marble, interrupted only by the barest suggestion of a mantel-shelf. A simple oak window-seat was tucked into the bay to one side, and above it the ceiling followed the curve of the ogee roof. The natural graining of oak and marble and the texture (never quite smooth) of stone and slate were expressed without elaboration. They were exposed with a latent power and sensuality that Voysey skirted demurely around with words:

We cannot be too simple. A true desire to be simple strengthens our sense of fitness, and tends to the perfecting of proportion and workmanship, and a more reverent regard for the natural qualities of material. Carving richly veined marbles and finely figured woods is only the action of irreverence and conceit. We ought to respect nature's veining too much to allow of our chopping it up with man-made pattern.[25]

Voysey wrote of 'spiritual significance', of reverence and of 'thought and feeling'. When 'purely sensuous enjoyment' entered into his writing it did so as a force to be powerfully checked by 'spiritual development'[26] or as a condemnation of the characteristics of Art Nouveau, which he considered to be 'distinctly unhealthy and revolting',[27] but his interiors belie the theories.

Voysey abandoned his quiet restraint in the hall at Norney. The honest expression of natural materials and the insistence on proportion, which endowed his interiors with a refined sense of dignity and harmony, were vamped up with curvaceous balconies, dramatic arches and a remarkable selection of windows. Of these, the most compelling was the great circular window above the porch, which Voysey used to light the staircase; the circle was sliced in half in a second window, which in turn echoed a semi-circular arched opening to the bedroom passageway. The play of a curve through three dimensions was a preoccupation throughout the design of the house. However apart from the semi-circles, the geometry was alluded to, rather than declared.

Voysey was evidently pleased with the hall at Norney because two large photographs of it were chosen to illustrate his 'Remarks on Domestic Entrance Halls' for *The Studio* in 1901. In spite of its eccentricities, it exemplified his demand for generous proportions and strong horizontal lines.[28]

13

13 *The library, Norney.*

14

On the same pages, the article was illustrated by another hall, designed five or six months after Norney, and no less experimental in its detailing. New Place was designed in the same year as Norney, less than ten miles away to the south-west, and the two houses were closely related in their attempt to extend the limits of Voysey's architectural vocabulary.

NEW PLACE, at Haslemere, was designed for the publisher A. M. M. Stedman, who changed his name to Algernon Methuen in 1899, and later became Sir Algernon Methuen. Like Norney it was designed not as a country retreat, but as the client's main residence. By 1896 Methuen was already conducting most of his work as a publisher from his home in Haslemere, commuting into London mid-week by train, and, on the days when he worked from home, ordering the office-boy to post him full details of the day's events, which he posted back by return 'with clear indications of the course of action to be followed in every matter'.[29] He may well have known Julian Sturgis's house on the Hog's Back, and he would almost certainly have been aware of Voysey's work through *The Studio*, but whatever the introduction between the two men might have been, in October 1897 Methuen commissioned Voysey to design a new house for him, sequestered away from view in a woodland estate of over forty acres in the heart of Surrey.[30]

The site for New Place was uneven, banking away to one side, and for the first time Voysey chose not to terrace out a platform for his building or to shape the plan around an existing level area as he had done at Perrycroft and Greyfriars. Instead he fitted the house around the contours of the site, skilfully exploiting the change in level to create an additional storey in one of the wings.

This manipulation of levels became the central idea behind the garden elevation that sprang forwards from the main body of the house in two gabled wings. The first of these, a single-storey wing headed by a polygonal bay housed the study. The second wing, rising through three storeys, took advantage of a dramatic terrace in the garden to drop down to a lower ground floor, so that it read as a two-storey wing, in keeping with the rest of the house from the raised part of the garden, but viewed from the lower level it had a quite different

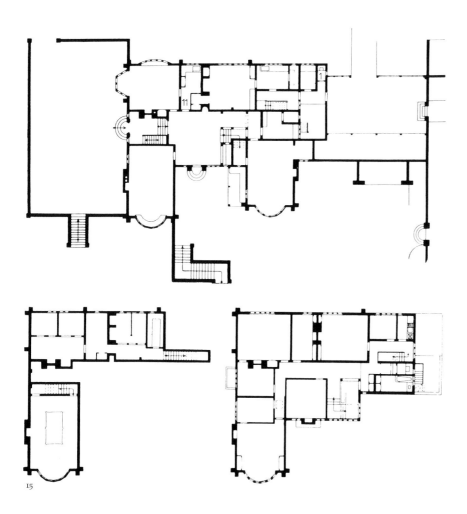

15

14 *Preliminary design, New Place,*
   Haslemere, Surrey, 1897.

15 *Lower ground, ground and*
   first-floor plans, New Place.

and emphatically vertical three-storey character. It was this duality, this transition from a predominantly vertical entrance front to a more complex horizontal one as the corner into the garden was turned that Voysey chose to present in the colour perspective of the house. In reality the transition from three to two storeys is even more dramatic because he underestimated the steepness of the incline in the perspective.[31]

Voysey had already designed gardens for his houses at Walnut Tree Farm and at Lowicks, but in both instances the houses had come first and the gardens had been added later. At New Place, Voysey blocked out the house and garden as a single entity and the conditions of the site were central to the design of both. In one of his earliest surviving drawings, a block plan of 5 December 1897, the existing ground level was outlined in red along the right-hand margin of the plan as a more or less steady incline, against which the principal levels of the house and garden were marked with pencil crosses: the level for the entrance-lobby floor; the billiard-room floor; the rose-garden; the kitchen-garden and the tennis-court were all carefully measured above or below the existing ground level, demonstrating that Voysey conceived the house and garden as a coherent whole. Just as the house exploited the incline of the site, the garden, too, was designed as a sequence of outdoor rooms, arranged in gradually ascending terraces from west to east. The house was connected to its grounds by a succession of formal vistas so that the drawing room, with billiard room on the floor below, overlooked a sunken garden with a rose-garden beyond framed by a 'battlemented Yew hedge';[32] and both the living hall and Methuen's study enjoyed views along long straight paths, leading the eye (and tempting the feet) across the formal garden to the grounds beyond, which Voysey suggested should be left 'more or less wild'.

Voysey's garden looks excessively formal on paper. The straight paths, the heart-shaped beds (which Voysey wanted planted with rue) and the geometric alignments have a daunting severity in plan, and it is often forgotten that many of the best gardens of the period were organized around equally rigid structures. It was the planting that was unruly and abundant, with indigenous shrubs, perennials and climbers scrambling over walls and

16

falling across the hard outlines of paths and borders, and wild gardens and woodland glades around the perimeters. Voysey's knowledge of horticulture was limited. For one of the borders he specified 'flowers big and tall', but by 1897 he was aware of the ideologies of William Robinson and Gertrude Jekyll: the bank between the bowling-green and the lower lawns was to have been planted with 'Briars, Blackthorn, other wild shrubs' and although the rose-garden was redesigned in 1902 by Jekyll, the overall layout of the garden still testifies to Voysey's skill and sensitivity in interlocking the house and its garden.[33]

Like Norney, the design of New Place continued to develop and change after the perspective was drawn in 1897, and some of the experimental details that Voysey had first introduced to Norney continued to preoccupy him at New Place.[34] The two houses were designed within months of one another and certain elements – the classicizing motif on the chimney-stack and the polygonal bay with its flat gable and buttresses capped with little hipped roofs – were lifted directly from one house to the next.[35] At New Place, however, the stone

16 Block plan, New Place, 5 December 1897.

arch set into the chimney-stack repeated the curve of a simple stone, round-headed porch over the front door, and this in turn was flipped through 90 degrees in the curvature of three stone steps, so that the geometric games were fired in quick succession. They were sharp and dry, and Voysey mixed his classicizing allusions with Medieval ones: the stone corbels to the porch caricatured a man's profile – not Voysey's on this occasion, but one suspects that he and Methuen would have shared in the joke – and at the back of the house two more caricature profiles were carved in wood above the garden door. Although Voysey employed different contractors for New Place and Norney, it seems likely that some of the specialist craftsmen worked at both houses. The elaborate, lead rainwater-goods with crenellated heads and decorative brackets were identical on both buildings.[36]

The composition of three gables fronting on to the garden was defined after the perspective was drawn. Where initially Voysey had designed the study wing with a hipped roof, this was replaced by a clean white gable and the polygonal bay was given a rounded roof of lead, which created a striking contrast within the triangular gable. Between the two wings Voysey projected the face of the house forwards from the main pile, like a wide square bay, which masked the sweep of the roof behind. The third gable, dissected by a chimney-stack, gave emphasis to the door into the hall. Voysey liked to gather his flues together and he often projected his chimneys on to the elevations as a vertical anchor, but the logic of locating a door beneath a chimney-stack, albeit one as artfully embellished as this, was questionable.

The main body of the house was contained within a deep rectangular plan with the hall at its heart and the drawing room and study projecting out into the garden. Compared with the hall at Norney, which was 34 feet in length, so that the double height of the space could be balanced, the hall at New Place was a relatively modest 21 by 20 feet, and like the other rooms in the house it had a low ceiling. As at Norney, Voysey designed an element of drama into the hall at New Place, but the theatrical entrance was separated from the main body of the hall itself. The massive front door opened on to an anteroom with a staircase to one side down to the billiard room, and a wide flight of

steps leading up to a pair of elegant glazed doors, which gave access to the main hall. Again Voysey experimented with geometry for dramatic effect and again he manipulated the round-headed arch, sometimes playfully, sometimes with ceremonial grandeur, setting up a subtle interplay of rhythms and repetitions which extended to every element of the design of the house.

The entrance to New Place, the gravity and scale of a relatively short sequence of arched openings and enclosures, was designed to impress as surely as the extravagant hall at Norney, but where the splendour of Norney was instantly and over-whelming apparent to the visitor, that of New Place was ordered and controlled, unfolding in a carefully devised series of stages. Each stage was lighter and more open than the last, more suggestive of other areas of the house. The round-headed arch gave a sense of continuity and repetition to the sequence, while at the same time, quite purposely conditioning the character of each area: the stone arch of the porch and the massive, oak front door were both heavy and monumental, in spite of the humourous caricatures; the anteroom within was tight and compact, with a concentrated formality, compressed between the solidity of the oak front door at one end and the transparency of the glazed double doors at the other (both doors were round headed); beyond the anteroom the hall itself was arranged with a gracious composure, which achieved a remarkable combination of harmonious balance and spatial dynamism.

The main staircase was framed within a composition of three arches in the east wall, just out of alignment with the arched doorway to the anteroom opposite. To one side a passageway effectively separated Methuen's study from the main living quarters and to the other a deep ingle-nook was tucked between the staircase and a window overlooking the garden, providing a space for intimacy away from the main thoroughfare. In the chimney-piece another arch was rounded into a semi-circle with a circle described within it, repeating the geometric games that Voysey had begun to play at Norney, and which had been incorporated into the chimney-stacks and porches of New Place. Although many of the grandiose elements that were explored in the Norney hall were present at New Place, the effect was restrained by a quality of

17

formal composure, of well-mannered politeness, which had been swept aside in the Baroque exuberance of Norney.

The allusion to vertical space in the staircase at New Place was much more discreet than that of Norney. The stairs were contained within their arched opening, rising in a short wide flight to a half-landing before turning out of sight, and although all the principal rooms in the house opened on to the hall it remained a comfortable living room, a space to sit and read or enjoy the company of friends with generous daylight and a wide door on to the garden terrace.

The idea of the main hall as a 'comfortable all-purpose room' was indigenous to the Arts and Crafts movement, and Voysey was too familiar with Tudor building traditions not to have made conscious references to the English Medieval hall, where eating and entertainment all took place in a single lofty space. Hermann Muthesius wrote of the profound influence of these English halls on European architecture, illustrating his words with photographs of Norney.[37] He described the heavy hall furniture, the simple table on which the servant would lay the outdoor clothes of callers whose short stay might not warrant the use of the cloak-room: coats would be carefully folded with hat and gloves always laid on top, and a stick or umbrella set to one side. Voysey, too, was exacting in his attitude to furniture and he designed a hall settle for Methuen in 1901 with carved profiles terminating the uprights.

The plan of New Place was arranged so that all the principal rooms faced southwards overlooking the garden; and Methuen's study was skilfully isolated, giving him access to the garden that was so important to him without proximity to the distractions of the drawing room. The service quarters were more closely integrated with the main house than is usually the case in Voysey's plans – he preferred to string them out as an extremity to the house or tuck them around a corner in a service wing – but they were confined to a corner of the plan, conveniently close to the dining room and hall, while maintaining a proper distance from the family areas of drawing room and garden.

The interiors were oak panelled, fastidiously detailed with built-in cupboards and shelves and characterized by an almost excessive preci-sion. The stone window surrounds, usually exposed, were covered with oak frames, but at least some of the panelling was added after the completion of the house. It was certainly designed by Voysey, but when the house was first completed some of the rooms were papered with patterned wallpaper. During a recent rewiring process this wallpaper was found underneath the panelling. Voysey's black book does not list the decoration of New Place as a separate project and so it would appear that the client changed his mind about the interiors very soon after the completion of the house.

The billiard room, an essential provision in any country house because 'on rainy days when the house is full of people, billiards is the only cure for deadly boredom',[38] was built into the lower ground floor, with a raised dais for non-players at one end overlooking the garden and a window-seat shaped into the bay. Muthesius selected this room as an ideal of its type, pointing out that the best billiard rooms had their own special entrance, 'by which visitors may enter in the evening and leave, possibly late at night, without coming into contact with the rest of the household'. Voysey designed the table and its lights.

The design for the table was originally made for the Reverend Leighton Grane and then sold to Thurston & Co., who offered it in their catalogue from 1900 for the sum of seventy guineas as a 'Voysey design... The table can be supplied in mahogany, walnut, or oak, and is fitted with the "Perfect" low cushions, slate bed, west of England cloth, and Thurston's patent bottomless pockets.'[39] Voysey would never have had the table made in anything other than oak; it was specified again in oak for The Homestead at Frinton, and perhaps for other Voysey houses.

The idiosyncratic details of Norney and New Place represented a self-conscious attempt on Voysey's part to introduce grandeur and monumentality to his more ambitious country houses. As early as 1896 he was rankled by the assumption that his abilities might be limited to the design of smaller, and more specifically to cheaper, country houses like Walnut Tree Farm and Lowicks. As he told *The Builder's Journal*, '...he does not wish these to be considered in any way as his particular *line*. He has simply executed them because he was

18

18 *The billiard room, New Place.*

commissioned to do so, and is equally prepared to devote his attention to any branch of Architecture that may be required of him.'[40]

Regrettably, designs for anything other than houses were very seldom required of him, but when they were, Voysey proved himself to be more than a match for the challenge; in his speculative (and unexecuted) designs made after the First World War, he relished the prospect of extending the language of Tudor and Gothic to meet the requirements of skyscrapers and government offices and shops.

The quest for grandeur (on the rare occasions when it was deemed appropriate) and the manipulation of changing levels in the site to create a series of elevations, which, while leading fluently from one to another were strikingly different in character, were refined through the experience and experiments of Norney and New Place. When Voysey began work on the designs for Broadleys the following year the flirtation with 'Wrenaissance' was over and he emerged as a fully mature architect, uncompromisingly assured of his own highly individual style.

BROADLEYS was one of Voysey's most strikingly successful houses. It was designed for a spectacular site on the banks of Lake Windermere, as a country retreat for Arthur Currer Briggs, the son of a Yorkshire colliery owner. Although it was not a large house, it combined a stately elevation in which three majestic bow-windows broke through the roof line on the lake side with an L-shaped plan, which half enclosed the entrance courtyard in a series of long low lines and cascading roofs.

Briggs would have arrived with his weekend guests by train to Windermere and then taken a steamer along the lake to Broadleys, approaching the house from the lake side.[41] The bank rose up steeply and Broadleys was set at the top of its site so that, approached from below, it would have been revealed gradually as a long horizontal expanse of Westmoreland slate roof, wrapped around the stone bow-windows and anchored to the site by its massive white chimney. The steep incline of the roof echoed that of the site and the green Westmoreland slate, graduated to emphasize the depth of its expanse, together with the local, green-stone terrace walls fixed the house to its location.

19 *Lake front, Broadleys, Gillhead, Cumbria, 1898.*

20 *Bedroom window and seat overlooking Lake Windermere, Broadleys.*

21

Voysey favoured Westmoreland slate whatever the location, but at Broadleys the entire house was constructed of rough green stone with walls two-feet thick 'to secure dryness and warmth'.

He might have chosen to leave the stone exposed, as he did in Broadleys' lodge-house and in the design of a house for W. E. Rowley at Glassonby, made (but never executed) in the same year, but, as *The Studio* observed in 1905, having made his reputation with white buttressed and rendered houses Voysey often found himself saddled with his own idiosyncrasies.[42] One wonders whether Voysey ever tired of his own cut-out hearts, but the roughcast render certainly palled at The Pastures in North Luffenham three years later, and the following extract from *The Studio* was illustrated by a photograph of Broadleys:

It is true there are many architects who, on principle, would employ only such building materials as are produced in the particular locality; but Mr Voysey is no purist, nor has he any prejudice against importing from wherever he may. At the same time, when a perfectly suitable material is ready to hand, he would naturally prefer to take advantage of it. And it is a mat-ter for regret to the artist should a client insist on having what he or she deems a thoroughly characteristic house instead of one more properly native to the soil.[43]

Voysey believed that sunshine was far more important to the orientation of a house than the prospect of a view: 'A view can be enjoyed out of doors; it is surely second in value to sunshine'; he wrote, 'No one in his senses will sit for hours in the house, looking at the view he has every day, no matter how beautiful it is.'[44] At Broadleys, however, the view across Lake Windermere was taken as the central idea behind the design and Voysey's favoured south-easterly orientation was forfeited so that the principal rooms could face out over the lake. The three bow-windows made an unequivocal statement in the main elevation, while ensuring that the principal interiors commanded panoramic views.

Although the prominant bow-windows recalled Georgian and Regency elevations, their arrangement within a strongly asymmetrical composition owed nothing to tradition. Voysey was careful to set them towards one end of the elevation, skilfully

22

21 *Perspective of Broadleys, 1898.*
22 *Veranda, south elevation, Broadleys. This veranda has since been filled in.*

23

balancing the composition with a massive chimney, which, like the bows, broke through the sweeping roof and then, with seemingly effortless assurance, he cut away the corner of the building on the ground floor. The daring quality of this deep veranda, covered by the main structure of the house above, which Voysey supported on four wooden Doric columns, was soon reassuringly clothed with wisteria, though in the early published photographs it dominated the south elevation of the house.[45]

Approaching Broadleys from the road side (by pony and trap along a dirt track in the early twentieth century), the deep veranda with its big roof formed part of a complex arrangement of projecting bays, each beneath its own sheltering roof, which was closed by a long, sleek service wing. It competed with the cluster of roofs around the simple entrance porch, establishing an irresistible sculptural pull, an indication that the artistic focus of the house lay beyond. There was no single artistic focus to Broadleys. The brilliance of the design unfolded in a sequence of subtle and sometimes surprising revelations.

The entrance courtyard, enclosed on two sides by the L-shaped plan of the house and signalled from the road by a Voysey lodge was designed to give an impression of relaxed, although distinctly artistic, rural domesticity. Broadleys epitomized the high-minded romantic ideal of the 1890s and early 1900s of a return to the simple rural life in idyllic surroundings with all its wholesome values, although it was an idealistic rather than a literal revival. But there was nothing cynical or fluffily sentimental in Voysey's design. The entrance was 'put around to the back for protection from the weather, and also to secure greater privacy on the terrace side', and the ground hugging lines reflected the 'terribly exposed' position of the house.[46] Every aspect of the elevations expressed the functions of the rooms within so that the square bay to one side of the entrance porch, marked by a continuous horizontal band of windows around three sides, housed the staircase and the long, low service wing expressed purposeful corridors within.

Once again Voysey was careful to separate the servants' quarters from those of the family and to ensure that family areas were not overlooked by the service wing. Rooms where servants might linger looked out over the grounds to the north, away from the terraced gardens and the courtyard, and the tradesman's entrance had its own small veranda, screened from the main house.

The ground fell away steeply on the north side of the service wing, and again Voysey adapted his plans to take advantage of the change in level, gaining a lower ground floor on the north side of the service wing. This north elevation, seldom shown in photographs of the house, was uncompromisingly vertical and austere in appearance, in sharp contrast to the other faces of the house, and where it met the lake front Voysey reinforced the aesthetic and structural differentiation with a pair of corner buttresses.

The front door, wide, 'like the arms we open to receive our friends', was housed within a simple porch that Voysey tucked under the pitch of a gable roof.[47] It opened into an inner porch with oak panelled walls and ceiling and a cloakroom to one side, before admitting the visitor to the hall where the long lines and intimacy of the entrance courtyard and porch suddenly gave way to a monumental double-height space. The stark grandeur of the main hall, dominated by the great stone bow-window was delivered with rare theatrical genius. The window, commanding magnificent views across the lake, was boldly off-centre, carrying up through the full height of the room and framed by a monumental stone arch. It drew the visitor right across the room and the same Prudham stone framed a deep ingle-nook fireplace with a 'stout copper flue and hood'.[48] Juxtaposed against these mighty arches a porthole window injected a note of humour on the other side of the room.

Structure and decoration in Voysey's buildings were conceived as a single entity. At Broadleys, the main structural walls were built of a double thickness of local stone like a cavity wall with smaller stones in between. The smallest useable stone for this kind of wall was at least eight inches thick so that it was not possible to construct an outer face and an inner face with a cavity between much under two feet thick in total.[49] The structure of the three projecting bays was different from that of the main house because they played no part in supporting the weight of the roof. Each bay had its own flat roof and each, in keeping with its principal function, comprised more window than wall. As a consequence the bays were built of a relatively thin skin of red brick, rendered like the stone walls, but hardly thicker than the solid stone window surrounds which they supported. The contrast between the thin, non load-bearing stonework in the bays and the massive thickness of the structural walls of the house was expressed in the hall in a manner that is so successful, as a statement of grandeur and monumentality, that its full structural significance is seldom appreciated. The massive stone arch framing the bow-window marked the place where the thick local stone walls of the house gave way to the thinner bays and by dressing the arch with the same sawn Prudham stone as the window Voysey accentuated the comparison.

The hall at Broadleys depended for its effect on the dramatic presentation of structural elements, on fine materials vividly juxtaposed one against another, on extravagant proportions, and, ultimately, on the magnificence of nature. Voysey had all the stonework, 'neatly dragged on all exposed faces', contrasting with the smooth texture of the simple oak window-seat and panelling, and in the ingle-nook with the rubbed green-slate seats. In the window, the arch, and the fireplace, the presentation of dragged stonework, unpolished oak joinery and white plaster was unashamedly naked of all decoration. The only decorative elements were two carved cariacature heads, and these were almost certainly portraits of Currer Briggs. Voysey wrote on the drawing for them, 'This nose must be sharp cut with its true fascits and not to be round and dumpling shaped', but even the heads had a structural relevance: they were carved out of the ends of the beams that supported the first-floor corridor.[50] The corridor above overlooked the hall through a glazed screen with 'two lights hung to open', as if the hall were a great Tudor courtyard and its events and entertainments might be viewed from the gallery.

The staircase was set discreetly into the corner of the room, partially enclosed by the drawing room and porch walls, but the modesty of its position was contravened by a flood of light that poured down the broad treads from the windows

24

wrapping around the landing on three sides. Voysey deployed his screens of closely packed balusters to maximum effect, constructing a series of geometric patterns, which changed as each half-landing was turned. The straight, oak newel posts were carried up to the ceiling and finished with square moulded cappings, and although these newels and the handrail were made by a local joiner, the balusters, inlaid with lead hearts, were made by the furniture maker A. W. Simpson of Kendal.[51] Simpson and Voysey had probably met through Arts and Crafts Exhibitions, but by 1899 they were friends, and ten years later Voysey was to build 'Littleholme' a few miles from Broadleys in Kendal for Simpson and his family.

By 1899 Voysey was in the habit of specifying a range of standard parts, some of which were specially made to his designs by small manufacturers who regularly supplied components for his houses. Most of his contracts and specifications are lost, but both Broadleys and Moorcrag were constructed by the local building firm of Pattinson, and the family firm – still in business – holds the most complete set of documentation for Broadleys that has survived for any Voysey house. The mortice latches with 'Voysey knobs' and bronzed rim-locks were supplied by Elsley & Company of Great Titchfield Street, London, as were the Voysey-pattern escutcheons and coat hooks. The tee-hinges and wrought latches that characterize Voysey's houses were supplied by W. B. Reynolds of 28 Victoria Street, London, and the elaborate hinges to the front door were itemized at a cost of four pounds and five shillings a pair, compared with fifteen shillings and six pence for the standard long wrought-iron Voysey hinges. Reynolds supplied the light fittings for the house (although later it was Elsley & Co. that manufactured Voysey lamps) and their account shows that four wooden standard lamps with 'moonlight shades' lit the principal rooms with a note that 'All glass and shades are very expensive.'[52]

It is not surprising that these relatively small details, standard to most Voysey houses, should have been ordered from London and that the tiles for his fireplaces were ordered from Leeds.[53] However Voysey insisted that the tapered earthenware chimney pots he preferred should be ordered from Nuneaton;[54] and even the source for the

cement was specified. It was to be supplied by Sir Michael Lakin's Company, Graves Bull and Lakin of Paddington.[55] The roughcast was made up in two coats:

…with well washed gravel or stone chips finished to a very rough surface with pebble or stone chips as approved; the last coat to be mixed pebbles or stone chips and cement mixed together and applied with a spoon while the second coat is soft. The first coat to be scored over to form key for second coat.[56]

The drawings for Broadleys, like those of Norney and New Place, went through a series of alterations before they were resolved. In particular, the decision to incorporate an extra bedroom into the house appears to have taken place either while construction work was in progress or, at the very latest, as the site was being cleared. Voysey made his first visit to Windermere for Broadleys on 8 and 9 May 1898. The following month his preliminary design for the house was drawn and he visited Currer Briggs in Leeds on 18 and 19 June, presumably in order to go over the drawings with him. By July substantial alterations had been made to the plans so that the three bow-windows of the lakeside elevation, the deep veranda, the staircase-tower, and the double-height hall were all in place, and Voysey returned to Windermere on 25 and 26 July, presumably to meet with his client, making a third visit on 25–27 September. By October there had been sufficient discussions with the client for Voysey to organize paying H. Gaye two guineas for the now famous perspective painting. It is interesting that even while the final design was being resolved Voysey was engaged in having samples made up of the details: he paid A. W. Simpson five shillings and six pence for a sample baluster less than a week later.[57]

On 2 December Voysey made a three-day visit to Windermere and a month later, on New Year's Day 1899, he travelled to Leeds where he would have consulted with his client. On 6 January he paid his typist £3.16.4, probably for typing the detailed specification which was to be read in conjunction with twenty-three drawings, most of which have not survived. He installed himself in the Windermere Palace Hotel on 10 January and he appears to have remained there until 18 January. It was during this stay that the final set

25

of drawings were probably made. They included three interior elevations showing the panelling, in addition to an exterior elevation and ground and first-floor plans, which incorporated the additional bedroom with its own gabled bay to one side of the porch.[58]

There is nothing in Voysey's expenses to suggest that he paid a clerk of works to oversee the construction, and we must assume that the provision in the specification for an 'office for the use of the Architect with desk, stool, basin, towel, soap and clothes brush' was for his own use. Site visits were made on a fairly regular basis, but perhaps inevitably given the distances Voysey had to travel and the number of other buildings that he was engaged upon at the time they were not particularly frequent. His office expenses show that a two-day visit was made to Broadleys every month between April 1899 and December 1900 (with the exception of August, September and October 1899) and that more often than not these visits coincided exactly with trips to Moorcrag. Faced with the moral dilemma of how to charge two separate clients for travelling expenses to the same location Voysey invoiced them both for the full amount. Although he favoured Müntzer as a builder, and he employed Pattinson at both Broadleys and Moorcrag, Voysey did not develop strong relationships with a limited number of builders who knew his ways, as he did with furniture-makers. In fact he often used a firm of builders for a single house, and then employed a different firm to build another near by. Nor can the frequency of his site visits be related to the distance of the site from London: his visits to New Place between 1897 and 1900 were hardly more frequent than those to Windermere.

The development of the design of Broadleys was almost as experimental as that of Norney and New Place, but at Broadleys the element of display was fully integrated within a complex and extraordinarily rational whole. No foreign elements were applied to the exteriors or the interiors, every detail was integrated into a unified whole. The designs for Broadleys were exhibited at the Royal Academy and at the Arts and Crafts Exhibition, and Voysey later chose Broadleys as one of the designs to represent his work in the Victoria and Albert Museum. He designed a kitchen dresser for the house and,

later, in 1904 he designed electric light fittings, a bed, a writing table and a copper jug with a sponge basket and soap dish for the house.[59]

Even during construction the house attracted attention. In 1900, Currer Briggs wrote to Pattinson saying that though Edward Tucker and Hubert Coutts could be shown over the building, no other visitors should be admitted without 'a permit'. The proliferation of Voyseyesque houses around Windermere suggests that Pattinson used the house to impress prospective clients.

Plans and photographs of Broadleys were published in Muthesius's *Das Englische Haus*, showing the dining room furnished with a Voysey table, beneath his light fitting, and a Voysey dresser and rush-seated chairs arranged around the walls. Muthesius described Broadleys as a medium to small-sized house, 'Built and designed throughout by C. F. A. Voysey', noting that:

He is able to call on the very best resources for wall-coverings, carpets and materials, since these are made to his design: English industry has benefited largely from Voysey in this field, in which he has almost become Morris's successor. But he uses pattern in his interiors less than the delight in ornament reflected in his materials and carpets might lead one to expect and his rooms have an air of pleasant restfulness in form and colour. Their underlying atmosphere is one of delicate, almost timid, modesty that recoils in horror from sudden flights of fancy.

He went on to describe Voysey as 'the most individualistic of the busy domestic architects in London today'. He was applauded for his 'courage in seeking new ways and displaying his own personal art to good advantage', and his architectural style was succinctly and accurately summarized. Already Voysey's influence on younger architects – the imitation of his buttresses and the adoption of roughcast as a 'fashionable finish for exterior walls' – was recognized. But although the 'decidedly long and low' proportions of his houses and the whiteness of his walls were later claimed to have had a profound effect upon German and European architecture, it was the unity of Voysey's approach and the unwavering consistency of his detailing that were to extend his influence beyond that of the Arts and Crafts movement and into the twentieth century and the Modern Movement.

26

26   The gable end of the lodge-house closes the third side of the entrance court.

2

NORNEY

1897

Norney, near Shackleford in Surrey, was designed for the Reverend Leighton Grane. In this house and New Place, its contemporary, Voysey sought to extend his architectural language, and to achieve an element of formal grandeur. The elevations, the interiors and even the hard landscaping of the garden explore a subtle repetition of geometric motifs and dramatic juxtapositions with a coherence that binds the disparate elements together.

3

4

1–3 *Entrance front. The principal rooms are distinguished by polygonal bays with over-hanging gables, whereas the service wing is marked by a row of three flat gables.*

4 *The curved stone walls and outer door to the porch were a late addition to the design.*

5

6

7

5 Garden elevation, drawing-room bay.
   The buttresses have their own
   miniature hipped roofs.

6 Voysey sundial, strategically placed
   to focus the view from the house.

7 The lodge-house at Norney is typical
   of Voysey's lodges in the way it
   manipulates elements from the design
   of the main house and presents them
   in a daring and stylized form.

102   NORNEY

8

9

10

8 *Garden elevation.*

9 *Summer-house.*

10 *Even the garden pond repeats architectural motifs from the house.*

11

12

13

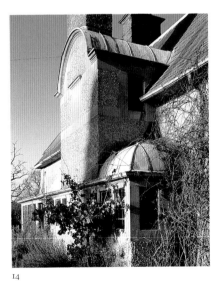

14

11 *The hall.*

12 *The library fireplace, manufactured*
    by Thomas Elsley.

13 *East wall of the bedroom directly*
    above the ingle-nook.

14 *Detail of east elevation.*

15 *East elevation.*

2

3

NEW PLACE

1897

New Place in Haslemere,
Surrey, was designed for the
publisher A. M. M. Stedman,
who changed his name to
Algernon Methuen in 1899.
It was the first house in which
Voysey manipulated a steeply
sloping site to create a lower
ground floor in one wing of
the house; as at Norney, he
introduced contradictory
architectural elements,
tightly worked into compact
compositions, in a deliberately
ambitious design.

4

1 *Front door. The simple stone porch
  is corbelled with caricature profiles.*
2 *Entrance elevation.*
3 *Porch corbel.*
4 *Hall window showing presentation
  of texture and finely crafted detail.*

5

6

7

5, 6 *From the raised terrace to the east,*
   the garden elevation reads as a
   coherent two-storey elevation.

7 *Garden court, with settle to one side.*
   The bell above the garden door would
   have summoned the family and guests
   from the garden for meals.

8

9

C F A VOYSEY

8, 9 *From the lower terrace, the vertical character of the end bay is revealed, creating a tension within the elevation.*

2

BROADLEYS

1898

Broadleys, on the banks of Lake Windermere, Cumbria, was designed for Arthur Currer Briggs, the son of a colliery owner. The design focused on a magnificent site with three bow-windows in the principal elevation, commanding panoramic views across the lake. Each elevation is quite different in character, creating a sculptural pull from the ground-hugging lines of the entrance courtyard, to the short south-facing elevation, which was daringly cut-away, originally in a veranda, to the lake elevation beyond.

3

1   *Lake elevation from the north.*
2, 3   *The site banks steeply away towards the lake and on the north side of the house, where Voysey took advantage of the sloping site to create a lower ground floor.*

4

5

6

4 A long, low service wing encloses
  the entrance courtyard.

5 The porch tucked into the gable
  of a guest bedroom.

6 Service wing, viewed from the porch.

II2   BROADLEYS

7

8

9

10

7   *Staircase. The balusters, inlaid
    with lead hearts, were made by
    A.W. Simpson.*

8   *Two caricature heads are carved into
    the beams which support the corridor
    above the hall.*

9   *Family and guests could look down into
    the double-height hall through a glazed
    screen in the corridor above.*

10 *The hall was designed for entertaining
    on a grand scale.*

The idealized image of the old English cottage, white-washed, with roses around the door, which had come to represent rural stability and historical continuity in a century of overwhelming change, was profoundly important to Voysey's clients, if not to Voysey himself. *Country Life* devoted an article in 1898 to the 'ideally perfect' old country cottage, where 'hollyhocks rise up over the hedges and rosy apples hang from gnarled trees'.[1] Sentiment, it said, was 'a very important factor in life, and the old-world associations that an English cottage possess are not to be dismissed lightly'. The article suggested that these cottages were the 'ancestral home(s)' of peasants whose families had lived there 'generation after generation, tracing back their holdings to feudal times'. But, disenchantment set in the moment the front door was opened, 'if you enter, the low damp walls, the cramped staircases, the arrangements for cooking, and other essential if sordid items of the daily life, quickly disillusion you'.

According to *Country Life*, there were two solutions to the practicalities of obtaining a perfect country cottage. The first was to find a cottage 'of poetry', evict the peasants and gut the interiors, 'although the cost of adapting them would be much greater than that of building a new house'. The second, and here the article revealed its true intentions, was to abandon the idea of an authentic old cottage altogether, and to commission Mr Voysey to build a new one:

The best plan is to forego all pretence of antiquity, and have a house that is modern in every respect, except that it is built to last, and is comfortable and commodious as well as picturesque.

Here Mr Voysey comes in, and he enters alone, for no architect at the present day has attempted what he has done over and over again.

Shaw was entertained, and then neatly dismissed as an alternative designer: 'A Norman Shaw cottage in its own way may be as perfect as a Voysey; but here a difficulty crops up – Mr Norman Shaw has retired from practice, and no longer designs cottages.' Only Voysey, it was claimed, could re-embody the spirit of the ideal cottage, never setting the picturesque above the practical and yet making 'utility the basis for aesthetic expression'.

THE MODERN
COUNTRY COTTAGE

2

115

1 *View of entrance front of Moorcrag, Gillhead, Cumbria, 1898–9.*

2 *Eagle modelled by Voysey and cast in bronze, c.1909.*

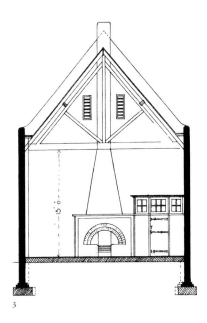

3

Voysey was at his best when he was most succinct, and the restrictions of the country cottage provided the perfect vehicle for his rigorous consistency and his exacting attention to detail. In addition, the commissions for smaller country houses came steadily throughout his architectural career and so they give a much clearer picture of the development and crystallization of his ideas than the spectacular show-pieces of Norney, New Place and Broadleys. They were not real cottages in the the old-world sense. They answered a contemporary set of requirements for modest and functional accommodation in a rural setting, usually with rail links to a city. They were much larger than the buildings we would recognize as cottages today, as they had to accommodate servants. They were founded on a vision of simple cottage life, rather than the grandeur of a country house, and they revitalized and rationalized the essential features of a cottage – the thick walls, stone floor, low ceilings, and the provision of a few well-sized rooms – and so they attracted a diverse clientele.

Voysey's country cottages appealed to the practical, as well as the nostalgic faculties of the middle-class industrialist or businessman with adequate resources for an unpretentious holiday house. These were the men that *Country Life* set out to assist. They also attracted patrons and practitioners working in every field of the arts, who shared Voysey's artistic convictions and his quest for honest simplicity. The prospect of abandoning urban life for an artistic country cottage, of opting for the simple life, or at least a semblance of it, where man and nature could live in harmony was intellectually attractive and at the same time financially viable. For many, including Voysey himself, the availability of building plots within a convenient distance of a railway line to London represented an attractive alternative to renting or buying a house in the city. In addition, the 'ideally perfect' concept of cottage life set the occupant apart from (even above) the English practice of associating property with wealth, and of judging an individual by his address. By commissioning a country cottage, the client asserted his independence from the swiftly changing and artificial values of city life and associated himself instead with the enduring attributes of the rural artisan as idealized and articulated by William Morris.

Voysey had always kept company with artists, and though his cottage designs were founded partly on those for estate cottages, dating back to his years with George Devey, they also drew on the discipline and creative stimulus of designing artists' studios. One of his first jobs in independent practice had been the design of a studio in 1884, for C. Christie, in Oakley Street, London, his designs for the Forster house and 17 St Dunstan's Road have already been described, and in 1892 he designed a row of four studios in Glebe Place, Chelsea for Conrad Dressler – a fellow Art Workers' Guild member who had sculpted the relief panels in the porches of the Hans Road houses. There is no record of the Glebe Place studios having been built, but Voysey did design a simple brick studio for Reynolds Stephens in the same year;[2] and in 1893 he designed an extraordinary studio, again unexecuted, for Miss E. Forster at Brook Green.[3]

Miss Forster's studio, like the family house in Bedford Park, was strikingly simple. It was three storeys high with a gable end part hidden behind a parapet, and its composition was dominated by the artistic distribution of arched and square-headed windows. Straight horizontals and gentle curves were emphasized by projecting lines of weathering, and the plan, like that of the St Dunstan's Road studio near by, was compact with a double-height studio to the rear and a sitting room with bedrooms above stacked up at the front. Apart from the provision of shutters fitted to the first-floor windows, the studio was stripped of all unnecessary detail. Perhaps the austerity and arrangement of the elevation was inspired by working for an artistic client, or perhaps Voysey was liberated by the idea of designing a great shed of a studio, with the most basic accommodation in front.

HILL CLOSE. Whatever the inspiration, Voysey's design for a studio-house for A. Sutro three years later was more conventional although it was hardly less succinct. Perhaps it was more traditional in appearance because it was designed as a definite project to be built at Studland Bay in Dorset or perhaps because the studio element was more integrated within the four-bedroom house. Hill Close was a country cottage and artist's studio combined, and the first plans and elevations were drawn up in January 1896 and published immediately in *The*

British Architect. The studio itself was clearly defined by an immense window in the end elevation and a square bay on the garden front. The scale of Sutro's work did not warrant a double-height space, but there was a raised gallery at one end of the studio and an area 'paved for animals' by the external door, presumably to accommodate his various models.

Because Hill Close was a country cottage Voysey gave full play to the contours of the graduated roof of local stone, bringing it down to touch the ground-floor windows on three sides so that it blended with the landscape, and only clipping it short to show the first-floor walls and windows at the front of the house. A witty gablet light, breaking through the front of the roof, pointed out the underlying triangle of the hipped roof and the long horizontal bands of windows, joined by continuous lines of dressed stone, were neatly balanced by buttresses. The plans accommodated complex changes in level, following the contours of the site to give additional height to the studio, and there was a clear division between areas of work – the studio and study, linked through the raised gallery on one side of the house, and the family areas of dining room and hall on the other.

The clarity and economy of Voysey's studio houses, like his lodges, suggest that he relished the challenge and focus of designing the most compact artistic dwelling; many of his artists studios and houses were designed for fellow members of the Arts Club and the Art Workers' Guild. The sharp artistic consciousness of these early designs was to have a decisive effect on his country cottages. He applied the same principles of clear artistic definition, economic planning, and the best materials and workmanship that the budget would allow, even to the smallest unit. In 1894 Voysey had been commissioned to design a new house for the Earl of Lovelace at Ockham Park in Surrey. The house was never built, but the following year, perhaps as compensation, he was commissioned to design an inn and a terrace of six estate cottages for the Earl of Lovelace at Elmesthorpe near Leicester.[4] The Wortley Cottages were not artistic middle-class retreats. Like Devey's estate cottages they were to be lived in by poorly paid families who had worked the land for generations – the very 'peasants' that *Country Life* idealized.

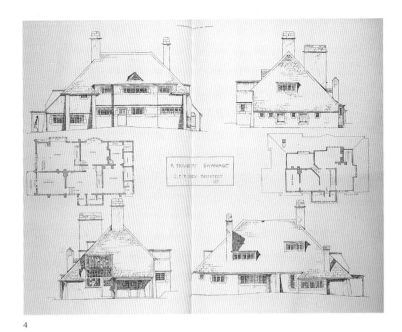

4

WORTLEY COTTAGES. In the design of the cottages, Voysey drew on vernacular traditions, and even in this relatively basic accommodation he was careful to provide two good-sized rooms – a living room and kitchen – on the ground floor of each cottage with three bedrooms on the floor above. The straight economy of the front elevation, framed by a corner buttress at each end, was enriched by projecting porches and the composition was crowned by a thatched roof that swept down over the porches and curved around the first-floor windows.[5] *The Studio* remarked that the great eaves of thatch brought over the porches gave a sense of shelter, which suggested 'a hen covering her chickens', and Voysey's provision of a bench outside each porch was claimed as an indication of his 'sympathy with the inmates – a reward of rest after honest labour'. It went on to state, 'In touches of this sort Mr Voysey betrays plainly the accord with humanity which softens the apparent austerity of his work. His "extras" do not take the form of ornament, ... yet when they are apparent, they are invariably planned to yield some little pleasure to the occupants.'[6]

5

4 *Plans and elevations, Hill Close,
Swanage, Dorset,* 1896.

5 *Wortley Cottages, Elmesthorpe,
Leicestershire,* 1895.

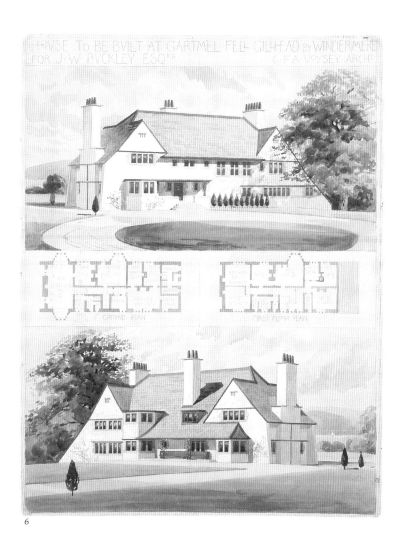

6

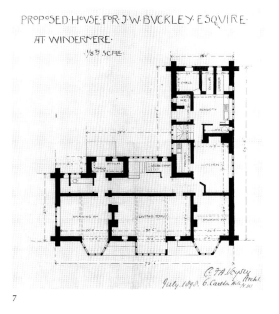

7

Though both *The Studio* and *Country Life* championed Voysey for his economy, it is very interesting that the *Country Life* article on cottages, which described and illustrated Voysey's cottages in detail, chose to cite his earliest houses as examples. The plans and elevations for Sir Michael Lakin's Cottage at Bishop's Itchington, designed a decade earlier and shown with and without half-timbering, were presented as: '… good to look at, good to live in, and give you your money's worth for money spent. They are comfortable and lasting, with a curiously home-like appearance, that makes them harmonise with pastoral scenery in a way few modern houses have done before.'

No mention was made of Voysey's most recent and more ambitious designs (although Norney and New Place were still only drawings and Broadleys not yet designed), and, although the estate cottages for Lord Lovelace would have been considered too economic for inclusion, the omission of any reference to Lowicks, Greyfriars and Hill Close is surprising. Nevertheless, *Country Life's* campaign together with articles in *The Studio* must have swayed many prospective clients in search of a country cottage.[7]

J. W. Buckley, a Manchester textile manufacturer, may well have been influenced by the *Country Life* article and its emphasis on utility, economy and the ideal of a modern country cottage that would blend with the landscape. He commissioned Voysey to design him a weekend retreat overlooking Lake Windermere within months of the publication of the article. Buckley may have known Voysey's textile designs and he might well have been friendly with Currer Briggs, for whom Voysey was about to design Broadleys, but whatever the clinching factor might have been, Moorcrag was designed as a modern country cottage with a very careful control on the budget and a clear intention that the house should reflect and harmonize with its spectacular site at Gillhead.

MOORCRAG was one of four houses all designed by Voysey around the Lake District in 1898. Two of these, Broome Cottage near Windermere and a house further north at Glassonby were never built, but Broadleys was almost exactly contemporary with Moorcrag.[8] However, where Broadleys was

6 *Perspective, Moorcrag, 1898–9.*

7 *Preliminary design, Moorcrag,*
   July 1898.

CHAPTER 8

designed with a strong element of display Moorcrag was private and domestic in character. The design of the cottage went through three distinct phases between July 1898 and June 1899 making it later than Broadleys and suggesting that the owner's taste and whims were taken into account to an unusual degree.

Initially, the house was to have been planned around an entrance court in an L shape like that of Broadleys with three bay windows, one square and two splay-sided, presumably looking out over the lake. Voysey made a second visit to the site on 27 May and the first preliminary design was simply dated 'July 1898'. Within days of this design, however, in a drawing dated 9 July, Voysey swung the service wing through 90 degrees, enclosing the house within a simple rectangular plan with the servants' quarters at one end and the family area at the other still arranged in three principal rooms, each with a bay window. The second plan afforded more generous living accommodation, with the central living room opened up into an immense living hall. The elevations reveal a simple white house with a deep sheltering roof interrupted on the entrance side by a cross gable, which kicked out to enclose the porch. On the garden side the roof wrapped around the first-floor windows and extended down around the bays in a protective gesture.

Almost a year passed before a third design for Moorcrag was '... shown to Mr. Buckley at Riggs Hotel, Windermere, June 23rd 1899 and approved by him and Mrs Buckley in the presence of Mr. Mawson'.[9] Thomas Mawson was the landscape designer for Moorcrag and Broadleys, and a local man. The agreed design was to become one of Voysey's most resolved and celebrated houses. On the entrance side the cross gable was shifted along to close the elevation at one end with a cat-slide roof which ran almost down to the ground. It was balanced by a second cross gable at the other end, but here the pitch of the roof stopped level with the first-floor windows, and it was held in check by a monumental chimney and reinforced by corner buttresses. Between the two gables, the strong horizontal of the roof line, just clipping around the gables at either end, was reiterated in horizontal bands of windows accentuated by long sharp lines of slate weathering and by the flat roof of the veranda that shaded the front door.

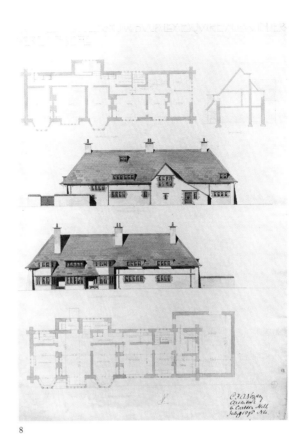

8

Immense slabs of the local green stone made up the steps to the front door, and the same stone, quarried twenty miles away at Buttermere, was used for the window dressings, the weather courses, some of the interior floors and the roof.[10] Like Broadleys, the walls of Moorcrag were two-feet thick and built of local green stone, the splay-sided bays were thinner and built of brick, and the slate roof was graduated to avoid 'the mechanical monotony of uniform slabs'.[11] Voysey's preference for slate rather than tiled roofs was again carefully justified: 'Mr Voysey, objecting personally to a hard surface which could not be expected to acquire the mellow tones of moss-grown age, never uses any save unpolished slate; but this he does introduce effectively in judicious combination with such materials as his experience has proved combine suitably with the slate.'[12] A slate roof, it was said, would hardly ever harmonize with brick walls, but, by implication, the aesthetic combination of slate and roughcast was perfectly acceptable.

Voysey used green-slate roofs with roughcast for houses all over the country, but he would have been aware of the seventeenth and eighteenth-

9

8 *Plans and elevations, Moorcrag,*
   9 July 1898.
9 *Garden elevation, Moorcrag,*
   photographed in 1902 before the
   parlour bay was tile hung.

century farmhouses and cottages in the Lake District, built according to vernacular traditions with white roughcast walls, sweeping green-slate roofs, and comprising a few good-sized rooms inside, simply arranged with whitewashed or panelled walls, low ceilings and slate floors.[13] At Moorcrag, Voysey brought the roof sailing down over the garden front and held it taut between two bays in a veranda that offered shelter from bracing winds and habitual rain. This roof had appeared in the earlier design between a pair of two-storey bays, but the line of the roof curving around the two-storey bay on one side and cutting across the gable to cover a single-storey bay on the other was more daringly assured in the final version.[14]

The strong defining outline of the cross gables on the entrance and garden elevations provided a frame for the artistic asymmetry of Voysey's compositions. If the genius of Broadleys had been founded on the design of a sequence of elevations and interiors, each one different from the last and yet contributing to a rich and coherent whole, then at Moorcrag it was founded on the poise and perfect balance of a building that abandoned all the traditional accoutrements of order and repose and yet achieved an extraordinary zenith of harmonious composure. In the main elements and in the detailing of the design, Voysey established a series of horizontal rhythms regulated by the strategic positioning of three massive white chimneys and he was relentless in his renunciation of symmetry.

The arrangement of the front door on one side and the south-facing veranda on the other, cast between the single and double-height bays, were emphatically asymmetrical; they were deliberately informal in character, horizontal in compositional value, and at the same time weighted to counterbalance the strong diagonal of the roof line and the change in site level at the other end of the elevation. At a detailed level the lines of slate weathering, particularly in the gables on both sides of the house, stepped down as the site sloped away, but the house never gave the impression of sliding down the hill. It was firmly anchored to its site and although a pattern in the fenestration would be repeated vertically (the ground-floor windows, for example, were similar to those directly above in one of the gables on the garden side), the patterning of the window dressings was deliberately different.

Moorcrag gives the appearance of having been designed as a direct response to the natural qualities of the site. 'A fine site,' according to Voysey, 'helps to create a beautiful house if the architect is careful not to come into competition with the country surrounding him, but endeavours to subject himself to nature's architecture.'[15] It has been suggested that the roof line sweeping down almost to the ground at the west end of the house, closest to the lake, made reference to the slope of the site, but the orientation of Moorcrag and the landscape detailing of Voysey's drawings would suggest that this was not originally his intention. None of the designs for Moorcrag show a north point and it seems likely, despite Voysey's site visits, that the house was designed without a correct understanding of the contours and geology of the site. Voysey's undated perspective painting of Moorcrag shows the lake in the background to both elevations, suggesting, rather optimistically, that it might have been viewed from the garden and from the entrance front as well. In the painting, the house commands a level site except for a manageable sloping away to one side, but in fact the site banks up steeply to the south and the east, and falls away sharply on the west side down to the lake, and more gently to the north.

Voysey arranged the principal rooms at Moorcrag to face south-west and so benefit from the afternoon sunshine, but in doing this he presented the principal views of the lake (on the north-west side) to the servants' quarters. In addition, the steep slope of the garden overshadowed the house depriving the parlour and hall of the low lines of sunshine for much of the year. Voysey had undoubtedly intended to level the site and terrace the garden, but he had underestimated the force and finance required to shift the local green stone. Having literally blasted through the rock face to forge the driveway from the road to the north of the house, the feasibility of levelling the site was probably found to be untenable and the house, as a result, became embedded in the landscape. Moorcrag was the only house for which Voysey did not survey the site himself. He paid Thomas Mawson for a survey of the land on 2 July 1898, and some of his designs must have been based on Mawson's calculations and on his knowledge of the local stone. It was the only occasion on which

10

Voysey's account book shows payments made to a second party for land surveys.

Voysey was obliged to compromise, too, on the arrangement of the interiors. He had intended the house to be served by a single staircase, but Mrs Buckley was appalled by his proposal that she should share the stairs to her country house with the servants. Voysey is said to have treated her snobbery with contempt, 'This is not a house! Its a cottage Madam'.[16] Mrs Buckley, however, won the point and a secondary staircase was inserted into a corner of the kitchen and buttressed in the front elevation. Voysey's early ideal of a vast open hall at the heart of the plan was relinquished to accommodate a cloakroom next to the porch and an enclosed study in the centre of the garden front.[17] It was replaced by a 'dining hall' running the full depth of one end of the plan, but the revision necessitated a long corridor, deprived of natural light, which dissected the house into north and south ranges. The early plan was more generous in light and living space, however any concessions that Voysey was obliged to make in the plan and position of Moorcrag were compensated for in the furnishing and decoration of the interiors.

The splay-sided bay in the parlour was reinforced by an emphatic oak beam and juxtaposed against a porthole window in a witty cross-reference to Broadleys. Voysey used the same local builders and joiner for both houses, but there were no double-height spaces or dramatic flourishes at Moorcrag.[18] The family areas were panelled throughout with simple, oak plank wainscoting up to the broad flat picture-rails, and the plaster above was left white.[19] The rooms were proportioned to emphasize length and width, 'which in a small house is more valuable than height', and the simplest mouldings were chosen for architraves, skirtings and picture-rails. Voysey, unlike some of his contemporaries, was ready to take advantage of machine production in many aspects of his work, but he advocated restraint in the application of any form of ornament:

Enough has been said to lead you to introduce ornament, that is, machine-made mouldings and pattern and decoration of any kind, only when it is needed on practical grounds, such as the moulding of a skirting board to avoid the wide ledge for dust at the top, or the rounding, splaying, or moulding of exposed

11

12

angles, or the emphasising of horizontalism with a view to suggest repose, or the binding together of points of interest by strings of moulding, delicate lines that express unity and rhythm.[20]

In the parlour, Voysey linked picture-rail and architraves to run around the room in a continuous line that cut around the splay-sided bay, made a square frame around the porthole window, and arched around a circular mirror over the fireplace. The moulding itself was plain, but the gathering of spatial and structural elements into an integrated pattern was sophisticated.

Voysey insisted that although fine materials added to the initial expense of a building, they would prove to be an economy in the long term. The oak joinery at Moorcrag, it was argued, could be justified because the cost of painting, decorating and upkeep generally would be reduced to a minimum.[21] However he very rarely found a client egalitarian enough to agree to his pronouncement that, 'If the money at our disposal will not pay for oak joinery everywhere, then let us have it nowhere … it would not be consistent with fitness to use deal in my kitchen that I might have oak in my hall; it

11 *Porthole window, parlour, Moorcrag.*

12 *The corridor, looking towards the 'dining hall', Moorcrag.*

13

We are only aware of the dining-room furniture at Broadleys through Hermann Muthesius's photographs, but it is known that Voysey designed table lamps and movable, electric wall-lamps, manufactured by Elsley's, which fitted on to the picture-rails at Moorcrag.[26] He also designed an oak bedstead for J. W. Buckley.[27] Voysey believed that furniture designed with thought and feeling had a purifying and enlightening influence on its users, and his views on beds, and in particular the horrors of brass bedsteads, epitomize the innocence and intensity of his design philosophy:

The proper ventilation of the bedroom and healthy conditions of rest do not entirely depend on air space or metal bedsteads. Indeed, the old four-poster was much more calculated to inspire right thoughts and feelings, and in a properly ventilated bedroom is as healthy and clean as any metal atrocity.[28]

The design of J. W. Buckley's bed was almost identical to the bed for E. J. Horniman six years earlier, and to Voysey's own bed at The Orchard, and it is interesting that, having found a vessel for 'glowing thoughts', Voysey saw no reason to tailor its design to the individuality of his clients. His success in integrating the design of furniture and interiors with the plans and elevations of his houses was described by a contemporary as 'epoch-making' in 1899;[29] and his practice of repeating or adapting successful elements from one design to another was thought no more unusual than the standard use of 'Voysey' doorhandles, strap-hinges and window-stays in most of his houses. There are remarkable similarities between the garden elevation of Moorcrag and an unexecuted design for Broome Cottage at Windermere of 1898 and on one occasion Voysey took the design of a house drawn up for a client at Bexhill, and built it for another in Surrey. But in spite of this economic recycling of designs and the restraint of his visual vocabulary, Voysey's repetition of motifs never resulted in the production of identical houses. Only unexecuted designs were extensively copied, and where the configuration of a bay or the cut of a roof was adapted from one house to another it was invariably woven into the context of a very different composition.

For Voysey, 1899 was one of the busiest and most lucrative years: he designed eight new buildings; revised the designs and managed the construction

would be regarded by some as mere vulgar display.' Vulgar display or not, Voysey was obliged to use deal in the kitchen, scullery, and servants' bedroom.[22] Their decoration conformed to his fallback position that:

We need not lay down velvet pile before the kitchen range; fitness must always be religiously regarded, but to have your kitchen dresser and your necessary details ugly and shabby is not right or necessary. Ugliness is a poison wherever it is found, and harmful to all concerned in its making, as well as in its use, therefore to be spurned at all costs.[23]

'Fitness' was served by white-tiled walls up to the picture-rails in the kitchen and scullery and the floors were of slate.[24] The simple, batten-and-ledge deal doors were stained green and there was a Voysey dresser in the scullery, again of green-stained deal. The curtains were probably supplied by Liberty and selected under Voysey's superintendence.[25]

An absence of early photographs of the Moorcrag interiors makes it impossible to know how many of the rooms were furnished by Voysey.

of some of his most ambitious earlier commissions; and some of his most successful decorative and furniture designs date from this period. His income doubled from just over £808 in 1895, to over £1,693 in 1899, representing a substantial increase even on the previous year's income of £1,466 and £1,461 for 1900. His designs were exhibited at the Royal Academy and in the Arts and Crafts Exhibition, and his flourishing practice attracted more articles in *The Studio* and *Country Life*. The practice remained small and distinctively individual, however, in the face of this sudden prosperity.

Before 1899, Voysey worked from a small studio at home. The offices at Broadway Chambers had been retained for three years until Voysey's marriage in 1885, when he moved to 7 Blandford Road, and the office then moved through a series of private houses, until in 1899 he separated his family house from his London office.[30] Voysey designed a 'House for Mrs C. F. A. Voysey' in the country, at Chorleywood, in Hertfordshire, and the family rented a house near by until it was ready in 1900.

The office moved to a more central position at 23 York Place, Baker Street. Voysey employed relatively few pupils for so prestigious and successful a practice, and we know very little about them. In his old age he made a list of all his pupils, amounting to thirty names, but of these no dates of pupillage are given for seventeen, and only three are known to have been employed before 1900.[31] The 1927 series of articles on Voysey, based on interviews with him, described the office as follows: 'In his most active years Voysey's staff seems to have consisted of no more than two or three pupils, and in an atmosphere of a happy family the letters were written by someone and press copied by somebody else. No telephone ever disturbed the tranquillity of Voysey's work.'[32] John Brandon-Jones, who knew Voysey and one of his pupils, and was himself assistant and later partner to Voysey's son, described the York Place office in more detail:[33]

His office consisted of two rooms, one opening into the other. Both were carpeted and hung with watercolour drawings and photographs, and the folding doors to the private office were usually left open so that the pupils might overhear and learn from conversations between the principal and his client or contractors. Voysey himself worked at the drawing-board alongside his pupils and clerks, and he encouraged them to read all the inward and outward correspondence so that they should learn all that they could of architectural practice.[34]

The very substantial collection of Voysey's drawings at the RIBA and at the V&A admit to no other designing hand than his, and, apart from the perspective watercolours, which were drawn up by H. Gaye for the Royal Academy Summer Exhibitions, Voysey made all his own drawings.[35] As with his decorative designs, his architectural drawings were made with remarkable speed and assurance. He would make a set of one:eight scale working-drawings for a house in a weekend, always drawing with a very hard 3H pencil, often on Imperial sheets of 'not-pressed' Whatman paper.[36] In spite of the volume of work during the busy years and the difficulties of travelling between Windermere, Surrey and London by train and then by pony and trap to make site visits, there is no evidence to suggest that Voysey employed a site clerk. He designed and managed every detail of his buildings, only allowing pupils to make the necessary copies, and even his letters to clients were handwritten in blue ink on small distinctive sheets of blue paper. They were press-copied by the pupils, but the specifications were typed.[37]

According to John Brandon-Jones, letters were dealt with promptly and normal office hours were strictly adhered to, 'overtime was never found necessary'. But Voysey did not take holidays. He lived for his work and letters from one of his clients, S. C. Turner, concerning the decoration of Capel House refer specifically to 'telephonic messages' from Turner to Voysey in 1906, and to weekend and evening meetings over dinner to discuss heraldic patterns and other matters. By 1906 the office was equipped with a telephone, and the lines between business and social meetings were fluid.[38] Voysey regularly entertained his clients and his builder at the Arts Club, in Piccadilly, and he was meticulous over his expenses: whenever he tipped a client's servant it was charged up to the job, and if he spent sixpence on a rose for 'drawing wallpapers' or three shillings and nine pence on a trip to the zoological gardens it was chalked up to professional expenses.[39]

M. H. Baillie Scott, writing in 1907, suggested that Voysey's office was quite different from those of most architects of the day:

14

14 *Movable electric wall lights, designed by Voysey to fasten to the picture-rail.*

15

16

THE ORCHARD. It had been Voysey's ambition to design his own house from his earliest years in practice. One of his first country-cottage designs of 1885 had ostensibly been drawn up to celebrate his marriage to Mary Maria Evans, in the hope that a friend might lend them the money to build it, and in 1897 Voysey had designed a cottage for himself at Colwall, within striking distance of Perrycroft.[41] The Colwall cottage was never built, but by 1899 Voysey had found a plot of land in an old orchard ten minutes' walk from Chorleywood station on the Metropolitan railway line to London. Like many of his clients he decided to build a country cottage for his wife and their three children and commute into work in the city.

Voysey rarely wrote specifically about his own work, but in 1901 he published an article in the *Architectural Review* devoted to The Orchard. In it he described the site and its indigenous flowers and trees with loving attention to detail.[42] The design of The Orchard at the peak of Voysey's career and his own account of the building offer an exceptional insight into the form that his carefully resolved design philosophy would take given an open site and release from the demands of a client. There were financial constraints: Voysey described The Orchard as, 'small, having only five bedrooms and a good-sized box-room'; for his favoured oak joinery he had to substitute deal, painted white; and there was no money for panelling, but if anything, the compact nature of The Orchard and the use of richly coloured wallpapers in place of Voysey's characteristic oak panelling made it even more striking as an expression of his personal taste.

15 *Perspective sketch, The Orchard,*
  Chorleywood, Hertfordshire, 1899.
16 *Garden elevation, The Orchard.*

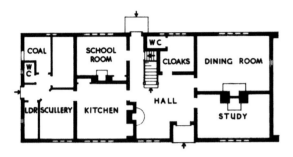

17

The Orchard was the quintessential Voysey house. It incorporated all his hallmark features in the most restrained and yet distinctive composition, perfectly balanced and with each component contributing towards a unified and harmonious total work of art. The relationship of the house to its site in plan and elevation; the expression of the plan in the elevations, and of the structure in the interiors; and the furnishing and decoration of the house were all carefully considered and arranged in accordance with Voysey's ideals and it soon became one of his most famous designs.

The plans were drawn up and construction was underway by September 1899 and the estimated cost was to be between £1,000 and £1,500.[43] The simple, flat elevations, roughcast beneath a slate roof, the gables defining the composition, the massive chimneys crashing up through the roof and the cat-slide roof over the service wing all testified to a strong allegiance to the design of Moorcrag – the two houses were designed within months of one another. But The Orchard dared to be even simpler than Moorcrag: there were no projecting bays and verandas; no massing of chimneys in the end eleva-

tion; and apart from the cat-slide, the sweep of the roof was more inhibited, remaining, for the most part, above the walls rather than flooding down between and across the gables.

Voysey clipped the roof line around the front of the gables, but he abstained from cutting into it with dormers so that the roof had a disciplined, clean-cut appearance with sharp folds and clear unbroken pitches.[44] The sensual presentation of green slate and the unbridled pitch of the cat-slide could not be justified as they might have been at Moorcrag by the nature and incline of the site.[45] At The Orchard they were exploited purely for their aesthetic qualities. The slates were laid in gradating courses, and Voysey described their colour as, 'a silvery grey tinged here and there with the tints found in the plumage of pigeons'.[46]

Strong horizontals were drawn across the elevations in lines of red-tile weathering and above the ground-floor windows the lines were continuous, arching up over the porch at the front and capping the half-glazed door into the garden. The fenestration, stone dressed in a series of flat patterns against the roughcast, was arranged in horizontal

17 *Plans and elevations, The Orchard, 1899.*

Only the narrowest strip of garden was laid between The Orchard and the lane, and a broad slate path led decisively straight to the front door. The house was arranged within a simple rectangular plan with the service area forming a square on the east side and the principal rooms – a hall, dining room and a study – to the west. The kitchen and scullery faced north, looking out over Shire Lane, 'so that the servants have the benefit of a cool aspect and all the life there is in Shire Lane, and the privacy of the garden and orchard is not impaired'.[51] Less ideally, the hall and study also had a northerly aspect, although Voysey described the advantages of this arrangement: 'The study looks out to a wood on the opposite side of Shire Lane, which by the grace of the Duke of Bedford is not to be bought or built upon, so that this room has a steady north light and plenty of it.'[52] Sadly, the wood has since had houses built upon it, and it is curious that Voysey arranged his hall in the north range of the house with the staircase and lavatory occupying the sunny southern aspect with its views out over the orchard.

Voysey described himself as a 'stickler for light' and yet only the school room and the dining room were south facing with views out over the garden.[53] When criticized for the smallness of his windows he countered that, 'Small windows, when rightly placed, in conjunction with white ceilings and friezes, may produce very light rooms, and have the advantage of preserving equable temperature throughout the year.'[54] Smaller windows, he continued, would save the expense of elaborate blinds and curtains, and so simplify the furnishing of the rooms in addition to making them easier to heat. His concern for light was far more complex than the straightforward provision of daylight:

The essential idea suggested by light is activity, and the chief material consequence is cleanliness. We all like abundance of light for work or play. It stimulates action. But we do not want windows that have to be covered up by the upholsterer morning, noon, and night. Precious as the light is, we must not be blind to the soothing mystery and charm of shadow and twilight. The suggestions of repose and mystery are sublime, and as necessary as the brilliant light.[55]

Voysey's reluctance to expose all his principal rooms to full sunlight (and he arranged his bicycle

bands and the Voysey front door was set within a recessed porch 'to ward off the cold winds' and emblazoned with a heart-shaped letter box.[47] The west elevation was left blank, apart from the signature porthole window, which lit the dining room, and the use of buttresses was restricted to the definition of this end wall.

Four years before the design of The Orchard, Voysey had lectured in Manchester on the importance of simplicity for 'The aims and conditions of the modern decorator'.[48] Later, he wrote that, 'Simplicity, sincerity, repose, directness, and frankness are moral qualities as essential to good architecture as to good men'.[49] Voysey demonstrated his characteristic honesty and candour in the positioning of the house at the front of its site, close to Shire Lane with the front elevation parallel with the lane:

Our need for economy will keep us near the entrance boundary ... our love of privacy, which is very much a matter of temperament, may be a good reason for leaving little or no garden between the house and the road. On a small site the entrance must be very evident, and overlooks the whole area on the roadside of the house.[50]

and coal-store in the south-east corner of the plan where the dining room would more usually be situated) differentiated The Orchard from the plans he designed for clients and demonstrated the Victorian element in his temperament. From a practical point of view, he would have understood the damaging effects of sunlight on patterned textiles and wallpapers and this would have offended his sensibility as a decorative designer, but his appreciation of the 'solemn mystery' of gloom and the value of 'a dim religious light' were unashamedly Gothic. None of the early photographs of The Orchard show gas or electric-light fittings, and this is more likely to have been determined by the lack of mains supplies available than by any preference on Voysey's part; however, in their place oil lamps and candles made to his designs appear in almost every room. His romantic sensibility was equally apparent and idiosyncratic in his specification of leaded-light windows:

It is pleasant to feel well protected when the weather is disturbed and angry; so you will not give me great sheets of plate glass, which look like holes in the walls both from within and from without. I much appreciate your regarding me, and suggesting to others that I am to be regarded as a precious thing, to be protected from all violent intrusion.[56]

At The Orchard and Moorcrag, Voysey introduced single, opening panes to his windows, 'so that he could enjoy the fresh air without suffering a draught', and they were fitted with his own patented window stays for greater versatility.[57]

Although his description of The Orchard and its surroundings revealed an attentive and affectionate observation of nature – he wrote that, 'Nightingales, larks, linnets, thrushes, blackbirds, wood pigeons, and even foxes, deign to keep company with the little white house' – the relationship between the house and its garden was remote.[58] There were no French windows or verandas linking the principal rooms with the garden, no strategically placed benches sheltered by bays or buttresses, and the principal door from the garden into the house gave access to a passage along the side of the staircase.[59] However if the continuation of the house into its garden was not a factor in the design of The Orchard, the view of the house as an integral part of the surrounding landscape was a con-

19

stant preoccupation. Even as an elderly man, Voysey preferred to give journalists and writers a photograph of the house with the old cherry tree and the younger trees of the orchard in the foreground, showing just one gable of the house with part of the roof and the windows below.[60]

On the other side of the staircase there was a small cellar beneath the lavatory, lit from a window above ground level; Voysey was assiduous in his attention to the details of plumbing and ventilation:

This [cellar] allows of easy access to all pipes, supplies, and wastes from the lavatories and bath-room over. The w.c. out of the lavatory on the ground floor is built sound proof, the w.c. on the floor above is exactly over it, and only the stupid local by-laws prevented the soil-pipe being carried through the two w.c.'s in a straight run to the drain; as it is, they had to be twisted and turned to the outside of the wall, thanks to the unpractical theorists who frame these regulations.[61]

The servants had their own w.c. under the cat-slide roof and there was a bicycle room close to the kitchen entrance, 'dry and not quite out of reach of

20

19 *Front door, The Orchard.*
20 *View of the house from the orchard.*

21

22

the influence of the kitchen fire'.[62] *Country Life* noted that the kitchen offices were given a great deal of room for so small a house: 'but the contentment of servants in the country is a thing of which it is quite worth while to make sure'.[63] On the first floor, Voysey exploited the steep incline of the cat-slide roof in a box room running the full depth of the house, 'in which floor space is far more important than head room'.[64]

Voysey's practical and economic approach to the mechanics of the plan was equalled by his consistent restraint and modesty, injected with an opulent manipulation of colour in the design of the interiors. It is tempting to see The Orchard interiors as a manifestation of Voysey's theories and his quotations spring irresistibly to mind: 'The hall should receive its guests with composure and dignity, but still with brightness, open arms, and warmth; warmth of colour as rich and luxurious as you like, but above all things, sober and reposeful, not dotted all over with bazaar and museum articles, and tables and chairs that repel you.'[65] The ceiling, frieze and woodwork at The Orchard were all painted white, but below the picture-rail the walls were covered with 'Eltonbury silk-fibre paper of a purple tone'; the fireplace was tiled with narrow, green Dutch tiles, supplied by Van Straaten; and set vertically with the central panel slightly lower than the sides, in a manner which was typical of Voysey, and in front of the fire, there was a thick Donegal tuft rug in 'dead peacock blue'. Voysey used similarly rich dense colours in his decorative designs, citing nature as his inspiration.

She furnishes with an abundance of the most soothing colour, vis, green; she uses her red most sparingly. In the spring she feasts us with delicate greens, greys, blues, purples, and later on, yellow, gradually warming and strengthening her colours as the summer sun increases its power over the eye; and as our eyes and our senses are tiring, come the more stimulating oranges and browns, the deep emphatic autumn colour . . . nature never allows her colours to quarrel. Her purple trees, with their gossamer of delicate spring green, dwell lovingly with the blue carpet of hyacinths. Harmony is everywhere. Nowhere without its dominating tint and jewel-like spots and patches of more brilliant colour. But the most brilliant colours are always in relatively small quantities. It is the relative quantities of colour that make for harmony.[66]

21 *The hall, The Orchard.*

22 *Study window, The Orchard, showing correct alignment of Voysey curtains.*

There were patches of brilliant colour at The Orchard in the turkey-red twill of the curtains, which Voysey liked to specify whenever the client would permit them. It was an exacting specification, indicative of the detailed attention that he gave to every aspect of his buildings: the top hem had to be one and a half inches, and the bottom hem one inch. The curtain rings were to be seven-eighths of an inch in diameter and fastened two and a half inches apart. Each light was to be covered by a single width of fabric: 'The several widths should not be joined together in any way and on no account should they be pleated or gathered.'[67] Only the narrow pelmet was allowed to be slightly gathered and the lengths of fabric were neatly aligned with the stone mullions.

Voysey was equally rigorous on the subject of hall floors and again The Orchard served as a paragon.[68] The Orchard hall and the kitchen offices were exquisitely paved with Delabole slate and the hall window was fitted with a long seat, which doubled as a chest for storing rugs. Voysey claimed that the hall fire, by virtue of its central position, kept the whole house warm in severe weather and early photographs show the fireplaces equipped with tongues, pokers, and shovels made to his designs and his hand-painted clock, 'Time & Tide Wait For No Man' on the hall mantel-shelf.

The study, the school room and the bedrooms were decorated with Voysey wallpaper, and the study and dining room were fitted with Voysey carpets. The dining room was papered with a plain, bottle-green, Eltonbury-silk paper, which contrasted with the red curtains around the porthole window, and with the blue and green carpet decorated with red and yellow flowers (which was also photographed in the bedroom). But if Voysey was extravagant in his use of colour the overall effect was restrained by his meticulous handling of proportions, and the consistent quality of his detailing.

All the rooms were furnished with Voysey's plain oak furniture, 'simply oiled'. He was by no means the only architect to decorate and furnish his houses, although as a contemporary noted in 1899: 'It was not so very many years since … the architect who wandered from the strait and narrow path and took to designing furniture, wall-papers, and so forth, had committed a species of professional suicide.'[69] Voysey cited William Burges,

23

designing water-taps and hair-brushes, and E. W. Godwin and A. H. Mackmurdo for their furniture, as his predecessors, together with A. W. N. Pugin and G. F. Bodley as designers of textiles and wallpapers.[70] However *The Studio* described Godwin as the architect who 'more than any other dissipated this absurd theory', and Voysey was heralded as the most 'completely successful in this respect'.

Voysey's furniture, like every other aspect of his work, was recognized as exceptional for the period, for, 'its broad simple effects, its reliance on proportion, its eschewal of useless ornament, and its strikingly original lines'. It was particularly appropriate to the plain lines and lifestyle of a modern country cottage, and according to *The Studio* in 1899 its influence established 'a school of its own'.[71]

24

If you can appreciate the reticence and severity of Mr Voysey's work, you can no longer tolerate the ordinary commercially designed product. His furniture deserves elaborate and patient study, for its one aim is 'proportion, proportion, proportion' and that is a quality most elusive and difficult even to appreciate, still less to achieve.[72]

23 *The dining room, The Orchard, viewed from the hall, showing Voysey's rich use of colour. Watercolour, published in 1901.*

24 *The dining room, furnished by Voysey, The Orchard.*

25

26

The rush-seated, high-back chairs with splats shaped around two cut-out hearts, which furnished the dining room at The Orchard, together with the lathe-back armchair, were identical to the ones photographed in the dining room at Broadleys.[73] Variations on the lathe-back chair, with and without arms, were used again at The Homestead, but with four lathes in the back in place of five. Characteristic profiles and motifs were repeated from one piece to another: the gentle curve at the top of a chair back and the projection of verticals beyond the line of duty – sometimes capped with circular plates – became part of a clearly defined and recognizable style. Plain oak surfaces were left unadorned and the oak was often carefully selected for the quality of its grain, but although Voysey was adept at modelling there is no evidence to suggest that he crafted his own furniture. F. Coote made up many of his designs from 1889 through the 1890s, and from 1901 F. C. Nielsen's prices were repeatedly given on his drawings. There were other, less predominant names: Thallon and J. S. Henry both made furniture for Voysey under the prerequisite that the standard of their craftsmanship and the quality of materials used were to be irrefutable down to the dovetails: 'A mean man will inevitably tend to shabbiness in the hidden parts of his work; he will put deal bottoms to his satinwood casket and fasten up his joinery with screws or nails to save the labour of dovetailing or mortising. How often we see effectiveness in the place of genuine quality.'[74] One of the furniture-makers who Voysey occasionally used, and whose affinity for the inherent beauty of wood may well have influenced his designs, was Arthur W. Simpson of Kendal.[75] The two men shared a profound admiration for Ruskin (Simpson had met him at his home, Brantwood on Lake Consiston) and they became life-long friends with a mutual respect for each other's work, so that when Voysey designed Broadleys he specified that Simpson should make the finely cut and inlaid balusters and the veranda seat.

Simpson often dined with Voysey when he was in London buying timber or for exhibitions, and there is a story that on one occasion when Voysey was in the Lake District he and Simpson took the train together from Kendal to dine at Riggs Hotel in Windermere. From the train, Simpson pointed

to a building and asked Voysey what he thought of it. Outraged, Voysey is said to have replied, 'Its damnable, Simpson. Damnable! Don't look at it; it'll spoil your taste!'[76] Later, in 1909, Voysey designed a house for Simpson – Littleholme in Kendal. Simpson's observation of the simple lines and fine proportions of Voysey's furniture clearly influenced his own designs. However, though he admired Voysey's buildings, the furniture at Littleholme was made to Simpson's designs.

Voysey's furniture was meticulously proportioned and often it was the proportions of the piece that gave it its elegant or sturdy character, as *The Studio* noted in October 1899:

He ... relies very much on grace of proportion, a feature to which reproductions on a reduced scale cannot, of course, do adequate justice. Indeed, the rigidly severe character of the joinery, accompanied by plain though elaborately-studied mouldings, make it seem almost bald, unless the objects themselves, completed full-size, are examined; in which event the restraint and refinement of the whole can hardly fail to be appreciated.[77]

Although Voysey's furniture was extremely simple, the detailing was refined by thought and feeling. The legs were often chamfered towards the base, so that while they were square in plan at the top, the corners were tapered away making them octagonal at the base; this detailing was appropriate to the function of the parts, as well as to the elegance of the piece as a whole – strength is required at the top of a chair leg, where it meets the seat while the leg can afford to be more slender and consequently weaker towards the base. Voysey claimed a deliberate avoidance of style and to reject mannerisms in his work. Nevertheless the chamfered legs, the tapering or capped uprights, the recurrence of pierced hearts, the gently curved tops and oak pelmets and his consistent use of straight lathes, arranged in groups in his bed-heads or with candid regularity in his chairs and chesterfield, all define an unmistakably individual style.

A sense of proportion, he wrote, was the consequence of temperament rather than learning and education, the expression of feeling far more than thought.[78] At The Orchard, this spontaneous expression of temperament and Voysey's discriminating sense of proportion and propriety suffuse every element of the house. Early photographs of

25 *Oak dining chair with arms and rush seat, c.1902.*

26 *Oak dining chair without arms. Various versions of this chair with slightly different proportions were made from 1902.*

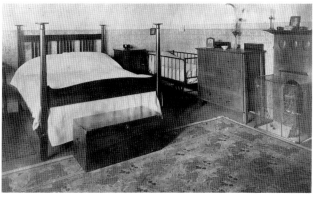

27

28

the interiors commissioned by Voysey ring with his voice and demonstrate that the wholesome goodness, which made so many imitations of his work irksome, was never overbearing in his own designs. Despite his condemnations of the 'useless and often gimcrack ornaments and nick-nacks' that cluttered 'nine thousand out of every ten thousand houses … the typical, hideous, carved coal-box, or a three-legged standard lamp with tiers upon tiers of silk petticoat and the like monstrosities',[79] The Orchard was not stripped of every vestige of sentimentality and nor was it as obsessively clean as some of Voysey's writings might suggest: the photographs show interiors peppered with small pictures, vases of peacock feathers and honesty, and an array of personal objects, and the dining room and study hearths were scattered with the residue of spent fires.

Voysey believed that beautiful surroundings had an inspirational and morally uplifting effect on people: 'All objects possess intrinsic qualities, having a direct influence on our minds and emotions.'[80] He once wittily quipped: 'If I cannot be graceful and comely, I can at least have a graceful and comely umbrella, and in that way help to keep up my interest in those qualities.'[81] And again, (with more than a hint of irony) he told *The British Architect:* 'Cold vegetables are less harmful than ugly dish covers. One affects the body and the other affects the soul.'[82] His philosophy of spiritual advancement through exposure to beauty was essentially Platonic and a 1901 edition of Plato's *The Republic* was found among Voysey's personal effects after his death. His interpretation of these ideals, however, was inextricably linked with his quest for a harmonious and peaceful environment through the perfection of proportions and the proliferation of restful horizontals. A sense of balance and calm was one of the most distinguishing features at The Orchard.

Even before The Orchard was complete it was the subject of an article in *Country Life*, who urged their readers to imagine the 'soft warm red of the tiled roof[!]'. In 1901 it was lavishly illustrated in Charles Holme's book on *Modern British Domestic Architecture and Decoration*. Inevitably it brought Voysey clients who would entrust him, not only with architectural commissions, but also with the provision of interior architecture and furnishing.

27, 28 *Bedroom, furnished by Voysey, and the study, The Orchard.*

2

3

MOORCRAG
1898–99

Designed for J. W. Buckley, the textile manufacturer, Moorcrag is almost contemporary with Broadleys, and the two houses are only a few miles apart on the banks of Lake Windermere. Both houses were designed as weekend and holiday retreats for wealthy industrialists, but whereas Broadleys surveys its magnificent view with an element of grandeur and display, Moorcrag is embedded in the hillside – the lines and local green slate of its roof, window-dressings and terraces fix it to the landscape.

C F A VOYSEY

1 *Entrance front.*

2, 3 *The roof sweeps down almost to the ground over the original servants' quarters, which, paradoxically, enjoy the best views across the lake.*

4

5

6

4–6 Garden elevation and veranda.

7

8

9

7 *The 'dining hall', which runs the full depth of the house.*

8 *Fireplace with simple oak mantel in the dining hall.*

9 *Landing.*

THE ORCHARD

1899

Voysey designed The Orchard at Chorleywood, Hertfordshire, for himself and his family. It was the quintessential country cottage: harmonizing with its natural environment, and at the same time offering modern, compact and distinctly 'artistic' accommodation. He described the roof as 'a silvery grey tinged here and there with the tints found in the plumage of pigeons'. All the furniture and fittings for the house were made to his designs.

2, 3 *West elevation. The pond is not original.*

4

5

4 *Front elevation. Voysey extended the
study window into a bay in 1913 for
a subsequent owner of the house.*

5 *Front elevation from Shire Lane.*

6 *Gable end showing dining-room and
bedroom windows looking out across
the garden to the orchard beyond.*

The role of the artist or architect as a complex designer of all things, whose creative abilities could be applied with equal facility to any field, was by no means new in Voysey's time. It had been at its height during the Medieval period and the Renaissance and was revived by the Arts and Crafts movement. Voysey and his contemporaries benefited from practical demonstrations and theoretical papers on a wide range of specialist arts and crafts techniques at the Art Workers' Guild, and there was a sense of camaraderie in exhibiting their crafts together under the umbrella organization of the Arts and Crafts Exhibition Society. In the 1890 exhibition, for example, Morris & Co. exhibited furniture and tapestries; A. H. Mackmurdo, W. R. Lethaby and Ernest Gimson all showed furniture; and in addition, Gimson exhibited a sampler and a plaster frieze and Mackmurdo showed a fireplace and grate. The Guild and the Exhibition Society gave designers and manufacturers a chance to meet and discuss technical and artistic innovations, and it was in this stimulating environment that Voysey's ambitions as a complex designer were nurtured and endorsed.

Voysey's versatility as a designer went beyond that of any of his contemporaries in both range and duration. Throughout his life he had pieces made up specifically for exhibitions, but many of his domestic objects – table-ware, cutlery and clocks – were designed primarily to satisfy his own curiosity or purely for the pleasure of the process of designing. They were made up for his friends and family, and sometimes a mirror or a clock was made for a particular client to complete a Voysey interior. Voysey's work as a furniture designer, because of its three-dimensional character and its close association with the proportions and materials of his interior architecture, can be considered as an extension of his architectural work. However, the relationship between Voysey's architecture and his decorative designs was more ambiguous.

Even through his busiest years in architectural practice, Voysey continued to produce decorative designs for wallpapers and textiles. He was one of the most prolific and pre-eminent pattern designers of his day. The same clear authoritative lines and coherent ideas, simply expressed, that underpinned the design of his houses were applied with equal

VERSATILITY: ARTIST, ARCHITECT & DESIGNER

2

1 'The Union of Hearts' decorative
    design, c.1898.
2 Badge design, Mary Maria Voysey with
    Priscilla in her arms, flanked by her
    angelic sons, Charles and Annesley.

3

name 'Halcyone' is emblazoned across a banner. There is a strong horizontal emphasis in the repeat of the pattern and in the shape of the nest and the banner, and the background is a rich scrumbled blue with a note from Voysey that, 'It is hoped that the broken effect of colour in the background can be got by mixing the colour of the bird and sea together *horizontally*.'[1] The dense blue background was common to many Voysey designs of this period, but even the handwriting of this note has a horizontality with emphatic dashes to the 't's.

Voysey explained the symbolic significance of the halcyon as a harbinger of calm:

The bird called the halcyon, concerning which the old fable runs, that she was the Daughter of Oedus & mourning in her youth for the lost husband, was winged by Divine powers, & now flies over the sea, seeking him whom she could not find.

Halcyone was the daughter of the winds. The bird known as the Halcyon is the kingfisher and is said to build its nest on the sea in the days when there is most calm hence we derive the expression halcyon days. It was believed that the Halcyon had the power of calming the sea.[2]

'Halcyone' was by no means the only decorative design in which symbolism played an important part. In a typescript, 'Symbolism in Design', Voysey outlined a highly evolved and personal allegorical system, and he defined the allegorical role of many of the motifs that recur throughout his work.[3] The heart signified 'the emotions and affections' and the spade was the sign of economics, 'it is the instrument by which material is made to fructify'. Birds, too, were vested with emotional import and different species were given quite specific connotations: 'The eagle which is the highest flyer and the furthest seer stands for aspiration, and revelation, the heavenward quest, which in other words, is true philosophy…' The crown or band, 'usually placed round the head is the original symbol of self-control, indicating the fact that the mind (that is, reason) must control the emotions'.

In 'The Union of Hearts', also designed around 1898, the entire design was made up of blue hearts surmounted by crowns and knotted together with red-tasselled cords symbolizing, according to Voysey's theories, the union of emotions and affections, governed by the restraining factors of self-control and reason. The knot is an ancient sym-

clarity to his pattern designs, and favoured motifs – birds, hearts and trees – recur as one of the more obvious links between his two and three-dimensional designs. Inevitably there were other links because the decorative and architectural designs were all founded on the same philosophy. Voysey's decorative designs deserve a more detailed analysis than can be explored here as an independent body of work with its own stylistic developments. Even a brief overview, however, demonstrates that the decorative and architectural designs ran along parallel courses, and the icons that Voysey was able to explore more freely in his decorative work, than in any other medium, offer invaluable insights into his personal use of symbolism.

As Voysey's reputation gathered momentum his designs became bolder in scale and colour, and the animals and birds that he had fought so hard to introduce in his early years became increasingly predominant. 'Halcyone', drawn in June 1898, is typical of this period in its uncompromising simplicity and strength of colour. A clear blue kingfisher, or bird, sits on her nest with an expression of brooding concentration and above her the bol of union associated with marriage, and, ironically, a framed section of this design decorated Voysey's flat in St James's Street where he lived and worked from 1917, after he and his wife had separated. Voysey made no distinction between designs drawn up for wallpapers and those woven into fabrics and even carpets, so that this design appears to have been manufactured as a wallpaper by Essex & Co., as a woven fabric by Alexander Morton, and as a carpet by Tomkinsons.

Voysey's allegorical definitions were highly individual. The crown, for example, is generally accepted as an emblem of sovereignty, either earthly or divine, and as a reward for victory in love or accomplishment in the arts. The eagle, far from being a symbol of aspiration and philosophy, has been accepted from Roman times as a symbol of power and victory. It is associated with sight, but also with pride. Voysey was aware of ancient symbolism, but he preferred, he said, 'to stimulate living thoughts and feelings' rather than to 'wander in the cemetery of ideas and collect the monuments and remains of a bygone age … an overdose of museum specimens, and the cemetery atmosphere had clouded over them like a pall, hiding all hope of the future'.[4]

In 1918, Voysey gave a lecture on 'Modern Symbolism' at Carpenters Hall in London, which resembled his father's sermons in fervour, and gives some indication of the intensity of his beliefs. It was reported in *The Architect & Contract Reporter*:

The printed page had had a long innings and had led some to forget the existence of ideas in things. Their materialistic temper had caused them to count only sensuous qualities in things material, and so they were contented with the pleasures derived from form and colour, light and shade, texture and tone. The time was, however, quickly coming when, as he had said, the unseen would be regarded as the glory of the seen; when qualities of thought and feeling would be looked for, and they would enjoy a second sight as of the eagle, which soared above the heavens, and they would then be enraptured with the vision of a glorious future and a clearer understanding of the present. That second sight could be cultivated through symbolism to a very great extent, for surely people saw what they looked for. …Objects of daily use would assume a significance they had not before, and instead of their being surrounded with deadly, dull, inanimate objects, these things would sing to them songs of joy, and carry them up into the clear blue sky of celestial thought and feeling.[5]

Voysey's condemnation of materialism and his insistence on the importance of 'ideas in things' and of 'thought and feeling' as fundamental to all creative activity were repeated again and again in his writings and lectures. His moral tone: 'What they enjoyed through their senses was on a lower plane to that which stimulated their intelligence and their love' was unmistakable. There were traces too of his instinct for the righteousness of martyrdom and poverty, recalling his father's trials, and, by 1918, his own precarious financial position: 'Material prosperity stimulated their interest in material things, as much as material things led them to seek prosperity. Sorrow and suffering stimulated their interest in spiritual ideas.'[6]

Symbolism was found in architectural language in the pointed arch or spire as an expression of conflict and movement, and of 'a struggling and aspiring age'. By comparison, 'A luxuriant self-indulgent age sought to avoid conflict and found its language in the round arch'. However, the round arch was not always sullied by self-indulgence. Voysey used it in many of his houses as a representative of repose. Voysey was not alone in his interest in redefining symbolism: W. R. Lethaby's *Architecture, Mysticism and Myth* was published in 1891; it is frustrating that the most essential element in the history of the period, the conversations over drawings and informal discussions before and after the Art Workers' Guild meetings, have not been recorded. Symbolism appears to have endorsed Voysey's graphic work, almost from the very first designs: a wallpaper designed for Wollams in 1885, now lost and known only by its name, was entitled 'Floral Ethics'; and the significance of the oak tree as a symbol for 'sturdy growth', the flame indicating the soul, and the fleur-de-lys as a representation of purity (all rather unorthodox definitions) remained constant throughout his long designing career.

An understanding of Voysey's 'second sight' is crucial to an informed appreciation of his work. It would be a mistake to read his graphic designs purely as coded messages for a deeper philosophy; they are often light-hearted and humorous in intent, and his list of definitions is far from complete. He was, nevertheless, insistent that, 'works of art were to be valued according to their spiritual qualities, the messages of love they were created to convey, and the emotions they were designed to

4

6

5

arouse'. The symbols themselves, he claimed (and his hearts are a pertinent example of this), were no more than a material manifestation of spiritual expression. When the symbol only was relied upon, and not what it stood for, it was indicative of laziness and of 'loving the wrong things'.

Voysey's decorative designs, and particularly the elongated flowing lines of his early work where the influence of Mackmurdo and the Century Guild is most apparent, had a formative influence on Art Nouveau. His designs were exhibited in the great Paris Exhibition, as early as 1889, and in 1893 his wallpapers were exhibited at the 'Salon de l'Association pour l'Art d'Anvers'. Through articles by Henry Van de Velde in the Brussels magazines *Emulation* and *L'Art Moderne,* and in *The Studio,* Voysey's designs, full of movement with bold calligraphic lines and clear colours, spread across Europe.[7] Later, as his style developed and became more succinct, tapestry designs like 'Martello', with its large-scale design and rich greens and blues continued to influence Art Nouveau designers abroad. Henry Van de Velde considered Voysey's wallpapers to be superior to anything else manufactured at the time, and Victor Horta used one of the Essex papers to decorate his Hotel Tassel and 'Flight' designed by Voysey in 1896 in his Hotel Solvay.[8]

Voysey's wallpapers were exhibited in the Paris Exhibition, again in 1900, by Essex & Co. and as part of a room setting by Heal's, who used the 'Squire's Garden' (manufactured by Essex) as a furnishing fabric and a wallpaper, and who included one of the 'New Three-Ply carpets' that they had commissioned from Voysey as part of their exhibit. *The Journal of Decorative Art* described Voysey as at the 'fountain head' of 'Art Nouveau' in 1900, but Voysey most certainly did not see himself as part of what he disparagingly described as the 'Spook school'. He criticized Art Nouveau for its lack of reverence, writing in 1904 that:

Atheism, conceit, and apish imitation seem to be the chief features ... Surely L'Art Nouveau is not worthy to be called a style. Is it not merely the work of a lot of imitators with nothing but mad eccentricity as a guide: good men, no doubt, misled into thinking that Art is a debauch of sensuous feeling, instead of the expression of human thought and feeling combined, and governed by reverence for something higher than human nature.[9]

4 *Machine-made carpet designed by Voysey for Alexander Morton & Co.*

5 *Fruit tree, tile.*

6 *Birds and cherries textile design, 1898.*

Voysey's use of colour was exceptional for the period, but not all his designs were dense or daring in their colour combinations or charged with a dynamic sense of movement. In 'The Callum', a wallpaper designed for Essex and Co. around 1896, a simple pattern of graceful foliage with yellow bud-like flowers was repeated against a cream background. It was a fluid and restful design, not unlike William Morris's more complicated branching Willow Boughs of 1887, except that where the Morris design has a continuous sense of movement across the wall, in 'The Callum', movement is limited to the foliage and flowers of the motif, and Voysey used the repeat to contain rather than to extend the fluid lines of the pattern. 'The Wild Olive', again designed for Essex & Co. as a wallpaper, was comparable in its sparing use of foliage and fruit against a pale ground, and there were other, more densely patterned paper and fabric designs, such as 'Purple Bird', where the foliage and birds were more formally arranged and the repetition of the design was much tighter and more overt.

The birds and trees that decorated Voysey's furniture hinges, bell-pulls and ventilator-grilles in his houses were transferred with wit and dexterity into his wallpaper and fabric designs. The tree whose branches traced a circle was adapted from fretted screen, to embroidered cushion, to fabric design, to tile decoration. The immense range and quantity of Voysey's surviving decorative designs demonstrate that this repetition of motifs was not a consequence of any limitations in his creative vocabulary. Instead it is evidence of his constant striving for a particular type of unity throughout the arts, which would allow him to express his philosophy of spiritual love, thought and feeling through a set of refined symbolic icons.

Voysey's conviction that the public should look beyond the charming patterns of birds and fruiting trees and recognize the sentiments that had inspired their design was perhaps optimistic. Certainly his contempt for the consumer who purchased a work on the strength of the reputation of its author alone, for its materialistic rather than artistic value, must have been exercised by Essex & Co.'s advertisement for 'many papers by C. F. A. Voysey, the Genius of Pattern. These supply the Something Distinctive for which you are looking.' Nevertheless he noted with apparent pride in his brief autobiographical notes that, 'The name of Voysey has frequently been used by journalists and Estate Agents advertising "Voysey houses".'[10]

Voysey's relationship with his manufacturers, too, was recorded with satisfaction in his autobiographical notes:

Mr Voysey has designed furniture of every kind required for a home and for many years was retainee by the manufacturers of Carpets, Curtains, Cretonnes and Wallpapers, who undertook to accept and pay for a given number of (his designs) per annum without option. An arrangement very seldom enjoyed by designers.

His first decorative designs were sold to the wallpaper manufacturers Jeffrey & Co., but by 1893 he had negotiated a regular contract with Essex & Co. for wallpapers and from 1895 with Alexander Morton of Darvel and Carlisle for his textiles. Minton Tiles and the Pilkington Tile and Pottery Company manufactured tiles decorated with his designs, and Tomkinson and Adam of Kidderminster produced Voysey carpets, but Voysey designed for many other leading manufacturers of the day. Carpet designs were commissioned by Heal's, textile designs were sold to Liberty and wallpaper patterns were manufactured by Sanderson's, as well as by many smaller specialist firms. It was Voysey's good relations with these clients for his decorative designs that kept him afloat financially (although at times 'within measurable distance of the workhouse') after the First World War, but in the first years of the twentieth century his architectural practice was buoyant enough.

Between 1899 and 1906 Voysey designed a number of small houses that can be regarded as a set of permutations on his formula for a country cottage, which he had evolved through the design of Moorcrag and The Orchard. Just as he reused decorative motifs in many different patterns or produced designs in various colour schemes to vary the effect, the concept of repetition for Voysey represented an opportunity for experiment and enrichment. It allowed him to compose patterns in his architecture that explored a delicate balance between constant themes and variations. As his commissions became more comprehensive, encompassing the design of the furniture and fittings for the house, Voysey was able to extend

7

7 Bird and vine decorative design, 1918.

NORTH WEST ELEVATION·

SOUTH WEST ELEVATION·

0 5 10 15 20 25 30 35 40 45 50 FEET

SOUTH EAST ELEVATION·

NORTH EAST ELEVATION·

8

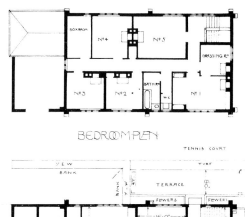

BEDROOM PLAN

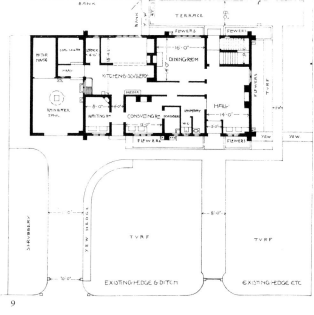

9

this idea of repetition and variation, bringing his full versatility as a designer into play. His houses were never predictable, just as his decorative designs were never dull. He had an extraordinary capacity for taking the familiar and finding a fresh revelation within it.

HOLLYBANK. In the autumn of 1903 Voysey was commissioned to design a house neighbouring The Orchard at Chorleywood in Hertfordshire. (A considerable area of open ground prevented it from being immediately next door.) Hollybank was nominally designed for the Reverend Matthew Edmeads (in Voysey's black book and in one of the drawings), but in practical terms it was designed for Edmead's son-in-law, Dr H. R. Fort, as a doctor's practice and family house. Though the background to the commission is unknown, Voysey would have been living at The Orchard during the construction of Hollybank, and it must be assumed that his supervision of the building would have been particularly attentive.

Hollybank was arranged in two distinct parts, with the waiting room, consulting room and dispensary on one side, and the living hall, dining room and staircase on the other. This was clearly expressed in the elevations where a pair of gables presided over two front doors. The door to the practice was round headed and set within a recessed porch, while that of the house was rectangular and sheltered by a simple canopy. A central buttress, meeting the angle between the two gables divided the elevation into two halves, and two straight wide paths of Delabole slate led from Shire Lane to the two front doors. Yew hedges were planted to screen the front garden of the house from the path to the surgery, and at the rear to shield the terrace and tennis-court from any view from the kitchen and scullery windows.

Again the house was positioned at the front of its site, close to Shire Lane, but unlike The Orchard (although *Country Life* might not have noticed) Hollybank was given a red-tile roof. The same red tiles were used to draw three crisp horizontal lines across the front and rear elevations. The simple composition of Hollybank with its massive white chimneys, crashing up through the deep sheltering roof, breaking the symmetry of the two cross gables and establishing an artistic balance in the

8, 9 Plans and elevations, Hollybank,
Chorleywood, Hertfordshire, 1903.

short south-west elevation represented Voysey at his most concise. There were no compositional risks at Hollybank: no runaway roofs or sculptural massing of forms. It was conceived as a neat economical statement, but one which was unmistakably related to its neighbour.

Inside, Voysey allocated the view along Shire Lane and to the wood beyond to the waiting and consulting rooms so that the doctor and his patients would benefit from a cool north-westerly light throughout the day. At the back of the house the kitchen and scullery were combined in one large room and divided from the surgery area by a massive round-headed door. There were two principal rooms, separated from the working area of the house by a second massive door: a dining room, with a south-easterly aspect looking out over the garden, and a living hall.

There were clear similarities between the inside of Hollybank and that of The Orchard. Both houses were contained within compact rectangular plans with generous service accommodation, a clearly defined study or work area, and a hall as the principal living room (although Voysey's son, Charles Cowles Voysey, always described the hall at The Orchard as a waiting room rather than a living room).[11] Voysey divided his interiors into a few good-sized rooms, rather than a warren of smaller spaces, and, by creating views from one room across a corridor or landing through to another, he generated a more complex and expansive sense of space that involved the dimensions of the entire house. The hall was central to this sense of space in both houses, although at Hollybank its position was shifted to the west end of the plan. Again the front door and porch took a corner out of the room and an imposing fireplace, tiled with luminous green vertical tiles, generated enough warmth to heat the entire house. But at Hollybank the front door was directly opposite a glazed door into the garden so that the depth of the house was immediately defined, and the staircase in the south-west corner of the room was partially screened by a wall with arched openings above the picture-rail.

The predominant use of arches throughout the interiors at Hollybank marks a transition in Voysey's work. Arches had been used in his earlier houses to denote an opening in a structural wall, and at Norney and New Place they had been incor-

10

porated into a complex system of geometry that had permeated every aspect of the houses. In his later interiors, Garden Corner, for example, and Brooke End, they were employed for their decorative effect, but it was at Hollybank that Voysey made his first concerted exploration into the decorative, as well as the structural, implications of the arch.[12] In the hall, a wide shallow arch sprang from the line of the mantel to frame a series of shelves set into the recess on one side of the fireplace and a dialogue was established between the round-headed doors to the dining room and service area, and the series of arched openings revealing the staircase.

Like The Orchard, Hollybank had five bedrooms and a box room, but Voysey squeezed a dressing room in at the top of the stairs, and in the master bedroom a gentle arch spanned the width of the room, defining a more intimate area for the bed. Again the budget precluded Voysey's favoured oak panelling, and the joinery was in deal, painted white, but drawers and fitted cupboards were built-in, and there was an oak wash-stand with cupboards underneath. All the bedrooms were fitted with Voysey's simple cast-iron fireplaces, embossed

10 *Front elevation, Hollybank.*

ledge was more streamlined in its moulding; and below this the projecting edge to the shelf was devoid of all ornament other than the smooth curve of its underside. The extreme plainness of this shelf, with only the form of an underlying curve betraying the authorship of its designer, was repeated in details and shelving throughout the house, and even the curve outlined in the top of the glazed panels was a recurrent theme, reappearing in other parts of the house.

Voysey was characteristically rigorous in attending to every detail for the smooth running of the house. He designed a fold-away butler's table to hinge out from the wall in the corridor between the kitchen and the dining room, and there was a smaller version of this for the bedrooms. Under the staircase the cupboard with the biggest lock and the most elaborate key was presumably intended for storing wine, where the temperature could be adjusted by a small window with a single, opening pane. There was no room for bicycles at Hollybank. Dr Fort was an early motorist and Voysey incorporated a 'Motor House' with its own pitched roof on the east side of the house. The gate to the driveway was ten-feet wide with massive strap-hinges and a latch exquisitely modelled into a caricature profile.[13] Inside the motor-house, Voysey made provision for an inspection pit with a wooden cover pierced by two hearts for hand holds. Thought and feeling extended even to the maintenance of the car.

Hollybank was completed in 1904, and the construction of the building must have coincided with that of Tilehurst and Myholme for Miss Edith Somers, a few miles away at Bushey in Hertfordshire. Miss Somers was a single woman with a philanthropic desire to run a boys' home. Tilehurst was designed as her home in 1903, and the following year Myholme was designed as a convalescent home for children. The two houses were little more than five miles from Hollybank and The Orchard, and one might have expected Voysey to use the same contractor for all four houses. Müntzer, whose home was in Surrey and offices were in London, might have quoted for them all, but Voysey employed Messrs J. Bottrill & Son of Reading to build The Orchard; A. J. Bates to build Hollybank; and C. Miskin and Sons of St Albans were the contractors for the two Bushey houses.

with three hearts like those at The Orchard and the same green cork was used to cover the bedroom floors and landing in both houses.

Voysey's regard for natural materials, and in particular for slate, was expressed in the use of Delabole slate throughout the ground floor of the house, apart from in the dining room, consulting room and waiting room. Slate would have been chosen not only for its hard-wearing, functional qualities and natural beauty, but also for its ability to reflect light. By using a single-floor covering throughout the service areas, corridors and hall, Voysey reinforced the impression of unity and continuity in a small house. The repetition of similar mouldings throughout the house and a careful, systematic ordering of decoration, at every level, reiterated this sense of unity on a more esoteric level. Voysey's exacting hierarchy of ornament was clearly, if subtly expressed in the cupboards built across two of the corners in the dining room: three projecting horizontals decorated the cupboards, each with a different moulding. At the top, the cornice moulding was delicately elaborate; beneath the glazed cupboard doors a second projecting

TILEHURST. Apart from his lodge-houses and estate cottages, Tilehurst was one of Voysey's smallest houses. Almost square in plan, it had a red-tile pitch roof that extended down to just above the ground on one side and was broken by a single chimney in the centre. The plan revolved around this central chimney, eliminating unnecessary corridors by fitting the staircase into an angle at the back of the hall and parlour fireplaces; very short passages linked the kitchen and hall with the staircase vestibule. Again Voysey made the hall the principal living room, with a small lobby, in this case, tacked on to the corner of the room, leading to the front door. A massive fireplace, tiled beneath a great oak lintel was the focus of the room and the slate floor, and white-painted joinery linked Tilehurst to the refined simplicity of The Orchard and Hollybank. The windows were large in proportion to the rooms, and the hall and adjoining parlour had a south-easterly aspect, looking out over the garden. A second window in the hall, running almost the full-length of the room in a long horizontal, faced south-west so that the room was flooded with light throughout the day, and the staircase, too, was abundantly lit from above by a large landing window.

Upstairs three bedrooms were lined up on the south-west side of the house, with fitted cupboards tucked under the pitch of the roof, and the bathroom, box room and a 'photographing room' were arranged around the staircase on the opposite side. On the landing two structural arches expressed the exceptional load of the roof and an airing-cupboard was built into the chimney breast so that the linen might be warmed by the residue of heat from the parlour and hall fires.

The planning at Tilehurst was masterly in its efficiency and attention to detail, and even in so small a house the proportions of the rooms were generous and meticulously calculated. Voysey's manipulation of light and his presentation of a restricted number of fine materials was no less effective for its economy, and the elevations depended on absolute restraint and simplicity for their effect. Unusually for Voysey the front door, with a flat projecting porch like that at Hollybank, was set at the side of the house and the kitchen door, round-headed with an arch of weathering, was set in the gable end, overlooking the road.

13

Tilehurst established an elemental design for a simple square or rectangular building beneath a pitch roof, with its gable ends fronting on to the road on one side and the garden on the other. Less than two years later, in 1905, Voysey was to take this elemental core and develop it in the design of Holly Mount for C. T. Burke, but whereas Tilehurst was designed for one of a row of building plots all facing on to Grange Road with town gardens to the rear, Holly Mount was designed for a substantial site surrounded by fields and woods, and Voysey was commissioned to design the furniture, as well as the house itself.

HOLLY MOUNT, near the town of Beaconsfield in Buckinghamshire, and The Homestead, commissioned in the same year at the resort of Frinton-on-Sea, in Essex, were designed as second homes for clients who were based in London during the week.[14] The publicity generated by The Orchard would undoubtedly have attracted clients to Voysey who were drawn by the idea of commissioning a house complete with all its furniture, designed as a single entity by one of the most

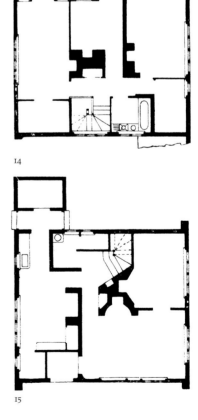

14

15

13–15 *Perspective and plans, Tilehurst, Bushey, Hertfordshire, 1903.*

fashionable architects of the day. However, there was a secondary, more pragmatic attraction to the diversity of Voysey's designing skills: most clients would have had an accumulation of furniture, which they would expect to take with them from one house to the next, but in the design of a second home there was an opportunity to make a fresh start; where clients had adequate financial resources but little time or inclination to shop for furniture the simplest, as well as the most ideologically correct option, would have been to entrust all matters of taste to Voysey, and commission the complete house.

The first ground plans for Holly Mount, including the layout for a formal garden, were drawn up in September 1905 and over the next twelve months the details of the plans and elevations were refined. Voysey retained the rectangular plan that he favoured for smaller houses, adding a deep square bay on to the front of the house to accommodate the staircase and a recessed porch, and all the essential ingredients for a small house were added in careful measure. There was almost nothing new in the design of Holly Mount: almost every element

can be associated with an earlier house, and yet, in spite of the familiarity of each of its parts, as a composition it was uniquely different from any other Voysey house, and at the same time in ethos and in detail it was absolutely consistent.

The long rectangular plan of Holly Mount and the deliberately composed gable ends beneath a steeply pitched, green-slate roof, elaborated on the extreme economy of Tilehurst. By adding a gabled, two-storey bay on to the front of the house, Voysey introduced a dialogue between the three gables, enriching the spatial quality of the elevations. The detailing was characteristically precise: stone kneelers to the gable ends picked up the base line of the bedroom window dressings (and Voysey was to develop this two-dimensional patterning of stone against roughcast further at The Homestead); and the horizontal lines of red-tile weathering were sharply drawn across the gable ends and around the front of the house, stopping short on one side of the entrance bay to signal the position of the staircase.

Voysey was less resolute than usual in his insistence on asymmetry. The entrance bay was positioned off-centre, but the front door, the name-plate,

16 *Slate name-plate, Holly Mount, near Beaconsfield, Buckinghamshire, 1907.*

17 *Hall fireplace, Holly Mount.*

18 *The parlour, Holly Mount. Photograph 1908–9.*

19 *Bedroom, Holly Mount. Photograph 1908–9.*

150   CHAPTER 9

the first-floor window lighting the staircase, and the chimney, breaking through the roof from behind, were all centrally aligned. Only the ground-floor window, wrapping around the corner on one side, contradicted the symmetry of the entrance bay, and one of the gable ends was emphatically symmetrical. Inside, the ideal of a living hall was relinquished, although the hall was still generously proportioned, and the alignment of the front door with the hall fireplace was far from accidental. The fireplace itself was not large, but its importance was accentuated by a tall surround of black slate, and early photographs show one of Voysey's tall clocks on the mantel-shelf.[15]

Voysey specified solid floors, 'avoiding the presence of damp, cold air under floors',[16] and slate for the path to the front door and for the porch and hall floors, because:

The disturbance of the senses is often very subtle. You go to call on a friend; you leave the York stone pavement and stand on mosaic or tiles, then on coconut mat, then possibly, on polished wood, and then on pile carpet; all varying sensations in rapid succession, which are more or less destructive of repose according to the sensitiveness of the visitor.[17]

However, his client proved insensitive to the sensations of feet, and was quick to cover the slate with a run of carpet, and in the parlour the floor was covered with a plain Voysey rug with a decorative border, but we must assume that Voysey concurred on the choice of the latter. He would not tolerate Persian rugs unless their owners knew how to interpret their symbolism recommending that it would be, 'more simple and sincere to have a plain British rug with no pattern on it at all'.[18] Voysey used arched openings for the front door and porch (echoed in miniature by the arched opening of the hall fireplace) and to accentuate the door between the hall and the parlour, so that the visitor to the house was presented with a sequence of wide round-headed doors. The doors to the kitchen and dining room, for family and servants, and to the bedrooms upstairs, were square headed, and consequently less conspicuous. Again the joinery was painted deal with black wrought-iron latches and tee-hinges. The staircase, tucked around the recessed porch, was a variation on Voysey's characteristic theme of screens of straight white balusters

with an oak handrail and newels, rising to the ceiling, but in spite of the familiarity of the component parts, no two Voysey staircases were exactly alike.

The house was simply furnished. Voysey's office and professional expenses books show that he regularly had sample pieces of furniture and metalwork made up to his designs, partly for exhibition purposes (and there are records of 'Carriage of samples to exhibition'), but also, in all probability, so that they could be taken to a newly completed house for consultation with the client, and to give the interiors a furnished effect for the photographer. The Holly Mount photographs, commissioned by Voysey in 1908 and 1909, show what was probably his preferred arrangement of furniture and the entire house furnished to his designs.

Voysey designed a number of upright and grand pianos. One of these, designed in May 1902 as a 'cottage piano for Mrs Voysey', presumably for The Orchard, was adapted for the specialist firm of Collard and Collard and exhibited at the Arts and Crafts exhibition of 1903. It was very like the piano in the parlour at Holly Mount, which was also supplied by Collard and Collard, with pierced hearts across the front to either side of the music stand and angle posts that rose above the height of the keyboard and were capped with circular plates.[19]

20

The original photographs published in 1911 show Voysey's usual twill curtains at the porthole window in the parlour and in one of the bedrooms, and the walls appear to have been whitewashed.[20] The bedrooms, too, were furnished by Voysey, and one of the 1911 photographs shows a Voysey washstand next to a small rectangular table and a very simple oak chest of drawers with a fine adjustable mirror designed by Voysey on top. The bedroom fireplaces appear in Elsley's catalogue. Like those at The Orchard they were cast-iron and elegantly proportioned, but they were more extravagantly curved and each one was decorated with a Voysey bird and fruit tree.

21

Some of the furniture at Holly Mount was almost identical to pieces designed for S. C. Turner at The Homestead.[21] The two houses were designed over the same period, both as complete houses for clients who gave Voysey an open brief in their furnishing and decoration and yet, in spite of the similarities in their detailing, the differences between them are far more salient than their similarities.

20 *Summer-house, Holly Mount (demolished).*
21 *Bedroom fireplace, Holly Mount.*

THE HOMESTEAD. The plan for The Homestead was L shaped, breaking the pattern of simple rectangular plans for smaller houses, which Voysey had used from Moorcrag onwards, but making a reference back to that of Annesley Lodge. The reason for this was given as, 'the outcome of the difficult levels of the site, and its prospect, together with the special requirements of the client'.[22] Voysey tucked the house into the corner of its plot with its two wings decisively fronting on to Holland Road to the north and Second Avenue to the east and in the crook of the L, sheltered from northerly and easterly winds and from the gaze of any passer-by, he provided a large south-facing garden, sloping very gently away from the house, open to views across the golf-course and to the countryside beyond.

The client was Sydney Claridge Turner, Secretary and General Manager of the Essex & Suffolk Equitable Insurance Society, who, like Burke, had his main residence in London.[23] He was a keen golfer, already a member of the club in the select and conservative seaside resort of Frinton-on-Sea, and when the opportunity arose to invest in a building plot overlooking the links he consulted Voysey and together they selected a corner site on Second Avenue and Holland Road, which was purchased for the sum of £375.

The contours of the site, falling gently away to the west along Holland Road, contributed towards the shape of the plan. By running the service wing along Holland Road, Voysey was able to accommodate and exploit this change in level. The placement of the service quarters in a long narrow wing allowed Voysey to effectively separate the servants from the main body of the house, giving both employer and employee a degree of privacy from one another.

Turner was a bachelor, and The Homestead, with its six bedrooms and a dressing room, would have been used for entertaining weekend guests, as well as for quieter golfing weekends. The main areas of the house were clearly differentiated from the service wing in the elevations, although Voysey was consistent in the quality and handling of materials throughout the house. The service wing angled back from the plane of the entrance porch to follow the line of Holland Road and delineate

22 *Entrance bay and service wing, The Homestead, Frinton-on-Sea, Essex, 1905–6.*

23 *Garden elevations, The Homestead.*

the acute angle of the plot, while the end bays of the main house were accentuated by a pair of dramatically asymmetrical gables and a deep-recessed porch with its arch picked out in red tiles, laid end on.

The style and function of each elevation was interpreted and expressed in the character of its Westmoreland slate roof, in a manner that was self-assured and indicative of extraordinary artistic freedom: the roof line to the service wing was relatively low and broken by small gables, giving it a modest domestic appearance: by comparison the gables to the entrance bay reared up in a dashingly elegant statement over the front door, the dining room, and the master bedroom; and around the corner, still fronting on to the street, the Second Avenue elevation was roofed with understated, perhaps rather aloof simplicity, telling very little of the private faces of the house. The modest simplicity of this Second Avenue elevation was disrupted by a sculptural massing of chimneys, breaking out from the plane of the elevation to house the deep ingle-nook in the parlour, and towering upwards, each with its own red-tiled set-off, in a proclama-

tion of the profound importance of the fireside, physically and symbolically, to the home.

The gable end facing southwards towards the sea was no less inspired. The strong diagonal of a cat-slide roof, sweeping down almost to the ground on one side, and the more inhibited limits to the roof line to Second Avenue defined the composition and described the dichotomy between the public and private faces of the house. The composition was balanced by a strategically placed buttress, which reinforced the structural load of the bedroom floors, and made a visual response to the verticality of the corner to Second Avenue. Within the gable end, Voysey signed his name with graphic simplicity. The three, vertical ventilation slits, just below the apex of the gable and the single light stone-dressed window, which were capped by a sharp horizontal of red-tile weathering, were characteristic of his work. The porthole window looking out towards the sea from beneath its jaunty line of weathering and the precision with which a minimum number of highly stylized components were arranged, like patterns on a page, represented a chic sense of poise that was unsurpassed.[24]

24 *Entrance bay, The Homestead.*

25 *The Homestead exploits its corner plot in an L-shaped plan to create a secluded rear garden.*

27

26

The garden elevations were sheltered beneath a cascade of sweeping roofs, anchored by a square tower at the juncture of the two wings of the house with windows wrapping around its upper storey to light the staircase within. Over the guest bedrooms and the parlour a massive, broad sweep of roof brushed the top of the parlour windows and covered a deep, west-facing veranda, which connected the parlour with the garden.

The grey roof of The Homestead was praised for its ability to blend with the surrounding landscape.[25] A row of elegant wrought-iron brackets, with heart-shaped tips supported the gutters, and the gutters themselves were wooden, V shaped and tarred inside. Three windows overlooked the garden from the first floor of the service wing, and Voysey exploited the change in level to ensure that the first of these, a single light, was at knee height in the corridor inside, and the second, a dormer, was above eye level. Only Turner's study or day room at the west end of the wing had a wide band of windows, tucked under the eaves, offering spectacular views southwards over the garden and golf-course beyond, towards the sea.

At The Homestead Voysey was given a rare opportunity to furnish an entire house, including the servants' quarters, in oak, making it one of his most resonant buildings. Oak lintels and beams were used in the structure, as *Country Life* noted in 1910, and like The Orchard, every detail of the building was designed by Voysey, but the budget for The Homestead was more generous than that of his own house.[26]

The studded, oak front door gave entrance to a relatively small hall with a cloakroom to one side, and, almost facing the front door, a superlative oak staircase. There was no secondary staircase at The Homestead. Turner, like most of the patrons of Voysey's cottages, was content to share his staircase with the servants. The walls were wainscoted to waist height, and dark grey 'tile paving' was laid throughout the ground floor of the house, with the exception of the dining room. These tiles, which Voysey had already used at Tilehurst, were French and had to be blacked and polished with boot polish by the parlour maid three times a week in order to look their best.[27] The Homestead was similar to Tilehurst, too, in the use of a name-plate of tile letters made to Voysey's design by Martin van Straaten and set into the roughcast.[28]

There were two principal ground-floor rooms: a dining room, conveniently close to the butler's pantry and the service wing, and a great parlour, L shaped to echo the main plan of the house. By cutting a corner out of the dining room, Voysey was able to open the hall out at an angle towards the parlour, and an arched opening, trimmed with red tiles like that of the porch, gave a clear directional link between the arched front door and the parlour.[29] Voysey had established a similar appeal to the sensibilities of visitors to Holly Mount, but at The Homestead the connection was more sophisticated.

The parlour was larger than the three bedrooms above it put together, but in spite of its size and the unrelenting use of hard surfaces – tiled floor, plain white walls without wainscoting or picture-rails, and simple oak furniture – this room, more than any other Voysey interior illustrates one of his most compelling statements:

Try the effect of a well-proportioned room, with white-washed walls, plain carpet and simple oak furniture, and nothing in it but necessary articles of use, and one pure ornament in the form of a simple vase of flowers, not a cosmopolitan crowd of all sorts, but one or two sprays of one kind, and you will then find reflections begin to dance in your brain; each object will be received on the retina, and understood, classified and dismissed from the mind, and you will be free as a bird to wander in the sunshine or storm of your own thoughts.[30]

28

A deep, splay-sided ingle established the fireplace as the focus of the room with a window to each side, so that sunshine and light for reading, as well as warmth, could be enjoyed by the fireside. White-delft tiles covered the walls of the ingle to reflect the light, and the delicacy of four Voysey picture tiles – two birds and two trees – on either side of the fire drew the visitor into the recess beneath a shallow arch of red tiles laid end on. Voysey's brick supplier, Mr Ames, recalled that Voysey selected the bricks to surround the hearth itself with the greatest care, asking first for one sample and then another. When he visited the house he was horrified to find that all the bricks had been black leaded – Voysey had selected them not for their colour, but purely for the quality of their surface texture, so that they would have a soft sheen when they were blacked.[31] Above the fireplace more birds and trees decorated Voysey's characteristic ventilator-grille and the practicalities, as well as the aesthetics of the fireside were treated with assiduous attention to detail, as *Country Life* noted with satisfaction:

In an exposed situation like that of The Homestead the treatment of chimneys demands great care, if the trouble of smokiness is to be avoided. Mr Voysey has gone about it in a thorough fashion. Under each grate is an inlet from the outer air, and in the chimney-breast an outlet leads to a separate shaft in the chimney-stack, a device efficient but costly.[32]

29

Voysey's use of colour was sharply defined throughout the parlour, and consistent with the rest of the house. Turkey-red curtains contrasted with green-ceramic tiled sills and the stone surround of the porthole window, which had no curtains, was simply ringed with green tiles. The handmade, red building-tiles, which Voysey used to edge his arches, were used to line a recessed niche with a green-ceramic tile base next to the door and a plain green carpet covered part of the floor. Green was undoubtedly employed for its restful qualities and two of Voysey's easy chairs, which

C F A VOYSEY

28 *The parlour, The Homestead.*
   Photograph pre-1911
29 *The dining room, The Homestead.*
   Photograph pre-1911.

30

31

were photographed drawn up towards the fireside, were upholstered in green. He used the same combination of red and green patches of colour against a white background in his elevations.

Under the porthole window the south end of the parlour was equipped with a Voysey billiard-table, lit by its own electric extrolier, as well as by ample daylight from three different aspects. Where the room projected westwards towards the garden a pair of massive oak braces supported the ceiling beam, which in turn took the load of the broad sweep of roof above. The structure was honestly, but never obtrusively, expressed throughout the interiors and Voysey made a point of exposing the oak lintels above the windows, often juxtaposing them against the fireplace lintels. The smooth, regular appearance of machine-worked oak was deliberately avoided: 'We are far too keen on mechanical perfection. That love of smooth, polished surfaces is very materialistic; it can be produced without brains, and in most cases can only be produced by the elimination of all human thought and feeling.'[33]

The great oak doors with their Z-shaped reinforcements and simple oak latches, locked by the insertion of an oak wedge or the twist of an oak piece, were supreme examples of thought and feeling and their generous proportions and textural surface variations represented Voysey at his most sensuous. Unlike Morris, who was an avid machine hater, Voysey sought to exploit the advantages of machine production, combining technology with the 'skill of hand and eye' of craftsmanship:

You have all observed the soft, yet massive, effect in old buildings, when the angles were put up by human eye, and compared them with the hard, unsympathetic, mechanical effect of the modern drafted angle.

I would not have you go back to all methods of hand labour and neglect the aid of the Machine. All we need is to recognise its material value, and its spiritual imperfection, and put into all our hand-work that thought and feeling which is the breath of life.[34]

Decisions about the furnishing of The Homestead began in earnest in August 1906. Voysey made his first visit to Nielsen on Turner's behalf on the third, and on the eighth he made a trip to Frinton, presumably to meet Turner on site. The two men had dinner together that evening at Voysey's club and it

must have been a good dinner because it cost thirteen shillings and six pence, compared to only five shillings and a penny spent on entertaining another of Voysey's clients, E. J. Horniman at his club the following day. Over the next twelve months Voysey made frequent visits to Frinton and to his furniture-maker, and Voysey and Turner evidently became great friends. They went together to see Thomas Elsley in October 1906, again after a site visit to Frinton, and Turner might have had a say in choosing the heart-shaped letter plate, bell-pull, fire-grates, fenders, and even the lampshades, as well as all the other specialist handles and ironmongery, which Elsley regularly supplied to Voysey houses. Voysey made numerous visits to Elsley for almost all his houses as a matter of course, but it was very unusual for him to take a client with him. Equally intriguing are the entries in Voysey's accounts for 'Expenses with Turner re Burke's House' (Holly Mount) in November 1907 and for 'Turner and self at Exhibition'.[35]

Voysey designed all the furniture for The Homestead and he arranged for photographs to be made of the house in November 1908. It was these photographs, taken before Turner had a chance to put his pictures on the walls or his knick-knacks on the mantel-shelves (except for an obligatory peacock feather and a few books on the trolley by the fire), which were reproduced in an article in *Country Life* in October 1910 and which give us one of the sharpest insights into the complete Voysey house. Some of the furniture, including the writing table and bed that were also used at Holly Mount, and an oak chesterfield were designed specifically for The Homestead in 1906–7 and in addition to these freestanding pieces, Voysey designed fitted furniture throughout the house. The bedrooms were furnished with chests of drawers and wardrobes built in to the pitch of the roof and one of the guest rooms, 'a bachelor's room' was furnished with, 'a fitment which comprises wardrobe, chest of drawers and washstand, an arrangemeament [sic] which economises space and gives a certain dignity to the room despite its smallness'.[36] The quality of furnishing in the servants' rooms was indistinguishable from that of the other areas of the house, making it difficult to be sure which of the bedrooms were allocated to servants' use. We do not know how many servants Turner employed at The Homestead. He would have brought his butler with him from London, but even as late as 1938 when the days of domestic service were well on the wane, The Homestead employed a cook, a housemaid, a gardener and a gardener's boy, and the cook and the housemaid lived in.[37]

The dining room was furnished with a round table and lathe-back chairs and a pendant, electric lampshade designed by Voysey. It was described by *Country Life* as:

...of an interesting shape, suggested by the fact that no one sits in the corners of a room. One of the angles is cut off and thrown into the hall, two more are fitted with big store cupboards and the fourth with a side-board. The more usual square is thus turned into an octagon, and the room adequately furnished without any loss of floor space.[38]

On the other side of the hall, and several steps lower down to follow the slope of the site, the butler's pantry was strategically placed between the dining room and the kitchens: '...it must be as close as possible to the dining room (because the butler serves at table), its position must be one from which he can observe the front-door of the house, so that he may attend to visitors the moment they arrive; it must be close to the owner's room, for he often needs the butler.'[39] The walls were lined with oak cupboards for table linen, glasses and crockery, and beneath the window a lead sink was originally provided for cleaning the silver. Even the kitchen and scullery – areas where the client would never venture – were furnished with an oak table and dresser designed by Voysey.

Partly as a result of its small scale, and in spite of the complexities of the site, The Homestead was one of Voysey's finest and most complete houses. The free handling of the elevations demonstrated has confidence and maturity and the synthesis of plan and elevation, of structure and decoration, was superlative. In its elevations it combined the daring lines and variations that Voysey had explored so successfully at Moorcrag, with the compact sense of unity that he had refined and perfected at The Orchard. Together with The Orchard it is one of the best documented and most rigorously consistent examples of a house as a total work of art, expressing every dimension of its author's versatility as a designer.

32

LITTLEHOLME, GUILDFORD. Early in 1906, Voysey began to make drawings for a house for one of his builders, George Müntzer. The Müntzer family had built Greyfriars, Norney, Vodin and Prior's Garth in Surrey, and they were to go on to build Voysey's most important London interiors at Garden Corner and Capel House. They worked for Sir Edwin Lutyens, as well as for Voysey, and in the design for Littleholme Voysey incorporated a first-floor balcony with a timber frame and its own hipped roof that might easily have been lifted from a Lutyens house, but the overall design had all the Voysey hallmarks. The site was on the side of a hill with spectacular views to the south, and Voysey included the terracing and general layout of the garden in his first drawings. The Müntzers were regular visitors to Gertrude Jekyll's house at Munstead Wood, and soon after it was completed, Littleholme was featured in her book *Gardens for Small Country Houses*. They must have admired the dovetailing of house and garden in Jekyll and Lutyens's gardens. At Littleholme, the house and its garden were planned as a single entity right from the start.

32 *Entrance front, Littleholme, Guildford, Surrey, 1906.*

Littleholme was contained within a rectangular plan, cut into a level terrace, with the earth banking up steeply on the north side and falling away in a series of level terraces to the south. A flight of stone steps led down to the front door and the front of the house was articulated by changes in the roof line and an elegantly asymmetrical cross gable. The door itself was oak with an imposing circular window, which allowed light into the porch. It was positioned with a low lavatory window to one side and a high bank of windows lighting the grand staircase on the other; the shape of the gable above brought the irregular composition into sharp focus. On the west side of the gable, the roof came down in a fluent sweep over the library windows, with a dormer window (originally designed as a miniature gable) breaking through above. On the other side, the plane of the elevation broke back and the roof line shot up to mark the service area of the house.

The garden elevation was designed with the same stylish assurance and economy of means. At its focus (although characteristically not at its centre), a wide veranda, outlined with an arch of tiles laid end-on, framed the main axis of the garden and established the critical relationship between the house, its garden and the landscape beyond. A glazed door, flanked by deep windows, gave entrance to the living hall where Voysey repeated the arch of red tiles around the brick fireplace, and long bands of windows in the dining room and drawing room to either side gave unrestricted views across the garden. Voysey projected the kitchen out into a deep square bay to give him grounds for the Lutyens-style balcony to the master bedroom above. Although the kitchen bay had windows on three sides they were high enough not to detract from the privacy of the garden.

Voysey had understood the importance of bedding a house into its landscape by extending the lines and patterns of the house into its garden from his earliest garden design for Lowicks in 1895. This was in spite of the fact that the relationship between his own house, The Orchard, and its garden and early photographs of that garden suggest that he was neither a sophisticated plantsman nor an enthusiastic practical gardener. (Our knowledge of Voysey's private life is too sketchy to know this for sure. The Orchard was equipped with a full-size

tennis-court, and yet we know nothing of Voysey's enthusiasm or otherwise for the game).[40] Nevertheless, his profound regard for nature and his 'respect for local conditions of climate and soil' were by no means limited to the design of the house. His roughcast walls were intended to be covered with creepers (at Broadleys Voysey specified that the brick layer should, 'Provide and fix 4 gross of galvanized iron eyes 2 feet apart where directed for fixing wires for creepers'),[41] and his gardens were carefully conceived to be enjoyed from the interiors of his houses, with long vistas drawing out the axis of a room, as well as from the terraces and verandas, which could be enjoyed on warmer days.

Voysey designed pergolas and summer-houses for his gardens and they were furnished with settles and garden-benches made to his designs. Sundials were strategically placed to focus formal vistas, and even the smallest garden was entered through a Voysey gate. At Littleholme, Voysey designed a lead gargoyle for one of the retaining walls to throw the water that drained down from above clear of the wall. It was illustrated in *Gardens for Small Country Houses* and was described as having, 'a delightfully grotesque quality that is suggestive of the mediaeval craftsman', but although parts of the garden at Littleholme were drawn up by Voysey, the laying out of the garden was credited to Thomas Young of Woking, and it was Young's drawing of the garden, conspicuously signed and dated 1907 that was reproduced.

Young was clearly influenced by Jekyll's ideas, and the garden at Littleholme is the closest Voysey came to a direct collaboration with Jekyll, although she worked on the planting at New Place some years after he had completed the house. Photographs of the house and garden, published in *Country Life* illustrating the lines of yew hedging in their infancy, show how successful the architectural lines of Voysey's hard landscaping could be when they were skilfully planted. The main axis north/south through the hall was brilliantly composed with a pergola extending the depth of the arched veranda and a wide paved terrace leading to a double staircase that descended to a small grass garden below. From the veranda and the terrace the view southwards towards Bramley and Ewhurst was spectacularly composed by the alignment of a square tank pool, a sundial and the

33

33 *Voysey contemplating his garden at The Orchard. He had already trained the ivy into a heart.*

158   CHAPTER 9

curved wall of a brick bastion all on the terrace below, and the formality of the composition, together with the prospect of a second view over the bastion wall drew the visitor down the double staircase into the grass garden.

The aspect and the view of the countryside beyond was open from the terrace by the house, but the lower terrace, wrapped around with yew hedges was secluded and planned to create an effect of orderly calm. The rectangular lawn was set within a frame of straight stone paths with the square pool at its centre, and although the bastion wall gave vistas over the lower orchard to the landscape beyond, the views out of the grass garden were structured by the high yew hedges. To the east and west arches were cut into the hedging to reveal views of the flower gardens on either side, and to the north, looking back towards the house, the high retaining walls and the steps down from the terrace above completed the sense of enclosure. Voysey himself looked out over the grass garden in the form of a stone devil perched on a wall between the double staircase, so that looking back towards the house he could be seen grinning a little ruefully beneath it.

To the west of the grass garden, flower-beds banked away in a series of shallow terraces, which mirrored the pitch of the roof. Local brick and the flints that were dug from the site were used in the retaining walls. The different levels were exploited to create areas of garden that were quite different in purpose and character from one another: there was a croquet lawn on one side of the house and a servants' garden on the other with a fruit garden laid out below the lower orchard, but even in 1907 the cost of laying out and terracing the garden on such a scale was considerable. Jekyll's book stated that the cost of, 'The mere work of digging and wall-building, the construction, in fact, of the carcass of the garden, cost over five hundred pounds, and this takes no account of the planting.' However, the money, it concluded, had been 'worthily spent'.

Littleholme was one of the last country cottages that Voysey built. Voysey extended the house almost as soon as it was completed, designing rooms into the roof with dormer windows in 1909, and in 1912 he designed a gardener's cottage for Littleholme, which he estimated would cost considerably less than the garden itself at about £300.[42] Characteristically Voysey designed this cottage

34

with the same attention to detail and utility that he applied to all his work, and when Littleholme was requisitioned by the Home Office during the Second World War the Müntzers moved into the gardener's cottage and remained there.

The popular appeal of Voysey's houses had led to many copies being made, even in the 1890s, and some of the local building firms that Voysey had employed had unscrupulously built Voysey adaptations or even replicas of his houses without the architect's consent. These houses had the superficial appearance of a Voysey house, but the resemblance seldom went beyond the elevations, and Voysey would have dismissed them as shams. Of all his builders Müntzer would have found it easy enough to build himself a house in the Voysey style, and the fact that he did not do so and that Voysey designed not only the house, but also the additions, and even the gardener's cottage, is evidence of the mutual respect and friendship between architect and builder.[43] Voysey was friendly with many of his clients, but for an architect to win the respect of his builder is an achievement of consequence.

34 *Garden elevation, Littleholme.*

2

3

HOLLYBANK

1903

4

Hollybank was built next
door to The Orchard in
Chorleywood, Herfordshire,
with a wide tract of open land
between the two houses. It was
designed for Dr H. R. T. Fort
with a doctor's practice on one
side and living accommodation
on the other. The dual purpose
of the building, with its two
separate front doors, is clearly
expressed in the twin gables
of the front elevation.

1 *Front elevation, this side of Hollybank*
   was designed as a doctor's practice.
2, 3 *The front door to the doctor's house at*
   Hollybank was distinguished from that
   of the practice by a simple flat canopy.
4 *Window detail.*

5

6

7

5 *The hall, looking northwards.*

6 *The landing.*

7 *Ground-floor lavatory with Voysey*
   towel-rail.

163   C F A VOYSEY

8, 9 *The garden elevation from a distance and from close-up showing the door into the hall.*

10 *Gate latch (no longer in situ).*

11 *Bedroom with fitted cupboards and wash-stand.*

12 *The dining room, Hollybank.*

1

2

3

1 The entrance elevation – a crisp and
   modern statement in cottage design.

2 Gable end, composed with a rare
   concession to symmetry.

3 Voysey designed rustic gates for many
   of his cottages. This is the last one to
   survive.

4

5

6

7   8

HOLLY MOUNT

1905

Holly Mount, near Beaconsfield in Buckinghamshire, was designed as a weekend retreat for C. T. Burke. Burke probably visited The Orchard and was encouraged to commission Voysey to design the house and all the furniture and fittings in it. When it was first completed, photographs of Holly Mount were published in England and Germany, promoting Voysey's reputation as a complex designer of everything for the home.

4, 5 Hall and landing.
6 Front elevation.
7 Piano case, designed for Collard and Collard, c.1903. It is similar to the one originally photographed in the parlour at Holly Mount.

8 Oak toilet glass, first designed c.1897. A version of the mirror appears in bedroom photographs of Holly Mount.

4

5

THE HOMESTEAD

1905–6

6

The Homestead at Frinton-on-Sea, Essex, was designed for a bachelor client, S. C. Turner, overlooking his favourite golf-links. Turner and Voysey selected the site together; the house was tucked into its corner plot with an L-shaped plan fronting decisively on to Second Avenue and Holland Road, sheltering a secluded garden to the rear. Each elevation expresses the function of the rooms within, and Voysey furnished all the interiors to the same high standard, from the pantry to the parlour.

1 Second Avenue elevation, and gable end facing south.

2 Porthole window looking towards the sea, south elevation.

3 Ingle-nook window, the pattern of stone dressings is deliberately asymmetrical.

4 A row of gables differentiate the service wing.

5 The Second Avenue elevation with its massing of chimneys marks the importance of the ingle-nook within.

6 Detail, service wing.

7

8

9

7 *The garden, sheltered from view and*
   from prevailing winds.

8, 9 *Timber gutters, V-shaped and tarred*
      inside, supported on elegant iron
      brackets with heart-shaped tips.

THE HOMESTEAD

10

11

12

13

10 *Bedroom fireplace directly above the ingle-nook.*

11 *Voysey designed the dining room without corners because he believed that nobody would choose to sit in the corner.*

12 *View of staircase looking towards the parlour.*

13 *The parlour, originally furnished with a billiard-table and Voysey chairs gathered around the ingle-nook.*

Voysey's buildings fall quite easily into specific groups: country houses, cottages, grander houses and houses that he treated as total works of art. For historical and comparative purposes it is useful to look at them in this context; by comparing similar buildings, the continuous themes, refinements and developments in Voysey's work clearly emerge. The disadvantage of fitting his houses into this artificial framework, and it is quite a serious disadvantage, is that they begin to look as if they were conceived with each other in mind. Voysey's cottages, for instance, were not designed as a single coherent body of work. Taken chronologically, they were interspersed with designs for a hospital, a school, a factory, various offices and with moderately sized houses, which demonstrate a considerable architectural range in the organization of plans and elevations. In this chapter, very different buildings are considered sequentially. While the cottages or grander houses can be related to the buildings in previous chapters as a group, they also give a clear indication of the diversity of Voysey's practice between 1899 and 1905, and of the way that his preoccupation with the Gothic emerged and reappeared from one building type to another.

Voysey's architectural language was deliberately restrained. Where his designs were innovative they were also founded on reason rather than on a contrived attempt to be different. It was the conditions of the site and the function of the building that dictated the design, and where, as in the case of the Sanderson Factory, these were extraordinary, Voysey responded with inventive solutions. His urban buildings were conceived quite separately from his country houses and yet when they are considered together chronologically, Voysey's urban, rural, commercial and domestic buildings are remarkable because they present a set of patterns and repetitions, as well as a vigorous and incisive exploration into the nature of architecture.

THE WINSFORD COTTAGE HOSPITAL. In April 1899 Voysey was commissioned to design the Winsford Cottage Hospital in Devon. Although it was a public building with a private benefactor he did not automatically develop a new architectural vocabulary, and given the strong philosophical base and careful reasoning behind his style it would

ARCHITECTURAL RANGE

2

1 *Garden elevation, The Pastures, North Luffenham, Rutland, 1901.*
2 *Side elevations, Vodin, Pyrford Common, near Woking, Surrey, 1902.*

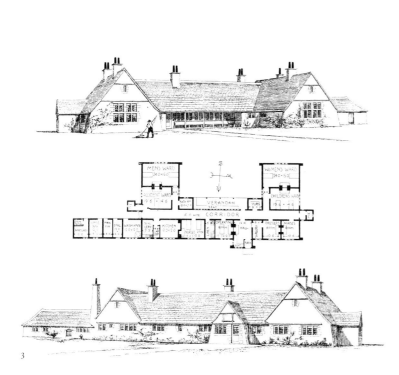

3

4

have been surprising if he had done so. Instead, he took into account the rural location and the small scale for the building and he designed a hospital, which from the outside might easily have been mistaken for a Voysey house. It was a single-storey building with a deep Delabole-slate roof and two projecting wings with a sheltered veranda between them. The building was set close to its boundary on the north side with a clear straight path to the front door, asymmetrically arranged in a gabled bay. A plaque in the gable gave details of the benefactor, but from the lane the first glimpse of the hospital was of a long, low roof half hidden behind the boundary hedge.[1]

The hospital was quite unlike a Voysey house inside. It was conceived to combine sanitary and practical considerations with a perceptive understanding of the requirements of patients and nursing staff alike. Voysey gave particular attention to providing draughts only where they were beneficial: 'the floors of the wards are boarded on solid beds of concrete, so that there is no cold damp air or any harbour for rats below,' and 'Cross-ventilation is provided in each ward by means of separate

air-flues.'[2] The floors were all on one level so that wheel-chairs and beds could be moved with comparative ease, and they were cheerful as well as practical: the hall, corridors and veranda were paved with a yellow-mosaic tile, contrasting with the green-painted doors, and the kitchen floor was made of massive slabs of slate.[3]

The plan was arranged with a row of small utilitarian rooms along the north elevation, with the mortuary at one end, the nurses room at the other and the operating room next to the entrance hall towards the middle. There were four generous wards: a men's ward and an accident ward in one wing, and a women's ward and children's ward in the other with only two beds in each (apart from the accident ward which was designed for a single bed). Both the men's and women's wards enjoyed southerly views across a garden to the landscape beyond and Voysey was careful to arrange the children's ward so that it would overlook the railway, 'which is the only entertainment near the site'. 'I mention these points,' he told *The Builder's Journal,* 'as the hospital faddists are apt to forget them.'[4]

3 *Plans and elevations, The Winsford Cottage Hospital, near Beauworthy, Devon, 1899.*

4 *Perspective and plans, Spade House, Sandgate, Kent, 1899.*

SPADE HOUSE. The first design for Spade House in Sandgate, Kent, was made within a month of the Winsford Cottage Hospital design, and again Voysey was preoccupied with the practicalities of invalid mobility. Though both buildings made reference to the comforting and regenerative associations of the cottage idyll, in character and organization they were quite different from one another. Spade House is famous for having been designed for the author H. G. Wells, and when it was first designed in March 1899, allowances had to be made for the prospect that Wells's health might have confined him to a wheel-chair. He was still a young man with a rising literary reputation, but his early career had been plagued by respiratory problems and kidney failure and so at Spade House, as he later wrote in his autobiography: 'The living-rooms were on one level with the bed-rooms so that if presently I had to live in a wheeled chair I could be moved easily from room to room. But things did not turn out in that fashion.'[5] Instead, Wells decided, while the building work was in progress, that a family would be in order, and in January 1903 Voysey was required to put an additional storey into the roof of the house for nursery accommodation.

Voysey could not have approved of H. G. Wells's championing of free love, his womanizing, or of his socialist theories, and it is difficult to imagine what sort of relationship the two men would have had. H. G. Wells's autobiography throws little light on the subject, stating only that:

We found a site for the house we contemplated, we found an architect in C.F.A. Voysey, that pioneer in the escape from the small snobbish villa residence to the bright and comfortable pseudo-cottage. Presently we found ourselves with all the money we needed for the house and a surplus of over £1,000.[6]

This would suggest that Voysey was chosen for his professional reputation, however, the two men clearly got on because in October 1911 Wells included Voysey in a private poem:

God is an Amoosing God, although he let that site,
What first we chose, be Toomerized, he more than
     made things right
By getting us a better site, a more amoozing chunk
And finding us the Voysey man and Honest Mr. Dunk.[7]

The site for Spade House was on a ridge, falling steeply away to the north and south, and the site for the house itself sloped away to the west. It enjoyed dramatic sea views to the south across Sandgate Bay and the English Channel – Wells's study was within the sound of the waves. The first preliminary design was made on 5 March 1899, and within a week a revised design had been drawn up. From the outset Voysey incorporated the slope of the site into the plan, putting the kitchen, scullery and servants' bedroom on the lower ground floor, and arranging the principal rooms together with the bedrooms, facing south towards the sea on the ground floor. Initially the bedrooms were in the centre of the plan with the living and dining rooms at opposite ends, each with a polygonal bay beneath a cross gable. Wells's library was in the north range of the house with a porthole window looking, rather quirkily, away from the sea, but a conservatory and a deep veranda linked the library with the garden.

There were similarities between this first design and the final design for Moorcrag, which was drawn a few months later. Voysey was obliged to simplify the design for Spade House. Perhaps the surplus of over £1,000 would not stretch to conservatories and polygonal bays, but the composition of a rectangular plan terminated at either end by a cross gable was developed to far greater effect the following June at Moorcrag. In the final design for Spade House the relationship between the house and its site was more rigid and the manipulation of changes in level in the site was squat and uncomfortable, even in the perspective drawing. The bedrooms were no longer at the centre of the plan, perhaps because Wells's health 'was getting better and better' and in their place two square bays, each with its own hipped roof, jutted out from the south elevation housing the study and the dining room. Between them, a sheltered veranda linked the dining room with the garden and Voysey provided a broad level path along a raised terrace, presumably so that Wells could propel himself along. In the event Wells recovered enough to pull a roller around his 'nascent garden', and photographs of the house during construction suggest that the ungainly severity of the raised, wheel-chair run was refined before the house was completed.

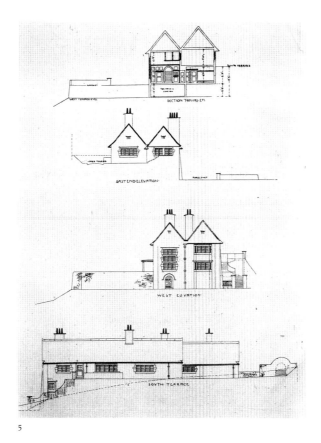

The walls may have been papered, like the dining room and hall at The Orchard, with a strong coloured, Eltonbury silk. When Wells finally sold Spade House, he claimed to have done so deliberately with Mr Lewisham of *Love and Mr. Lewisham* in mind: 'because I felt that otherwise it would become the final setting of my life'.

OAKHURST was designed while the construction of Spade House was nearing completion, in August 1900. The two houses, however, were very different in appearance and organization. Oakhurst had the appearance of a big house with a long, two-storey entrance elevation fronting on to a drive and forecourt. It looked bigger than it was because the site banked up steeply to the south and east allowing only a short single storey on the garden side; Voysey's brightly coloured perspective of the house presented the long entrance front and the towering west elevation. By incorporating the steep slope of the site into the house, he was able to present a sharp contrast between this verticality and the two single-storey elevations. The plan was divided into two piles, a north and south range each with its own pitch roof, and this division was clearly expressed in the short, east and west elevations.

There were two clients, Mrs E. F. Chester and her sister, but the two women fell out during the building process, and the sister built another house, Ashhurst, near by.[9] The house was at Fernhurst in West Sussex, and we must imagine Voysey travelling between his rented house in Chorleywood, across to Kent to oversee the construction of Spade House, up to the Lake District to keep a check on Moorcrag, to Hereford and Worcestershire where he was building a house and a lodge, and as far west as Halwill, in Devon, where the Winsford Cottage Hospital was being worked on, all in 1900, while The Orchard was being built. Voysey travelled everywhere by train and he once cut a colleague at the Arts Club, who hoped he might have read his book on the Spanish Renaissance, with the remark, 'I have only one book in my office, and it is a Bradshaw's Railway Guide, which, I am sorry to say, I have to use much oftener than I like.'[10]

Voysey's perspective of the final design gave the house a graduated slate roof and a heart on the front door. No explanation is given for the substitution of red tiles for slates, but by October 1899 when the plans and elevations were published in *The British Architect*, as an example of a 'cottage on a sloping site', the heart was inverted and a tail had been added. In his autobiography H. G. Wells proudly accounted for the naming of the house: 'Voysey wanted to put a large heart-shaped letter plate on my front door, but I protested at wearing my heart so conspicuously outside and we compromised on a spade. We called the house Spade House.'[8]

H. G. Wells and his wife Amy Catherine lived at Spade House for ten years, and *Kipps, Anticipations, A Modern Utopia, Mankind in the Making, Ann Veronica, Tono Bungay* and *The New Machiavelli* were among the books written in his simple study there. Though photographs of the study and of George Bernard Shaw's visit to the house in 1902 show that Voysey may have had a say in the decoration of the house, he did not furnish it. It was painted white above the picture-rail and the joinery and fitted bookshelves were also white.

Oakhurst was uncompromisingly plain. It was given a budget generous enough to afford oak panelling in some of the interiors, and yet there were no sweeping roof lines, and the many gables and projecting bays, which had adorned Voysey's houses of two and three years earlier, were omitted. To some extent the use of tiles instead of slates inhibited Voysey's roofs – and Oakhurst had a tile roof – but the functional austerity of the elevations with the grouping of windows into bands or blocks, as almost the sole decorative element, indicates a confidence in simplicity that was not altogether justified.

Inside, Voysey provided an immense double-height hall, hence the great blocks of windows in the entrance and west elevations, lined with oak and with a deep fireplace, and an ingle-nook seat placed rather curiously in the corner away from the warmth of the fire. The position of the staircase, too, was planned for dramatic effect rather than expedience. It was strategically placed just off-centre in the end wall of the hall, flanked by a doorway to either side. This central position was achieved at the expense of the most obvious source of natural light. In spite of the immense hall windows it was necessary to insert a roof-light above the staircase in order to satisfy Voysey's dictum that the staircase must always be 'amply lighted'.

The hall and dining room were arranged on the west side of the ground floor, overlooking the garden, and the parlour was on the floor above with the bedrooms. Both the landing and a window from the parlour looked down into the hall, and Voysey was able to give the dining room and the parlour above it openings directly into the garden, by virtue of the steep terracing. The service area, for the main part, was strung along the north frontage, with views out over the drive and in the basement below the hall a tool house and stokehole probably housed a boiler for central heating. Mrs Chester clearly insisted on the most modern home comforts because in 1901 *The Builder's Journal* noted that, 'Electric light will be provided by the engine that pumps the water.'[11]

Although Oakhurst was relatively modest in size, with six bedrooms, Voysey concentrated his resources on the four principal rooms – the double-height hall, the dining room, parlour and the master bedroom – and the scale and proportions of these rooms, together with their relationship to the terraces outside, gave the house a sense of simple nobility and grandeur.

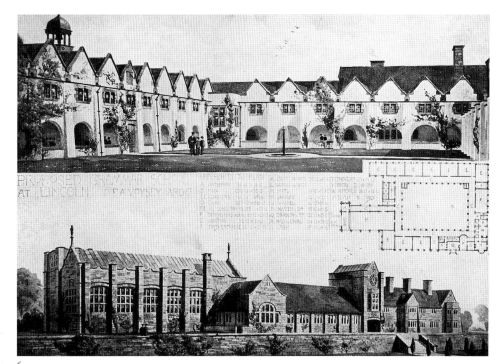

6

DESIGN FOR LINCOLN GRAMMAR SCHOOL. Within a year of the design for Oakhurst, in the summer of 1901, Voysey was invited to enter a competition to design a new grammar school for Lincoln.[12] The invitation came about because he had designed a house, Priors Garth, for the new headmaster, F. H. Chambers, and it is ironic that this house in Surrey was almost immediately converted into a school, while Voysey's competition entry was unsuccessful.

The competition entry broke the mould of Voysey's earlier architectural designs and gave him a highly plausible reason to return to the Gothic influences of his early architectural education. The scale of the proposal for Lincoln Grammar School together with the conditions of a site 'exposed to violent winds' caused him to abandon domestic models and to produce a design that was radically different from his earlier work. The school was to have been an impressive stone building on a raised terrace with a towering entrance bay and buttressed wings to either side, beneath a deep sheltering roof of handmade, sand-faced red tiles. The tradition of old English schools and colleges was

6 *Perspective and plan, Lincoln Grammar School, unexecuted design, 1901.*

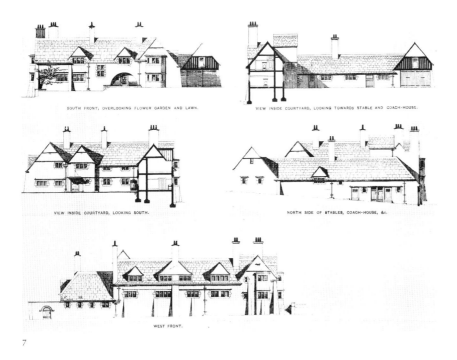

SOUTH FRONT, OVERLOOKING FLOWER GARDEN AND LAWN.

VIEW INSIDE COURTYARD, LOOKING TOWARDS STABLE AND COACH-HOUSE.

VIEW INSIDE COURTYARD, LOOKING SOUTH.

NORTH SIDE OF STABLES, COACH-HOUSE, &c.

WEST FRONT.

7

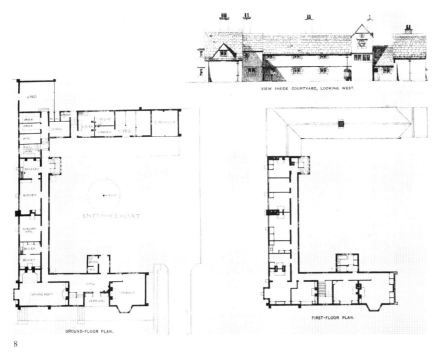

VIEW INSIDE COURTYARD, LOOKING WEST.

GROUND-FLOOR PLAN.

FIRST-FLOOR PLAN.

8

clearly evoked in the plan and elevations, with four wings arranged around a sheltered quadrangle, and Voysey called his knowledge of Tudor buildings into play in the diversity of the entrance elevation and of the cloistered faces of the quadrangle with their many gables. Though Lincoln Grammar School was by no means a Mock Tudor design, it permitted him to re-examine the rationale and detailing of Medieval and Tudor architecture. It was clearly stamped with Voysey's individual style: the great hall projected out from the quadrangle in a separate wing with blocks of mullioned windows indicating the double-height space within and towering piers set up a jaunty rhythm with the syncopated line of the parapet. A note of humour was added to the roof with two figures looking very like masters posted above the gables at either end of the hall, looking down into the quadrangle and surveying the landscape beyond.

Although it failed to win the competition, the design for Lincoln Grammar was extremely important to Voysey. He exhibited the perspectives in the Royal Academy Summer Exhibition of 1905, and they were published in *Building News* with a description, which included a fastidious account of the ventilation and ended with the stoic remark: 'My design was rejected on the ground that it was too severe, and I am pleased to say the design of Mr. Leonard Stokes was accepted instead.'[13] The design for the grammar school represented a turning point in Voysey's career. It marked the onset of what was to become an increasingly dogmatic preoccupation with the Gothic; by the time the drawings were exhibited Voysey had already taken extracts from the plan and elevations and incorporated them into buildings as diverse as The Pastures, the Sanderson Factory, Vodin and a house at Higham.

THE PASTURES, in North Luffenham, adopted two of the elements in the grammar school design, and if Voysey had had his own way it would have taken three. It was designed within months of the school, in November 1901, and the site was pegged out on 7 and 8 January 1902.[14] The plan of the house, again after the manner of an Oxford college, was arranged in three long wings, each one room and a corridor deep, around a courtyard. Voysey would have been quite conscious of the English

Medieval connotations of such a plan, but at The Pastures he combined traditional references with a personal and contemporary relevance. The court-yard plan was designed around an existing old wal-nut tree and so the architecture became quite liter-ally a frame for the beauty of nature and the spread-ing form of the tree became a focus, and perhaps an analogy for the design of the house.

Voysey had intended to build the house of local stone, but according to *The Studio*, he had come up against the fixed ideas of his client on the subject of materials and had lost:

Thus the house designed by Mr. Voysey for Miss G.C. Conant at North Luffenham, near Stamford, Rutland, not withstanding the district yields excellent building stone, was required to have brick walls covered with cement rough cast. Happily it was roofed, after the manner of an Oxford college, with slabs of local stone.[15]

Miss Conant was clearly a force to be reckoned with. In addition to her insistence on roughcast, she had Voysey incorporate a clock-tower into the design to house a fourteenth-century bell, 'weigh-ing upwards of three hundred weight', whose ham-mer had to be plugged with wood so that when it struck the hours its harsh metallic clang might be softened, and the parlour walls were lined with pink silk.[16]

Miss Conant's accommodation was like a Voysey cottage forming the shortest arm of the composition; the central arm housed the service accommodation, with its tall clock-tower marking a step down in roof line to the single-storey stores; and the stable block closed the third side of the courtyard. Each arm had a distinctive character of its own, derived from the function of the rooms within, and this, together with the change in roof line and the courtyard plan, made reference to the tradition of the Tudor or seventeenth-century house, which had been extended in an ad hoc man-ner over generations, as maintenance requirements and the changing needs of the owners dictated.

There was a strong sense of unity at The Pastures, which showed no sign of improvisation, but there were deliberately disparate elements too, in the half-timbered cross gable, which terminated the stable wing, and the deep-arched veranda on the south side of the house. This wide arch with a

9

10

first-floor window and gable above was very like the sequence of bays which were repeated to form the cloistered courtyard of the Lincoln Grammar School, and one wonders whether or not Voysey was conscious of the similarities. The courtyard plan ensured a greater sense of privacy between Miss Conant and her servants by keeping their respective accommodation and even their views across the grounds quite separate. Perhaps this independence was more important to a single client (and The Homestead was designed with the same clear delineations), who might have felt out-numbered by the servants, than one with a family.

Voysey used the sweep and contours of the roof to define the character of each wing, just as he had done three years earlier at Broadleys, and he was to do again at The Homestead. A pattern of gables set within broad gestural expanses of roof covered Miss Conant's wing, while the roof of the servants wing formed a long, high and narrow line above the corridor on the courtyard side. On the other side of the ridge, where it covered the ser-vants' bedrooms, it was punctuated by dormer windows with their own miniature gables coming

11

9, 10 *Garden elevation of The Pastures, showing veranda and extension to parlour bay. The bell-tower, viewed from across the courtyard.*

11 *Early photograph of the garden elevation of The Pastures.*

up through the roof, and making a pattern with the chimneys and buttresses, which dominated this side of the house. The break to a single storey with a much deeper roof, three-quarters of the way along this elevation, very much in the ad hoc tradition, was adroitly managed with a strategically placed chimney and the long, low lines of the stable block, with its deep roof brushing the tops of the ground-floor windows, consolidating the effect of confidence and artistic assurance of the composition as a whole.

Within the courtyard the front door was immediately apparent as part of a projecting bay, which housed a lobby with a cloakroom to one side. It was an understated entrance, sheltered only by a simple flat-roof with a porthole window to one side, but the door itself was massive. Although it was some distance from the service wing, Voysey ensured that the front door and all the comings and goings of the courtyard were directly overlooked by the butler's pantry. Beyond the entrance lobby the principal rooms – the living hall with the parlour on one side and the dining room on the other – were arranged in a line facing southwards with views

across the garden. However, no repetitions were permitted in this by now very familiar arrangement. The hall was wide and shallow because a deep veranda was cut into the south face of the house, linking the hall through a glazed door with a sheltered transitional space between the house and its garden. Both the parlour and the dining room were given bay windows overlooking the garden.

The stonework around Voysey's windows was always solid. It was set flush with the roughcast on the exterior, presenting a contrast in colour and texture, and the joints between individual stones were crisply defined. In general, Voysey windows were distinguished by a complete absence of decorative mouldings. The mullions and architraves were cut square, and only the sills were bevelled so that rain water would run off; the interior sills were flat. Where the walls varied in thickness, at

Broadleys for example, Voysey maintained the same distance between the exterior stone face and the surface of the glazing throughout the house, and this was a constant factor in all his mature houses. The glazing was slightly recessed, giving the windows definition within the elevation, without having the deep, punched-out appearance of those in Charles Rennie Mackintosh's Hill House (1902–3). Any variation in wall thickness was compensated for in the interiors by setting the windows into recesses and so the thickness of the wall, and consequently a feeling of protection, was felt inside the house without detracting from the balance of parts in the elevations.

The long dining room at The Pastures was fitted with two fireplaces, one to heat the room, with seats in the wall to either side, and a more intimate fireplace in its own deep ingle. According to *The Studio* all the fireplaces were 'of special design, different in every room' (they are now boarded up) and their tiles were made by Mr C. Dressler of Marlow. A contemporary watercolour suggests that the pink parlour walls were more the colour of black currants mixed with cream and the woodwork throughout the house was 'enamelled in white'.[17] The parlour fireplace was contained within a tall wooden frame as Voysey's fireplaces often were, with a minimal mantel-shelf at picture-rail height. Above the hearth the central panel of tiling was made up of white narrow tiles, set vertically with a decorative roundel in the centre, and flanked to either side by a chequer-board effect of larger square black and white tiles. Voysey's fenders were invariably very plain and in the parlour a set of black (presumably wrought-iron rather than brass) Voysey fire-irons and a Voysey kettle-stand were set within the copper fender.[18] The mantel-shelf was adorned with a Voysey clock, and bookshelves were set into the arched recesses to either side of the chimney breast.

The parlour curtains conformed to Voysey's general specification in size and cut, but they were a deep blue-green. Red would have clashed with the wall colour and the floor was carpeted 'with self-coloured Austrian pile carpets'.[19] The ground floor of the house was paved with large slabs of Castle Hill stone,[20] and although Voysey was thwarted in his desire to build the main structure of local stone, he did use a local contractor,[21] and the

12

12 *Watercolour of the parlour, The Pastures. Published in* Moderne Bauformen *in 1911.*

178   CHAPTER 10

garden walls and terraces, like the roof, were built of local materials.

VODIN. Voysey may have adopted a courtyard plan and made efforts to build in local stone at The Pastures in order to explore some of the Gothic elements in the Lincoln Grammar School design, however, when a few months later, in the design of Vodin, he gathered his rooms together under a single roof and returned to a simple rectangular plan, the influence of the Grammar School design was still explicit. Vodin was designed for a level site at Pyrford Common, near Woking in Surrey, and the preliminary design was drawn in August 1902. Like Oakhurst and The Pastures it combined familiar Voysey elements with stylistic innovations, but it was notable too because it adapted one of the bays from the Grammar School design and transposed it on to the front of the house. The secondary staircase at Vodin was projected out into a tall bay with its own gable breaking through the roof line and buttressed so that it had a Medievalizing influence on the entrance front. The composition and effect of this bay were very similar to the design of the buttressed and gabled bay set to one side of the entrance to the Grammar School.

The front door at Vodin was accentuated by a projecting porch with a shallow stone arch, which sprang from corbels set into the buttresses to either side. The economic virtuosity of using buttresses to give the porch its depth and the deliberate juxtaposition of finely crafted stonework set into the coarser roughcast distinguished the house as an exceptionally assured, though never contrived, example of Voysey's mature style.[22] Above the front door, a porthole window was tucked under the eaves, perhaps making a whispered reference to the relationship between the stone porch and circular window at Norney, and the buttresses were used to frame a series of miniature compositions in each of the elevations, as well as to add rhythm and surface variation to the whole.

The garden elevation faced south and the garden door was set within a niche (a miniature variation on The Pastures porch) and framed by a stone-dressed arch – this time flush with the surface of the roughcast – and the stonework of the niche was bonded with the window-dressings to either side. The pattern of windows was idiosyncratic,

13

14

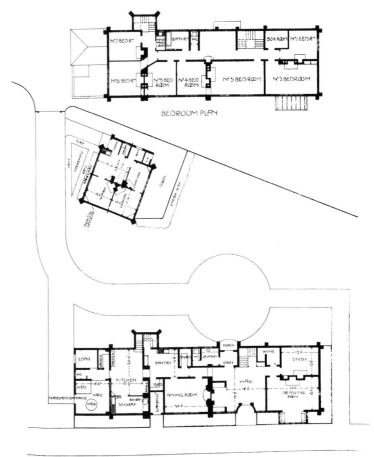

15

13–15 Plans and elevations, Vodin, 1902.

were to be grown against the back wall, where they would have been viewed from the house.

In January 1904, before the main house and lodge were completed, Voysey designed a 'motor house' for Vodin and an 'Electric light generating house' to complete the group of buildings. A new wall with an arched opening linked the lodge with the motor-house and divided them from the house. No photographs or records have come to light to tell whether Voysey furnished the house, but the budget was generous enough for him to have done so.[23] He recorded the total cost of the house as £6,617.8.3 in 1902 and *The Studio* published a perspective of it in 1904, stating that it had recently been 'built and decorated throughout' by Voysey: 'the dining room is lined with oak, the wood being left, as Mr Voysey prefers it, in the natural state, without staining, oiling, fuming, polishing or doctoring of any kind. The large window of the dining room contains a specially designed heraldic panel with the owner's arms in painted glass.'[24] Apart from the dining-room window, *The Studio* might have been describing any of Voysey's oak-panelled houses, but the consistent handling of materials that runs as a constant factor throughout his work was given a very different interpretation when the function of the building and the prerequisites of the site demanded it.

with portholes in all but one of the elevations and clear correlations between, for example, the two blocks of staircase windows in the front elevation and between the long bands of windows to the dining room and the drawing room overlooking the garden, with one projecting out in a bay in each case.

The plan of Vodin was characteristic of Voysey's more straightforward houses. The service quarters were very compact, as they had been at Moorcrag, because a separate lodge housed the servants' kitchen, parlour and bedrooms, so that only a kitchen, scullery and a butler's pantry needed to be provided within the main house. Nevertheless, Voysey was obliged to provide a secondary staircase for the servants' use, and he had done the same for Oakhurst. Had he become more lenient towards the bourgeois affectations of his clients? Or had Mrs Buckley set a precedent at Moorcrag, which, once permitted, could no longer be denied with such rectitude? The lodge house was carefully positioned to create a courtyard in front of the house. It had its own small garden with flowers facing the driveway and Voysey specified that roses

THE SANDERSON FACTORY. Voysey would have first encountered the Sanderson family in his capacity as a decorative designer, but in September 1901 he first designed a new veranda and then a summer-house for Harold Sanderson's house at 57 Harvard Road in Chiswick. Harold Sanderson was responsible for selecting decorative designs for the company while his brother Arthur took care of 'the counting house arrangements'. According to *The Journal of Decorative Art* in 1905, it was Harold's 'qualities of discernment and artistic perception which have been the determining factor in giving their papers that standing which they have in the market to-day'.[25] It was undoubtedly Harold who appointed Voysey as the designer for an extension to their main factory in Barley Mow Passage.

The site for the extension was ill lit and enclosed by existing buildings. The new building was to be linked to the main factory on the other side of Barley Mow Passage. Voysey responded by designing a rectangular box faced with white-glazed bricks to reflect the light, which was linked to the main factory by an iron bridge like a railway carriage caught between the two buildings at third-floor level.[26] It was an uncompromisingly functional building, quite unlike the roughcast houses with their sweeping roofs in appearance, and yet at the same time it was absolutely consistent with Voysey's design vocabulary, and with his philosophy that 'True architectural beauty, to my mind, must be wedded to structural function.'[27] The structure was clearly expressed in the elevations by a series of projecting piers, which supported the floors and roof and acted, in addition, as ventilation shafts. Voysey employed the most modern materials available using massive, steel-framed windows to light the factory (these were divided into small panes and the upper windows were fitted with exterior fabric blinds) and concrete floors supported by steel joists, which bore on to riveted main beams spanning between the piers and a central line of cast-iron columns. The diameter of these columns reduced progressively through each of the floors, indicating a reduction in structural load in a refined example of structural expression.

Voysey lectured that meanness and greed were the parents of concrete construction, that it was the shopkeeper, 'out to make money' by seizing every inch of space, who had furthered its development and that because, 'when any new inventions first appear (like the railway train or the motor), they are made in the form of that which they are destined to replace', society would have to suffer a great many concrete buildings 'made to look like stone or brick, and even at times like half-timber work.'[28] He worried that unlike brick or timber, with concrete, 'the man that mixes the material must exercise his conscience, and who can measure the amount or tell its value,' and he stated unequivocally that 'Concrete in itself is an ugly thing.'[29] But concrete construction, he argued, provided it was kept in its place and the unique character of the material was understood, could be made a 'ministering angel'.

At the Sanderson Factory, Voysey's use of concrete floors supported by columns and beams allowed each of the four floors to be completely open in plan so that great runs of tables or of block-printing machinery on the pattern-book making

floor could be lined up without interruption. The stencilling room was on the top floor, lit from above by a half-glazed, half-slate roof and this north light allowed Voysey to use a porthole window in each of the bays in the north and south elevations on the fourth floor, establishing a contrast with the banks of windows below. The roof was concealed behind a tall parapet, which has been described as 'disconcertingly reminiscent of a Voysey bed-board!'[30] The combination of rising pilasters capped with squares of Portland stone and a shaped parapet did establish an overt link between Voysey's furniture and his architectural design, but it also, like the porthole windows, made a witty gesture of authorship.

In addition to its functional and structural integrity, the Sanderson Factory, like all Voysey designs, was appropriately decorated. The use of white-glazed bricks for a dark enclosed site was a logical extension of the use of this type of brick for light wells and area walls, which Voysey and other architects of his generation employed as a matter of course, but Voysey drew horizontal lines around his factory with Staffordshire blue bricks, 'as black as they could be got'.[31] The six-foot-deep plinth might have been blacked so that it would not show the mud and dust splashed up from the street, but the blue-black string-courses and window surrounds, like the parapet, were purely for decorative effect. Cast-iron quadrants were tucked into the corners of the piers, just above ground level, and these had a more practical function. They were designed to discourage drinkers from urinating on the factory after an evening at the Barley Mow!

The fact that the Sanderson Factory stands apart from the main body of Voysey's work is more an accident of history than of design. Certainly it was Voysey's only design for a factory, but it was not the only building he designed with a rectangular plan and tall elevations punctuated by projecting piers with a shaped parapet concealing the roof. If Voysey's design for Lincoln Grammar School had been built then its hall would have warranted a close comparison with the Sanderson Factory, and his designs for the Carnegie Library and Museum for Limerick, drawn c.1904, would have developed elements of both buildings in local chalk stone, patterned with a chequered band of dark grey and pale stone. If Voysey had been given more inner-city

17

17 Silver water jug, c.1912, and pepper pot.

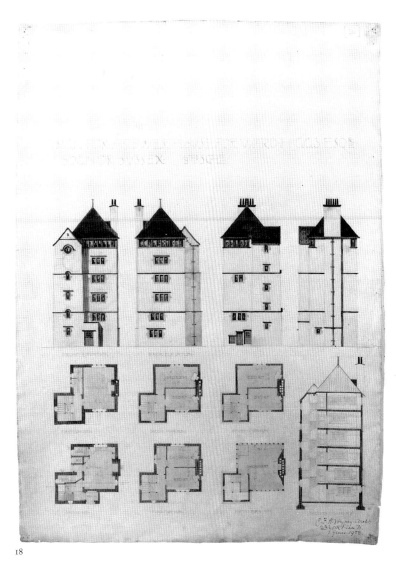

18

19

commissions, too, this form of tall self-contained building might have broadened his reputation, but his attempts to break away from the low-spreading lines and deep-sheltering roofs of the country houses that had made him famous, like his efforts to use local materials, were seldom successful.

TOWER HOUSES. Throughout his career Voysey was fascinated with towers. He slipped them in at the pivot of his plans or used them to counterbalance long horizontals. He designed them as free-standing buildings, but apart from the Forster house in Bedford Park they were rarely built. In 1903, Voysey designed a tower house for Ward Higgs for a site in Bognor, Sussex. It had six floors with a square, corner turret continuing the staircase and a lift. The kitchen occupied the ground floor with the dining room directly above, and the five bedrooms and a dressing room occupied the next three floors up. On the top floor beneath a hipped roof, there was the Edwardian equivalent to a penthouse, a smoking room with almost continuous bands of windows on three sides. Another tower house was designed two months later for M. T. La Thangue for a wedge-shaped site in Bedford Park. It was a tall, narrow building arranged on four floors. However, neither this nor the Ward Higgs house was ever built.

WHITWOOD HOUSES AND INSTITUTE. Like many of his contemporaries Voysey was interested in the social effects of good housing, and in 1904 he was commissioned to design a Workman's Institute and housing at Whitwood in Yorkshire. The commission had come from Henry Briggs & Son, and the 'Son' was Currer Briggs for whom Voysey had designed Broadleys six years earlier. The project was conceived with very similar principles to those behind Bournville and Port Sunlight, to design a village of decent workers housing with its own village hall, built in the form of an institute, around the Briggs's colliery at Whitwood near Normanton. Voysey's absence from the garden-suburb movement is a notable one, although he did design a house in 1909 for Hampstead Garden Suburb, which was never built.[32] As early as 1877, while he was still articled to J. P. Seddon he had made plans for model dwellings for a Miss Morfit;[33] his lodge-houses and service

18 *Unexecuted design for a tower house for Ward Higgs at Bognor Regis, Sussex, 1903.*

19 *Perspective, Whitwood Houses and Institute, Whitwood, near Normanton, Yorkshire, 1904.*

wings demonstrated a keen interest in designing compact and economical, though none the less comfortable accommodation throughout his career.

At Whitwood he adopted an economic pattern for two rows of terrace houses, forming an L shape with the Institute and a single, detached house incorporated into a simple tower at their juncture. There were clear links between the twenty-nine terrace houses and the thatched Wortley Cottages of 1896 in the organization of houses into pairs with a cross gable at either end and the way that the roof line was broken by a row of dormers. The Institute was designed in response to a growing concern at the levels of drunkenness among the working classes, as an alternative to the more usual public house, with two billiard rooms and a smoking room and only a very small bar. There was a covered veranda for sitting out and a reading room with a large central table designed by Voysey, along with sturdy chairs.

The intention was to distract the 'mining artisans' away from the excesses of drink, and Voysey, although he was by no means a teetotaller, might well have approved of the sense of mission behind this Edwardian idealism. In spite of the economy of his design, only the Institute and one of his rows of terraces were erected, and he told *The British Architect* that, 'The Company found it necessary to build the houses so cheaply that architectural superintendance of the work was perforce left out of court,' but the following year he was commissioned by the Earl of Ellesmere to design an 'improving' pub.[34]

THE WHITE HORSE INN, at Stetchworth, near Newmarket, was the second pub to be built to Voysey's designs. The first was at Elmesthorpe, commissioned with the Wortley Cottages by another Earl, the Earl of Lovelace, and in both buildings Voysey adopted a rustic old English plan with the inn fronting on to the road and a stableyard behind. At the White Horse Inn the stableyard was almost entirely enclosed with stables and coach houses on two sides, and the inn adopted a T-shaped plan so that the service wing ran back along the third side of the stableyard and the inn turned the corner of the fourth side, allowing the tap room to overlook the stables on one side and the road on the other.

20

The long, low lines of the inn with its sheltering roof had a wholesome domesticity and its relationship with the stables, clearly in evidence from the road, recalled the centuries old heritage of the inn as a resting place for travellers, rather than a setting for drunken ribaldry. A large kitchen was provided so that food could be served, as well as drink, and the 'Coffee Room' with a deep veranda leading into the garden vied with the tap room for size and importance. The garden boasted a bowling-green to draw drinkers out into the fresh air, and to emphasize the family orientation of the place it was photographed with a row of children in front of the porch – not a drunkard in sight – for publication in *Moderne Bauformen* in 1911. A few years later, during the First World War, Voysey served the Liquor Control Board in a similar attempt to divert the working classes from their drinking. He designed posters depicting the healthy life with exemplary messages like 'Love and the Pilgrim' and 'Tis Love, 'tis Love that makes the World go round'. Voysey would have been confident of the psychological effect of his decoration in 'improving' pubs.

20 *The White Horse Inn, Stetchworth, near Newmarket, Suffolk, 1905.*

21

In both the Whitwood Institute and the White Horse Inn, Voysey concentrated on refining a rural architecture that was entirely appropriate to its function. The sheltering roof and enveloping plan of the inn, and the straightforward honesty of a row of workers' cottages were firmly rooted in the mainstream of his architectural language, and, apart from the crenellations to the Institute tower, he made no attempt to incorporate Gothic experiments into the design of either. This was not an indication that he had abandoned the Gothic experiments of Lincoln Grammar School. It shows that in the first years of the twentieth century his interest in Gothic was intermittent, and that it was exercised where it was deemed appropriate to the function of the building.

When Voysey was commissioned to design a large house for Lady Henry Somerset at Higham, near Woodford in Essex, in 1904, shortly before the design of the Whitwood Institute, he recognized in the scale of the commission together with the social position of the client a perfect justification for architectural innovation. Just as the commissions for Norney and New Place had encouraged

him to extend his architectural range to include classicizing elements seven years earlier, the house at Higham gave him a rare opportunity to exercise his exuberance and experiment with Gothic.

THE HOUSE AT HIGHAM, WOODFORD. Voysey believed that, 'qualities like grandeur, splendour pomp, majesty and exuberance' were 'suitable only to comparatively few' houses.[35] The house at Higham was to have been built of stone and like The Pastures it had strong Medievalizing elements, but these were incorporated into a highly individual and eclectic composition. In the first perspective drawings for the house Voysey presented the entrance front as a long, two-storey elevation interrupted by a square clock-tower, which housed the entrance porch, and with a wide front door set within a shallow recess, studded and tee-hinged with a heart-shaped Voysey letter-plate. The inspiration for the clock-tower and some of its detailing came directly from the Lincoln Grammar School design, but the house lent itself to a Tudor or Medieval interpretation because it was designed to house a double-height chapel and a priest's room on the west side of the entrance. This was expressed in the front elevation by four, closely packed buttresses, which carried the structural load and also, quite consciously, made reference to Medieval buttresses. This development of a referential, as well as a structural role for Voysey's buttresses was not entirely new: the buttresses to the clock-tower at The Pastures and to the stair-tower at Vodin had been used for their stylistic associations, as well as their structural support.

Though in the west elevation Voysey marked the chapel by outlining a cross in the stonework of the gable, his stylistic references were deliberately mixed. Beneath the cross a narrow, projecting course traced the line of a rising semi-circle, and the same motif was repeated on the face of the chimney-stacks. If the rising semi-circle was reminiscent of New Place, so too were the polygonal bay windows overlooking the garden on the southeast side of the house, with their domed and leaded roofs set into the gable ends of two projecting wings, but the garden elevation was very different in style from that of New Place. In between the projecting wings Voysey designed a long, covered veranda with its roof supported by a series of stone

arches. Directly above there was a winter garden –
a romantic balcony overlooking the formal garden
– closed by a parapet, whose curvilinear top
repeated the outline so familiar in Voysey's furniture and in the parapet of the Sanderson Factory.

Sadly, Lady Henry Somerset declined to build
this romantic design in stone, and Voysey was
obliged to scale down his exuberance and settle, yet
again, for a version in roughcast. In the final design
only the lower part of the tower was stone faced,
the chapel was moved, and the dormer windows
overlooking the garden were removed. The house
was not built exactly to Voysey's designs and
according to *The British Architect* of 1906 it was
'being built without the superintendence of the
architect',[36] although no details were given
explaining why.[37]

Perhaps if Voysey had had the social aptitude
and persuasive powers of Lutyens, whose work he
admired, he would have had more success in
acquiring and retaining aristocratic and influential
clients. He did have aristocratic clients, and in his
autobiographical notes he was careful to list them
in order of precedence, but their commissions were
relatively modest. Perhaps if his manner had been
lighter and his nature less sincere, he could have
walked Lady Henry Somerset around the garden
after dinner and charmed the stonework out of her.
Instead his clients came to Voysey because, unlike
Lutyens, he could be relied upon not to induce
them to double the budget for the house, and
because he would consider the utility and fitness of
every aspect of the brief and design a home that
was warm and reassuring, as well as finely crafted.
Voysey's 'good value for money' reputation would
hardly have attracted extravagant clients, and his
friends were men from the Arts Club. He did not
mix in socially elevated circles, and when he did
mix with the aristocracy by all accounts his attitude
to them was distinctly deferential.

The boundaries of Voysey's architectural range
were established not least by the expectations of his
clients, and by his own regard for those expectations. When he was given complete freedom of
expression, in some of his later competition entries,
for example, the resultant designs were startlingly
unorthodox. His failure to win competitions irked
him and he complained that the names of jurors
were published so that entrants might know which

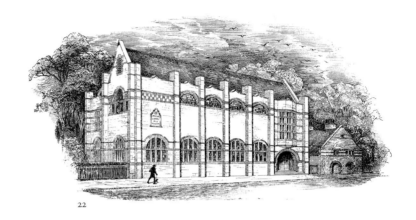

22

style to favour. Unfortunately, by the time Voysey
had enough spare time to make speculative competition designs he was constrained by a new set of
self-imposed restrictions, as he defended the corpse
of English Gothic design. To some extent the diversity of his designs was masked by the uniformity of
his materials. If, as he had wished, some of his
houses had been built of local stone, then he might
have enjoyed a stronger reputation for versatility.
But more than anything Voysey's designs
responded directly to the function of the building
and the conditions of the site. If he had been more
successful in securing commissions of a non-
domestic nature – schools, offices, factories and so
on – and if the sites for these buildings had presented him with restrictions in scale and outlook,
then Voysey would have employed the most innovative building technology and materials to over-
come those restrictions. The Sanderson Factory
demonstrates beyond reasonable doubt that the
familiar view of Voysey is a partial view. A more
challenging flow of commissions would have stimulated an extraordinarily inventive and articulate,
architectural language.

22 *Perspective, Carnegie Library and*
Museum, Limerick, Ireland.
Unexecuted design, 1902.

2

THE PASTURES

1901

The Pastures was designed
for an open site in North
Luffenham, Rutland, for
Miss G. Conant. The house
was planned around a courtyard, with an old walnut tree
at its centre. Voysey wanted
to build the house of local stone
but Miss Conant insisted on
having a characteristic Voysey
house with roughcast render
walls. They compromised
on the roof and the hard
landscaping of the garden.

3

4

1 *Garden elevation, showing addition to
   the parlour, designed by Voysey in 1909.*
2 *Garden elevation facing south with
   sheltered veranda set within an
   arched recess.*

3 *Detail of parlour bay window.*
4 *End bay, west elevation, showing
   two-storey square bay.*

5

6

7

5 *View from the east across the courtyard.*

6 *Gable at the east end of Miss Conant's*
   accommodation.

7 *Detail of the stone roof to the stable wing.*

8

9

10

11

8 Clock-tower, designed to house
   a fourteenth-century bell.
9 Detail of the entrance bay and the east
   end of Miss Conant's accommodation.
10 Heart detail on front door.
11 Approach to The Pastures.

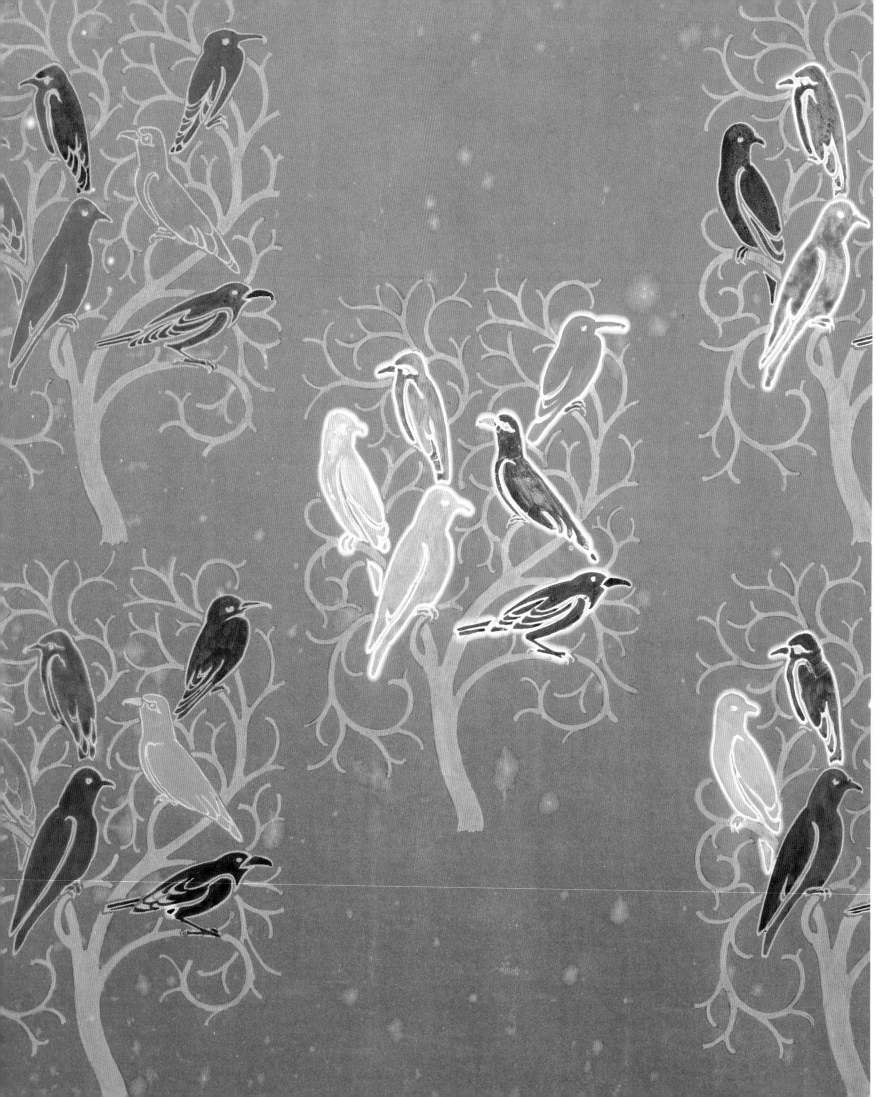

Throughout his career Voysey altered and extended existing buildings, stamping them with his individual style, often without regard for their own period integrity. One of his first jobs in independent practice had been to decorate a library for L. B. Knight Bruce in Sunbury-on-Thames in 1882, and to install a new oak gallery there. In 1890 he built new bays and a porch on to Russell House in Hampstead for the Aumonier family, and he designed numerous new studios to extend the houses of his artist friends in St John's Wood, including substantial studios for George Frampton. Sometimes these smaller jobs would be carried out for an existing client and sometimes an extension to a London house would lead to a commission for a country cottage. It is not possible to evaluate them in any detail here except where they were considered in Voysey's own time to make a significant contribution to his output.

For Voysey, an invitation to extend or refurbish a house represented an opportunity for far more than a superficial change of decor or the provision of a little more space. The interiors at 37 Bidston Road, Birkenhead, at Garden Corner in Chelsea and at the Essex and Suffolk Equitable Insurance Society offices, in Capel House, were exceptional because they were designed with a disproportionate attention to detail and a degree of completeness, which was rarely possible in the design of an entire house. Not only did Voysey design all the furniture (and even the pen-trays at the Essex and Suffolk), but he plotted the precise position for each piece within the room. The fact that he recognized the importance of these interiors as consummate designs is evident from the number and quality of photographs that he commissioned of them. His enthusiasm was shared in England and Germany. *The Studio, Dekorative Kunst* and *Moderne Bauformen* all published copies of Voysey's photographs; the images are remarkable not only for the exceptionally concentrated and comprehensive quality of the interiors that they portray, but also as examples of architectural photography.

37 BIDSTON ROAD. Voysey was commissioned to design a new dining room for Mrs Van Gruisen at 37 Bidston Road, Birkenhead, Cheshire, in 1902. He made radical alterations to the room, blocking

INTERIORS
AND EXTENSIONS

1 *Decorative design, undated.*
2 *Iron fireplace, from Elsley's catalogue of Voysey designs.*

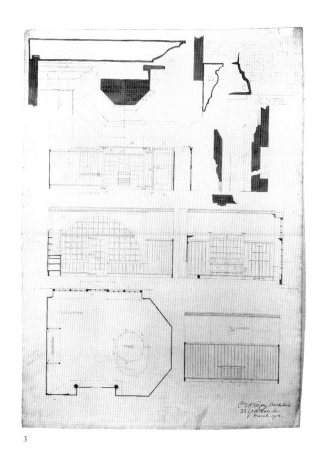

3

4

5

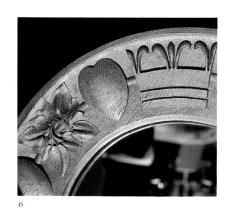

6

3 *Plans and elevations, dining room, 37*
Bidston Road, Birkenhead, Cheshire,
March 1902.

4, 5 *Dining Room, 37 Bidston Road,*
photographs published in Dekorative
Kunst *and* The Studio *between 1902*
and 1904.

6 *Detail of circular mirror, 'carved in*
oak and gilded with grains of wood
left open', 1901.

up already existing windows and stripping out fireplaces, and his plans and elevations show that each piece of furniture designed for the room was located on the plan to establish an exacting relationship between fixed and movable elements.

A small round table, which according to Voysey's drawing would seat seven, was centred on the short end wall with a circular mirror directly above it, and the sideboard or dresser was exactly in the centre of the opposite wall with another circle, a round dumb-waiter, to one side. In fact the table was moved closer to the wall for the photograph, but the pendant light not quite exactly above it shows the permanent position closer to the fireside. The room itself was typical of Voysey's interiors, wainscoted in oak with a deep, white frieze and a low ceiling (albeit one sporting a cornice). A wide fireplace, characteristically tiled within a simple oak frame, was equipped with Voysey fire-irons and trivet, and the circular theme was reiterated in a fender decorated with pierced hearts. Almost the entire wall on one side was cut away beneath a wide arch and glazed with a glass door in the centre, and the shape of the arch above the wainscoting traced an exact semi-circle.

None of the dining-room furniture was exclusive to Mrs Van Gruisen, although in 1902 drawings were made for the dining table and chairs, the dresser, the dumb-waiter and the circular mirror, 'carved in oak and gilded with grains of wood left open', all with Mrs Van Gruisen's name on them.[1] In fact an almost identical mirror had already been designed the previous year for Ward Higgs and the chairs appear in a number of Voysey interiors. Variations on the dresser design had been made, as early as 1899, for the Earl of Lovelace and for three other clients;[2] yet Voysey invariably made new drawings for each client, even where the variations on an existing piece were minimal.

Although the 'remodelling of interiors in already existing, commonplace houses' was described by Aymer Vallance as, 'Less satisfactory work to the artist', the Bidston Road dining room was illustrated and described in The Studio;[3] photographs of it were exhibited in the Arts and Crafts Exhibition of 1903, and published in Dekorative Kunst and in Hermann Muthesius's Das englische Haus. In the same year as Bidston Road, Voysey designed furniture for another house in Birkenhead, Hollyhurst

at 30 Shrewsbury Road, for a Miss McKay, and designs for some of the furniture were repeated in both houses.[4] Miss McKay appears to have had her guest room decorated and furnished by Voysey in 1902, followed by the dining room in 1909 and another of the bedrooms in 1912.

The redesign of the dining room at 37 Bidston Road was followed in 1905 by the bedroom, and again where changes were necessary they were made unflinchingly. The existing windows were blocked up and replaced by a new band of Voysey windows and a Voysey fireplace faced with Van Straaten's tiles replaced the original one. The room was wainscoted to a height of six foot and simply furnished in oak. As with The Homestead, with which it was contemporary, some of the furniture was fitted. A simple, fitted wardrobe with a full-length, looking-glass fixed to its door, a wash-stand with a round-headed cupboard above, and a chest of drawers beneath another cupboard lined the wall next to the door, and these were distinguished by the insistence on fine proportions and understated craftsmanship, which characterized all Voysey's work. Freestanding bedroom furniture was also commissioned, and again Voysey's drawing showed the position for each piece, as well as its price, so that we know that two single beds at a cost of £6.7.0 each were to have been pushed together at one end of the room with a bedside table to either side. A 'light chair' (one of the rush-seated, oak chairs with a single splat pierced by a heart) was to have cost £2.5.0, and Voysey intended it to stand next to the dressing-table beneath the window.

GARDEN CORNER. Another important interior from this period was Garden Corner in Chelsea, London, where the remodelling was much more ambitious. Voysey stripped away the original interiors of an entire house and replaced them with his own uncompromising designs. Only the most confident client with a deep purse and nerves of steel would have taken this twenty-year-old, Late Victorian, semi-detached house with high ceilings and massive windows and invited Voysey to rebuild the interiors. The house was E. J. Horniman's London base; Horniman had already commissioned Voysey to design and extend Lowicks for him in 1894 and 1904–5, respectively. By 1906 when

7

8

the decision to redesign the interiors of Garden Corner was made Horniman and Voysey were life-long friends.

False ceilings were inserted 'to increase the restful proportions of the room', the principal staircase was ripped out and replaced and Voysey windows, doors and fireplaces were substituted for the originals. Where the tall windows of the living room could not be altered, Voysey built a plaster, barrel-vaulted ceiling to reflect the light downwards and give an impression of low proportions, and this room was extravagantly decorated as *The Studio* described in October 1907:

The drawing-room is L-shaped, one arm being treated with oak 6 ft. 6 ins. high, with plaster barrel ceiling above, and the other section is lined with Westmoreland green slate unpolished, and twelve water-colour drawings, representing the months, by Lilian Blaterwick ... are let into the slate and held in position by small silver moulded strips.[5]

A wide fireplace was tiled with gold mosaic almost to picture-rail height, and Voysey inserted a large circular window in a deep recess at one end of the room. In the dining room a second, smaller port-hole window was inserted into an arched recess and Voysey built a new stone window into the library overlooking the Physick Garden. Voysey was commissioned to furnish the house with free-standing, as well as fitted furniture, and this, together with the oak joinery throughout the house was 'left quite clean from the plane, without stain, varnish, or polish' in contrast to the oak veneer, stained a nut brown, which had originally lined the walls and which had been 'torn off the walls' once Voysey had condemned it.[6]

The new interiors at Garden Corner were extravagantly artistic, partly because the need to incorporate some of the original high ceilings into the predominantly horizontal, low lines of Voysey's style created an artistic tension, but also because it pushed Voysey into exaggerating his design in order to match the scale and presence of the original. The sweeping arcs of the ceiling and the dramatic, glazed arches of the hall recalled the dining-room interior of Bidston Road and the decorative arches at Hollybank, but the detailing of the staircase with glazed panels and a metal arch

9

10

springing from the first-floor newels, from which a lantern was suspended, suggest that Voysey enjoyed setting his usual reticence to one side.

The lantern over the staircase may have been designed by C. R. Ashbee, who designed the electric pendants in the dining room 'and a few others' in the house, but there can be no mistaking the authorship of the four-poster bed in the principal bedroom, with each of its posts surmounted by a bronze bird standing on a ball. The same bird could be found perched on the firedog in the dining room and a smaller version of it was available through the Elsley catalogue. Voysey would undoubtedly have modelled these birds himself.[7] His professional expenses regularly accounted for visits to the Zoological Gardens (in one instance, specifically to study eagles) and for modelling wax and tools.[8] The bedroom furniture was ingeniously practical as well as artistic: 'The bedstead, jewel-safe writing-table, wardrobe, and all the usual bedroom equipment are fixed and fitted in to utilise every inch of space, and at the side of the bed the cabinets are fitted with sliding shelves, to bring the morning tea-tray over the bed.'[9]

In addition to restyling the interiors at Garden Corner, Voysey made them lighter and more efficient. The basement was rearranged and 'lined throughout with van Straaten's white Dutch tiles'. The secondary staircase which had been a 'narrow dark slit by the side of the grand stairs' linking the seven floors was replaced by an electric lift, 'fitted with a specially designed plain oak cage to match the new joinery', and every floor was provided with a bathroom and a housemaid's closet. Where 'Darkness and gloom' had prevailed, the interiors were transformed into the brightest and most stylish accommodation by Voysey, and the client was evidently delighted. Voysey continued to work for Horniman, designing additional furniture for the house in 1909 and 1912, and in 1913 he designed a 'Pleasure Ground', which was financed by Horniman, for Kensal New Town with a roughcast shelter and boundary walls, a flower garden, waterways, and an oak bridge and pergola. Even after the sale of Lowicks, Horniman remained at Garden Corner, and as late as 1933, when Voysey was seventy-six he was employed to oversee repairs to the roof garden for Mrs Horniman there.

9, 10 *Landing and principal bedroom,*
Garden Corner. Photographs 1907.

The Studio featured nine photographs of the Garden Corner interiors together with a summary of the work and a review of 'The Characteristics of Mr. C. F. A. Voysey's Architecture' by his friend and rival, M. H. Baillie Scott in October 1907. Scott's own career was already well established at the time of writing, but Voysey had been a powerful influence on his early work and his homage was both perceptive and affectionate:

The essential characteristic of Mr. Voysey's work is its absolute sincerity. The outward aspect of his buildings is comely because all is well with them within. So they seem to smile pleasantly upon us, instead of grinning through conventional masks replete with all the usual superficial features. And this beauty which is "an outward and visible sign of an inward and spiritual grace," is a beauty of which we never tire, and which is above all the changing whims of fashion.[10]

WOODBROOK. In Alderley Edge, Cheshire, Voysey began by designing a new house for his client, but circumstances limited him to altering and extending an existing house. The initial design was for an L-shaped house, drawn for A. Heyworth in June 1905, but within a few months Voysey was at work designing alterations and extensions to Heyworth's existing yellow-brick house. Again the interiors were substantially altered with Voysey fireplaces replacing the originals and large, semi-circular windows built into the drawing room and the play room. New furniture was designed for the house and in 1915, Voysey designed a studio for the garden.

Voysey's relationship with Heyworth, like his relationship with Horniman and with Van Gruisen must have been a good one because in 1919 he was commissioned to design a pair of semi-detached cottages at Alderley Edge and these were intended to be used as models for twenty cottages with green-slate roofs and roughcast render walls.

HAMBLEDON HURST. In the same year A. H. Van Gruisen commissioned Voysey to extend a house at Hambledon in Surrey. The two-storey wing, which he built on to the west side of the house, together with remodelled offices and a motor-house with a pigeon-house above, was very different in style to the restrained simplicity of Van Gruisen's rooms at Bidston Road. The extension to Hambledon Hurst formed a Gothic wrapping

around the original house (which was only about twenty years old), with a lantern and crenellations complicating the roof line and elaborately shaped chimneys declaring Voysey's rejection of the Classical Revival and his position as Pugin's last disciple. (Although it is difficult to imagine what Pugin would have made of these tributes in rough-cast render.)

The extension to Hambledon Hurst was one of Voysey's last executed buildings, and it demonstrated a steadfast determination to preserve the English Gothic tradition, with distinctly unfashionable Gothic eccentricities infiltrating the reasoned simplicity of Voysey's mature style and as such it belongs with his late works. The refurbishment of the Essex and Suffolk Equitable Insurance Society's offices in Capel House, New Broad Street, by comparison, fits more easily into Voysey's main body of work. There were clear links between the decoration and furnishing of these offices and Voysey's alterations to Bidston Road and Garden Corner.

THE ESSEX AND SUFFOLK EQUITABLE INSURANCE SOCIETY OFFICES. The Essex and Suffolk Offices were exemplary as progressive and innovative workplaces at a time when office design was in its infancy. Again the client was already well known to Voysey. Sydney Claridge Turner was Secretary and General Manager of the Essex and Suffolk Equitable Insurance Society, and in 1905 he had commissioned Voysey to design The Homestead, in Frinton-on-Sea. Until 1906, the Essex and Suffolk, like every other regional insurance company was prohibited by law from doing business within ten miles of the Royal Exchange in London. Turner was responsible for petitioning Parliament to negate this law together with a host of other restrictions, and when in 1906 he was successful, the Society went into a period of rapid expansion acquiring offices in Manchester, Liverpool, Birmingham and London, in addition to their head office in Colchester. Voysey was invited to decorate and furnish these new offices over the next few years but the first and most important of these commissions was the invitation to decorate and furnish the Society's prestigious offices in the City of London, at Capel House, in August 1906.

Capel House in New Broad Street was a new purpose-built office-block by Paul Hoffmann, and

11

11 '*Bronze Electric Pendant with Iced Shade*'. *Voysey's pendant lights were very expensive; they were manufactured by Elsley and sold for £6.10.0.*

196   CHAPTER 11

12

the Essex and Suffolk had taken rooms on the ground and lower ground floors. The Homestead was still being built at the time of the commission and Voysey had already designed some of the free-standing and all the fitted furniture for the house. Turner was evidently preoccupied with the expansion of the Society and so it is understandable that he entrusted Voysey, just as he had done with The Homestead, with the design of everything for the new London offices from the proportions of the rooms down to the inkstands and the pen-trays on the desks.

The fitting out of Capel House was not yet complete when Voysey took over responsibility for the Essex and Suffolk's rooms, and he insisted that one of the passage walls be removed, and that the construction of the staircase and the provision of doors, window fittings, lavatories and many other details, which might otherwise have fallen under Hoffmann's jurisdiction, should be under his sole control. Hoffmann's stanchions in the clerks' office and the manager's office caused considerable aggravation, as Voysey explained in a letter to Turner on 20 August, two days after his official appointment:

13

12 *General Manager's room, Essex & Suffolk Equitable Insurance Society Office, Capel House, New Broad Street, London, 1906.*

13 *Clerks' office, Essex & Suffolk Equitable Insurance Society Office. Showing the load-bearing piers which caused Voysey so much trouble.*

designs was applied with equal clarity to the workplace, and the rooms in Capel House were generously lit and finished with the finest materials and workmanship that could be afforded, as Voysey explained in 1909:

The principle we worked on was to have everything durable, and minimise the cleaning as much as possible. Thus the upkeep is reduced to a minimum. All the woodwork and furniture is in oak, left in its natural colour. The counters are gilded, with quarter-plate glass on the top. All the windows are glazed with Chance's Norman slabs, and there are twenty-seven panels of stained glass representing the arms of towns in which the Society does business; so no blinds or curtains are needed.[12]

The offices were exceptional in their time for their open-plan and clearly defined work areas. Oak screens wrapped around the desks and long, low cabinets divided the large rooms into separate work areas, but partitions were kept to an absolute minimum.[13] Electric lighting, too, was used to distinguish and define the different parts of the offices with small bell-shaped, pendant lights on heart pulleys hanging over the desks in the accounts department, the colonial department and the typewriting room, and with large glass bowls with ornate metal rims lighting the main thoroughfares and the General Manager's room.[14] Every file had its place in an oak filing-cabinet, every claim-form an oak tray, and even the calendars on the desks were designed by Voysey.

Voysey was fond of designing monograms, and he designed high-backed chairs for the Essex and Suffolk with the Society's monogram stamped into their leather backs for the main office and the General Manager's rooms.[15] Simple lathe-back chairs and the rush-seated chair with the heart pierced in its splat were used in the remaining offices, and the dining room was furnished with Bentwood chairs. The Society's directors did not share Voysey's determination that a building should be finished to the same high standard throughout, in spite of the fact that S. C. Turner had been one of Voysey's most exceptional clients in this respect at The Homestead. In December 1906 he wrote to tell Voysey that the Committee of Directors liked his plans for Capel House but that they were:

I was not able to make any details until I have seen Mr. Hoffmann & heard from him what girder he would require to put in along the clerks office. So I called on him this morning & I find he has some very important stanchions on special foundations which he declared he cannot move. The one in the manager's room will drive us to square the door tight up into the corner, which will not look at all well. And the one in the clerks office will have to be left under the big girder and be cased in to look like a marble column, so says Mr. Hoffler.[11]

The problem with the stanchion in the clerks' office was that its position interfered with a row of columns, which Voysey had planned to build across the room. He must have been diplomatic with Hoffmann because he claimed, 'I left him in a good mood, and promising to get the plans [for Voysey's alterations] passed by a side door without loss of time.' Pressure was brought to bear on the owners of Capel House, and it was agreed that the stanchion in the clerks' office should be replaced with load-bearing piers, in accordance with Voysey's design, and clad to his specification.

The same rigorous attention to fitness and proportion that formed the basis of Voysey's domestic

...in hopes that it will be possible to carry out the work at considerably less than the nett sum of £2,000 which you have roughly estimated. They feel that whilst no pains should be spared to make the public offices as dignified and handsome as possible, it may perhaps be possible to effect some economy in the basement, especially as we now have in mind putting the typewriting office on the ground floor and using the front room downstairs more or less for the storage of papers.[16]

In the same letter the Directors wanted to know how much extra it would cost to cover the ground floor with Belgian black marble in place of the black tiles from Van Straaten's that Voysey had specified. Regrettably no written reply has survived. Turner also appears to have pressed Voysey for the design of a clock, which could work the dials on many faces around the offices. On 19 December 1906 Voysey wrote him a careful letter saying that this would not be advisable:

I have just seen Dent and they say they can make you a clock that shall work many dials in different places: But they do not recommend it nor could they guarantee any arrangement of the kind. What they suggest is a good clock in one place say the clerks office that shall work the dial in your room as well and from which the time can always be taken to set the other smaller or cheaper clocks by. They want to make the cases and dial themselves and are going to give me an estimate as soon as I can supply them with a drawing of the case and faces we want. They will also give us a price for the one Master Clock to do all the work if you like but if they say it cannot be relied on is it not a pity to bother about it.[17]

He met with Turner the next day, and evidently Turner gave his approval for the mechanism with two dials because the following February Voysey did make a drawing for an excessively prominent clock-case in the clerks' office with a large octagonal face, and on the other side of the wall the same mechanism worked a different clock face in Turner's office. The clocks presided over both offices as a testament to Voysey's diplomacy (and Turner's obsession with time keeping perhaps), and they were still in place when the Essex and Suffolk moved out of Capel House in *c.* 1950.[18]

Voysey's bright open spaces with large windows and the spaces ordered and defined by long, low lines of desks and cabinets should be seen in the context of the warren of tiny rooms, divided by high partition walls, many without a window, which characterized the majority of offices of the period. The dependence on good proportions and the repetition of themes and motifs, which distinguished his domestic work, were particularly apparent in the open spaces of Capel House. His love of heraldry as a disciplined and historically charged means of incorporating strong colour into a decoration was imaginatively explored in the stained glass and the shields worked into the fireplaces. Like his interiors at Bidston Road and Garden Corner, the Essex and Suffolk offices were extremely influential and well publicized. Voysey paid Charles Latham the substantial sum of twelve pounds and fifteen shillings for photographs of the offices in July 1907, ordering an additional twenty-six photographs the following month. The German periodical *Moderne Bauformen* published five photographs of the offices in 1911, a perspective drawing of the clerks' office was exhibited at the Royal Academy Summer Exhibition of 1909 and *The Builder* published Voysey's description of the work in the same year.

Despite this critical acclaim and consistently successful relationships with influential clients (Voysey continued to furnish and decorate the Essex and Suffolk's regional offices until 1910, and between 1907 and 1908 he designed a series of small houses for Turner at Frinton), Voysey's architectural practice was showing the first symptoms of decline as early as 1907. He wrote to Turner in January of that year complaining of the inconvenience that 'we St John's Wood & Hampstead people are suffering' at the hands of the omnibus company (Turner had a London house in Circus Road, St John's Wood) suggesting that, 'As I have not quite enough to do I think I ought to go round with an address of complaints & get signatures?' Within a dozen years the not having quite enough to do had escalated to being 'within measurable distance of the workhouse'. While the repercussions of the First World War and the sort of Gothic detailing, which made the extensions to Hambledon Hurst so eccentric, can be held responsible for part of this decline, it is not so easy to explain the gradual slipping away of commissions in 1907, when Voysey was only fifty years old with an international reputation and at the height of his creative powers.

The decline of Voysey's practice was not brought about by any single decisive blow. Commissions for buildings decreased in number after 1906, but it is significant that of the seventeen commissions for new houses, which Voysey received between the beginning of 1907 and the end of 1910, twelve were never built. Of the five houses, which were built during this period, four were designed in 1909 (the fifth being Littleholme in Guildford, designed in 1906–7). History has made these houses into 'late works' but when Voysey designed them, at the age of fifty-two, he probably did so in the belief that his practice was regaining momentum after a fallow period of a few years. The 1909 houses show some shifting of orientation and one of the houses, 'Lodge Style' represented a stylistic tirade against changes in fashion in architectural design. It was this house, together with Voysey's lectures and writings, which consolidated the terms of his defiant architectural stance.

LITTLEHOLME, KENDAL, on the outskirts of Kendal, in Cumbria, was designed for Voysey's friend and fellow member of the Art Workers' Guild, A. W. Simpson. It was a small, almost square house, with a steeply pitched roof and a central chimney so that it looked like a house in a child's drawing. It was designed and built of local stone, without a trace of white roughcast, and Voysey sheltered the front door within a wide arched porch, which must surely have been influenced by Charles Harrison Townsend's arched entrances to the Bishopsgate Institute (1892–4) and the Whitechapel Art Gallery (1899–1901), in London, and perhaps by a knowledge of H. H. Richardson's houses in America and the house that Richardson designed at Bushey in Hertfordshire.

Voysey had recessed the garden door within a wide arched porch at The Pastures eight years earlier and at Littleholme in Guildford, but at Simpson's house the width of the porch, taking up almost a quarter of an otherwise simple, flat elevation was more pronounced and Voysey framed the opening with a heavy oak canopy. Simpson's furniture was uncompromisingly plain, depending upon proportions and the grain of the wood for its effect, and the simple lines and weighty presence of the canopy (and the house itself) reflected his style.

LATE WORKS AND

LECTURES

2

1 'Alice in Wonderland', textile design,
    c.1930.
2 House for Arthur à Beckett Terrell,
    Ashmansworth, Berkshire, October
    1914. Unexectuted.

3

4

Littleholme was designed with the strong solid lines of an artisan's stone cottage, and built with a craftsman's regard for good materials, however simple. It was built by a local contractor, J. W. Howie of Kendal; and the oak doors, floors and cupboards inside were made by another local firm, Hayes and Parkinson of Kendal. Simpson's own firm, 'The Handicrafts', was responsible for much of the furniture, and Simpson undoubtedly had a hand in the detailing of the interiors.

The Simpson family diaries and recollections give a marvellous insight into the construction of the house.[1] It was designed with alacrity: Voysey went over the site with A. W. Simpson on 19 June; the plans and elevations were drawn up the following day, and the site was pegged out before he returned to London on 21 June. There was no living hall. Instead Voysey provided an L-shaped parlour with a deep ingle-nook at one end and a dining area around the corner. Oak fitted cupboards from floor to ceiling separated the dining room from a generous kitchen, and sliding doors enabled food and dishes to be passed between the two rooms. In the parlour the ingle area was defined by a massive oak

beam and braces, and Voysey provided space on either side of the fireplace so that Simpson could design a drop-leaf desk on one side of the ingle for himself and a sewing cupboard on the other side for his wife Jane; these were made at 'The Handicrafts' and built in. As at The Homestead, the ingle was naturally lit and the oak lintels above the windows were exposed.

The walls were simply covered with 'one-coat plaster' and distempered white, without wainscoting or wallpaper and their thickness, which gave protection from harsh weather, was emphasized in the deep window-sills tiled with green-glazed, Dutch tiles. The skirtings too were tiled with 'green glass tiles, let in flush with the plaster'.[2] Voysey had drawn his favourite turkey-red curtains on to the elevations, and although in early photographs the shape and tone of the curtains appear to conform to his specification, in fact, they were made up in a Sundour fabric of shot green-blue at Jane Simpson's request. The whole of the ground floor, apart from the main area of the parlour, was paved with Staffordshire stable tiles and this included the ingle, but the parlour floor was of oak.

3, 4 *Parlour and dining room, Littleholme, Kendal, Cumbria, 1909. These photographs, showing the interiors furnished by Simpson, were published in England and Germany in 1911.*

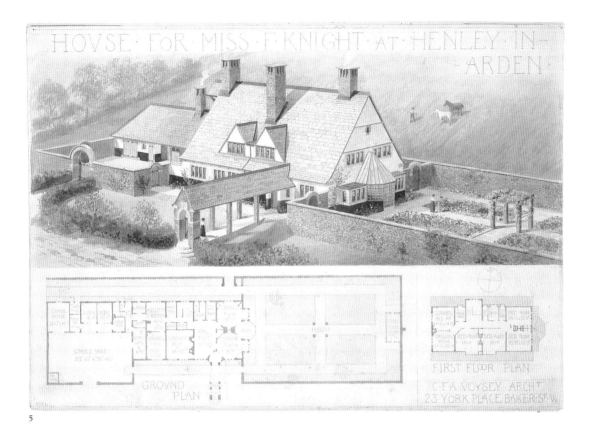

5

According to Simpson family records, there were delays in the construction of the house and A. W. Simpson finally insisted that the family would move in on June 16, 'come what might'. It was still unfinished on the appointed day and only three of the doors were hung: the front door, the back door and the one to the lavatory. Hubert Simpson is said to have spent most of 17 June waxing the oak parlour floor and when the family's friends arrived in the evening they tied polishing cloths to their shoes and danced it to a sheen.[3]

Although Littleholme was a modest cottage in a remote part of England, it was reviewed in *The British Architect, Architectural Review, The Craftsman* and in Germany, in *Moderne Bauformen*. There was no indication that demand for Voysey houses was slipping, and the photographs of the little stone house with its simple interiors furnished by Simpson might have suggested that he was moving away from the white roughcast walls and sweeping roofs that had characterized his style for so long. It was most probable that the stone walls of Littleholme were a response to local building traditions, however, because Voysey designed another small cottage in 1909 for his brother Arthur Annesley Voysey as a holiday house, which was designed and built with his characteristic roughcast walls and stone window-dressings.[4]

BROOKE END. The third 1909 house, Brooke End at Henley-in-Arden, was designed in typical Voysey style; the predominance of arched openings and octagonal rooms inside mark it out unmistakably as a late work. It was designed for three sisters, who were all portrayed in Voysey's perspective of the house surveying the formal gardens. The house was contained within a simple rectangular plan beneath a steeply pitched slate-roof, but it was exceptional in two respects: Voysey designed a long projecting porch with its own gable on to the front of the house and an octagonal conservatory extended the house into its garden and took the corners out of the two end rooms so that the dining and drawing rooms were also octagonal in plan.

Voysey sandwiched the house between a stable-yard and stable on one side, and a walled garden on the other and the stone-dressed openings in the garden walls were aligned along straight paths to

6

5 *Bird's-eye perspective, Brooke End, Henley-in-Arden, Warwickshire, 1909.*

6 *Holiday house designed for Voysey's brother Annesley, at Slindon, Sussex, 1909.*

7

tive for Lincoln Grammar School in the Royal Academy Summer Exibition of 1905, or maybe the two men had come up with the model of an Oxford College together. Whatever the background to the commission, Voysey relished the opportunity of building in stone and the invitation to design a building in the English Medieval style coincided with his rising passion for defending Gothic architecture in the face of the Classical Revival. The case that he presented for the Gothic in Lodge Style, he was to articulate in writing six years later with the publication of his book *Individuality*.[5]

Voysey, like A. W. N. Pugin and G. E. Street before him, did not want to make copies in the Tudor style. He argued instead for a revival of the individualistic spirit and moral strengths of the Medieval period so that 'a noble national architecture' might evolve as a 'living natural and true expression of modern needs and ideals' without imitation or 'any revival of any particular style, either native or foreign'.[6] He had no desire to be tied to the faithful reproduction of a style, and the use of each of the architectural elements that he adopted was justified by its practical as well as its spiritual strengths.

Lodge Style was designed with a liberal mixture of stylistic elements and even Voysey's description of it as a 'bungalow' (a very modern word for 1909) demonstrated a strong hold on the present.[7] The house was built of Bath stone beneath a Gloucestershire stone roof, and although it was planned around four sides of a quadrangle, the front elevation with its square tower and Gothic entrance was more like a parish church than an Oxford college. Lodge Style contradicted fundamental Gothic principles by applying Tudor details, all exquisitely crafted in stone, to an otherwise characteristic and emphatically horizontal Voysey house. If it had been called 'Gothic Style', it would have summarized Voysey's intentions because beneath the carved details and the pointed arches his distinctive motifs were never far from the surface. The gables and fluctuations in roof line, the windows arranged in horizontal bands tucked under the eaves, and even a veranda recessed beneath a wide porch like the one at The Pastures were all incorporated into the design, although the windows were shaped into drop arches and the bay windows were corbelled out on

make a series of formal patterns. The same blue and red brick, which was used for the garden walls, was continued in the piers and gable end to the long front porch and the pointed arch above the gateway was dressed with stone and adorned with a plaque bearing the sisters' initials in a touch of purely Gothic detailing, but aside from the porch there was nothing eccentric in the design of Brooke End. Voysey allowed an original Medieval door and a decorative ceiling-boss, which had been salvaged from a nearby building to be incorporated into the library, but in contrast to these historical elements he designed simple, wooden wall sconces and pendants for the electric light-fittings, and the interiors were elegant and immaculately crafted.

LODGE STYLE, at Combe Down, near Bath, was very different. It was designed for the owner of a Bath stone-quarry, who wanted a house reminiscent of Merton College, Oxford. Given this predilection for a specific style and the client's desire to build a show house out of his own stone, Voysey was a surprising choice, but perhaps the client, T. Sturge Cotterell, had admired Voysey's perspec-

7 *Voysey's room. Possibly his office at York Place, 'filled with beautiful things'.*

204   CHAPTER 12

curvaceous stone mouldings.

Lodge Style was decorated with three pieces of sculpture: a stone gargoyle, a statue of a Medieval burgher standing piously on top of one of the buttresses and an angel bearing the date of construction. All three pieces exemplified the specific recommendations that Voysey published on sculpture in *Ideas in Things* in 1909:

...a feeling for simplicity and restfulness will result in economy of labour and material, and perhaps leave us with a little spare cash to devote to one spot of sculpture, one point of pre-eminent interest in which we might suggest some merriment like the old grotesques. If, however, we use figure sculpture, let it not be a gentleman without his hat, or a lady with nothing on. For in this climate such exhibitions only excite our pity and discomforting sympathies.

Inside the house, Voysey left the walls unplastered so that the stonework was exposed, and the chimneypieces were cut out of the stone, depending for their effect on the craftsmanship of the mason in carving out Voysey's fine mouldings. The only plaster work in the house was the covering of the coved ceilings and it is interesting that Voysey rejected the Tudor-style ceiling with ribs and bosses: 'I ask for no cornices which produce lines of shade, no ornament on my ceiling which I cannot look at without paining my neck – ornamental ceilings are fit only for large rooms and halls.'[8] The rooms were distinguished by a remarkable simplicity, which was Medieval in general effect, rather than through a plethora of carved detailing. The joinery was in oak; all the floors except the bedroom and drawing-room floors were paved with Bath-stone slabs and blue Bath stone was used for the skirting.

Lodge Style was important as a testament to Voysey's personal interpretation of Gothic principles. It was a form of Gothic with the verticals omitted. Its design coincided with his lecture, *Ideas in Things*, which was published alongside lectures by M. H. Baillie Scott, Chas Spooner, Guy Dawber, R. W. Schultz and others, but it was an important house too, because the conditions of the brief gave Voysey an opportunity to develop and extend his characteristic style. If he had been typecast by the success of his early houses and obliged by insistent and unimaginative clients into reproducing their

long low lines, sweeping roofs and roughcast render walls then Lodge Style would have provided him with a chance for a clean break. The Medieval windows and doors, the battlements and the gables made it different in external appearance from Voysey's earlier houses, but essentially the rhythm and proportions of the plan and elevations were entirely consistent with the main body of his work. There was no frustrated desire for a profound and radical change.

Voysey's unfaltering constancy and his ability to create an almost unlimited variety of patterns and permutations within the fixed and self-imposed parameters of his architectural vocabulary were among his most resonant strengths, but this lack of diversity might also be thought of as a weakness. Certainly the architectural range and visual risk taking in Sir Edwin Lutyens's oeuvre, and to a lesser extent in M. H. Baillie Scott's, seem astonishingly adventurous by comparison with the quiet resolution of Voysey's restraint, but equally, the virtuosity and theatrical appeal of Lutyens's achievements would be found wanting if they were judged by the criteria of depth and integrity that distinguished Voysey's work. Nobody would criticize a tennis champion for being fairly useless at golf. By restricting his architectural language Voysey was able to indulge in a complex and finely orchestrated sequence of rhythms and repetitions in each of his houses, so that every component part, no matter how small, contributed to the whole.

He was typical of his generation in writing and lecturing about his work, and in defining the philosophy behind it, but the fact that his practice consistently conformed to the theory made him exceptional. He was not an intellectual, and the repetition in his writings was never as erudite as the pattern making in his architecture. However, the main stays of his philosophy remained constant throughout his career and the repetition of an idea from a magazine interview to a lecture to a passage in a book would not have been so apparent in Voysey's lifetime, when an idea could span a period of several decades.

In 1906 Voysey published a small book, *Reason as a Basis of Art*, in which he quoted Plato and Michelangelo as his intellectual mentors: Plato, he said, had defined the importance of a 'brave and sober-minded' character to the creation of 'grace,

8

9

8 *Entrance, Lodge Style, Combe Down, Bath, Avon, 1909.*
9 *Angel, Lodge Style.*

rhythm, and harmony'; and Michelangelo had said, 'The ideal of beauty is simplicity and repose.'[9] He did not state his sources. Three years later his lecture, 'Ideas in Things' was one of the most complete and comprehensive accounts of his building philosophy and he continued to publish on 'Copying and its relation to art', 'Patriotism in architecture', 'The Quality of fitness in architecture', 'The Aesthetic Aspects of Concrete Construction', 'On town planning', 'Lettering' and 'Unfamiliar uses for stained glass', even when he was an elderly man in his seventies. His recommendations were invariably based on an invincible line of logic, but his arguments were never commonplace. He had an extraordinary tendency to splice his own idiosyncratic assumptions, prejudices and open-hearted faith into an otherwise factual account of events, and for Voysey spiritual and physical considerations were inseparable:

What *do you want to build, is no more important a question than* why *do you want to build? After all the knowledge of material requirements and conditions has been gathered together and classified we shall find all this knowledge worse than useless, until we bring to bear upon it the moral, intellectual and spiritual sides of our nature.*[10]

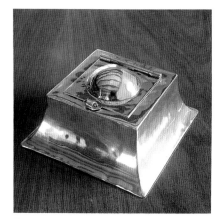

10

He was careful to answer criticisms in his writing, often veiling his defences in general terms in a manner that made him infuriatingly supercilious and oddly vulnerable at the same time. His remarks about unconventional dress in *Individuality* were particularly revealing. The cross-hatching of repetitions and justifications that recur again and again throughout his writings tell as much about his personality, his insecurities and obsessions, as about his vision of architecture.

In 1941, C. R. Ashbee described Voysey's idiosyncratic jackets with affection.[11] However, he also remarked that 'the Englishman in Voysey can turn round sharp and snap'.[12] As Voysey's dress became increasingly snappy after 1900 (his jackets still sported lapels when he was photographed at The Orchard), so too his temper became sharper. To some extent Voysey's disposition was directly related to the amount of pain that he suffered from his stomach ulcers, but in his later writings there are passages that show a disillusioned bitterness, which must be attributed to the decline of his practice:

To be popular we must synchronize with our times, we must sympathize with the thoughts and feelings of the multitude, we must catch the temper of the moment and harmonize with popular sentiment. In a materialistic age we have to make matter our first concern. Good business habits and good bargaining will count for more than ethical qualities. The successful architect to-day is not the spiritual leader and raiser of popular taste, but he who can minister most smoothly to the thirst for ease and comfort, and teach men how to multiply material gain. Making things look better than they are is sure to be amply rewarded by a people grown indifferent to truth and shy of sincerity.[13]

Voysey was never prepared to synchronize with the times in order to be popular and although the decline of his practice was partly caused by changing social conditions as the Edwardian, country-house lifestyle faded into obsolescence, even before the First World War he was unfashionable. Voysey would not be carried along by changing architectural fashions, but he did not simply hold fast to his position of individuality. He deliberately reproached the fickle trends of what he described as a 'materialistic age' by accentuating the element in his work that was most unfashionable. He had been sympathetic to the Gothic since his earliest introduction to architecture. He had absorbed the writings of A. W. N. Pugin and John Ruskin, even before he had learnt to draw, and the practical example of J. P. Seddon was seminal to his development as a designer. His early and mature buildings were not overtly Gothic, but they were founded on Gothic principles, and when the pioneering values and achievements of these figures were rejected as passé, brushed aside as unfashionable, Voysey came out fighting. He recalled his hereditary characteristics, passed down from John Wesley through the exemplary role of his father, and he staunchly defended his position even when it lost him commissions and ultimately deprived him of his living.

There can be little doubt that Voysey re-enacted the martyrdom of his father, in the same way that he had translated his father's teaching into a rational design philosophy. There was a quality of moral purity associated with martyrdom, but there might also (and we will never know this for sure) have been an intimacy and companionship between Voysey and his father in the years of his architectural decline. In 1906 Voysey sold The Orchard and moved to 14 Briardale Gardens, within a few minutes walk of Annesley Lodge, and this coincided with the surfacing and ultimately with the predominance of Gothic elements in his work. Voysey's grief after his father's death in 1912 may have sparked off an emotional crisis, and the evangelical quality in his writing, and to some extent in his architectural stance, became more entrenched after 1912. It might also be relevant that Pugin and Ruskin were associated with Voysey's family background and so in defending their doctrines Voysey may have believed that he was upholding the values of his father and of his grandfather. For Voysey the Gothic tradition in English architecture had a hereditary as well as a national significance.

Voysey's last house was built in 1911 when he was only fifty-four, but he continued to design buildings and enter competitions well into his seventies. The house was a typical rectangular building with roughcast walls beneath a green-slate roof, designed for a Robert Hetherington and built in Belfast, Northern Ireland. In the same year Voysey extended and refurbished a perfume shop in Old Bond Street for J. & E. Atkinson, working Gothic tracery above one entrance and modelling a royal coat of arms above another. There was some antagonism between Voysey and his client and in 1925 the shop was rebuilt.[14] His Gothic inclinations were even more openly expressed the following year when he designed a shop at 145 Victoria Street, London, for Perry & Company. The stone facade was decorated with Gothic tracery and the display window was round headed with a grid of leaded lights giving the effect of a fortress where precious things were stowed away. The design was never built.

Some of Voysey's Gothic designs must have been conceived in a spirit of bloody-mindedness. If a competition entry would not be fashionable it might at least take his aesthetic postulations to their extreme limits. Not all of his late works were Gothic, however, and a number were designed to be built and then thwarted by circumstances or a breakdown in client relations. In 1910 Voysey designed two office tower-blocks for Spicer Brothers in Tudor Street, in the City area of London, and it is particularly regrettable that these bold and simple blocks, which would have predated Berlage's Holland House by four years, were never built.[15] Voysey's office expenses show that

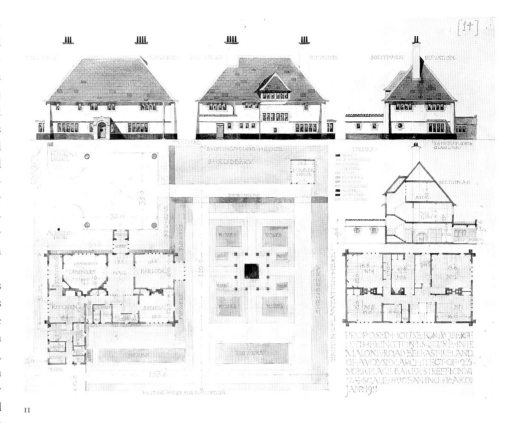

11

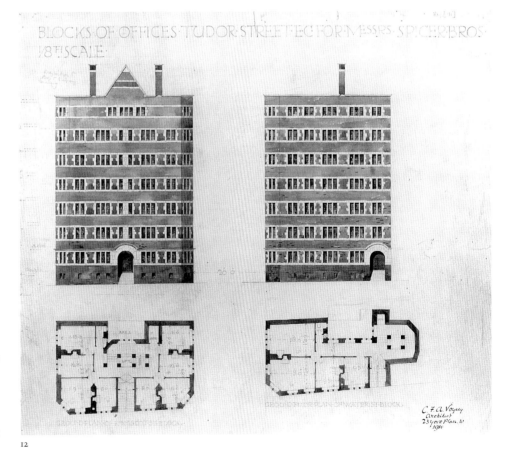

12

11 *House in Malone Road, Belfast, Northern Ireland, 1911.*

12 *Office-blocks for Spicer Brothers, Tudor Street, London. Unexecuted design, 1910.*

building contracts were drawn up and foundation work began on site. For over a year from February 1910 he made regular visits to see his client, and to the LCC, but the account ended with legal expenses.

Like the Sanderson Factory, the offices for Spicer Brothers were tall streamlined buildings, quite different from Voysey's houses, but at the same time clearly identifiable as his work. They were to have been seven-storeys high with an additional half basement, and the smooth, yellow-brick elevations would have been patterned with bands of stonework, linking the window dressings. The plinths would have been black brick and above the ground-floor windows a projecting string-course would have cut a sharp horizontal line around the building, wavering only to trace an arch over the main entrance. Like Holland House, the design of the Spicer Brothers' offices was governed by fitness, and the decorative effect of the building would have been dependent on Voysey's refined and imaginative use of relatively simple, but inherently rich materials.

Thirteen years later he designed a very different tower block for the Devonshire House site in Piccadilly. In a letter to *The Builder* he recommended that the site should be used for apartments surrounded by greenery and fresh air rather than for commercial use, which would increase traffic congestion. The tower was to have been one of three, based on 'Pugin's Victoria Tower at Westminster'. It was 300-feet high, and Voysey had set out to prove that a Gothic building could incorporate as much glass as one designed in any other style. Le Corbusier had designed the Ville Contemporaine the previous year, and although Voysey's Gothic turrets and finials were idiosyncratic, the concept behind his design – tower blocks soaring above the tree tops of a surrounding park – was exceptionally modern.

In 1912, Voysey designed a village hall for Porlock to be built of stone with crenellated parapets and adorned by a statue of an angel. The following year he designed an extension for Simpson's house in Kendal, again making defiant use of crenellations. Neither the hall nor the extension was built and the number and scale of commissions coming into the office slowed to a trickle. In 1914 Voysey designed three houses which might have set his career back on course: one for his brother

Ellison in Wilmslow; one at Thatcham for H. Tingey; and an extraordinary house with a castellated tower surmounted by a windmill at Ashmansworth for Arthur à Beckett Terrell, but the war intervened, the projects were abandoned, and Voysey's career slipped into obscurity.

There is a romantic perception that the decline of Voysey's architectural practice led to a steady degeneration into poverty; that financial pressures forced him to sell The Orchard; and that he suffered a martyr's fate, living his last years alone in a two-roomed flat, always remaining constant to his art. As with many good stories there is more than a grain of truth in this one, but Voysey's own rudimentary financial accounts suggest that it was not altogether the whole truth, and the causes of his decline were more complex. Voysey's income from professional fees rose steadily in his early years of practice, from £377 in 1885, the year that he married, to an average income of about £1,500 per year for the peak years from 1898 to 1905. In 1906 fees fell by thirty-eight per cent from £1,575 the previous year to £973, but in 1907 his income shot back up to a record high at £2,197, and then dropped again in 1908 to £634. The following two years were a little better financially, probably because the fees for the 1909 houses were coming in, but from 1911 to 1914 Voysey's average income from fees amounted to £558 per year.[16]

The massive fluctuations in income and the sudden reduction after eight years of affluence, and apparent financial security, must have been as alarming as the deterioration in living standards, which the reduction in income induced. Voysey's professional disappointments were exacerbated by his inability to sustain the same level of provision for his family and a third area of pressure, the well-being of his own elderly parents, became an increasing preoccupation from 1906. In October 1906, Voysey and his family left The Orchard and moved to Hampstead. *The Tatler* noted Voysey's regret at having to part with the house, stating that he was obliged to move to town 'for business and private reasons'.[17] However, given their new address and the date of the move, before Voysey's income could be seen to be in permanent decline, it must be assumed that they left The Orchard not least to care for the seventy-eight-year-old Reverend Voysey and Frances Maria. Another reason for the move was

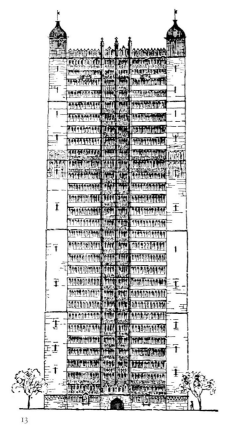

13

education. Voysey was interested in progressive education and the children were sent to King Alfred School, within walking distance of Briardale Gardens. The family moved again, to Erskine Hill in the suburbs of north London after Reverend Voysey's death, but by this time Voysey's income from fees was reduced to a third of what it had been during the peak years, and there were serious difficulties, too, in his marriage.

The exact cocktail of factors that caused Voysey's architectural decline cannot be defined, but his father's old age and death, his own dogged determination to uphold Pugin's Gothic values, financial problems, the failure of his marriage and bouts of ill-health, which are generally believed to have been caused by stomach ulcers, would all have been in the mix between 1906 and 1914. He must have been disillusioned, too, perhaps even bewildered, at the twist of fashion away from his work after so many years of having his opinions sought after and his designs eagerly awaited. In 1913 the office in York Place was closed and Voysey moved his studio briefly to 25 Dover Street, Piccadilly, where his builder, Müntzer, had his offices, and then to 10 New Square, Lincoln's Inn. During the war years his income from fees fell to their lowest ever levels: £238 for 1915 – considerably less than his income of thirty years earlier – and there was hardly any improvement over the next two years.

By 1917 Voysey had abandoned the idea of a separate house and office. His marriage to Mary Maria had become increasingly unhappy, and when their youngest son, Annesley, came of age they separated, and Voysey went to live and work in a small flat at 73 St James's Street. Voysey's niece, describing her visits to stay with 'Uncle Charles', remembered the flat's primrose-yellow walls and a plain blue curtain dividing the living and sleeping areas of the room, and she recalled their walks along Piccadilly together in the 1920s when she would wear the special primrose-yellow dress that he had designed for her twenty-first birthday;[18] 'He had a very delightful habit, that although he'd been divorced or separated from his wife for years and years and years, when he sat down at a restaurant he always sat facing his wife'; he would ask the waiter the direction of Welwyn Garden City, where she lived and seat himself accordingly. 'I think when they were together it wasn't so easy.'[19]

They generally went out for tea rather than lunch or dinner, because care had to be taken over the cost of things, but Voysey's financial position was not as consistently bleak as is generally supposed. By the end of the war, after three fallow years and the expense of moving and, presumably, of providing a separate home for Mary Maria and their daughter Priscilla, Voysey's finances had become desperate and he was obliged to write to friends and former clients asking for the loan of money or the means of earning it. In April 1918 he wrote to Morton, who had manufactured his textile designs for over twenty years:

My dear Morton.
Again I am out of work and now in a very terrible plight. Within measurable distance of the workhouse. It is hard at 61 to get any kind of post. Can you help me by giving me anything to do?[20]

Later, when his highly prized retainer fee of £200 per year was threatened he wrote even more explicitly: 'It is very painful to me to go beggin on my own behalf. Without that 200£ I should have to leave my flat, sell all my furniture and bury myself in a slum.' But interspersed with the fallow periods there were prosperous years when Voysey's income would shoot back up. In 1920 his fees amounted to £1,448 and the following year they were £1,177. Given the precision of his office accounts, it is difficult to believe that he made no financial provision for his old age, but if he did then either his investments failed or else they were spent keeping Mary Maria in Welwyn Garden City. The romantic story of Voysey as an abandoned hero who ended his life in poverty is fuelled by the fact that his old age exceeded the period of time in successful practice. Voysey was sixty when he moved to St James's Street and he lived to be eighty-three. He never officially retired, continuing to design well into his seventies, but his annual income only fell below two hundred pounds after 1924, by which time he was sixty-seven.

As Voysey's architectural practice diminished he became increasingly dependent upon the income that he could derive from his wallpaper and fabric designs, and some of his most memorable patterns were drawn up after 1914. Around the turn of the century the birds and animals, which had patterned

14

14 *'River Rug', 1903.*

his early papers began to take on a more narrative role, and in 1903 he designed a 'River Rug', which was made up and exhibited in the Arts and Crafts Exhibition that year. Apparently he intended to sell the design to amateur rug-makers. Black swans, white swans, boats and fishes animated the course of the river as it ran vertically through the rug and on its banks Voysey painted a series of tales from rural life: farmers followed their ploughs and hunters their hounds; the country pursuits of shooting and fishing were drawn within a pattern of lanes, which led to Voysey-style cottages and there was a fine Voysey house with a peacock in its formal front garden and an orchard to the rear.

In his textile designs, and particularly in the later works, Voysey expressed a charmed view of the world that was fresh and simple and touchingly naive. C. R. Ashbee described, 'The abundance, the delicacy, the grace of his designs for textiles, wall papers and inlay. They appealed to innocence because they had the child-like, – a certain universal quality we loved in him.'[21] Around 1919 he designed 'The Huntsman' for a machine-woven textile and the same gentle sense of narrative and expressive

quality of line gave the huntsman his streamlined posture full of purpose and determination, while every detail of the deer expressed nervous uncertainty. Even the fish had expressive faces and a rudimentary castle gave a sense of time and place to the action.

Between 1929 and 1930 Voysey produced a series of nursery designs for textiles and wallpapers, including a textile and a set of tiles for Minton's based on the story of 'Alice in Wonderland'. They coincided with the long awaited arrival of his grandchildren, Elizabeth and John in 1927 and 1929, and they owe something of their humour and spontaneity to Voysey's affection for the two children.[22] He was described as 'a stern father, an awe-inspiring father-in-law, but a delightful grandfather' and some of the picture letters which he made

for them still survive.[23] 'The House that Jack Built' was designed in September 1929, and was sold to Morton 'with all copyrights' the following November. However, the enormous rat (bigger than the house) and the pencilled figure of a priest, believed to be a caricature of Voysey's brother Annesley, who was a Unitarian minister, in the first drawing, were omitted in the final design.[24]

An 'Alice in Wonderland' textile with figures based on the original Tenniel illustrations to the book was equally light-hearted and again the design was printed by Morton Sundour, but Voysey's relationship with Morton was not always easy. In April 1931, within a year of selling Alice he wrote: 'At your last visit you had not a word of praise for my work and after I had shewn you between 40 and 50 desigs [sic] you asked if I could not shew you something *fresh!*'[25]

Voysey very seldom expressed any bitterness at his circumstances, leading Ashbee to write that if fate was cruel, 'with Voysey somehow it didn't seem to matter much'. But in 1919 he had written to A. W. Simpson:

I often feel that loneliness you describe, especially do I feel that want of a sympathetic enjoyment of the beautiful. Though a member of the top Arts Club in the top Metropolis of the world, yet I am alone without one soul in whom to confide and with whom to enjoy truly the beauty of man made things.[26]

As Voysey grew older and designed less, he spent an increasing amount of time at the Arts Club and the Art Workers' Guild, where he had many good friends. He was described in 1927 as having, 'probably more friends than acquaintances, and it is hard to imagine that he has one enemy in the whole world'.[27] Although the letter to Simpson expressed a deep sense of isolation, Robert Donat described a much happier side to Voysey with a strong sense of humour and an avid enthusiasm for oysters.[28] He also recounted Voysey's innocence in a world of twentieth-century celebrities and movie stars, when he persuaded Voysey to go and see one of his films.[29] However according to Donat, even as a frail old man, Voysey was never to be pitied: 'not that your sympathy would be spurned, not that your sympathy would be wasted. Simply that your sympathy is not needed.' His loneliness was, according to Donat, an obligatory part of his artistic sensibility.[30]

15 *'The White Rabbit' from a set of* Alice in Wonderland *tiles designed for Minton, 1930.*

16 *Picture letter: 'My dear grand children, I hope you are busy working at something nice for someone. Service*
is the safest road to happiness. You will delight in realizing the pleasure you give to others. I would like to know what things you most delight in, and do something that adds to your well being.'

17 'The House that Jack Built'
textile design, September 1919.

2

3

LITTLEHOLME

1909

Littleholme in Kendal, Cumbria, was designed for Voysey's friend the furniture-maker, A. W. Simpson. In his own work Simpson depended upon bold shapes and the grain of the wood, simply worked; in the timber canopy over the porch Voysey paid homage to Simpson's style. Although the house was designed as a simple artisan's cottage, built of local stone, Voysey sheltered the front porch within a massive stone arch, which was surely inspired more by American architecture than by vernacular tradition.

4

5

CFA VOYSEY

1 *Front and side elevation.*
2 *Garden elevation.*
3 *Stone porch and timber canopy. If not inspired by H. H. Richardson, then*

perhaps the element of shelter was influenced by the local climate.
4 *Ingle-nook in the parlour.*
5 *Landing.*

1

2

3

*1–3 Garden elevation. An extraordinary
combination of the long, low lines and
architectural motifs of a characteristic
Voysey house, with Tudor Gothic
detailing.*

214

4

5

LODGE STYLE

1909

The site for Lodge Style at Combe Down, near Bath, in Avon, was adjacent to the stone quarry where its owner, T. S. Cotterell, had his business. He wanted a show-house, which would display the beauty of his stone and the skill of his masons. Voysey found the commission to be a perfect vehicle for his militant (and unfashionable) promotion of Gothic architecture. The house was designed as a miniature quadrangle to remind Cotterell of Merton College in Oxford.

6

215   C F A VOYSEY

4 *Entrance front.*

5 *View across the courtyard.*

6 *The stone interior walls and floors of the parlour were exposed, and only the ceilings were plastered.*

The extent of Voysey's influence is conspicuous today in Britain's suburbs, in the white roughcast houses of the Twenties and Thirties with their miniaturized Voysey motifs. However the implications of Voysey's international reputation, his influence on his contemporaries and on a later generation of Modernists are more profound. Voysey was never interested in foreign travel either to study European architecture or to promote his own career. As a young architect his failure to make a tour across Europe made him exceptional, although George Devey must have encouraged him to do so and A. H. Mackmurdo would have regaled him with tales of the Italian Renaissance. As an old man he quoted John Ruskin as saying: 'That knowledge is got by travel – but wisdom by staying at home.'[1] Perhaps during his training years Voysey could not afford to travel, but even in the 1890s when his European reputation began to grow and his work was exhibited in Paris his only recorded visit abroad was a brief trip to Holland, and as early as 1895 he was lecturing against the imitative revivalism that had 'brought into our midst foreign styles of decoration totally out of harmony with our national character and climate'.[2] The campaign against foreign styles intensified as 'Classicism of the Georgian type became fashionable and corrupted even the Great Lutyens'.[3] However, his diatribes against the folly of adopting foreign styles for English architecture did not disaffect the growing interest in his work abroad and nor did it prevent him from designing houses in his own characteristic style for sites in Egypt and America.

Very little is known of Voysey's commissions abroad and his own record of work is unreliable on the subject. In his autobiographical notes he claimed to have 'built over 117 private houses in England, Ireland, Wales, Austria, America & Egypt', but the only American building recorded in his black book was a 'House for Mrs. Tytus at Ashintelly, Tyringham, Mass. U.S.A.' in 1905, and this was almost certainly never built.[4] Robb de Peyster Tytus was an American millionaire and Egyptologist, who had bought an estate of eight-hundred acres at Tyringham after his honeymoon in 1902. The site was immediately named Ashintully, but shortly after the land was acquired

AN INTERNATIONAL

REPUTATION

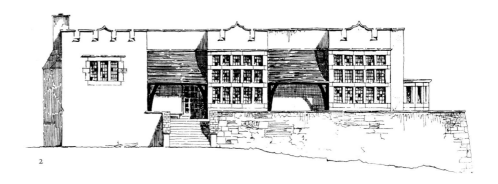

1 *Voysey's preferred view of The Orchard was of a gable end, partially obscured by fruit trees.*

2 *Elevation for House at Aswan, Egypt, 1905.*

4

3

5

Mr and Mrs Tytus went to Egypt, where they lived in a house-boat on the Nile, while Mr Tytus assisted Howard Carter in his exploration of Egyptian tombs.

The circumstances of Voysey's introduction to the family remain a mystery. He designed a half-timbered house, arranged around a courtyard for Tytus and the drawings were published in *The British Architect* in 1908.[5] However, when the Ashintully house was finally built between 1909 and 1911 it was designed by an American architect Francis V. L. Hoppin, in a style that Voysey would have found deplorable. Photographs survive of an immense Neo-Georgian mansion house built of grey Vermont marble, whose most notable characteristic was its size. It was one of the largest and grandest houses in Berkshire, USA, but there are no records of an additional Voysey structure on the site.[6]

The 'House at Assuan, Egypt' was listed within a few entries of Ashintully in Voysey's black book for the year 1905, but the Egyptian house was for an English client, Dr H. E. Leigh Canney of 31 Belsize Square in London, and the drawings are in the RIBA collection. They show a two-storey, rendered house with Voysey's characteristic stone-dressed windows and a typical round-headed front door recessed within a porch. Voysey gave the house a flat roof with a castellated parapet to take account of the climate, but the prospect of a house without a chimney must have been inconceivable to him because a massive chimney-like structure projected out from the front elevation, apparently housing only cupboards and a larder inside. Voysey's office expenses for the commission were unusually scant: the house was dated October 1905 and there were no expenses for client visits or for typing the specification. The only expenses for the house at Aswan were two relatively large sums for postage in 1906, suggesting that the extent of Voysey's involvement was limited to the provision of drawings. Nevertheless there were photographs of the house, newly built, in his collection.

Evidence for the Austrian house is more elusive still, unless Voysey was referring to a house he designed at Helenthal, which he described alternately as within Austria and Czechoslovakia. Voysey designed furniture and decorations for a room in Vienna for 'Messrs Hofler Rama & Co.' in 1898, and according to his black book the 'Work was put up in Lodz, Russia'. In 1912 he designed burial grounds for a Carl Low at Helenthal, and ten years later he designed a house there for the same client.[7] Drawings for the house survive at the RIBA, and Voysey applied for a passport and visas in September 1922, charging his expenses to Low, but there is no known evidence to confirm either that Voysey made visits to Czechoslovakia or that the house was ever built to his designs.[8]

Whether Voysey actually built houses in Europe and America, or not, is only a partial indicator of the extent of his influence. By 1897 his reputation as an architect was international and illustrations of his work in *The Studio* were eagerly awaited and collected by designers all over Europe. Magazines like *Dekorative Kunst* and, later, *Moderne Bauformen* published special articles on his work. Architects in Holland, Scandinavia, Germany and Austria were influenced by his designs and he was visited by a deputation of Dutch architects who wanted to express their admiration for his buildings. C. R. Ashbee, whose own influence on European and American architecture was considerable, wrote that, 'No architect of the Guild has, I think, had more influence abroad, in his generation, than Voysey',[9] and Pevsner wrote that his designs, 'revolutionized the minds of the most go-ahead young artists on the Continent'.[10]

Hermann Muthesius was an avid supporter not only of Voysey's houses, but also of his interiors, his decorative designs and his furniture. In *Das englische Haus,* one of the most influential architectural books at the beginning of the twentieth century, Muthesius described Voysey as 'by far the most active and best-known architect' of his group and summarized his work with remarkable accuracy and economy. Pevsner later described it as 'the ultimate recognition of his European importance'.[11]

Muthesius's appreciation of the quality of completeness in a Voysey house, not only the designing of fireplaces and fabrics, although these were described, but the manner in which exterior and interior were conceived together in a seamless exploration of rhythm and form was incisive. He described Voysey as Morris's successor in his designs for wallpapers, carpets and materials; the

fact that he designed for industry rather than exclusively for hand-crafted production was specially noted. Voysey's furniture, too, and its importance as an integral part of his interiors was described and illustrated and when Holly Mount, Littleholme and The Homestead were photographed for *Moderne Bauformen* their furnished interiors were given priority:

In his furniture too C.F.A. Voysey is an exception among the members of the London group. Like the others he too designs almost exclusively in untreated oak, he too is plain to the point of being primitive, he too forces the construction on the attention. But beyond the construction, his furniture has higher artistic qualities, his pieces have style and a personal idiom. And above all, they are designed as elements in the concept of the interior.

The connections between Voysey and American architects, like H. H. Richardson, Greene and Greene and Frank Lloyd Wright, are more difficult to assess. He would almost certainly have known the house that Richardson designed for the Royal Academician Sir Hubert von Herkomer at Bushey, in Hertfordshire, in 1884, with its characteristic, arched front porch;[12] he would have known the work of his American contemporaries through the pages of *The Studio* and other magazines. Later, Ashbee forged a direct link between British and American architects, and Voysey must have listened to his accounts of Frank Lloyd Wright and the building of the first Taliesin during their evenings together at the Art Workers' Guild, but neither Wright nor Voysey were easily influenced by the achievements of other men, and nothing that Voysey wrote made reference to Wright's achievements.

Voysey's designs were published in America later than in Europe. In 1903 the New York *House & Garden* magazine reviewed the seventh Arts and Crafts Exhibition in London and the next edition featured an article on 'Some recent work by C. F. A. Voysey, an English architect'. The following year the Boston *Architectural Review* gave an account of the English Arts and Crafts movement, concluding that in spite of 'all its affectations, with all its straining for novelty, with all its mistakes' the Arts and Crafts movement had revived English handicraft and produced some

6

6 *Electric fire, designed by Voysey for his son, Charles Cowles Voysey.*

'delightful buildings'. The writer concluded that there was little to be learnt from the English country-house plan: 'The dining-room is never, as invariably in this country, connected with the kitchen by means of the butler's pantry. It is often so situated that the meals have to be carried down a long passage half across the house from the kitchen to the dining-room…' This aside, the English and American suburban houses were very similar.[13]

Two of the houses that the article had been considering were Moorcrag and New Place, but the unconditional approval, which Voysey generally enjoyed in the European press was withheld. Far from being championed as one of the front-runners of the Arts and Crafts movement, it was suggested that he had been 'somewhat injured' by the eccentricities of the movement: 'His work is well considered and is not without attractiveness, but the sloping buttress-like terminations to the gable ends of his stucco-covered houses, the exaggerated forms of over-hanging gables, are notes of affectation which mar otherwise pleasant compositions.'[14] The same magazine, however, published two more photographs of Moorcrag three years later, 'with the fullest appreciation of its perfect composition and its exquisitely English domestic quality'.[15]

Voysey seldom commented on the interpretation or extent of his influence in England and abroad. In his autobiographical notes he recorded with evident satisfaction, 'Has had One Man Shows in Holland and America got up and paid for by those countries without the faintest suggestion or request from him.' His work was exhibited in New Zealand, in 1906, and in Finland, in 1909, but in spite of his international reputation Voysey retained his insularity: 'If a foreigner chose to admire and emulate his work that was very nice for the foreigner, and in a quiet way Voysey enjoyed his flattery, but he never thought of returning the compliment.'[16]

After the First World War, as the course of architecture turned away from the Classical Revival towards Modernism, 'homes for heroes' sprang up along the arterial routes of metroland, and Voysey's influence inspired the work not only of a new generation of architects, but of builders too. For the speculative builder of the Twenties and Thirties Voysey's cottage designs replaced the pattern-books of former generations. His characteristic motifs were easily reduced in scale, they were cheap to build, and their mixture of reassuringly traditional elements with a crisp, clean and essentially modern quality of lightness and utility was exactly what the market demanded. Thousands of little white houses with roughcast-render walls, cat-slide roofs, and quaint little recessed porches, asymmetrically arranged in gabled entrance bays, sprang up in suburban estates all over the country. Voysey's own practice of repeating and rearranging very similar component parts from one cottage to another provided a perfect model for variations within a similar housing type in order to add diversity to an estate, and the sentimentality of Voysey's designs, stripped of all integrity, was exploited for its prettiness.

Voysey remained an active member of the Art Workers' Guild, whose membership of bright and progressive young men of the 1880s continued to share advice and companionship well into the twentieth century as they grew old together, and the Guild became less of a missionary force to educate the 'Philistine world' and more of a sanctuary away from it. In February 1924 Voysey was elected its Master and under his leadership meetings were convened to consider: 'Why is Archaeology detrimental to living Art?' and 'Does the Artist learn more from Art than from Nature?', as well as to hear papers on 'Ferro-concrete and Cement-casting', Chinese Sculpture and European Lacquer. John Leighton wrote an affectionate poem recalling Voysey's manner in the Chair:

His diffident flutterings will not last long,
For he's Voysey! he's Voysey! he's Voysey!
And that small silver voice will grow brazen and strong,
And get noisy! get noisy! get noisy!
His efforts (if any) shall pass for a whim
But the Guild's little faults we'll attribute to him,
And we'll say 'sotto voice' with countenance grim,
It's Voysey! it's Voysey! it's Voysey!

When striking ideas in the course of debate
Hit Voysey – hit Voysey – hit Voysey.
He will welcome dissent when he knows it's too late,
Wit Voysey! Wit Voysey! Wit Voysey!
If we venture to differ his glasses will glare,
He will earn in his person respect for the chair;
And whatever our sentiments, no one will dare
Twit Voysey, Twit Voysey, Twit Voysey.[17]

7

For fifteen years, between 1912 and 1927, Voysey's British reputation went through a period of dormancy. The main current of architectural events by-passed him and he was left to design and to publish his thoughts in the quiet back-waters of his flat in St James's Street. *Individuality* was published in 1915 and reviewed by Halsey Ricardo in the *RIBA Journal*. It was commended by Voysey's contemporaries, but it probably had very little impact on the rest of the architectural world at the time. In 1927, however, a concerted effort was made to revive Voysey's reputation. A dinner was given in honour of his seventieth birthday by the President and Council of the RIBA and a statement written and signed by his friends was published in the *RIBA Journal*.[18]

It was signed by some of the most prestigious architects of the day, including A. H. Mackmurdo, Sir Edwin Lutyens, Walter Cave and C. R. Ashbee, as well as by manufacturers like W. Bainbridge Reynolds and W. Aumonier. Voysey had persistently rejected 'the honours and priviledges of membership' of the RIBA 'for no other reason than that he has held strong views on architectural training at variance with the prevailing custom' (he supported the pupillage system). Nevertheless, he was reported to have been both honoured and moved by 'the undercurrent of esteem and almost brotherly regard', which distinguished the evening.

In the same year an anonymous series of articles on 'C.F. Annesley Voysey – The Man and His Work' was published in *The Architect and Building News*. They were written by a friend (John Brandon-Jones has suggested that H. B. Creswell may have been the author), whose first task, 'at the instigation of the Editor' was to subdue 'the extreme restiveness of Voysey at the approach of an interviewer'. Voysey, he wrote, after 'avoiding capture' with obstinate tenacity, greeted the proposal for a series of articles with the words 'Why can't you wait till I'm dead?'

The articles presented Voysey as a design hero and a harbinger of the Modern Movement:

Voysey ... is like a rock ... inveterate in his likes and dislikes, unyielding to any fashions of thought or of sentiment, unmoved by changing vogues, a man whose artistic convictions are at one with his spiritual ideals and identified with his

8

whole attitude to life and to work; he remains complete and sufficient, staunch and immovable. He changes not; men may come and men may go, wars and revolutions along with them, but Voysey goes on for ever.[19]

In spite of Voysey's admonishments to, 'Write about what you don't like. Criticise my work. Say how bad it is', the articles eulogized his achievements and reiterated his opinions, setting the tone for future descriptions of the architect, 'who has long ago found clear answers to the questions that harass most of us throughout our lives, and who dwells in a compact impregnable system of his own'. A few years later John Betjeman as a young editor at the *Architectural Review* adopted Voysey as one of three 'true pioneers'; the other two were Ruskin and Le Corbusier. At Betjeman's instigation the Batsford Gallery, in London, organized a Voysey exhibition in association with the *Architectural Review* in 1931, and Betjeman publicized the event in a four page article on the individualism of Voysey and his 'brave and outspoken' opinions.[20]

Voysey found himself launched back into a very

8 *Statement in homage to Voysey on his seventieth birthday, written and signed by his friends.*

different architectural world to the one that he had entered forty years before. He must have gritted his teeth at some of Betjeman's observations:

I remember asking Mr. F. H. Newberry, who taught Charles Rennie Mackintosh at the Glasgow School of Art, from whom his pupil derived his inspiration. And I learned that it was from Voysey, who was at that time starting practice. Mackintosh did more probably than anyone else for a healthy, simple architecture abroad. So Voysey has not fought in vain.

Voysey disliked Mackintosh's work and he would have recoiled, too, at the frequent associations that Betjeman made between his work and the Modern Movement. In 1934 in a lecture to the Architectural Society of the Bartlett School, he laid his position on Modernism clearly on the line:

Modern architecture is pitifully full of such faults as proportions that are vulgarly aggressive, mountebank eccentricities in detail and windows lying down on their sides. Like rude children we have broken away and turned our backs on tradition. This is false originality, the true originality having been, for all time, the spiritual something given to the development of traditional forms by the individual artist.[21]

9

The dye was cast, however, and Voysey's brave and outspoken opinions could do nothing to change it. Photographs and descriptions of his work were included in Nikolaus Pevsner's *Pioneers of the Modern Movement* published by Faber & Faber in 1936, and in the Dutch *Elseviers maandschrift*; and when J. M. Richards made the pilgrimage to St James's Street he was surprised to find, having made the mistake of admitting that he wanted to talk about his Penguin book on modern architecture, in which Voysey was to appear as a pioneer, that Voysey 'objected indignantly … to being included among the originators of an architecture he heartily disliked'.[22] He was included just the same.

In 1936 Voysey was one of the first to be made 'Designer for Industry' by the Royal Society of Arts, and in February 1940, at the age of eighty-two, he was awarded the RIBA Royal Gold Medal, 'the highest award British architecture can give'.[23] The following month J. J. P. Oud wrote to congratulate him:

Dear Mr Voysey,
As there are not such a lot of characters in architecture I am very glad to learn that one of the best of them is honoured now by the gold medal of the R.I.B.A. You are one of the most admired examples out of my youth and I am still admiring you in the same degree up to now.[24]

According to John Brandon-Jones:

Voysey was never quite sure whether to be pleased or amused or distressed by his rediscovery and the honours that followed; but he certainly felt that many of those who sung his praises had completely misunderstood his philosophy and the lessons that he had tried to teach.[25]

If circumstances had been different, if for example Voysey's Gothic competition entry for the government buildings of Ottawa of 1914 had been successful, then his position in history might have been quite different. He might have been cast in the final chapter of the Victorian era rather than in the prelude to a modern one, and perhaps he would have been more comfortable among the Victorians, but he was not an altogether unwilling partner in the creation of his own legend.

When the RIBA Gold Medal award was announced Voysey was suddenly the subject of more general media interest, and again his circumstances were moulded and clipped in the interests of a strong narrative. Robert Donat described him 'writhing beneath the lash' of an insistent interviewer more intent upon a human interest story than on what Voysey really wanted to say and he was caricatured as 'a man too old, too frail, too disappointed' to appreciate his medal. The *News Chronicle* quoted him as saying 'I hope they send me the medal by post … And then I hope I may die',[26] and an article in *The Daily Mail* by Rhona Churchill was headlined: 'Medal? What use to Me? – I need Friends.'[27] The latter attracted the sympathy of a widow who wrote to Voysey, pitying him his loneliness and inviting him to share her rooms. He sent her letter directly to his daughter Priscilla with a note: 'You will readily [sic] understand my disgust on the receipt of this dear Priscilla. I am as jovial as anybody.'

The revival of interest in Voysey's work and the claims for his influence had little effect on his financial situation, and he continued to live in the small flat in St James's Street and to spend his days at the Arts Club in Dover Street, until, in March 1940, ill-health prevented him from continuing to live alone and he went with his son, Charles Cowles Voysey, to spend the last months of his life in Winchester. Even in the Park House nursing home his taste for fine things continued. *The Times* was delivered daily and regular deliveries of six bottles of his favourite sherry were despatched from London – no mean feat during the war years. He died on 12 February 1941. It was still wartime and the two large chests of his drawings, which he had kept in his rooms at St James's Street, were sent for safe keeping to join the RIBA drawings collection, and after the war they remained with the RIBA. Together with the substantial collection of decorative designs and the architectural designs, which Voysey himself selected to represent his work at the Victoria & Albert Museum, they form a formidable monument to his life's work.

Memorials to his life and work were written by some of the most influential writers of the day; J. M. Richards, John Betjeman and Nikolaus Pevsner wrote his obituaries in the architectural press, and Robert Donat broadcast a fond account of 'Uncle Charles', which was published in *The Architect's Journal*. They were unanimous in their affection for the man and their unreserved admiration for his work. Robert Donat's study has already been recounted at length, but Richards wrote of him as 'a gentle, courteous man who received one in his characteristically furnished study at the top of a long flight of stairs in St James's and talked about times and events that no one else remembered,'[28] and Pevsner wrote with great affection:

So the dear old gentleman with the shrewd and kindly face walks no longer every morning up St. James's Street. No longer will that little figure, somewhat lonely and somewhat pathetic, be seen in his large armchair in the Arts Club. No longer will his gentle voice, growing irritable only when talked to admiringly about his work, be heard; no longer the genuine humility and gracious courtesy of his manner be heard and seen. How patient he was with the eagerly searching visitor, how obliging – only a little fidgety when asked to part for a time with photographs or drawings of his buildings or designs. He hated negligence. A record of the transaction was at once taken and signed by the borrower, and soon the blue cards began to arrive with alarmed questions about the safety of his property.[29]

His importance as a precursor of Modernism was upheld. Pevsner recalled that William Marinus Dudok in Amsterdam had described him as England's greatest living architect and Richards insisted that Voysey's work had come 'as a revelation to the academy-ridden Continent' at the turn of the century, but Voysey's vigorous protests at being associated with contemporary architecture were also recorded. The fact that he never consciously sought to create a new style, that 'the unity of all the parts of a house, however insignificant, and the maintenance of quality in them all was one of the things he stood for' and that, 'gratifying as it is to see his bonds with the present done justice to, it must not be forgotten that the essence of his work and his personality does not belong to our age but to an age gone for ever' were noted with insight and compassion. If Voysey could have read his obituaries he probably would have approved.

10

11

10 *Oak bed, towel-rail, bedside table and lamp.*

11 *Voysey's own easy chair, designed in 1900.*

NOTES

CHAPTER 1

1 Anon, 'C.F. Annesley Voysey – the man and his work – 1', *The Architect and Building News*, VOL. CXVII, 21 January 1927, p. 134.

2 John Betjeman, 'Charles Francis Annesley Voysey, the architect of individualism', *Architectural Review*, VOL. LXX, 1931, p. 93.

3 Charles Voysey (1828–1912) was vice-principal, in conjunction with his brother, of Kingston College. The exact time of Voysey's birth was recorded in a notebook by his mother, now in a private collection.

4 Reverend Charles Voysey and Frances Maria had four sons and six daughters, but Frances Maria's notebook lists eleven, of which one was stillborn at seven months in June 1854.

5 Quoted in John Brandon-Jones, 'C.F.A.Voysey', *Victorian Architecture*, ed. Peter Ferriday, (London, Jonathan Cape, 1963), p. 269.

6 Charles Voysey, 'Defence of the Rev. Charles Voysey, BA. Vicar of Healaugh, on the hearing of the Charges of Heresy preferred against him in the Chancery Court of York on the 1st December, 1869' (London, 1869).

7 M. D. Conway, 'The Voysey case from a heretical standpoint', (1871), p. 4.

8 'The prosecution of the Rev. C. Voysey', *The Times*, 16 August 1869, p. 7.

9 Anon, 'C.F. Annesley Voysey – the man and his work – 1', art. cit. p. 134.

10 *Ibid.*

11 *The Times*, 24 March 1871, p. 7.

12 'Autobiographical notes by C. F. A.Voysey' were loaned in their handwritten form by Voysey's son, Charles Cowles Voysey, to John Brandon-Jones, who donated a typed transcript to the RIBA Library [Voc/1/6(iv)]. A slightly longer version of this autobiography is in a private collection.

13 *Ibid.*

14 These ages are approximate to within a few months, taken from the family tree in George Stevenson, *Memorials of the Wesley Family: Including Biographical and Historical Sketches of all the Members of the Family for Two Hundred and Fifty Years* (London, S. W. Partridge & Co., 1876) and from Frances Maria's book, but the exact date of the family's move to Healaugh is not known.

15 This photograph remained in Voysey's collection throughout his life and is now in a private collection. The handwriting on the back is C. F. A.Voysey's.

16 C. F. A.Voysey, *Individuality* (London, Chapman and Hall Ltd, 1915). A few later sketches by Voysey of rural cottages, however, have survived.

17 *Ibid.*

18 Thomas H. Mawson, *The Life and Work of an English Landscape Architect: an Autobiography* (London, The Richards Press Ltd, 1927), pp. 78–9. According to Mawson, however, 'the two men came to have a great regard for each other, and both agreed, I think, that their fathers had acted a little precipitately'.

19 *Ibid.*

20 Nikolaus Pevsner, 'Charles F. Annesley Voysey', *Architectural Review*, VOL. LXXXIX, May 1941, p. 112.

CHAPTER 2

1 The family first moved to Camden House in Dulwich, and then in 1882 to Woodlawn House, which still stands at 105 College Road.

2 Camille Pissarro, *Dulwich College*, 1871.

3 *Building News*, 1869.

4 This book by Sir Henry Ellis, *The Elgin and Phigaleian Marbles of the Classical Ages in the British Museum* (London, Nattali and Bond), was found in Voysey's personal collection after his death, with an inscription on the frontispiece in his father's hand: 'Charles F. Annesley Voysey Feb 1870'. It is now in a private collection.

5 Interview with C. F. A. Voysey in *The Leeds Mercury*, 10 April 1936, and complete autobiographical notes, private collection.

6 So I am told by John Brandon-Jones.

7 This information is given in an annotated copy of the Dulwich College Register, compiled in 1926 by T. L. Ormison.

8 John Brandon-Jones, 'C.F.A. Voysey', *Victorian Architecture*, ed. Peter Ferriday (London, Jonathan Cape, 1963), p. 270.

9 C. F. A. Voysey, *Individuality* (London, Chapman and Hall Ltd, 1915).

10 *Ibid.*

11 Letter of 8 November 1910 to the *Evening Standard*.

12 Paper on 'City Offices' in the RIBA *Transactions*, 1864–5.

13 J. Coates Carter, 'John Pollard Seddon', *Journal of the RIBA*, VOL. XIII, 1906, p. 221. Carter joined the Seddon office as an improver in 1880, possibly overlapping with Voysey's time there by a few months.

14 C. F. A. Voysey's articles of clerkship. Private collection.

15 The Architectural Association archive records Voysey on the membership roles from the session for 1873–4 to the 1879–80 session, and again, after an unexplained gap between 1880 and 1885, from the 1885 session onwards. His election as a member on 20 December 1878 appears to have been a formality.

16 Obituary, 'Mr. J.P. Seddon', *The Builder*, VOL. XC, 10 February 1906, p. 150.

17 C. F. A. Voysey, '1874 & After', *Architectural Review*, VOL. LXX, October 1931, p. 91.

18 Quoted in John Brandon-Jones, art. cit.

19 Voysey's collection of books passed on his death to his son, Charles Cowles Voysey, and then to a private collection. Those with his bookplate on the frontispiece are often dated in his hand. They include: *An Address Delivered by William Morris at the Distribution of Prizes to Students of the Birmingham Municipal School of Art on February 21 1894* (Chiswick Press, Longman, 1898) – with Voysey's bookplate dated in his hand 6 April 1899 – and *Art and the Beauty of the Earth*, William Morris, (Chiswick Press, Longman, 1898) – with Voysey's bookplate dated in his hand 6 April 1899.

20 'Charles F. Annesley Voysey, 1858–1941: a tribute by Nikolaus Pevsner', *Architectural Review*, May 1941, p. 112.

21 Voysey's contemporaries made regular pilgrimages to Webb houses; and from 1889 The Red House, designed by Webb in 1859 for William Morris, was the home of Charles Holme, who promoted Voysey's work through *The Studio*, so it is conceivable that Voysey may have visited him there.

22 In 1935 W. R. Lethaby's book, *Philip Webb and his Work* was published.

23 C. F. A. Voysey, '1874 & After', art. cit. p. 91.

24 Quoted from Anon, 'C.F. Annesley Voysey – the man and his work – 1', *The Architect and Building News*, VOL. CXVII, 21 January 1927, p. 134.

25 There is a sketch design for this mosaic in the RIBA Drawings Collection, with Voysey's address given as 7 Blandford Road, Bedford Park, suggesting a date of 1885. It is inscribed with the date, August 1887, and this may have been the date when the mosaic was executed.

26 Quoted from Anon, 'C.F. Annesley Voysey – the man and his work – 1', art. cit.

27 James Williams, 'George Devey and his work', *Architectural Association Journal*, VOL. XXIV, no. 266, April 1909, p. 99.

28 Quoted in Jill Allibone, *George Devey, Architect, 1820–1886* (Cambridge, The Lutterworth Press, 1991).

29 Percy G. Stone, 'The late George Devey, Fellow, born 1820, died 1886', RIBA *Journal of Proceedings*, 18 November 1886, p. 46.

30 *Ibid.*

31 James Williams, 'George Devey and his work', art. cit. p. 101.

32 C. F. A. Voysey, '1874 & After', art. cit. p. 91. This statement is queried and rationalized in Jill Allibone, op. cit.

33 See Seddon's designs for Birchington on Sea, V&A D1424–'96, 28 Jan, 1880.

34 Devey's designs for Penshurst were well known among the architectural profession, and the Architectural Association made a visit to the village in 1886.

35 James Williams, art. cit. p. 96.

36 *Ibid.* p. 97. Devey was involved in alterations to 'Swaylands' at Penshurst between 1879 and 1882, while Voysey was an improver in the office.

37 I am indebted to Jeremy Moore for bringing my attention to this sketch in the J. Fremlyn Streatfield Collection: V.1194 VOL. 21, p. 99, Kent Buildings, Kent Archives Office. It was made and dated in 1884 of a building, which is believed to have been demolished c.1874, suggesting that it was made from a photograph.

38 John Williams, op. cit. pp. 96–7.

39 The remaining drawings are in the archive of Pattinson of Windermere.

40 *Ibid.* p. 97.

41 *Ibid.*

42 The drawing for these 'five different types of houses', dated 1876 or after, is in the RIBA Drawings Collection. Voysey was later to make a number of designs for specu-

lative developments including the miners' institute and houses at Whitwood, near Normanton in 1904–5.

43 RIBA Drawings Collection, Devey drawings for Brampton Ash, Northants, for Lord Spencer, 1880 [dev.iv.].

44 Anon, 'C.F. Annesley Voysey – the man and his work – I', *The Architect and Building News*, VOL. CXVII, 21 January 1927, p. 134.

CHAPTER 3

1 His age is given as 26 in Anon, 'C.F. Annesley Voysey – the man and his work – I', *The Architect and Building News*, VOL. CXVII, 21 January 1927, p. 134, and this same article gives his age as 'seven years old when he left Healaugh', when he was in fact within a few months of fourteen years old. Extract from Anon, 'C.F. Annesley Voysey – the man and his work – II', *The Architect and Building News*, VOL. CXVII, 4 February 1927, p. 219.

2 Kelly's *Street Directory* for 1882, compiled the previous autumn, lists 'Charles F. Annesley, architect', at 8 Queen Anne's Gate in its commercial section. He is listed the following year at Broadway Chambers. The rate books show that 8 Queen Anne's Gate and Broadway Chambers were rented to a number of tenants. Voysey was not the ratepayer for either property, his office – probably a single room – would have been sub-let to him and so we cannot ascertain the exact dates of tenancy at Queen Anne's Gate, but the move to Broadway Chambers is recorded among his private papers, now in a private collection.

3 Proof of a pen drawing, RIBA Drawings Collection [564].

4 The earliest of these was an anonymous 'plans for model dwellings' for a Miss Morfit in 1877, and

the following year Voysey designed some cottages for J. T. Trench in Kenmore, Co. Kerry in Ireland, although there is nothing to determine whether they were ever built.

5 Jill Allibone, *George Devey, Architect 1820–1886* (Cambridge, Lutterworth Press, 1991), p. 23.

6 Anon, 'C.F. Annesley Voysey – the man and his work – II', *art. cit.*, p. 219.

7 Anon (possibly Hermann Muthesius), 'CFA Voysey', *Dekorative Kunst*, I, Munich, 1897.

8 'G', 'The revival of English domestic architecture. VI. The work of Mr. C. F. A. Voysey', *The Studio*, VOL. XI, 1897, pp. 17–18.

9 C. F. A. Voysey, 'Ideas in things', *The Arts Connected with Building*, ed. T. Raffles Davison (London, Batsford, 1909).

10 'G' *art. cit.* p. 22.

11 Aymer Vallance, 'Mr. Arthur H. Mackmurdo and the Century Guild', *The Studio*, April 1899, p. 184.

12 A. H. Mackmurdo, 'Autobiographical notes', held in manuscript form at the William Morris Gallery, Walthamstow.

13 Aymer Vallance, *art. cit.* p. 186.

14 A. H. Mackmurdo, *art. cit.*

15 Aymer Vallance, *art. cit.* p. 189.

16 Letter from C. F. A. Voysey to A. H. Mackmurdo, 3 April 1930, William Morris Gallery, Walthamstow. Thornicroft's House, now 16 Redington Road, Hampstead, was designed by Mackmurdo.

17 C. F. A. Voysey, '1874 & After', *Architectural Review*, VOL. LXX, October 1931, p. 92.

18 *Ibid.*

19 Aymer Vallance, *art. cit.* p. 189.

20 A. H. Mackmurdo, *art. cit.*

21 John Brandon-Jones, 'C. F. A. Voysey', *Victorian Architecture*, ed. Peter Ferriday (London, Jonathan Cape, 1963), p. 275.

22 Anon, 'Men who build. No.45. Mr Charles F. Annesley Voysey', *The Builders' Journal and Architectural Review*, 9 September 1896, p. 68.

23 'Dinner to C.F. Annesley Voysey', *Journal of the Royal Institute of British Architects*, VOL. XXXV, 26 November 1927, p. 53.

24 C. F. A. Voysey, 'The aims and conditions of the modern decorator', lecture delivered by Voysey on 15 February, 1895 at the Art Gallery, Mosley Street, Manchester, and published in the *Journal of Decorative Art*, VOL. XV, p. 82.

25 Charles Cowles Voysey, in an unpublished letter to *The Architect's Journal*, 22 February 1941.

26 H. J. L. J. Masse, *The Art Workers' Guild 1884–1934* (London, Art Workers' Guild, 1935).

27 Quoted in *ibid.*

28 *Ibid.*

29 Art Workers' Guild, minutes of meetings, October 1885.

30 Anon, 'C.F. Annesley Voysey – the man and his work – II', *art. cit.* p. 220.

31 *The British Architect*, 25 June 1880.

32 John Brandon-Jones, 'C. F. A. Voysey: an introduction by John Brandon-Jones', *C. F. A. Voysey, Architect and Designer, 1857–1941* (London, Lund Humphries in association with Brighton Art Gallery and Museums, 1978), p. 10.

33 *The Architect*, VOL. XL, 1888, p. 76.

CHAPTER 4

1 It is generally assumed that the 'Design for a Cottage' was designed in 1885, because when it was published in *The British Architect* the illustration was inscribed '7 Blandford Road Bedford Park'. This was Voysey's address from June 1885, and the design is generally thought to have coincided with his marriage.

2 'G', 'The revival of English domestic architec-

ture. VI. The work of Mr. C. F. A. Voysey', *The Studio*, VOL. XI, 1897, p. 21.

3 *The Architect*, VOL. XL, 1888, p. 76.

4 I am indebted to Pat Greger-Murray for bringing my attention to this will, and for so generously sharing her research into the Greaves family history with me. The legacy was quite a small one by Greaves's standards and was probably made to help fund Voysey's case in the Healaugh trials.

5 Anon, 'C.F. Annesley Voysey – the man and his work – III', *The Architect and Building News*, VOL. CXVII, 18 February 1927, p. 315.

6 Although an alternative cement manufacturer was also recommended. See Voysey's specification for Broadleys, RIBA Library.

7 Plans and elevations published in *The British Architect*, VOL. XXXI, 1889, following p. 248. The octagonal hall may have been influenced by Seddon's designs for seaside houses at Birchington of c.1881.

8 A design for a bungalow at Bellagio was published in *The British Architect*, on 10 June 1898, relating to an entry in Voysey's black book for a 'Design for house at Bellagio for E. Allport, Esquire' in 1889.

9 *The British Architect* published plans and elevations for a drinking fountain 'to be erected to the memory of Mrs Henrietta Bellended Sayer at Southampton' on 10 May 1889, and for a 'Dove-cot for M.H. Lakin Esqre' on 30 August 1889.

10 'Domestic architecture. By C. F. A. Voysey. No.2 – a tower house', *The British Architect*, VOL. XXXI, 25 January 1889, p. 70.

11 *Ibid.*

12 *Ibid.*

13 According to his obituary in *The Builder*, of 16 January 1904, Snell, 'continued to retain

a keen interest in all matters relating to the planning of hospitals and their ventilation' even in his retirement.

14 C. F. A. Voysey, 'Remarks on domestic entrance halls', *The Studio*, VOL. XXI, 1901, p. 243.

15 *The British Architect*, VOL. XXXVI, 18 September 1891, p. 210; *The Builder's Journal & Architectural Record*, VOL. IV, 1896, p. 68.

16 Voysey noted on a scrap of paper that he 'Took 11 Melina Place for 14 years' on 25 March 1891, but the census for 16 April 1891 found the Voysey family still in residence at 45 Tierney Road, Streatham Hill, so presumably decorations were completed before the family moved in.

17 John Brandon-Jones, 'C. F. A. Voysey', *Victorian Architecture*, ed. Peter Ferriday (London, Jonathan Cape, 1963), p. 280.

18 Voysey's 'New Wing to The Cliff, Warwick' for M. H. Lakin is listed in the black book, and I am indebted to Mrs Pat Greger-Murray for describing his alterations to the interior of the house.

19 'G', 'The revival of English domestic architecture. VI. The work of Mr. C. F. A. Voysey', *art. cit.* p. 20.

20 *Ibid.* p. 25.

21 *The British Architect*, *art. cit.* p. 209.

22 A. W. N. Pugin, 'The true principles of pointed or Christian architecture', London 1841, p. 47 (London, Academy Editions, 1973, p. 47).

23 *The British Architect* of September 1891 states that 'the house is to be built on the Parade at Bedford park', suggesting that construction of the Forster house began after September 1891. The first drawing for a house for J. W. Forster was made in 1888, therefore, Walnut Tree Farm was designed and built between this early

drawing and the completion of the final design of the Forster house.

24 *The British Architect*, VOL. XXXIV, 24 October 1890, p. 302.

25 'G', 'The revival of English domestic architecture. VI. The work of Mr. C. F. A. Voysey', *art. cit.* p. 20.

26 *Ibid.*

27 'Houses for people with hobbies, Walnut-Tree Farm, Castlemorten', *Country Life*, 28 October 1899, p. 525.

28 *Ibid.*

29 *The British Architect*, VOL. XXXIV, 19 September 1890 and 24 October 1890.

30 'Houses for people with hobbies, Walnut-Tree Farm, Castlemorten', *art. cit.* p. 525.

31 'G', 'The revival of English domestic architecture. VI. The work of Mr. C. F. A. Voysey', *art. cit.*

32 *Ibid.* p. 24.

33 *The American Architect and Building News* published plans VOL. XXX, 1890, p. 75, pl. 775; *The Studio* published a perspective and photograph of the exterior in VOL. XI, 1897; and *Country Life* reproduced plans, elevations and a photograph on 28 October 1899.

34 Catalogue of the 1904 St Louis International Exhibition, The British Section, 1906.

35 The design published in *The British Architect*, 18 December 1891 was described: 'This cottage was designed for an artist, for whom Mr.Voysey is building one, a little, but not much, larger.'

36 The design published in *The British Architect* on 18 December 1891 had a smaller studio with a gallery across one corner.

37 *The British Architect*, 18 December 1891, p. 456.

38 Compare these profiles with the portrait of Voysey by Harold Speed of 1896 in the National Portrait Gallery.

39 *The British Architect*, 1 January 1892, p. 5.

40 *Ibid.*

41 An additional elevation for the Swan Walk houses was published, substituting simple triangular gables behind a parapet, and incorporating carved angels set into niches between the second floor windows.

42 *The British Architect*, 18 March 1892, p. 208.

43 'G', 'The revival of English domestic architecture. VI. The work of Mr C. F. A. Voysey', *art. cit.*

44 Conrad Dressler was to commission Voysey to design a row of four studios for him in Glebe Place, Chelsea, the following year.

45 'G', 'The revival of English domestic architecture. VI. The work of Mr C. F. A. Voysey', *art. cit.* p. 23.

46 *Ibid.*

47 H. T. (possibly Horace Townsend), 'Artistic Houses', *The Studio*, VOL. I, 1893, p. 222. The treatment of the decorative panel in the accompanying photograph on p. 225 might suggest that the safety panel was not at that time erected, and was touched in by hand on the photograph.

48 According to *The Builder*, VOL. LXXI, 29 August 1896, Mackmurdo's 12 Hans Road was built in 1893, but T. Raffles Davison's 'Rambling Sketches' of 14 and 16 Hans Road, published in *The British Architect* on 9 February 1894, show a gaping hole in the terrace where number 12 should have been.

49 I am grateful to John Brandon-Jones for telling me this anecdote, told to him by one of Voysey's pupils, Haslam. In later years the friendship between Voysey and Mackmurdo appears to have been restored.

CHAPTER 5

1 Unpublished letter from Charles Cowles Voysey to Mr Wright at *Architectural Review*, 21 February 1941. Private collection.

2 Mrs E. Hall, Voysey's niece, in conversation with the author, 16 January 1993.

3 Anon, 'An interview with Mr. Charles F. Annesley Voysey, architect and designer', *The Studio*, VOL. I, 1893, p. 232.

4 *Ibid.*

5 Hampson, iii. 167.

6 The artist, F. Salisbury, was also a member of the Arts Club. Having been commissioned to make a portrait of Wesley he noticed that Voysey resembled the engravings of Wesley that he had been sent, and, without knowing his descendency asked Voysey if he would sit for the portrait. Voysey was delighted by the coincidence.

7 Robert Donat, 'Uncle Charles', *The Architect's Journal*, VOL. XCIII, 1941, pp. 193–4.

8 *The Studio* interview, *art. cit.* p. 232.

9 *Ibid.*

10 Voysey showed eleven pieces in the second exhibition of the Arts and Crafts Exhibition Society in 1889, of which ten were designs for printed fabrics or wallpapers. The exception was a cinerary urn in copper and iron – one of a number of crematory urns designed by Voysey in the 1880s.

11 *The Studio* interview, *art. cit.* p. 233.

12 Contemporary photographs show that Voysey's study, the play room, and at least two of the bedrooms at The Orchard and the hall at Annesley Lodge were patterned with Voysey wallpapers.

13 *The Studio* interview, *art. cit.* p. 233.

14 *Ibid.*

15 C. F. A. Voysey, 'The aims of a modern decorator', a lecture given in Manchester, 15 February 1895; published in *The Journal of Decorative Art*, VOL. 15, April 1895, pp. 82–90.

16 C. F. A. Voysey, speech recorded in 'Dinner to C. F. Annesley Voysey', *Journal of the Royal Insti-* *tute of British Architects*, VOL. XXXV, 26 November 1928, p. 53.

17 *The Studio* interview, *art. cit.* p. 233.

18 These monoprints were found in an envelope, labelled 'Hyslop's Prints' with Voysey's papers after his death. They are now in a private collection.

19 When I opened Voysey's copy of this book, published in 1905 by Frederick Warne & Co an old leaf, pressed and dried, fell from between its pages.

20 C. F. A. Voysey, 'The aims of a modern decorator', *art. cit.*

21 *The Studio* interview, *art. cit.*

22 *Ibid.*

23 *The Studio* interview, *art. cit.* p. 235.

24 *Modern British Domestic Architecture and Decoration*, ed. Charles Holme (London, *The Studio*, 1901), pp. 185–9.

25 C. F. A. Voysey, *Individuality* (London, Chapman and Hall, 1915).

26 C. F. A. Voysey, 'Symbolism in design', unpublished manuscript in the RIBA Drawings Collection, 1930.

27 The crest was worked into Barry's terracotta panels below the windows of the centre block.

28 C. F. A. Voysey, 'The aims of a modern decorator', *art. cit.*

29 Mrs E. Hall, Voysey's niece, in conversation with the author, 16 January 1993.

30 *The Studio* interview, *art. cit.* p. 237.

31 C. F. A. Voysey, 'The aims of a modern decorator', *art. cit.*

32 *Ibid.*

33 Anon, 'Men who build. No. 45. Mr. Charles F. Annesley Voysey', *The Builder's Journal & Architectural Review*, VOL. IV, 9 September 1896, p. 67.

34 C. F. A. Voysey, 'Domestic furniture', *Journal of the RIBA*, VOL. I, pp. 415–18.

35 *Ibid.*

36 'Architectural notes', *The Studio*, VOL. I., 1893, p. 37.

37 This date can be surmised from the address on the sheet – Broadway Chambers, Westminster – the offices Voysey inhabited from 1882 to 1885.

38 See *The Pugin Family* catalogue in the RIBA Drawings Collection.

39 C. F. A. Voysey, 'Domestic furniture', *art. cit.*

40 *Ibid.*

41 *Ibid.*

42 *Ibid.*

43 A copy of Elsley's catalogue of designs by C. F. A. Voysey is in the RIBA Drawings Collection. The cover for the catalogue was almost certainly designed by Voysey, and Lutyens used switch plates and probably other metalwork by Voysey at Goddards.

44 'The Arts and Crafts Exhibition, 1896, (Third Notice)', *The Studio*, VOL. IX, 1896, p. 190.

45 *Ibid.*

46 *Ibid.* p.196.

47 C. F. A. Voysey's black book.

48 Anon, 'Men who build. No. 45. Mr. Charles F. Annesley Voysey', *art. cit.* p. 69.

49 *Ibid.* p. 67.

50 C. F. A. Voysey, 'The aims and conditions of the modern decorator', *art. cit.*

51 *Ibid.*

52 'Men who build. No.45. Mr. Charles F. Annesley Voysey', *art. cit.* p. 68.

53 *Ibid.* p. 6.

54 See John Brandon-Jones, 'An architect's letters to his client', *The Architect and Building News*, VOL. CXCV, 1949, pp. 494–8.

55 *Ibid.*

56 C. F. A. Voysey, 'Autobiographical notes', typescript in the RIBA Library.

57 Anon, 'Men who build. No.45. Mr. Charles F. Annesley Voysey', *art. cit.* p. 67.

58 *Ibid.*

CHAPTER 6

1 Hermann Muthesius, *Das englische Haus,* first published by Wasmuth, Berlin in 1904. English edition published by Granada Publishing Ltd, Crosby Lockwood Staples, 1979, p. 70.

2 *Ibid.*

3 Voysey's black book lists the house under 1893 and the earliest plan is dated 29 December 1893, but the elevation for the garden front was completed 3 February 1894.

4 C. F. A. Voysey, black book.

5 *The British Architect*, VOL. XLIV, 13 December 1895, p. 418.

6 The tower was more detached from the service wing of the house before Voysey extended the house in 1903–4 and 1907. The porthole windows and lead roof are reminiscent of the Forster House.

7 C. F. A. Voysey, 'Ideas in things', *The Arts Connected with Building*, ed. T. Raffles Davison (London, Batsford, 1909).

8 C. F. A. Voysey, 'The English home', *The British Architect*, VOL. 75, 27 January 1911, pp. 60, 69 & 70.

9 This was said by Betjeman as he opened the door to The Orchard during the television film *Metroland*.

10 C. F. A. Voysey, 'Ideas in things', *art. cit.*

11 C. F. A. Voysey, 'The English home', *art. cit.*

12 *Ibid.*

13 C. F. A. Voysey, 'Ideas in things', *art. cit.*

14 C. F. A. Voysey, 'Remarks on domestic entrance halls', *The Studio*, VOL. XXI, 1901, p. 243.

15 *Ibid.*

16 *Ibid.*

17 'Country cottages and Surrey hills', *The British Architect*, VOL.XLI, 29 June 1894, p.451.

18 *Ibid.*

19 *Ibid.*

20 C.F.A. Voysey, 'Ideas in things', *art. cit.*

21 Hermann Muthesius, *op. cit.* p. 10.

22 C. F. A. Voysey, 'Ideas in things', *art. cit.*

23 Auction sale details: 'By order of E.J. Horniman, Esq., J. P. "Lowicks" Frensham'. For auction held by Messrs Wilson & Gray, 22 July 1914.

24 Quoted in Duncan Simpson, 'C.F.A. Voysey, an architect of individuality', *Double Lives*, William Plomer (London, Jonathan Cape, 1943).

25 Although he is known to have designed an oak chest, a frame and a kitchen dresser for Perrycroft, these were designed in 1907 and 1908 to coincide with extensions to the house.

26 And in the same year, 1894, his black book shows that he was given the laying out of the garden at Walnut Tree Farm.

27 Auction sale details, *op. cit.*

28 *Ibid.*

29 Hermann Muthesius, *op. cit.* p. 10.

30 Peter Davey has pointed out to me that few architects refuse a client wielding a cheque book. Whether or not Voysey was one of these is open to speculation.

31 According to Voysey's niece, Mrs E. Hall, Reverend Voysey regularly removed the dummies from babies' mouths on Hampstead Heath as a point of principle, and he was held in awe by all who knew him, including C. F. A. Voysey.

32 Stuart Durant suggested, in his book *C.F.A. Voysey* (London, Academy Editions, 1992) that Annesley Lodge may have been financed by Devey's bequest to Reverend Voysey of £2,000, but this bequest was made in 1886, nine years before the design of the house.

33 C. F. A. Voysey, 'Ideas in things', *art. cit.*

34 The Building Act insisted that the area was to be 'throughout the width of the building' and there was a dispute as to whether the south-east or the north-east side of Voysey's plan should be classified as the width. See *The British Architect*, VOL. XLV, 28 February 1896, p. 148.

35 When the plans and elevations were published in *The British Architect* (28 February 1896) the two aspects of the entrance elevations were shown in place of the more usual all round view.

36 C. F. A. Voysey, 'Ideas in things', *art. cit.*

37 *Ibid.*

38 *Ibid.*

39 Voysey's white book of office expenses, now in a private collection, lists expenses for curtain hooks, 'Rods to 1st curtains of study' and 'Curtains and tablecloth' for Annesley Lodge between April and June 1897.

40 'G', 'The revival of English domestic architecture. VI. The work of Mr. C.F.A. Voysey', *The Studio*, VOL. XL, 1897, p. 18. It is in this article that it was said of Lowicks, 'The Ideal of a modest country house is surely realised here' (see chapter title).

41 'Voysey's books of professional and office expenses, now in a private collection, show regular and relatively large sums spent on photography and itemize expenses incurred in visiting houses re photography.

42 Reverend Voysey's will is in a private collection.

CHAPTER 7

1 Hermann Muthesius, *Das englische Haus* (Berlin, Wasmuth, 1904).

2 The house was also known as Merlshanger and as Wancote.

3 Anon, 'Men who build. No. 45. Mr. Charles F. Annesley Voysey', *The Builders' Journal and Architectural Review*, VOL. IV, 9 September 1896, p. 68.

4 C.F.A. Voysey, 'Ideas in things', *The Arts Connected with Building*, ed. T. Raffles Davison (London, Batsford, 1909).

5 Excluding an additional six sheets for the stables and lodge.

6 C. F. A. Voysey, 'The aims and conditions of the modern decorator', a lecture given in Manchester, 15 February 1895; published in *The Journal of* *Decorative Art*, VOL. 15, April 1895, pp. 82–90.

7 *The British Architect*, VOL. XLII, 6 July 1894, p. 6.

8 *The British Architect,* VOL. XLIX, 29 April 1898, p. 291.

9 C. F. A. Voysey, *Individuality* (London, Chapman and Hall Ltd, 1915), p. 25.

10 C. F. A. Voysey, 'The English home', *The British Architect*, VOL. 75, 27 January 1911.

11 C. F. A. Voysey, *Individuality, op. cit.* p. 25.

12 *Ibid.*

13 Anon, 'Men who build. No. 45. Mr . Charles F. Annesley Voysey', *art. cit.* p. 68.

14 Correspondence between the Reverend Leighton Grane and Lord Middleton, and between Lord Middleton and his son, St John Brodrick MP is in the collection of Mr R. Clapshaw.

15 Letter from Reverend Leighton Grane to Lord Middleton, dated 4 March 1897.

16 An octagonal bay in the dining room, designed, like that of Walnut Tree Farm, to catch the sunshine throughout the day, was replaced by a curved polygonal bay to match those in the drawing room and library, and the front porch was marked, 'make round window smaller and higher and add hood for projecting porch'.

17 'Some recent designs for domestic architecture', *The Studio*, VOL. XXXIV, 1905, p. 152. These are the same photographs by F. Müntzer, first published in *The British Architect*, VOL. LII, 6 October 1899, pp. 234–5.

18 The wrought-iron stay appears in the above photograph, fastened above the circular window, and in the perspective drawing, fastened below the window. There is a drawing for it, dated 15 December 1897, in the RIBA Drawings Collection [125.4].

19 Voysey had already used an ogee-shaped roof in the white tower in the entrance courtyard at

Perrycroft, and in an extension of 1908 he used a similar section of roof to those at Norney.

20 C. F. A. Voysey, black book.

21 *The British Architect*, VOL. 67, 6 October 1899, p. 238.

22 Letter from Reverend Grane to Lord Middleton, 1 May 1900.

23 I am indebted to Frederick Müntzer's granddaughter, Miss D. Müntzer for this information.

24 I have this information from the present owners of Norney. The wall is plastered and so its structure cannot be inspected. I hope that if such an opportunity arises I shall be invited!

25 C. F. A. Voysey, 'Ideas in things', *art. cit.*

26 C. F. A. Voysey, *Individuality, op. cit.* p. 98.

27 C. F. A. Voysey's remark from 'L'Art Nouveau: What it is and what is thought of it, a symposium', *The Magazine of Art*, VOL. 2, 1904, pp. 211–12.

28 C. F. A. Voysey, 'Remarks on domestic entrance halls', *The Studio*, VOL. XXI, 1901, p. 242.

29 Maureen Duffy, *A Thousand Capricious Chances. A History of the Methuen List 1889–1989*, (London, Methuen, 1989).

30 Voysey's white book of office expenses show that his first visit to Haslemere for A. M. M. Stedman was made on 13 October 1897.

31 The perspective watercolour was made by H. Gaye.

32 The garden and its planting is described in detail in W. Duggan, 'The Gardens at New Place, Haslemere', *The Garden*, 6 August 1921.

33 Gertrude Jekyll redesigned the rose-garden. See drawings at Reef Point Gardens Collection.

34 The perspectives for Norney and New Place were both drawn by H. Gaye, as were the perspectives for Greyfriars and The Hill at Thorpe

Mandeville in 1897–8.

35 The earliest surviving block plan for New Place is dated 5 December 1897, whereas the preliminary drawing for Norney was made the previous May.

36 Thomas Elsley supplied a range of Voysey rainwater-goods, but there are no down pipe brackets in their catalogue and it is now known whether or not their crenellated rainwater-heads were in production as early as 1897.

37 Hermann Muthesius, *Das englische Haus, op. cit.* p. 203.

38 *Ibid.* p. 89.

39 A drawing for this table, and Thurston's records are deposited at the Victoria & Albert Museum.

40 Anon, 'Men who build. No. 45. Mr. Charles F. Annesley Voysey', *art. cit.* p. 68.

41 Country houses on the banks of Lake Windermere were equipped with their own jetties and often with their own boathouses, although none of Voysey's designs for a boathouse for Broadleys were built.

42 Aymer Vallance, 'Some recent work by C.F.A. Voysey', *The Studio*, VOL. XXXI, 1905, p. 127.

43 *Ibid.*

44 C. F. A. Voysey, 'Ideas in things', *art. cit.*

45 This veranda has been filled in.

46 '"Broad Leys", Windermere', *The British Architect*, VOL. LII, 13 October 1899.

47 *Ibid.*

48 'Specification for works' for Broadleys. A copy of this is deposited at the RIBA Library.

49 I am grateful to Alan Rhodes for sharing his working knowledge of the structure of Broadleys and Moorcrag with me.

50 Drawing for grotesque in RIBA Drawings Collection [138.5].

51 The balusters were priced at 2s.4d. each, and Simpson also made the deal veranda seat at Broadleys.

52 From W. B. Reynolds's account for light-fittings in the archive of Pattinson of Windermere.

53 From The Teale Fireplace Company of Leeds.

54 From Stanley Brothers Ltd, Nuneaton.

55 Sir Michael Lakin was one of Voysey's earliest patrons. He commissioned The Cottage at Bisthop's Itchington.

56 This specification for roughcast in Voysey's handwriting is in the archive of Pattinson of Windermere. They suggest that the pebbles for the roughcast were probably dredged from the Lake to ensure textural variation.

57 See Voysey's white book of office expenses.

58 These drawings are in the archive of Pattinson of Windermere.

59 These items cannot be positively associated with Broadleys, although the RIBA Drawings Collection catalogue for Voysey suggests that they are connected with the Broadleys drawing of 1904.

CHAPTER 8

1 E. B. S., 'Country cottages', *Country Life*, VOL. III, 19 February 1898, pp. 195–7.

2 At 7 Hill Road, St John's Wood, London.

3 Drawings of alternative plans and elevations for this studio were published in *The British Architect*, VOL. 50, in August 1898, but according to Voysey's black book it was designed in 1893.

4 The inn was built of local bricks with a green-slate roof and an arrangement of windows and chimneys that was characteristic of Voysey's style. J. W. Forster painted the signboard.

5 The cottages were rebuilt by Voysey with slate roofs after a fire in 1914.

6 'G', 'The revival of English domestic architecture. VI. The work of Mr. C.F.A. Voysey', *The Studio*, VOL. XI, 1897, p. 24.

7 *Ibid.*

8 Voysey made his first site visits for both houses on 8 and 9 May 1898. The preliminary design for Broadleys was dated June 1898 and the first drawings for Moorcrag were made the following month.

9 Plans and elevations inscribed by Voysey in the Victoria & Albert Museum, no. E255, 1913.

10 *The Architect and Contract Reporter*, VOL. 78, 8 November 1907, p. 296.

11 Aymer Valance, 'Some recent work by Mr. C.F.A. Voysey', *The Studio*, VOL. XXXI, 1905–6, p. 130.

12 *Ibid.*

13 See Gill Cottage and The Homestead, within two hundred yards of Moorcrag on the Cartmel Fell Road, built in 1719.

14 Photographs of Moorcrag, published in 1902 in *The Builder's Journal & Architectural Record*, show that the two-storey bay was not originally tile hung and there was no door from the parlour on to the veranda. By 1907, however, when photographs of Moorcrag were published in *The Architect*, both the tile hanging and the door were in place.

15 Voysey quoted on the design of Broome Cottage at Windermere in Horace Townsend, 'Notes on country and suburban houses designed by C.F.A. Voysey', *The Studio*, VOL. XVI, 1899, p. 160.

16 Robert Gilchrist recounted this story. He knew Mrs Spellar, one of the Buckley daughters who lived in the house until the 1970s.

17 See RIBA Drawing [140.2] dated 9 July 1898.

18 The builder was G. H. Pattinson and the joiner was John Edmondson, both of Windermere.

19 According to *The Builder's Journal & Architectural Record*, VOL. XVI, p. 176: 'every room is oak-lined to a height of 6 ft.

6 in., with plain white plaster above'. Not every room was panelled to this height, but there is no evidence to suggest that other colours were used.

20 C. F. A. Voysey, 'Ideas in things', *The Arts Connected with Building*, ed. T. Raffles Davison (London, Batsford, 1909).

21 *The Architect & Contract Reporter*, VOL. 78, 8 November 1907, p. 296.

22 The servants' quarters at Moorcrag were compact because their living accommodation was arranged over the coach house and in a separate, much older building on the site, Crag Lodge. The single servant's bedroom was the housekeeper's room in case she was required during the night.

23 C. F. A. Voysey, 'The English Home', *The British Architect*, VOL. 75, 27 January 1911.

24 Probably with the same white tiles that were used at Broadleys, from Martin van Straaten of 30 Little Britain, London EC. The present owners of Moorcrag were told that these tiles had been shipped from Delft as ballast, and Voysey's book of office expenses records a visit to Van Straaten's on April 1 1901 for Moorcrag.

25 Voysey's office expenses record 'Expenses to Liberty's re curtains' for Moorcrag on 15 April 1901 and he travelled to Windermere on the same day.

26 These were photographed at the house in 1976 before the dispersal of the Buckley family effects. See National Monuments Record photograph BB76/1869. They also appear in the Elsley catalogue of Voysey designs.

27 The design for this bed, dated February 1901, is in the RIBA Drawings Collection [169], and it remained in the house until the dispersal of the Buckley effects, after 1976.

28 C. F. A. Voysey, 'Ideas in Things', *art. cit.*

29 Horace Townsend, 'Notes on country and suburban houses designed by C.F.A. Voysey', *The Studio*, VOL. XVI, 1899, p. 157.

30 See list of office addresses.

31 A copy of this manuscript list is in the RIBA Library.

32 Anon, 'C.F. Annesley Voysey. The man and his work – v', *The Architect & Building News*, VOL. CXVII, 4 March 1927, p. 406.

33 He knew R. H. Haslam, who was Voysey's pupil from 1895.

34 John Brandon-Jones, 'C.F.A. Voysey', *Victorian Architecture*, ed. Peter Ferriday (London, Jonathan Cape, 1963), p. 276.

35 Gaye does not appear on Voysey's list of pupils, but he was employed to make perspective drawings of Greyfriars, The Hill at Thorpe Mandeville, New Place and Norney, all in 1897. In the catalogue to the Batsford Gallery exhibition of 1931 Voysey wrote that of the twenty perspectives exhibited, fifteen were by Howard Gaye F.R.I.B.A. and the remaining five were his own drawings.

36 Voysey's son, Charles Cowles Voysey, described his father's working method in an unpublished letter to *The Architect's Journal* on 22 February 1941.

37 According to Voysey's office expenses book, typing was regularly sent out to a Miss Waite.

38 Voysey's office expenses show telephone charges from 1906 and his book of professional expenses, also in a private collection, has an entry for 'Telephone for office' and the relatively very high cost of £7.10.0 made on 11 September 1906. See also letters from S. C. Turner, General Manager of the Essex and Suffolk Equitable Insurance Company dated 14 and 29 Novem-

ber 1906. These letters are in the archive of Guardian Royal Exchange Limited.

39 See Voysey's professional and office expenses books.

40 M. H. Baillie Scott, 'On the characteristics of Mr. C.F.A. Voysey's architecture', *The Studio*, VOL. XLII, October 1907, pp. 19–24.

41 There are two designs for this cottage in the RIBA Drawings Collection and it is listed in Voysey's black book as 'House at Colwall for self'.

42 C. F. A. Voysey, '"The Orchard," Chorley Wood, Herts', *Architectural Review*, VOL. X, 1901, pp. 32–3.

43 This figure was given in A. M. Shaw's 'Houses for people with hobbies. The Orchard', *Country Life*, 30 September 1899. Plans and a perspective sketch of The Orchard were published in the article, but Voysey's own black book rather curiously dates the house 1900.

44 The dormers in the end elevations were later additions.

45 Voysey rather curiously described the roof as of 'green American slates in graduating courses' in *Architectural Review*, 1901.

46 C.F. A. Voysey, 'The Orchard', *art. cit.*

47 *Ibid.*

48 The lecture was given on 15 February 1895 and published in *The Journal of Decorative Art*, VOL. XV, April 1895, pp. 82–90.

49 C. F. A. Voysey, 'The English home', *art. cit.* pp. 60, 69 & 70.

50 C. F. A. Voysey, 'Ideas in things', *art. cit.*

51 C. F. A. Voysey, 'The Orchard', *art. cit.*

52 *Ibid.*

53 See Horace Townsend, *art. cit.* p. 160.

54 C. F. A. Voysey, 'Ideas in things', *art. cit.*

55 *Ibid.*

56 *Ibid.*

57 This quote from Voysey's daughter, Priscilla, was recounted to me by the present owners of The Orchard, who were visited by Priscilla Voysey.

58 C. F. A. Voysey, 'The Orchard', *art. cit.*

59 I am reminded by John Brandon-Jones that Philip Webb and Richard Norman Shaw also deliberately refrained from using French windows.

60 Nikolaus Pevsner, 'Charles F. Annesley Voysey', *Architectural Review*, vol. LXXXIX, May 1941, p. 113.

61 *Ibid.*

62 A. M. Shaw, 'Houses for people with hobbies. The Orchard', *Country Life*, 30 September 1899, p. 389.

63 *Ibid.*

64 *Ibid.*

65 C. F. A. Voysey, 'Remarks on domestic entrance halls', *The Studio*, vol. XXII, 1901, p. 244.

66 C. F. A. Voysey, 'Ideas in Things', *art. cit.*

67 This specification is taken from a letter from Voysey to one of his clients, S. C. Turner of 18 October 1906. The letter is in the archive of Guardian Royal Exchange Limited.

68 C. F. A. Voysey, 'Remarks on domestic entrance halls', *art. cit.* pp. 244–6.

69 Horace Townsend, *art. cit.* p. 157.

70 C. F. Annesley Voysey, '1874 & After', *Architectural Review*, vol. LXX, October 1931, p.91.

71 Horace Townsend, *art. cit.* p. 157.

72 Anon, 'Some recent designs by Mr. Voysey', *The Studio*, vol. VII, May 1896, pp. 209–19.

73 See Hermann Muthesius, *The English House* (Crosby Lockwood Staples, Granada Publishing Ltd, 1979), pl. 78.

74 C. F. A. Voysey, *Architectural Association Notes*, vol. XIX, May 1904, p. 73.

75 It is not known how Voysey and Simpson met, but the two men knew one another by 1896 when a bedroom or invalid's chair designed by Voysey and executed by Simpson was exhibited at the Arts and Crafts Exhibition Society Show. It is not possible that they met through the Art Work-

ers' Guild because Voysey introduced Simpson to the Guild and he was not formally elected a member until 1913.

76 I am indebted to Arthur W. Simpson's granddaughter for this information.

77 *The Studio*, vol. XVIII, October 1899, p. 46.

78 C. F. A. Voysey, *Individuality* (London, Chapman & Hall, 1915), pp. 115–16.

79 C. F. A. Voysey, 'The aims and conditions of the modern decorator', *The Journal of Decorative Art*, vol. 15, April 1895, pp. 47–8.

80 C. F. A. Voysey, 'The English home', *art. cit.* pp. 60, 69 & 70.

81 C. F. A. Voysey, 'Ideas in things', *art. cit.*

82 *The British Architect*, vol. LXXIII, 4 March 1910, p. 160.

CHAPTER 9

1 Victoria & Albert Museum, E152 – 1974.

2 Note in Voysey's hand on a similar 'Halcyone' design for wallpaper or textile in the RIBA drawings collection [708], dated 31 March 1904.

3 This is an unpublished typescript in the RIBA Drawings Collection.

4 'Modern symbolism', report of a lecture delivered by Voysey on 6 February 1918 at Carpenters' Hall, London. *The Architect & Contract Reporter*, vol.99, 15 February 1918, pp.102–3.

5 *Ibid.*

6 *Ibid.*

7 Henry van de Velde published articles 'Artistic wallpapers' in *Emulation*, vol. XVIII, Brussels 1893, and on 'Essex & Co.'s Westminster wallpapers', *L'Art Moderne*, vol. XIV, Brussels, 1894.

8 According to Elizabeth Aslin in *C.F.A. Voysey: Architect and Designer 1857–1941* (London, Lund Humphries with Brighton Museum and Art Gallery, 1978), p. 100.

9 C. F. A. Voysey, quoted in 'L'Art Nouveau: What it is and what is thought of it, a symposium', *The*

Magazine of Art, vol. II, 1904, pp. 211–12.

10 C. F. A. Voysey, 'Autobiographical notes', typed by John Brandon-Jones from a manuscript in Voysey's hand, and now in the RIBA Library.

11 I am indebted to John Brandon-Jones for this information.

12 Although arches were used decoratively and structurally at The Pastures in 1901.

13 This latch appears to be identical to one designed for an entrance gate at Moorcrag in 1900. See RIBA Drawings Collection [140.5].

14 C. T. Burke lived at 24 Charles Street, Hatton Gardens, and S. C. Turner at 37 Circus Road, St John's Wood.

15 Photograph published in *Moderne Bauformen*, vol. X, 1911, p. 255. Voysey later designed two clock cases for C. T. Burke in c.1921.

16 C. F. A. Voysey, 'The English home', *The British Architect*, vol. 75, 27 January 1911, pp. 60, 69 & 70.

17 C. F. A. Voysey, 'Ideas in things', *The Arts Connected with Building*, ed. T. Raffles Davison (London, Batsford, 1909).

18 C. F. A. Voysey, 'The English home', *art. cit.*

19 Voysey's white book of office expenses shows a visit to 'Collard & Collard re piano' on 25 November 1908.

20 Although, according to his niece, Voysey had a liking for primrose-yellow walls and this would hardly show in a black and white photograph.

21 A drawing for a writing table for Turner, designed in February 1906 was annotated, 'Both sides to have drawers below desk and add. looking glass for Burke & One as this & one with glass. This one to have 2 cupbds & no drawers' (RIBA Drawings Collection [425]). The single bed at Holly Mount, too, was very similar to one

designed for Turner in November 1906, except that the head-and-tail boards to Turner's bed were each pierced with a single cut-out heart. However, The Homestead furniture was probably slightly earlier than that for Holly Mount. Voysey's office expenses show that he made his first visit to Nielsen on Turner's behalf in August 1906, compared to January 1908 for Burke. The bed at Holly Mount was probably made by Thallon in April/May 1906.

22 M. Macartney, 'Recent English domestic architecture', *Architectural Review*, 1911.

23 He also had rooms in Colchester, close to the head office of the Essex & Suffolk Equitable Insurance Society.

24 On a more practical level, Voysey incorporated fewer windows in this south-facing elevation because it faced another building plot.

25 W., 'The lesser country houses of to-day: The Homestead, Frinton-on-Sea, designed by Mr. C. F. A. Voysey', *Country Life*, 1 October 1910, pp. 7–11.

26 *Ibid.*

27 The words 'Produits Ceramiques Refractaire de Marchienne Au-Pont' are written on the reverse of the tiles. A description of their maintenance was give to me by Mrs Rosalie Smith, who worked as a housemaid at The Homestead from 1938.

28 Voysey's white book of office expenses shows that these letter tiles were first used at Bushey and paid for on 27 June 1904. They were supplied to The Homestead on 8 February 1906.

29 Although the tiling was more decorative over the porch.

30 C. F. A. Voysey, 'The English home', *art. cit.*

31 I am indebted to John Brandon-Jones who knew Mr Ames, of Ames and Finnis, for telling me this story.

32 W., 'The lesser country houses of to-day. The Homestead, Frinton-on-Sea, designed by Mr. C. F. A. Voysey', *art. cit.*

33 C. F. A. Voysey, 'Ideas in things', *art. cit.*

34 *Ibid.*

35 Voysey's book of professional expenses.

36 W., 'The lesser country houses of to-day. The Homestead, Frinton-on-Sea, designed by Mr. C. F. A. Voysey', *art. cit.*

37 I am grateful to Mrs Rosalie Smith, who worked at The Homestead as a housemaid from 1938, for describing the household management of the house after the war.

38 W., 'The lesser country houses of to-day. The Homestead, Frinton-on-Sea, designed by Mr C. F. A. Voysey', *art. cit.*

39 Hermann Muthesius, *Das englische Haus*, (Berlin, Wasmuth, 1904), p. 100.

40 See cutting of sales details c.1906, RIBA Collection of Photographs.

41 There is a copy of the specification for Broadleys at the RIBA Library.

42 See drawing in RIBA collection [46.9].

43 Müntzer's son, Tom, was a pupil with Voysey and designed the extensions to Priorsfield School.

CHAPTER 10

1 Voysey's office expenses show that a shield for the cottage hospital was carved by A. W. Simpson in Kendal, but this may have been the slate plaque or a wooden shield inside the entrance hall.

2 'A cottage hospital', *The Builder's Journal & Architectural Record*, vol. XVIII, 3 June 1903, p. 231.

3 Chips in the paintwork at the hospital at the time of writing show the original finish to have been green paint or stain on heavy deal doors.

4 'A cottage hospital', *art. cit.*

5 H. G. Wells, *Experiment in Autobiography*, vol. II (London, Victor Gollancz Ltd and The

Cresset Press Ltd, 1934), p. 639.

6 *Ibid.*, p. 638.

7 *Ibid.*, p. 460. This was a personal poem written to celebrate the first seven years with his second wife.

8 *Ibid.*, p. 638.

9 I am indebted to Mr Patrick Wright for this information.

10 T. H. Mawson, *The Life and Work of An English Landscape Architect: an Autobiography*, 1927, p. 78. In fact Voysey's office expenses show that he had a number of books in his office.

11 *The Builder's Journal & Architectural Record*, vol. XIII, 20 February 1901, p. 44.

12 According to his white book of office expenses Voysey made his first site visit to Lincoln on July 10 & 11, 1901. His postage expenses suggest that the design was probably drawn up by September 1901 and he paid a lithographer, presumably for the perspective reproduced in *The Building News* in February 1903.

13 *The Building News*, vol. 89, 21 July 1905, p. 76. Voysey admired Leonard Stokes's work and recommended him as an appropriate architect to design the London County Council offices.

14 According to Voysey's white book of office expenses his first site visit was made on 28 November 1901 and a man and boy were paid one shilling and sixpence for helping to peg out the site on a second visit on 7 & 8 January 1902.

15 Aymer Vallance, 'Some recent work by Mr. C.F.A. Voysey', *The Studio*, vol. 31, 1904, p. 127.

16 *Ibid.*

17 This watercolour was reproduced in *Moderne Bauformen*, x, 1911, pp. 248–9.

18 Voysey's office expenses for The Pastures include a visit to 'Elsleys re fire irons' on 7 September 1903.

19 Aymer Vallance, 'Some recent work by Mr. C.F.A. Voysey', *art. cit.*

20 *The Builder's Journal & Architectural Record*, vol. XVI, 26 November 1902.

21 According to *The Builder's Journal & Architectural Record*, this was S. F. Halliday of Stamford.

22 Both Vodin and Oakhurst were built by Frederick Müntzer, who had built his first Voysey house at Norney. Tom Müntzer was one of Voysey's pupils from 1899, so that Voysey must have been confident of the complete understanding and co-operation of his builder at Vodin.

23 Except for an entry in his office accounts; he paid Nielsen £3,15,0 for a table and charged it to Vodin.

24 Aymer Vallance, 'Some recent work by Mr. C.F.A. Voysey', *art. cit.*

25 'Wallpaper Manufacturers Ltd, Sanderson & Son Branch', *The Journal of Decorative Art and British Decorator*, part 297, September 1905, p. 17.

26 This iron bridge was removed after 1928 when the main Sanderson Factory was gutted by fire, but it is shown in a 1904 photograph in *The Journal of Decorative Art and British Decorator*, Part 297, September 1905, p. 16.

27 C. F. A. Voysey, 'The aesthetic aspects of concrete construction', *The Architect and Engineer*, vol. 57, May 1919, pp. 80–2.

28 *Ibid.*

29 *Ibid.*

30 John Brandon-Jones and others, *CFA Voysey: Architect and Designer, 1857–1941* (London, Lund Humphries with Brighton Museum and Art Gallery, 1978).

31 *The Builder's Journal & Architectural Record*, vol. XVII, 25 February 1903, p. 32.

32 Voysey's black book includes the following entry for 1909: 'Design for house for Miss Ling for Garden Suburb Development Co., Hampstead.'

33 C. F. A. Voysey, black book.

34 *British Architect*, VOL. LXIX, 1908, pp. 208 & 334.

35 C. F. A. Voysey, 'The English home', *The British Architect*, VOL. 75, 27 January 1911, pp. 60, 69 & 70.

36 *The British Architect*, VOL. LXIV, 1906, p. 78.

37 However, Voysey's office expenses show that he had the specification typed in July 1904 and that the 'Form of contract' was paid for out of his office expenses on 6 February 1905.

CHAPTER 11

1 See drawing for this mirror in RIBA Drawings Collection [305].

2 See RIBA Drawings Collection Catalogue [339].

3 Aymer Vallance, 'Some recent work by Mr. C. F. A. Voysey', *The Studio*, VOL. 31, 1904, pp. 130–1.

4 Voysey's white book of office expenses suggests that he started work in Birkenhead for Mrs Van Gruisen and Mrs McKay at the same time, charging his first visit to Birkenhead to both clients on 5 February 1902.

5 *The Studio*, VOL. XLII, October 1907, p. 25.

6 *Ibid.*

7 They are similar to a kestrel which he modelled and kept in his own collection.

8 See Voysey's book of professional expenses, now in a private collection, for 17 February 1908, although this date is later than the Garden Corner interiors.

9 *The Studio*, VOL. XLII, October 1907, p. 25.

10 'M. H. Baillie Scott, on the characteristics of Mr. C. F. A. Voysey's architecture', *The Studio*, VOL. XLII, October 1907, pp. 19–24.

11 This letter of 20 August 1906 is in the archive collection of the Guardian Royal Exchange Assurance Company.

12 *The Builder*, VOL. XCVII, 1909, p. 466.

13 Voysey's office expenses list frequent visits to Nielsen for Capel House suggesting that all the furniture there was made by him.

14 The large, glass light-fittings appeared in Elsley's catalogue of Voysey designs and it is probable that they supplied the small pendant lights too. Voysey's office expenses show that he visited 'Elsleys re electric fittings' on 23 August 1907 and on 18 August 1908 for Capel House.

15 Two of these chairs are now at the V&A and at the William Morris Gallery.

16 This letter is in the archive collection of the Guardian Royal Exchange Assurance Company.

17 *Ibid.*

18 Capel House was scandalously demolished in the 1980s. The board room was reconstructed in the basement of a new building on the site.

CHAPTER 12

1 See Eleanor Davidson, *The Simpsons of Kendal, Craftsmen in Wood 1885–1952* (Lancaster, University of Lancaster Visual Arts Centre, 1978).

2 *The British Architect*, VOL. LXXII, 1909, p. 363.

3 I am grateful to Miss Jean Simpson for this information.

4 The holiday cottage is at Slindon, near Bognor Regis, Sussex.

5 C. F. A. Voysey, *Individuality* (London, Chapman and Hall Ltd, 1915).

6 *Ibid.*

7 Voysey titled his preliminary design for Lodge Style 'St Winifred's Bungalow for T. Sturge Cotterell Esquire'. See RIBA Drawings Collection (34.1).

8 C. F. A. Voysey, 'Ideas in things', *The Arts Connected with Building*, ed. T. Raffles Davison (London, Batsford, 1909).

9 C. F. A. Voysey, *Reason as a Basis of Art* (London, Elkin Mathews, 1906), pp. 15 & 28.

10 C. F. A. Voysey, 'The aesthetic aspects of concrete construction', *The Architect and Engineer*, VOL. 57, May 1919, pp. 80–2.

11 C. R. Ashbee, *Masters of the Art Workers Guild From the Beginning Till A1934D*, bound typescript in the Archive Collection of the Art Workers' Guild, 1941.

12 *Ibid.*

13 C. F. A. Voysey, *Individuality, op. cit.*

14 See *The British Architect*, VOL. LXXVII, 1912, p. 274.

15 Voysey was probably familiar with Berlage's work from his visit to Holland in 1906.

16 Voysey's rudimentary accounts of income from fees are hand written on two sheets of paper, now in a private collection.

17 *The Tatler*, supplement no. 259, 13 June 1906.

18 Mrs E. Hall, Voysey's niece, described this dress in conversation with the author on 16 January 1993 as having a tight bodice and a long full skirt, made of a shot cotton (probably curtain fabric, she thought) with a thin black ribbon-tie around the neck and on the sleeves.

19 Mrs E. Hall in conversation with the author, 16 January 1993.

20 Correspondence between Voysey and Alexander Morton at the V&A.

21 C. R. Ashbee, *Masters of the Art Workers Guild From the Beginning Till A1934D, op. cit.*

22 Elizabeth Annesley Voysey and John Conway Voysey were the children of Voysey's younger son, Annesley Voysey and his wife Phylis.

23 This was said by Voysey's daughter-in-law, Phylis, and told to me by Elizabeth Annesley Voysey.

24 See John Brandon-Jones's note, pencilled on to the design in the RIBA Drawings Collection [794].

25 Letter from Voysey to Morton, dated 10 April 1931 in the V&A.

26 I am grateful to Miss Jean Simpson for bringing my attention to this letter.

27 Anon, 'C.F. Annesley Voysey – the man and his work – 1', *The Architect and Building News*, VOL. CXVII, 21 January 1927, p. 133.

28 Robert Donat, 'Uncle Charles …' *The Architect's Journal*, VOL. XCIII, 1941, pp. 193–4.

29 *Ibid.*

30 *Ibid.*

CHAPTER 13

1 C. F. A. Voysey, 'The aims and conditions of the modern decorator', a lecture given in Manchester, 15 February 1895, and published the following April in *The Journal of Decorative Art*, VOL. XV, pp. 82–90.

2 C.F. A. Voysey, '1874 & After', *Architectural Review*, VOL. LXX, October 1931, p. 92.

3 Voysey's book of professional expenses makes reference to another design for a house in America, for Dr Fort, presumably the same Dr Fort for whom Hollybank was built: on 2–4 August 1910 he listed 'Expenses with Dr Fort re house for America'. No further details are given.

4 *British Architect*, 20 April 1908.

5 I am indebted to Kathleen Reilly of the Berkshire Athenaeum for material relating to Ashintully and the Tytus family.

6 Voysey's black book lists '2 designs for Burial Grounds for Herr Carl Low, Helenthal, Iglau, Moravia, Austria', for 1912.

7 See RIBA Drawings Collection catalogue [54].

8 C. R. Ashbee, *Masters of the Art Workers Guild From the Beginning Till A1934D*, bound typescript in the Archive Collection of the Art Workers' Guild, 1941.

9 Nikolaus Pevsner, 'C.F.A. Voysey, An Appreciation', *Architectural Review*, VOL. LXXXII, 1937, p. 36.

10 Nikolaus Pevsner, 'Charles F. Annesley Voysey, 1858–1941', *Architectural Review*, VOL. LXXXIX, May 1941, p. 112.

11 Herkomer and Voysey were both members of the Arts Club, Dover Street, Piccadilly.

12 H. Lanford Warren, 'Recent domestic architecture in England', *Architectural Review*, Boston, VOL. XI, January 1904, p. 12.

13 *Ibid.*

14 Anon, 'Current periodicals, a review of recent American and foreign architectural publications', *Architectural Review*, Boston, VOL. XIV, December 1907, p. 248.

15 John Brandon-Jones, 'C.F.A. Voysey', *Victorian Architecture*, ed. Peter Ferriday (London, Jonathan Cape, 1963), p. 286.

16 John Leighton, 'The future of the past',

10 Nikolaus Pevsner, 'Charles F. Annesley Voysey, 1858–1941', *Architectural Review*, VOL. LXXXIX, May 1941, p. 112.

17 H. B. C.[F] (presumably H.B. Cresswell), 'Dinner to C.F Annesley Voysey', *Journal of the Royal Institute of British Architects*, VOL. XXXV, 26 November 1927, pp. 52–3.

18 Anon, 'C.F Annesley Voysey – the man and his work – 1', *The Architect and Building News*, VOL. CXVII, 21 January 1927, p. 133.

19 John Betjeman, 'Charles Francis Annesley Voysey, the architect of individualism', *Architectural Review*, October 1931, pp. 93–6.

20 C. F. A. Voysey in a lecture to the Architectural Society of the Bartlett School, published in summary in *The RIBA Journal*, VOL. XLI, 1934, p. 479.

21 Sir James Richards, Preface in Duncan Simpson's book, *C.F.A. Voysey an Architect of Individuality* (London, Lund Humphries, 1979).

22 'Charles Annesley Voysey, Royal Gold Medallist', *The RIBA Journal*, VOL. XLVII, 18 March 1940, p. 97.

23 Letter dated 23 March 1940, from Oud to Voysey. Private collection.

24 John Brandon-Jones, 'Charles Francis Annesley Voysey', *C.F.A. Voysey Catalogue of the Drawings Collection of The Royal Institute of British Architects* by Joanna Symonds, Gregg International, 1976.

25 *News Chronicle*, 21 February 1940.

26 *The Daily Mail*, 21 February 1940.

27 J. M. Richards, 'C.F.A. Voysey' (obituary), *Architectural Review*. VOL. LXXXIX, March 1941, p. 59.

28 Nikolaus Pevsner, 'Charles F. Annesley Voysey, 1858–1941', *art. cit.*

VOYSEY'S OFFICE ADDRESSES

1881	8 Queen Anne's Gate
25 March 1882	Broadway Chambers, Westminster
24 June 1885	7 Blandford Road, Bedford Park
24 June 1888	'Staumoor', 17 Tierney Road, Streatham Hill
25 March 1891	11 Melina Place, St John's Wood
1895	6 Carlton Hill, St John's Wood
1899	23 York Place, Baker Street
1913	25 Dover Street
30 July 1913	10 New Square, Lincoln's Inn
1917	73 St James's Street

LIST OF WORKS

There are three main sources from which a complete list of Voysey buildings can be compiled. The first is Voysey's own record of all his building projects, written in a black book, which is now in the RIBA library. This catalogue includes unexecuted and built works and lists minor alterations and additions, as well as, decorations and crematory urns. It does not include decorative or metalwork designs, and it is by no means comprehensive in its inclusion of furniture designs. It can safely be assumed, however, that if a building is not listed in the black book then it was not designed by Voysey. There are many projects catalogued in the black book that were never built, and no differentiation is made between the projects which were executed and those which were not. The black book is invaluable for dating as

well as validating projects. In general, the dates given for each project should be taken as the date of the commission, but the black book was probably not started until Voysey's practice was well established so that the dates for the earliest entries, written from memory, are less accurate. Some projects are listed twice, where a delay occurred between the design and execution of a building, or where alterations and additions were made at a later date.

The second source of information is the extensive collection of Voysey drawings. In 1913 he gave a selection of designs, which he had chosen to represent his work, to the Victoria and Albert Museum. This collection is particularly strong in its range and quality of decorative designs. The drawings for objects (the painted clock for example) and buildings

are also known to have been important to Voysey. In 1940, when ill health made it impossible for Voysey to continue living alone in his flat in St James's Street, the two chests of drawings, which he had kept in his rooms, were moved for safe-keeping to be stored with the treasures of the RIBA. After the War they were presented to the RIBA Drawings Collection by Voysey's son, Charles Cowles Voysey, and in 1975 they were painstakingly catalogued by Joanna Symonds.

There are 88 designs for buildings at the RIBA; 208 designs for textiles and wallpapers; 260 designs for furniture; 206 graphic designs; and eight designs for extensive alterations to existing buildings. Only nine of the buildings that Voysey is known to have built are not represented in the RIBA Collection, and these are: The Cottage, Bishop's Itchington; the final design for the Forster house, Bedford Park; the Wentworth Arms Inn, Elmesthorpe; the Pavilion at Oldbury Park, Brimingham; The Orchard, Chorley Wood; Priors Garth, near Puttenham; Tilehurst, Bushey; White Cottage, Wandsworth; and the final design for the bungalow at Barnham Junction, Sussex. The two collections of drawings, therefore, at the V&A and the RIBA offer a remarkably complete record of Voysey's work. In addition, Voysey donated seventy designs for badges and bookplates to the British Museum (although these are not relevant to a list of his buildings).

A third major source of information is the white book in which Voysey recorded his office expenses from 1897 to 1936. Although this is a record of relatively minor expenses: travelling costs; telegrams and later telephones; and the typing of specifications, etc., it offers a definitive guide to the dates and frequency of Voysey's site

visits (and much more besides, which has yet to be analysed). The white book is in a private collection. Finally, Voysey's scrap-book of photographs and press coverage of his work is annotated with the cost of many of his buildings. Where this is handwritten in Voysey's hand over or next to a photograph of the building it is included in the list with an asterisk. Other costs given are taken from contemporary publications.

Although every effort has been made to validate the entries in this list of works I am painfully aware of its deficiencies. There will be drawings in private collections of which I am unaware, and I have been unable to gain access to all the buildings that Voysey may have extended. Where I have been unsure whether or not Voysey extended or altered an existing building I have included it in the list, on the grounds that it is easier to edit material out in the future than to write it in, but I should be very grateful for any information regarding Voysey's drawings, correspondence and extant evidence of building work. Please contact me through my publisher.

Voysey is rightly famous for his versatility and consistency in designing all things for the house, and I am aware that in listing his buildings I am only representing a part of his output. The addition of an exhaustive catalogue of his furniture, bookplates and decorative designs, however, would make this list prohibitively long and it would in any case duplicate much of the material in the excellent RIBA catalogue of Voysey drawings.

EXECUTED BUILDINGS
in chronological order

1 COTTAGES
    at Northampton
D 1881
CL George Devey
DR No drawings have been
    located either in the
    Devey collection at the
    RIBA or with Voysey's
    drawings
N Voysey includes these in
    his black book, although
    they are believed to have
    been designed by Devey
    and executed under
    Voysey's supervision so
    that technically they
    are Devey's houses
R Jill Allibone, *George
    Devey, Architect, 1820–1886*
    (Cambridge, The Lutter-
    worth Press, 1991)
2 RIVERMEAD
    Sunbury-on-Thames,
    Surrey.
    Summer-house and
    house alterations
D 1882
CL L. B. Knight Bruce
DR No drawings located
N According to the black
    book, Voysey decorated
    the library and provided
    a new oak gallery in
    Knight Bruce's house
    in Sunbury-on-Thames.
    The summer-house
    was of brick and stone.
3 THE COTTAGE
    Bishop's Itchington, nr
    Warwick.
D 1888
AD New wing added 1900
CL Sir Michael Lakin
DR No drawings located,
    although the drawings
    for 'Design for a Cottage'
    of c. 1885 on which this
    design was based are
    in the RIBA Drawings
    Collection [147]
£ £559*
R Drawings exhibited in
    *Arts and Crafts Exhibition
    Society* IV, 1893, no. 430.
    Referred to in BA. XXX,
    1888, p. 407; BA. XI, 1893,
    p. 292; St. IV, 1894, p. 34;
    and CL.III, 1898, pp. 196–7
N A new porch has recently
    been added to the side of
    The Cottage, but Voysey's
    elevations and some of
    the interiors remain in
    good condition.
4 WALNUT TREE FARM
    Castlemorton, Malvern,
    Heref. & Worces.

Farm and stables
D 1890
AD Alterations and garden
    laid out 1894
CL R. H. Cazalet
DR Drawings for house and
    stables, RIBA [24]. In addi-
    tion there are photo-
    graphs at the RIBA of
    a model of Walnut Tree
    Farm, made by
    A. Creswick
£ £1,120*
R Drawings exhibited at:
    Royal Academy, 1895,
    no. 1496; Arts and Crafts
    Exhibition Society, v,
    1896, no. 657 (photo-
    graph exhibited); and the
    British Section of the
    St Louis Internation
    Exhibition, 1904. Draw-
    ings or photographs
    reproduced in: BA. XXXIV,
    1890, pp. 208 & 302; *The
    American Architect &
    Building News*, XXX, 1890,
    p. 75, pl. 775; BA. XLVI,
    1894, pp. 417 & 420; BA.
    XLIV, 1895, p. 419; *Academy
    Architecture*, II, 1895, pp.
    10 & 143; *Builder's Journal
    & Architectural Record*, IV,
    1896, pp. 68 & 72; St. XI,
    1897, pp. 17 & 22; *House
    Beautiful*, VII, 1899,
    pp. 24–7; Sir Isidore
    Spielmann, *Catalogue of
    the 1904 St Louis Interna-
    tional Exhibition, The
    British Section*, 1906,
    no. 243; and *The Architect*,
    LXXVI, 1906, p. 404
N Soon after it was com-
    pleted the house became
    known as Bannut Tree
    House, and it is now
    known as Bannut Farm
    House.
5 COTTAGE
    at Llandrindod, Wales
D 1890
CL E. L. Lakin
DR No drawings located.
6 14 SOUTH PARADE
    Bedford Park, London.
D 1891
AD Addition by Voysey in
    1894
CL J. W. Forster
DR Original drawings not
    located, but plans and
    elevations published
    in BA
R BA. XXXVI, 1891, pp.
    209–10; *Builder's Journal
    & Architectural Record*, IV,
    1896, p. 68; and St. XI,
    1897, pp. 20 & 25
£ Contract price noted

in *The Studio* 1897 as
    £494 10s
N Voysey prepared prelimi-
    nary designs for a house
    in Bedford Park for Mrs
    Wilson in 1888 & 1889.
    These designs are in the
    RIBA [88].
7 STUDIO HOUSE
    17 St Dunstan's Road,
    Hammersmith,
    London W6.
D 1891
CL W. E. F. Britten
DR The RIBA hold only a
    drawing for a sundial
    for W. E. F. Britten [87]
B Messrs Hall, Beddall
    & Co.
R BA. May 1892; BA. XLIII,
    1895, p. 146; and St. II,
    1897, p. 12
N The fine wrought-iron
    railings were made by
    W. B. Reynolds.
8 14 & 16 HANS ROAD
    London SW3.
D 1891–2
CL Archibold Grove
DR RIBA [76]
B Messrs Thomas Gregory
    of Clapham Junction
R BA. XXXVII, 1892, p. 210; BA.
    XLI, 1893, p. 96; St. I, 1893,
    p. 225; *The Builder* LXXI,
    1896, p. 229; St. XI, 1897,
    p. 23; *Dekorative Kunst*,
    1897, p. 255; *The House*,
    IV, 1898–9, p. 163; and
    Magazine of Art, XXII,
    1899, pp. 457–65
N Voysey designed
    a terrace of three houses,
    12, 14, and 16 Hans Road,
    but a dispute with the
    client over fees led to
    A. H. Mackmurdo being
    commissioned to build
    number 12. Although
    Voysey's black book
    dates these buildings
    1891, the preliminary
    drawing for them is
    dated 15 May 1892.
9 48 GLEBE PLACE
    Chelsea, London.
    Row of four studios
D 1892
CL Conrad Dressler
DR No drawings located
R BA. 1 January 1892 and
    2 December 1892
N There is little evidence to
    suggest that these studios
    were built.
10 PERRYCROFT
    Colwall, Herefordshire.
    New house, stables and
    lodge
D 1893

AD New stables, 1903; summer-house and garden walling, 1904; alterations and additions, 1907; coachman's cottage, 1908; additions to lodge, 1914; and alterations and additions, 1924
CL J. W. Wilson
DR RIBA [32], and there are drawings for the coachman's cottage in a private collection
£ The cost of the house without out-buildings was given as £4,900; and was given by Voysey as £4,386* and as £6,607* including stables
B W. Porter of Malvern
R Drawings exhibited at the Royal Academy 1905–6, no. 1452. Referred to in BA. XLI, 1893, p. 454; BA. XLII, 1894, pp. 5–6; BA. XLIV, 1895, p. 120; *The Builder's Journal and Architectural Record*, IV, 1896, pp. 67–8; *Dekorative Kunst*, I, 1897, p. 246; St. XXI, 1901, p. 244; *The Architect*, LXXVI, 1906, p. 404; and T. Raffles Davison, *Modern Homes*, 1909, pp. 20–21.

11 COTTAGE
Alton.
Cottage and out-buildings
D 1894
CL Mrs Mary Scott
DR No drawings located.

12 LOWICKS
Sandy Lane, Frensham, Surrey.
House, stables and garden
D 1894
AD Alterations, 1898; alterations and addition, 1904; alterations to stable and entrance, and addition to garden, 1907; and new summer-house and additions to house, 1911. Entirely new system of drainage, alterations to E.C.s and enlargement of garage for C. Kerr, 1916. (Lowicks was sold by Horniman in 1914.)
CL E. J. Horniman
DR RIBA [40]
£ £2,137*
R BA. XLII, 1894, p. 328; *The Builder's Journal and Architectural Record*, IV, 1896, p. 69; St. XI, 1897, pp. 16, 18 & 23; *The House*, IV, 1898–99, p. 162; and St. XXI, 1901, p. 246.

13 THE WENTWORTH ARMS INN
Elmesthorpe, Leics.
D 1895
CL Earl of Lovelace
DR The RIBA has drawings for the signboard only [38]
B Messrs Brown & Son of Wellingborough
£ Contract price given as £1,562
R BA. XLV, 1896, p. 42
N Voysey's black book includes 'Painting signboard for Wentworth Arms' in 1930.

14 ANNESLEY LODGE
8 Platts Lane, London NW3.
D 1895
AD Alterations, additions, general painting & repairs for C. Horsley, 1913
CL Reverend Charles Voysey
DR RIBA [84]
£ £2,000*. It was also noted in Voysey's hand that the house was sold for £2,800, presumably in 1913
R Drawings exhibited, Royal Academy 1896, no. 1741 with Hill Close. Referred to in: *The Architect* XLV, 1896, p. 148; St. XI, 1897, p. 18; and St. XXI, 1901, p. 245
N Reverend Voysey remained at Annesley Lodge until his death in 1912. In his will he bequeathed it to his seven children, recommending that its value might be enhanced if they wait and find a buyer who appreciated the importance of the man who had lived there. It was apparently purchased by C. Horsley, shortly after 1912. The house has now been divided into flats.

15 HILL CLOSE
Studland Bay, Swanage, Dorset.
D 1895–6
AD Lodge and motor-house for Sir H. Cook, 1913
CL A. Sutro
DR RIBA [128]
R Drawings exhibited at Royal Academy 1896, no. 1741 with Annesley Lodge. Referred to in: BA. XLV, 1896, p. 42; *Dekorative Kunst*, I, 1897, p. 254; St. XI, 1897, p. 21; St. XXI, 1901, p. 246; Hermann Muthesius, *Das englische Haus*, II, 1904–5, p. 205; Hermann Muthesius, *Das moderne Landhaus*, 1905, p. 146; and W. Shaw Sparrow, *The Modern Home*, 1906, p. 54.

16 WORTLEY COTTAGES
Elmesthorpe, Leices.
D 1896
AD Rebuilding six cottages, 1914
CL Earl of Lovelace
DR RIBA [37]
£ £220* each. Total £1,194*
R BA. XLVII, 1897, p. 24; St. XI, 1897, p. 19; *Dekorative Kunst*, I, 1897, p. 246; St. XXXI, 1904, p. 133; and M. B. Adams, *Modern cottage architecture*, 1904, p. 8
N According to Voysey's black book, some rebuilding of the six cottages was necessary in 1914.

17 GREYFRIARS HOUSE,
The Hogg's Back, nr Puttenham, Surrey.
Stables and lodge
D 1896
CL Julian Sturgis
DR RIBA [117]
£ £4,191*
R Drawings exhibited by the *Arts and Crafts Exhibition Society*, V, 1896, no. 596 and at the Royal Academy 1897, no. 1797. Referred to in: *The Builder's Journal and Architectural Record*, IV, 1896, p. 70; *Academy Architecture* XII, 1897, p. 37; *Architectural Review*, I, 1897, p. 327; *The Builder's Journal and Architectural Record*, VI, 1897–8, p. 333; *Dekorative Kunst* I, 1897, pp. 245 & 250; BA. XLIX, 1898, p. 292; *The Builder's Journal and Architectural Record*, X, 1899–1900, pp. 48 & 56; *House*, IV, 1898–99, p. 162; *The Builder*, LXXIX, 1900, p. 192; W. Shaw Sparrow, *The British Home of Today* 1904, p. 6; Hermann Muthesius, *Das moderne Landhaus*, 1905, pl. 145; *The Architect*, LXXVI, 1906, p. 404; Hermann Muthesius, *Landhaus und Garten*, 1907, p. 156; W. Shaw Sparrow, *Our Homes and How to Make the Best of Them*, 1909, p. 100
N Also known as Merlshanger and Wancote.

Significant alterations and additions have been made to the house since Voysey's time.

18 HOUSE
Riggindale Road, Streatham, London.
D 1897
CL Free Church Trustees
DR No drawings located
N No references to this building have come to light either in archive repositories or in Voysey's office expenses, suggesting that it was designed but not executed.

19 DIXCOT
North Drive, Tooting Beck Common, Lambeth, London.
D 1897
AD Alterations to study and billiard room, 1916
CL Richard Walter Essex
DR RIBA [81]
R BA. L, 1898, p. 6; St. XVI, 1899, p. 162; *The Builder's Journal and Architectural Record*, XI, 1900, p. 326; C. Holme, *Modern British Domestic Architecture and Decoration*, 1901, p. 63
N Disagreements between Voysey and his client caused him to abandon the design, and a revised version was built under the supervision of Walter Cave. According to John Brandon-Jones the dispute was with Essex's wife. Voysey continued to design furniture for Essex.

20 NORNEY
Shackleford, Surrey.
House, stables and lodge
D 1897
AD 1903 additional wing and alteration to house, the new stable and the second lodge may date from this period of work
CL Reverend Leighton Grane
DR RIBA [125]
B F. Müntzer
R Drawings exhibited by the *Arts and Crafts Exhibition Society*, VI, 1899, no. 664 and by the *Arts and Crafts Exhibition Society*, VII, 1903, no. 394b. Referred to in: *Dekorative Kunst*, I, 1897, p. 243; BA. L, 1898, p. 130; *Architectural Review*, V, 1898, p. 240; BA. LII, 1899, pp. 234–5; St. XXI, 1901, pp. 242–3; Hermann Muthesius, *Das englische Haus*, III, 1904–5, p. 175; St. XXIV, 1905, pp. 151–2; Hermann Muthesius, *Das moderne Landhaus*, 1905, p. 148; *The Builder*, XCV, 1908, p. 406; and *The Architect* LXXVI, 1906, p. 404
N Correspondence between the Reverend Leighton Grane and Lord Middleton, from whom the site was purchased, is in the collection of Mr Clapshaw.

21 THE HILL
Thorpe Mandeville, Northants.
D 1897
CL J. C. E. Hope Brooke
DR RIBA [131]
£ £2,862*
R Drawings exhibited at the Royal Academy, 1898, no. 1759. Referred to in: BA. XLIX, 1898, p. 346, *The Builder's Journal and Architectural Record* VII, 1898, p. 396; *The Builder* LXXV, 1899, p. 349
N Voysey also designed a series of buildings at Brackley for Hope Brooke in 1897, including: 19 cottages, a pair of semi-detached houses, a dairy shop and a shop, none of these appear to have been executed.

22 NEW PLACE
Haslemere, Surrey.
House and garden design
D 1897
AD Design for lodge, gardener's cottage, stables and summer-house, 1899; and formal garden and new gates, 1901
CL A. M. M Stedman, later known as Sir Algernon Methuen
DR RIBA [49]
R Drawings exhibited by the *Arts and Crafts Exhibition Society*, VII, 1903, nos. 394 l & y. Referred to in: *Dekorative Kunst*, I, 1897, p. 242; St. XXI, 1901, p. 242; *Dekorative Kunst*, XI, 1902–3, p. 370; *House and Garden*, III, 1903, pp. 254–8; *Architectural Review* (Boston), XI, 1904, p. 12; *Builder's Journal and Architectural Record*, XX, 1904, p. 262; W. Shaw Sparrow, *The British Home of Today*, 1904, E21; Hermann Muthesius, *Das englische Haus*, II, 1904–5, pp. 113–14 & 124–5; Hermann Muthesius, *Das moderne Landhaus*, 1905, pp. 146–7; *Dekorative Kunst*, XIV, 1906, pp. 194–5; W. Shaw Sparrow, *Our Homes and How to Make the Best of Them*, 1909, p. 238; W. Duggan, *The Garden*, 6 August 1921 (reprinted as Anon.) and *New Place Haslemere and its Gardens*, 1921 (privately printed for Methuen)
N The house was known as 'Hurtmore' until January 1900.

23 BROADLEYS
Gillhead, nr Cartmel Fell, Windermere, Lancs. House and lodge
D 1898
CL Arthur Currer Briggs
DR RIBA [138]; V&A [E.252 1913]; and there is a set of drawings for the house as built in the archive collection of Pattinson of Windermere
B Pattinson of Windermere
£ £5,085 4s. 11d. (according to Pattinson's accounts). Voysey gave the cost as £5,592*
R Drawings exhibited at the Royal Academy, 1899, no. 1725 and by the *Arts and Crafts Exhibition Society*, VII, 1903, no. 394j. Referred to in: BA. LI, 1899, p. 256; St. XVI, 1899, p. 158; *The Builder's Journal and Architectural Record*, XVI, 1902–3, p. 389 and XVII, 1903, p. 29; St. XXI, 1904, p. 127; Hermann Muthesius, *Das englische Haus*, I, 1904–5, pp. 159–64; and *The Architect*, LXXIX, 1908, p. 208
N Broadleys is now the Windermere Motor Boat Club. A copy of Voysey's specification for the building is held at the RIBA Library. The gardens were laid out by Thomas Mawson.

24 MOORCRAG
Gillhead, nr Cartmel Fell, Windermere, Lancs.
D 1898
AD Stables 1900. By 1907 the bays on the garden elevation had been slate hung, possibly not under Voysey's superintendence

CL J. W. Buckley
DR RIBA [140]; and V&A [E.255 1913]
£ £4,827*
B Pattinson of Windermere
R Drawings exhibited by the *Arts and Crafts Exhibition Society*, VII, 1903, no. 394K and 394dd. Referred to in: *The Builder's Journal and Architectural Record*, XVI, 1903–4, pp. 176–7 & 182; *Architectural Review* (Boston), XI, 1904, p. 12 and XIV, 1907, p. 248; St. XXXI, 1904, p. 128; *The Architect*, LXXVIII, 1907, p. 296; and *The Studio Yearbook* 1907, p. 41
N The site for Moorcrag was surveyed by Thomas Mawson, who later laid out the gardens. The house has been sympathetically divided into two.

25 SPADE HOUSE
Radnor Cliff Crescent, Sandgate, Kent.
D 1899
AD Additional storey, 1903
CL H. G. Wells
DR RIBA [123]
£ £1,760*
R BA. LII, 1899, p. 292; H. G. Wells, *An Experiment in Autobiography*, vol II, 1934, pp. 638–9
N The house has suffered extensive alterations and is now a private nursing home.

26 OAKHILL
54 Hill Grove Crescent, Kidderminster, Worcs.
D 1899
CL F. J. Mayers
DR RIBA [56].

27 WINSFORD COTTAGE HOSPITAL
Halwill Junction, nr Beauworthy, Devon.
D 1899
AD Additions 1924
CL Mrs M. L. Medley
DR RIBA [47]
£ £2,215*
R *The Builder's Journal and Architectural Record*, XVII, 1903, p. 231
N According to Voysey's office expenses the carved shield at the hospital was carved by A. W. Simpson in Kendal. The building is still in use as a hospital.

28 GORDONDENE
15 Princes Way,

Wimbledon, Merton, Surrey.
House and stables
D 1899
CL Cecil Fitch
DR RIBA [85]
R See John Brandon-Jones, 'An Architect's letters to his client', *Architect and Building News*, CXCV, 1949, pp. 494–8 for correspondence between Voysey and Fitch. The house and stables have been demolished.

29 THE ORCHARD
Shire Lane, Chorleywood, Herts.
D 1899
AD New bay windows added to front of house (study), 1913
CL C. F. A. and Mary Maria Voysey
£ £1,000 – £1,500. Voysey gave the cost as £2,000*
B J. Bottrill & Son of Reading
DR Geffrye Museum; Collection of Brian Blackwood; and the RIBA has drawings for furniture for The Orchard
R *Country Life*, VI, 1899, pp. 389–90; *Architectural Review*, X, 1901, pp. 32–8; Charles Holme, *Modern British Domestic Architecture and Decoration*, 1901, pp. 181–94; *Tatler*, Supplement no. 259, 13 June 1906; and *The Ideal House*, USA, January 1907, pp. 3–11
N Voysey left The Orchard in 1906. He made alterations to the house for the subsequent occupant, R. H. Selbie, in 1913.

30 OAKHURST
Ropes Lane, Fernhurst, Sussex
D 1900
CL Mrs E. F. Chester
DR RIBA [39] and collection Mr Moore
£ £3,562*
R Drawings exhibited by the *Arts and Crafts Exhibition Society*, VII, 1903, no. 394i. Referred to in: *The Builder's Journal and Architectural Record*, XIII, 1901, pp. 37 & 44 and *House and Garden*, III, 1903, pp. 258–9
N The house was extended in 1919, and in 1949 divided into two. It is now known as 'Ropes and Bollards'.

31 PRIORS GARTH
Puttenham, nr Guildford, Surrey.
D 1900
CL F. H. Chambers
B F. Müntzer
DR The RIBA holds a drawing for the gate to Priors Garth only [118]
R *The Builder's Journal and Architectural Record*, XVI, 1903, B4
N The design was adapted from an 1898 unexecuted design for a house at Bexhill (RIBA[15]). Chambers never moved into the house and in 1901 it was purchased by Leonard Huxley and his wife Julia, who converted it to a 'High Class School for Girls', in 1901–2. Thomas Müntzer, Voysey's pupil, designed extensions to the school in 1904; it is now known as Priors Field and still in use as a school. In 1901, Voysey made a design for Lincoln Grammar School for F. H. Chambers and he later designed his gravestone.

32 THE PASTURES
North Luffenham, Rutland.
House and stables
D 1901
AD Additions and alterations including the addition of a two-storey square bay on south elevation, 1909
CL Miss G. Conant
B S. F. Halliday of Stamford
DR RIBA [109]
£ £6,110*
R Drawings exhibited at the Royal Academy 1906, no. 1548. Referred to in: *The Builder's Journal and Architectural Record*, XVI, 1902–3, pp. 245 & 248; St. XXXI, 1904, p. 127; *Moderne Bauformen*, X, 1911, pp. 248–9; and *The Architect*, CII, 1919, p. 352 and CXVI, 1927, p. 133.

33 SANDERSON & SONS FACTORY
Barley Mow Passage, Chiswick, London.
D 1902
CL Sanderson & Sons, wallpaper manufacturers
DR RIBA [63]
R *The Builder's Journal and Architectural Record*, XVII, 1903, pp. 26 & 32; *The Journal of Decorative Art and Wallpaper News*, Sept. 1905, part 297, special supplement, pp. 16–23
N A 1904 photograph shows the factory with connecting bridge to the 1884 Sanderson's Factory on the other side of Barley Mow Passage.

34 VODIN
Old Woking Road, Pyrford Common, nr Woking, Surrey.
House and lodge
D 1902
AD Motor-house and electric-light generating house, 1904
CL F. Walters
B F. Müntzer
£ Given in the black book as 'Total cost £6,617.8.5'. Not clear whether this applies to the house and lodge or to all four buildings. Also given in Voysey's scrap-book as £4,700* and £6,617.8.5*
DR RIBA [119]
R *The Builder's Journal and Architectural Record*, XVII, 1903, p. 208 and XVIII, 1903, p. 112; St. XXXI, 1904, p. 132; and BA. LXVI, 1906, p. 111
N Now known as 'Little Court'.

35 TWO COTTAGES
Polecat Lane, Shottermill, Haslemere, Surrey.
D 1903
CL A. M. S. Methuen
DR RIBA [50]
R *The Builder's Journal and Architectural Record*, XX, 1904, p. 265 and BA. LXV, 1906, p. 292
N There are no surviving semi-detached cottages in Polecat Lane that correspond to the RIBA drawings.

36 TY-BRONNA
St Fagan's Road, Fairwater, nr Cardiff, South Glamorgan.
D 1903
AD Stables, 1904
CL W. Hastings Watson
DR RIBA [23]
£ £3,115*
R *The Builder's Journal and Architectural Record*, XIX, 1904, p. 308 and W. Shaw Sparrow, *The Modern Home*, 1906, p. 55
N Now owned by South Glamorgan Health Authority.

37 WHITE COTTAGE
68 Lyford Road, Wandsworth, London SW18.
D 1903
AD Furniture 1912
CL C. T. Coggin
DR Drawings at the house
N Voysey designed furniture for Coggin in 1912, presumably for White Cottage, and drawings for a chest of drawers are at the RIBA [235].

38 TILEHURST
10 Grange Road, Bushey, Herts.
D 1903
CL Miss E. Somers
B C. Miskin and Sons, St Albans
DR No drawings located
£ £1,103*
R W. Shaw Sparrow, *The Modern Home*, 1906, p. 54 and M. E. Macartney, 'Recent English domestic architecture', *Architectural Review* 1908, p. 173.

39 HOLLYBANK
Shire Lane, Chorleywood, Herts.
House and doctor's practice, and garage
D 1903
CL Dr H. R. T. Fort (although nominally built for the Reverend Matthew Edmeads)
B A. J. Bates
DR RIBA [29]
£ £1012* also given as £2,000*
R *The Builder's Journal and Architectural Record*, XX, 1904, pp. 270–1.

40 MYHOLME
Merry Hill Lane, Bushey, Herts.
Children's home
D 1904
AD Alterations, 1911
CL Miss E. Somers
B C. Miskin and Sons, St Albans
£ £1,549* also given as £1,588*
DR RIBA[22]
N Voysey's black book dates Tilehurst as 1903 and Myholme as 1904, but his white book of office expenses shows that he first visited the sites for both buildings on 9 December 1903.

41 HOUSE
at Higham, Woodford, Essex.
D 1904
CL Lady Henry Somerset
DR RIBA [78] and V&A [256 & 257.1913]
R Drawings exhibited at the Royal Academy 1908, no. 1668. Referred to in: BA. LXIV, 1905, p. 440 and LXIV, 1906, p. 78
N The house was built 'without the superintendence of the architect'.

42 WORKMEN'S INSTITUTE AND COTTAGES
Whitwood, Normanton, Yorkshire.
D 1904
CL Henry Briggs & Son
DR RIBA [137]
£ £12,950*
R *Dekorative Kunst*, XIV, 1906, pp. 193 & 196–7. Referred to in: BA. LXIX, 1908, pp. 208 & 334
N Only one of the two terraces of housing was executed, and Voysey noted in 1908 that: 'The Company found it necessary to build the houses so cheaply that architectural superintendence was perforce left out of court.' The Institute has been converted into a public house.

43 WHITE HORSE INN
Stetchworth, Cambs.
D 1905
CL Earl of Ellesmere
DR RIBA [126]
R BA. LXIV, 1905, p. 440 and LXVI, 1906, p. 274; *Moderne Bauformen*, X, 1911, p. 174; *The Architect*, CI, 1919, p. 54; and *Country Life*, 6 August 1927
N Now known as the White Horse Stables.

44 HOUSE
at Aswan, Egypt.
D 1905
CL Dr H. E. Leigh Canney
DR RIBA [8]
R BA. LXV, 1906, p. 94
N There are photographs of this house in the RIBA collection of photographs, with inscriptions in Voysey's hand on the reverse.

45 HOLLY MOUNT
Amersham Road, Knotty Green, Bucks.
D 1905
CL C.T. Burke
DR RIBA [10]
£ £1,429* and the summer-house marked as costing £315 6s*
R BA. LXVIII, 1907, p. 60; *The Studio Yearbook* 1910, p. 81; *Moderne Bauformen*, X, 1911, pp. 255–6; M. Macartney, *Recent English Domestic Architecture*, 1911, p. 167; and *The Architect*, vol. CII, 1919, p. 352
N The RIBA hold photographs of the house and of a summer-house, which is no longer extant.

46 THE HOMESTEAD
Second Avenue, Frinton-on-Sea, Essex.
D 1905–6
CL Sydney Claridge Turner
DR RIBA [41]
£ £2,405*
R BA. LXV, 1906, p. 310; BA. LXVII, 1907, p. 370; *Country Life*, 1 October 1910, pp. 7–11; *Moderne Bauformen*, X, 1911, pp. 251 & 252; M. Macartney, *Recent English Domestic Architecture*, 1911, pp. 167, 169 & 170; L. Weaver, *The House and its Equipment*, 1912, pp. 18 & 20.

47 LITTLEHOLME
Upper Guildown Road, Guildford, Surrey.
D 1906–7
AD Dormer-windows and rooms in roof 1909; gardener's cottage 1911; and alterations 1925
CL George Müntzer
B F. Müntzer & Son
DR RIBA [46]
R BA. LXXVIII, 1907, pp. 5, 6, & 60; *The Architect* LXXIX, 1908, p. 304; BA. LXXVII, 1912, pp. 452 & 454 and LXXVIII, 1912, p. 390; *The Architect*, CI, 1919, p. 68; and G. Jekyll & L. Weaver, *Gardens for Small Country Houses*, 1912, pp. 76–80 & 162
N The main house has been divided into two.

48 HOUSE
at Gray's Park, Stoke Poges, nr Slough.
D 1906
CL J. Hatton
DR The RIBA hold drawings for a house for J. Hatton at Stoke Poges, but they do not match any extant houses. There are also drawings in a private collection
£ £1040*
R BA. LXVI, 1908, p. 184.

49 LODGE STYLE
Shaft Road, Combe Down, Bath, Avon.
D 1909
CL T. S. Cotterell
DR RIBA [34]
R Drawing exhibited at the Royal Academy, 1909, no. 1450. Referred to in: BA. LXXII, 1909, pp. 111 & 114; *The Builder*, XCVIII, 1910, p. 264; *The Studio Yearbook* 1910, p. 82; BA. LXXVII, 1911, p. 361; and *The Architect*, CI, 1919, p. 54.

50 LITTLEHOLME
103 Sedbergh Road, Kendal, Cumbria.
D 1909
CL A. W. Simpson
DR RIBA [55] and Cumbria Record Office
£ £967*
R BA. LXXII, 1909, pp. 363 & 366; *The Craftsman*, XX, 1911, pp. 276–86; M. Macartney, *Recent English Domestic Architecture*, 1911, pp. 171–2; *Moderne Bauformen*, X, 1911, p. 250; and *The Builder*, 1 June 1923, p. 891.

51 HOUSE
Slindon, nr Barnham Junction, Sussex.
D 1909
CL Arthur Annesley Voysey
DR RIBA [9] and V&A [E.253 1913 V.I].

52 BROOKE END
New Road, Henley-in-Arden, Warwickshire.
House with stable and garden
D 1909
CL Miss F. Knight
DR RIBA [51]
£ Marked in Voysey's hand: 'Contract price including garden £3672.16.11.'
R *The Architect*, LXXXIV, 1910, pp. 232 & supplement p. 18, and BA. LXXIII, 1910, pp. 345 & 348.

53 HOUSE
Malone Road, Belfast, Northern Ireland.
D 1911
CL Robert Hetherington
DR RIBA [14] and private collection
R BA. LXXVIII, 1912, pp. 316-8.

54 PUBLIC GARDEN
East Row, Kensal, Kensington & Chelsea, London.
Shelter and playground
D 1913
CL E. J. Horniman
DR RIBA [69]
R BA.LXXX, 1915, pp. 273 & 276.

55 WAR MEMORIAL
Wells Road, Malvern Wells, Worces.
D 1919
DR RIBA [104]. The model for a pelican is in a private collection, and a perspective by Charles Cowles Voysey is in the collection of John Brandon-Jones
R *The Builder*, CXVIII, 1920, p. 84.

56 WAR MEMORIAL
High Street, Potters Bar, Herts.
D 1920
DR RIBA [116]
R *The Architect*, CIV, 1920, p. 426 and *The Builder*, CIXX, 1920, p. 575
N The Memorial was moved to its present position at the junction of The Causeway and Hatfield Road in 1974.

57 HOUSE
at 'Helenthal, Iglau, Czecho Slovakia'.
D 1922
CL Karl Lowe
DR RIBA[54]
R *The Builder*, CXXV, 1923, pp. 288–9
N Not known whether it was built.

ADDITIONS & ALTERATIONS

I WOODLAWN HOUSE
105 Dulwich Village, London.
Alterations and additions
D 1883
CL Reverend Charles Voysey
DR No drawings located
N This Georgian house was let to Reverend Voysey in 1882 and was his home until 1890. The insertion of an interior corridor and some division of the rooms on the first floor, and alterations around the main-landing area were probably designed by C. F. A. Voysey. Two round bays may have been added to the rear elevation for Reverend Voysey c. 1882, but there are no distinctive features identifying C. F. A. Voysey's hand.

2 THE THEISTIC CHURCH
Swallow Street, Piccadilly, London.
Alterations, additions and decoration
D 1885

AD Voysey's white book of office expenses lists repairs to The Theistic Church between 1897 and 1902, and in 1905, and the removal of the spire at the Theistic Church in 1901
CL The Theistic Church Committee
DR No drawings located other than a drawing for lettering *The Theistic Church*, RIBA Drawings Collection [598], and for a lamp for the Theistic Church [90]
N The church has been demolished, but there are photographs of its interiors in a private collection.

3 RUSSELL HOUSE
South End Road, Hampstead, London.
Alterations and additions
D 1886
CL Frederick Aumonier
DR No drawings located
N Voysey designed wall-papers for Aumonier, and Russell House was the family home. According to his black book he produced designs for alterations and additions to the house in 1886 and added new bays and a porch in 1890. The bays and porch are roughcast with stone dressings.

4 THE CLIFF
102 Coventry Road, Warwick.
New wing and alterations to Regency House
D 1889
AD New fireplace and chimney-piece, 1914; alterations to sitting room, 1919
CL Sir Michael Lakin
DR No drawings can be definitely assigned to this project, although 'Suggestion for Treatment of a Domestic Window', RIBA Drawings Collection [166], may have been drawn for The Cliff
R BA. 26 April 1890
N The Cliff is now divided into two houses with Voysey's very substantial wing comprising the main part of one.

5 DEUDRAETH CASTLE
Penrhndeudraeth,

N. Wales.
Alterations and additions
D 1891
CL O. Williams.

6 7 HILL ROAD
St John's Wood, London. Studio
D 1892
CL Reynolds Stephens
N This is a very simple separate brick building at the rear of the house. Now radically altered.

7 CHAPEL TO ALMS HOUSE
Howard Hospital, Castle Rising, nr Lynn, Norfolk.
Decorations, new glazing, altar and reredos
D 1893
AD 1895 cross and candle-sticks for chapel
DR Design for cross and reredos, RIBA [25].
N Voysey's office expenses state that work began at the Castle Rising Chapel in 1893. In 1897, he listed a cost of £1. 9. 6. against '2 Candlesticks, Gilded' and in 1898, he listed expenses for the carving and gilding of angels. There is a drawing at the V&A for an embroidered decoration for the chapel [E. 5185, 1919, V. I].

8 54 CIRCUS ROAD
St John's Wood, London. Veranda
D 1894
CL M. R. Corbet
DR No drawings located.

9 10 & 12 MARLBOROUGH HILL
St John's Wood, London.
Additions and general repairs
D 1894
CL Arthur Lucas
DR No drawings located
N Demolished.

10 33 ADDINGTON SQ.
Additions, alterations, repairs and decorations
D 1894
AD 1895 Altar and cross, decoration of rooms and staircase
CL Trinity College, Cambridge. Mission, chuch house
DR No drawings located.

11 10 HILL ROAD
St John's Wood, London.
Repairs and alterations
D 1894
CL W. Reynolds Stephens
DR No drawings located.

12 3 COLLEGE GARDENS
Dulwich, London.

Alterations and additions
D 1894
CL J. R. Adams
DR No drawings located
N Building now demolished.

13 25 WILTON PLACE
Knightsbridge, London.
Alterations and additions
D 1894
CL R. J. Fennessy
DR No drawings located.

14 THE KNIGHTS OF ST JOHN TAVERN
7 Queen's Terrace, St John's Wood, London.
Decorations, alterations and repairs
D 1894
CL St John's Wood Arts Club
DR No drawings located.

15 83 LAVENDER HILL
Battersea, London.
Alterations and additions for Essex & Co.'s paper-hangings showrooms
D 1895
CL R. W. Essex
DR No drawings located
N Essex & Co. moved to 83 Lavender Hill in 1896, and Voysey probably converted the building for their use. According to *The Studio* of 1893 (p. 37) he had already designed a metal grille and possibly other decorations for an earlier showroom for Essex & Co.; Voysey's black book lists a 'Front elevation of Essex Mills, Lavender Hill' in 1896.

16 62 ACACIA ROAD
St John's Wood, London.
Gallery for studio
D 1895
CL Edward Onslow Ford, A.R.A.
DR No drawings located.

17 OCKHAM PARK
Surrey.
Alterations and additions to old house and estate
D 1895
AD Further additions include: gates, stable wall, staircase, pump, shed and arcade etc., 1901; additions and rebuilding of tower and alterations and additions to Chancellors Room, 1903; and new bathrooms and sanitary arrangements, 1932
CL The Earl of Lovelace, and after 1907 the Dowager Countess of Lovelace

DR RIBA [112]
N Voysey designed a new house for the Earl of Lovelace in 1895, but this was not built. His alterations and additions to the old house were destroyed in a fire of 1948.

18 WOODCOTE LODGE
West Horsley, Leatherhead, Surrey.
Addition
D 1897
AD New drawing room, hall and entrance, 1899
CL Sir Henry Roscoe
DR No drawings located
N Voysey's office expenses show frequent visits to Woodcote Lodge between January 1897 and January 1901.

19 REDE COURT
Nr Rochester, Kent.
Decoration of drawing room
D 1897
AD Furniture for Rede Court 1898 and pigeon-cote for Rede Court, undated
CL W. H. Tingey
DR RIBA [120] (pigeon-cote only).

20 12 CHATSWORTH ROAD
Brondesbury. Veranda
D 1897
CL P. Heffer
DR No drawings located
N Voysey's office expenses show that a specification was typed for this veranda in July 1897. No other documentation located.

21 SHERE
(Exact location unknown.)
Alterations and additions to house
D 1897
CL Somerset Beaumont
DR No drawings located, although Voysey's office expenses show that a specification was typed and site visits were made.

22 32 QUEEN'S GROVE
St John's Wood, London.
Two new studios
D 1897
CL George Frampton, A.R.A
DR No drawings located
N These very substantial and functional brick buildings still stand. The first extends the house at first-floor level with a wide access opening beneath.

23 OAKHURST
Oxted, Surrey.
Alterations and additions to house
D 1898
CL C. C. Macrae
DR No drawings located, although Voysey's office expenses show that a specification was typed and frequent site visits were made beween February 1898 and March 1899.

24 23 QUEENSBOROUGH TERRACE
Bayswater, Westminster, London.
Decorations and furniture
D 1898
CL W. Ward Higgs
DR RIBA [86]
R *The Furnisher*, I, 1899, pp. 108–11.

25 15 ABBEY ROAD
St John's Wood, London.
Repairs and new studio
D 1898
CL Herbert Draper
DR No drawings located.

26 78 FINCHLEY ROAD
London.
Alterations and additions
D 1898
CL C. F. M. Cleverley
DR No drawings located
N Demolished.

27 77 HARLEY STREET
London.
Alterations and additions
D 1898
CL William Johnson Walsham (surgeon).
DR No drawings located and Voysey's office expenses are limited to a payment to Gaye for measuring and a single site visit, so that the additions may not have been executed.

28 16 CHALCOT GARDENS
Englands Lane, London.
Additions
D 1898
CL Adolphus Whalley
DR No drawings located
N Very interesting substantial wing in stock brick with stone dressings, and gable fronting on to the street. Some interior fittings and fireplaces survive. It was the home of Arthur Rackham, a friend of Voysey.

29 SIMONSTONE HOUSE
Blackburn, Lancs.
Additions, alterations, repairs and decorations.

D 1899
CL A. Heyworth
DR No drawings located.

30 BURY HILL PARK
Oldbury, Birmingham. Pavilion
D 1899
CL J. W. Wilson
DR No drawings located
R Photograph of 'Keeper's Lodge, Entrance to Bury Hill Farm' in RIBA Photographs Collection.

31 DOLLIS BRAE
Totteridge, Barnet, London.
Alterations and additions
D 1899
AD New veranda, drawing-room window and garden entrance, 1902–3
CL C. Stewart King
DR Drawing for veranda seat for Dollis Brae, RIBA [328]
N Voysey designed new chimney-pieces for this house in 1897.

32 61 HAMILTON TERRACE
St John's Wood, London.
New studio buildings
D 1899
CL George Simonds, sculptor
DR No drawings located
N George Simonds was first master of the Art Workers' Guild. The main house has a small side extension, evidently designed by Voysey. The separate studio building is now converted to a house at 15 Hall Road.

33 73 FITZJOHN'S AVENUE
Hampstead, London.
Additions, alterations and repairs
D 1900
AD New bay, 1901; new drawing-room window, 1902; new veranda, 1903; and decorations and furniture, 1909
CL P. A. Barendt
DR RIBA [72] for the veranda and also furniture designs 1902–3
N Voysey's additions to the front of the house are clearly visible from the road.

34 MADRESFIELD COURT
nr Malvern Link, Worcestershire.
Two semi-detached cottages
D 1901
CL Earl Beauchamp
DR Unexecuted design; RIBA [100]

BIBLIOGRAPHY

'The Practice of art to-day in our own country', *Hampshire Chronicle*, CXX (1892), no. 6449, p. 3.

'Domestic furniture', *RIBA Journal*, I (1894), pp. 415–18.

'The Aims and conditions of the modern decorator', *Journal of Decorative Art*, XV (1895), pp.82–90.

'The Orchard, Chorleywood, Herts', *Architectural Review*, X (1901), pp. 32–8.

Contribution to 'Liverpool cathedral: a protest and petition', *Architectural Review*, X (1901), p. 172.

'Remarks on domestic entrance halls', *The Studio*, XXI (1901), pp. 242–6.

Contribution to 'L'Art Nouveau: what it is and what is thought of it – a symposium', *Magazine of Art*, II (1904), pp. 211–2.

'On Craftsmanship', *Architectural Association Notes*, XIX (1904), pp. 71–3.

'London street architecture and its possibilities', *Architectural Association Notes*, XX (1904), pp. 1–2.

Reason as a Basis of Art, Elkin Mathews, London, 1906.

'Ideas in things', *The Arts Connected with Building* ed. T. Raffles Davison, London, Batsford, 1909, pp. 101–37.

'Ideas in things', *British Architect*, LXXI (1909), pp. 150–1 & 158–62.

'Castles in the air', *British Architect*, LXXIII (1910), pp. 148–61.

'Copying and its relation to art', *British Architect*, LXXIII (1910), pp. 169–70.

'The English home', *British Architect*, LXXV (1911), pp. 60 & 69–70.

'Patriotism in architecture', *Architectural Association Journal*, XXVIII (1912), pp. 21–5.

'The Quality of fitness in architecture', *The Craftsman*, XXIII (1912), pp. 174–82.

'Open letter to the RIBA', *British Architect*, LXXVIII (1912), pp. 368–9.

Individuality, London, Chapman & Hall, 1915.

'Modern Symbolism', *Architect & Contract Reporter*, XCIX (1918), pp. 102–3.

'Carpenters' Hall lectures: modern symbolism', *The Builder*, CXIV (1918), pp. 156–7.

'On town planning', *Architectural Review*, XLVI (1919), pp. 25–6.

'Self expression in art', letter to *RIBA Journal*, XXX (1923), p. 211.

Tradition and Individuality in Art, unpublished typescript in RIBA Drawings Collection, 1923.

'Some fundamental ideas in relation to art', *RIBA Journal*, XXXI (1924), pp. 303–4.

'Review of AA students' work at Devonshire House', *Architectural Association Journal*, XL (1924), pp. 49–50.

Report of speech given at 'Dinner to C.F. Annesley Voysey', *RIBA Journal*, XXXV (1927), pp. 52–3.

'The Arts and Crafts Exhibition of 1928', *RIBA Journal*, vol. XXXVI (1928), p. 113.

'Modern Symbolism', *The Builder*, CXXXVI (1929), p. 634.

Symbolism in Design, unpublished manuscript in RIBA Drawings Collection, 1930.

'English church art', review of English Medieval Art Exhibition at the V&A and of Modern Church Art at Caxton Hall, *RIBA Journal*, XXXVII (1930), p. 644.

The Value of Hidden Influences as Disclosed in the Life of One Ordinary Man, unpublished manuscript, copy in RIBA Drawings Collection, 1931.

'1874 and after', *Architectural Review*, LXX (1931), pp. 91–2.

Review of Graily Hewitt, 'Lettering', *RIBA Journal* XXXVIII, 1931, p. 682.

Review of 'The Art of lettering and its use in diverse crafts and trades', *RIBA Journal*, XXXVIII (1931), pp. 732–3.

Introduction to a catalogue of an exhibition of the work of C. F. A. Voysey at the Batsford Gallery, 1931.

'Unfamiliar uses for stained glass', *Apollo*, XVII (1933), pp. 153–4.

Letter, *The Architect's Journal*, LXXXI (1935), p. 408.

'Architecture and archaeology', *RIBA Journal*, XLVI (1936), p. 34.

Aymer Vallance, 'The Furnishing and decoration of the house. Part 2: walls, windows and stairs', *Art Journal*, LIV (1892), pp. 306–11.

Anon., 'An Interview with Mr. Charles F. Annesley Voysey, architect and designer', *Studio*, I, pp. 231–7.

Henri Van de Velde, 'Artistic wallpapers', *Emulation*, XVIII, Brussels 1893, pp. 150–1.

Henri Van de Velde, 'Essex and Co's Westminster wallpapers', *L'Art Moderne*, Brussels, XIV (1894), pp. 253–4.

Anon., 'Art in decoration and design', *The Builder*, LXVIII, 1895, p. 151.

E. B. S., 'Some recent designs by Mr. C.F.A. Voysey', *The Studio*, VII (1896), pp. 209–18.

Anon., 'The Arts and Crafts Exhibition, 1896', *The Studio*, IX (1896), pp. 190–6.

Anon., 'Men who build: No.45: Mr Charles F. Annesley Voysey', *The Builder's Journal & Architectural Record*, IV (1896), pp. 67–70.

Reverend Charles Voysey, *Theism, the Religion of Common Sense*, London, 1896.

F. E. von Bodenhausen, 'Englische Kunst im Hause', *Pan*, II (1896–7), Berlin, pp. 329–36.

'G', 'The Revival of English domestic architecture: the work of Mr. C.F.A. Voysey', *The Studio*, XI (1897), pp. 16–25.

Thiebault Sisson, 'L'art decoratif en Angleterre: "Arts and Crafts"', *Art et Decoration*, I (1897), Paris, pp. 19–22.

Lewis F. Day, 'Art in advertising', *Art Journal*, LIX (1897), pp. 49–53.

Anon., 'C.F.A. Voysey', *Dekorative Kunst*, I (1897), Munich, pp. 241–80.

E. B. S., 'Country Cottages', *Country Life*, III (1898), pp. 195–7.

Anon., 'Academy architecture', *The Builder's Journal & Architectural Record*, VII (1898), pp. 414–6.

Anon., 'The Work of Mr. C.F.A. Voysey', *House*, IV (1899), pp. 161–5.

Anon., 'A House for a man with a hobby', *House Beautiful*, VII (1899), pp. 24–7.

Anon., 'Architecture at the Royal Academy', *British Architect*, LI (1899), p. 306.

Horace Townsend, 'Notes on country and suburban houses designed by C.F.A. Voysey', *The Studio*, XVI (1899), p. 157–64.

Aymer Vallance, 'British decorative art in 1899 and the Arts and Crafts Exhibition', *The Studio*, XVIII (1899), pp. 38–49 & 185.

E. F. V., 'Recent industrial art', *Art Journal*, LXI (1899), pp. 90–2.

Anon., 'Houses for people with hobbies: "The Orchard", Chorley Wood', *Country Life*, VI (1899), pp. 389–90.

Anon., 'Houses for people with hobbies: "Walnut Tree Farm", Castlemorton', *Country Life*, VI (1899), pp. 524–6.

James L. Caw, 'The Mortons of Darvel', *Art Journal*, LXII (1900), pp. 7–11 & 78–82.

M. P. Verneuil, 'Le Paierpeint a l'exposition', *Art et Decoration*, VIII (1900), pp. 83–90.

Charles Holme, 'Modern British domestic architecture and decoration', *The Studio*, 1901, pp. 181–94.

T. Raffles Davison, 'The Recent advances in architecture – country houses', *Magazine of Art*, n.s. I, 1903, pp. 477–82.

Edward W. Gregory, 'The Seventh exhibition of arts and crafts in London', *House & Garden*, New York, III (1903), pp. 208–213.

M.B., 'Some recent work of C.F.A. Voysey, an English architect', *House & Garden*, III (1903), New York, pp. 255–60.

Anon., 'The Arts and crafts exhibition at the New Gallery', *The Studio*, XXVIII (1903), pp. 28 & 179.

Anon., 'Hauser von C.F.A. Voysey', *Der Baumeister*, 1903, Berlin, pp. 61–4.

Maurice B. Adams, *Modern Cottage Architecture*, London, Batsford, 1904, pp. 7–8.

W. Shaw Sparrow, *The British Home of Today*, London, Hodder & Stoughton, 1904, after pp. 54, 55 & 64.

Aymer Vallance, 'Some recent work by Mr. C.F.A. Voysey', *The Studio*, XXXI (1904), pp. 127–34.

Warren H. Langford, 'Recent domestic architecture in England', *Architectural Review*, (Boston), XI (1904), pp. 5–12 & 196.

Hermann Muthesius, *Das englische Haus*, 3 vols., Berlin, Ernst Wasmuth, 1904–5.

Walter Crane, *Ideals in Art*, London, George Bell & Sons, 1905, pp. 146–7.

Hermann Muthesius, *Das moderne Landhaus*, Munich, Bruckmann, 1905, pp. 145–9 & 190–1.

Anon., 'Some recent designs for domestic architecture', *The Studio*, XXXIV (1905), pp. 151–2.

Henry F. Ganz, 'Houses, Cenegie Library and Museum, textile designs', *Moderne Bauformen*, Stuttgart, IV (1905), pp. 95–102 & 106.

J. Taylor, 'C.F.A. Voysey', *Upholstery Dealer & Decorative Furnisher*, VII (1905), New York, pp. 19–26.

J. H. Elder-Duncan, *Country cottages and weekend homes*, London, Cassell & Co., 1906, pp. 96–7 & 186–7.

W. Shaw Sparrow, *The Modern home*, London, Hodder & Stoughton, 1906, pp. 54–5 & after p. 64.

A. B. Daryll, 'The Architecture of Charles Francis Annesley Voysey', *Magazine of Fine Arts*, II (1906), pp. 191–6.

P. G. Konody, 'C.F.A. Voyseys neuere arbeiten', *Dekorative Kunst*, XIV (1906), pp. 193–8.

Hermann Muthesius, *Landhaus und Garten*, Munich, Bruckmann, 1907, pp. 156–7.

Anon., 'The Orchard, a house', *Ideal House*, January 1907, pp. 3–11.

Mervyn E. Macartney, 'Recent English domestic architecture', *Architectural Review*, London, 1908, pp. 171–3.

T. Raffles Davison, *Modern Homes*, London, George Bell & Sons, 1909, pp. 20–1 & 119–23.

W. Shaw Sparrow, *Our Homes and How to Make the Best of Them*, London, Hodder & Stoughton, 1909, pp. 100, 199, & 238.

Hugh Stokes, 'Ideals in art', *Art Chronicle*, I (1909), pp. 37–8.

H. W. Frahne, 'Recent English doemstic architecture', *Architectural Record*, XXV (1909), New York, pp. 259–70.

Lawrence Weaver, 'Small country houses of today', I, *Country Life*, London 1910, pp. 139–44.

Paul Klopfer, 'Voyseys Architektur-Idyllen', *Moderne Bauformen*, IX (1910), Stuttgart, pp. 141–8.

Mervyn E. Macartney, 'Recent English domestic architecture', *Architectural Review*, London, 1911, pp. 167–72.

Anon., 'Special Furniture', *Craftsman*, New York, XX (1911), pp. 476–86.

C. H. Boer, 'C.F.A. Voyseys Raumkunst', *Moderne Bauformen*, Stuttgart, X (1911), pp. 247–56.

Lawrence Weaver, 'The House and its equipment', *Country Life*, 1912, pp. 18, 20, 35 & 38.

Anon., 'Interiors of small houses', *Illustrated Carpenter & Builder*, 5 January 1912, pp. 12–26.

The Craftsman, XXIII (1912), New York, pp. 174–82.

Halsey Ricardo, review of C.F.A. Voysey's *Individuality*, *RIBA Journal*, XXII (1915), p. 336.

T. Adams, 'The True meaning of town planning, a reply to Mr. C.F.A. Voysey', *Architectural Review* XLVI (1919), pp. 75–7.

L.P. Butterfield, *Floral Forms in Historic Design*, London, Batsford, 1922, pls.10 (3, 9), 11 (2, 9, 10), 17.

Alan Sugden & John Edmondson, *A History of English Wallpaper 1509–1914*, London, Batsford, 1926, pp. 175–7, pls. 145–8.

T. H. Mawson, *Life and Work of an English Landscape Architect: an Autobiography*, 1927, pp. 39–42.

R. Randal Phillips, 'The Modern English home', *Country Life*, 1927, p. 170.

Anon., 'C.F.A. Voysey: the man and his work', *The Architect & Building News*, CXVII (1927), pp. 133–4, 219–21, 273–5, 314–6 and 404–6.

John Betjeman, 'Charles Francis Annesley Voysey, the architect of individualism', *Architectural Review*, LXX, 1931, pp. 93–6.

John Betjeman, 'The Death of modernism', *Architectural Review*, LXX (1931), p. 161.

H. M. Fletcher, 'The Work of C.F.A. Voysey', *RIBA Journal*, XXXVIII (1931), pp. 763–4.

H. Furst, 'Exhibition of the work of C.F.A. Voysey at the Batsford Gallery', *Apollo*, XIV (1931), p. 245.

John Betjeman, *Ghastly Good Taste*, London, Chapman & Hall, 1933, p. 104.

M. & C. H. B. Quennell, *A History of Everyday Things in England*, London, IV, Batsford, 1934, pp. 106–7.

P. Morton Shand, 'Scenario for a human drama: VII: looping the loop', *Architectural Review*, LXXVII (1935), pp. 99–104.

Nikolaus Pevsner, *Pioneers of the Modern Movement*, London, Faber & Faber, 1936, pp. 141–54.

Henry-Russell Hitchcock, 'Late Victorian architecture 1851–1900', *RIBA Journal*, XLIV (1937), pp. 1029–39.

Nikolaus Pevsner, 'An Appreciation', *Architectural Review*, LXXXII (1937), p. 36.

Nikolaus Pevsner, '1860–1930', *Architectural Record*, LXXXI (1937), New York, pp. 2–3.

Anon., 'C.F.A. Voysey's eightieth birthday', *Deutsche Tapeten-Zeitung*, 1 June 1937.

Art & Industry, XXII (1937), p. 31.

Anon., 'C.F.A. Voysey', *Royal Society of Arts Journal*, LXXXVI (1938), p. 344.

Nikolaus Pevsner, 'A. Mackmurdo', *Architectural Review*, LXXXIII (1938).

Editor, 'Royal Gold Medallist', *RIBA Journal*, XLVII (1940), p. 97.

Anon., 'C.F.A. Voysey', *Architect & Building News*, CLXI (1940), pp. 196–7.

John Betjeman, 'C.F.A. Voysey', *The Architects' Journal*, XCI, 1940, pp. 234–5.

Editor, 'The Royal Gold Medal award to Mr. C.F.A. Voysey', *The Builder*, CLIX (1940), p. 237.

John Summerson, 'Mr. Voysey: veteran Gold Medallist', *The Listener*, XXIII (1940), pp. 479–80.

John Betjeman, 'C.F.A. Voysey', *Architectural Forum*, LXXII (1940), New York, pp. 348–9.

J. M. Richards, *An Introduction to Modern Architecture*, Harmondsworth, 1940.

J. M. Richards, *Architectural Review*, LXXXIX (1941), pp. 59–60.

Nikolaus Pevsner, 'Charles F. Annesley Voysey, 1857–1941', *Architectural Review*, LXXXIX (1941), pp. 112–3.

Howard Robertson & Noel D. Sheffield, *RIBA Journal*, XLVIII, 1941, p. 88.

Anon., *The Architects' Journal*, XCIII (1941), pp. 124, 126.

Robert Donat, 'Uncle Charles ...', *The Architect's Journal*, XCIII (1941), pp. 193–4.

John Betjeman, 'C.F.A. Voysey', *The Architect's Journal*, XCIII (1941), pp. 257–8.

Anon., 'Two great domestic architects, Norman Shaw and C.F.A. Voysey', *The Builder*, CLX (1941), p. 355.

Kay Fisker, 'Tre pioneer fra aarhundredskiftet: C.F.A. Voysey, M.H. Baillie Scott, H. Tessenow', *Byggmasteren*, XXVI (1947), pp. 221–32.

John Cloag, *The English Tradition in Design*, London, 1947.

John Brandon-Jones, 'An Architect's letters to his client', *Architect & Building News*, CXCV (1949), pp. 494–8.

Martin S. Briggs, 'Voysey and Blomfield, a study in contrast', *The Builder*, CLXXVI (1949), pp. 39–42.

Thomas Howarth, *Charles Rennie Mackintosh and the Modern Movement*, London, Routledge & Kegan Paul, 1952, pp. 236–51.

Frank D. Salisbury, *Sarum Chase*, London, John Murray, 1953, pp. 119–20.

Guy Aldred, *No Traitor's Gait!*, Glasgow, Strickland Press, 1955.

John Brandon-Jones, *C.F.A. Voysey: A Memoir*, London, Architectural Association, 1957.

John Brandon-Jones, 'C.F.A. Voysey', *Architectural Association Journal*, XXVIII (1957), pp. 239–62.

Henry-Russell Hitchcock, *Architecture: Nineteenth and Twentieth Centuries*, Harmondsworth, Penguin, 1957, pp. 275–7.

Editor, 'Voysey centenary', *RIBA Journal*, XLIV (1957), p. 297.

Peter F. Floud, 'Voysey wallpaper', *Penrose Annual*, LII (1958), pp. 10–14.

Nikolaus Pevsner, *An Outline of European Architecture*, Penguin, 7th edn. Harmondsworth, 1963, pp. 393–4.

John Summerson, 'Some British contemporaries of Frank Lloyd Wright' in *Studies in Western Art: Problems of the Nineteenth and Twentieth Centuries*, ed. Rudolf Wittkower, Princeton, 1963, pp. 78–87.

John Brandon-Jones, 'C.F.A. Voysey' in *Victorian Architecture*, ed. Peter Ferriday, London, Jonathan Cape, 1963, pp. 267–87.

Julius Posener, *Anfange des Funktionalismus*, Berlin, Ullstein, 1964, pp. 71–94.

Robert Schmutzler, 'C.F.A. Voysey' in *Art Nouveau*, London, Thames & Hudson, 1964, pp. 186–9.

Margaret Richardson, 'Wallpapers by C.F.A. Voysey', *RIBA Journal*, LXXII (1965), pp. 399–403.

Julius Posener, 'Il funzionalismo comincia in Inglhilaterra', *Edilizia Moderna*, no. 80 (1965), pp. 54–64.

Judith Bock, *The Wallpaper designs of C.F.A. Voysey*, New York University MA thesis, 1966.

S. Tschudi Madsen, *Art Nouveau*, London, Wiedenfeld & Nicolson, 1967, pp. 101–2.

Nikolaus Pevsner, *Studies in Art, Architecture and Design*, II, London, Thames & Hudson, 1968, pp. 186–9.

Robert Macleod, 'Charles Rennie Mackintosh', *Country Life*, 1968.

Henry-Russell Hitchcock, 'English architecture in the early twentieth century: 1900–1939', XVIII (1968), Rome, pp. 6–9.

Elizabeth Aslin, *The Aesthetic Movement: Prelude to Art Nouveau*, London, 1969.

David Gebhard, *Charles F.A. Voysey: Architect*, catalogue of an exhibition at the University of California, Santa Barbara, University of California, 1970.

Robert Macleod, *Style and Society: Architectural Ideology in Britain 1836–1914*, RIBA, London, 1971, pp. 111–14.

J. Morton, *Three Generations of a Family Textile Firm*, 1971, pp. 96, 113–9, 177–8, 248–9 and 286–7.

David Gebhard, 'The Vernacular transformed', *RIBA Journal*, LXXIX (1971), pp. 97–102.

Mark Girouard, *The Victorian Country House*, Oxford University Press, 1971.

David Gebhard, 'C.F.A. Voysey – to and from America', *Journal of the Society of Architectural Historians* (USA), 1971, Philadelphia, pp. 304–12.

Gillian Naylor, *The Arts and Crafts Movement*, London, Trefoil Publications, 1971.

James Kornwolf, *MH Baillie Scott and the Arts and Crafts Movement*, Baltimore, 1972.

Alan Johnson, *C.F.A. Voysey: Architectural Theory and Practice*, dissertation for BA Degree, University of Manchester, 1972.

John Brandon-Jones, 'Architects and the Art Workers' Guild', *Royal Society of Arts Journal*, CXXI (1973), pp. 18–21.

Louis Hellman, 'Voysey in Wonderland', *Building Design*, no. 169, 28 September 1973, pp. 18–21.

Joanna Symonds, *CFA Voysey: Catalogue of the Drawings Collection of the Royal Institute of British Architects*, Farnborough, Hampshire, 1975.

David Gebhard, *Charles F.A. Voysey, Architect*, Los Angeles, Henessy & Ingalls, 1975.

Alistair Service, *Edwardian Architecture and its Origins*, London, 1975.

Alistair Service, *Edwardian Architecture*, London, 1977.

Mark Girouard, *Sweetness and Light: The Queen Anne Movement, 1860–1900*, Oxford University Press, 1977.

John Brandon-Jones and others, *CFA Voysey: Architect and Designer, 1857–1941*, Brighton, 1978.

Eleanor Davidson, *The Simpsons of Kendal, Craftsmen in Wood, 1885–1952*, University of Lancaster, 1978.

Duncan Simpson, *CFA Voysey: an Architect of Individuality*, London, 1979.

Peter Davey, *Arts and Crafts Architecture: The Search for Earthly Paradise*, London, Architectural Press, 1980.

Charles C. Oman and Jean Hamilton, *Wallpaper: a History and Illustrated Catalogue of the Collection at the Victoria and Albert Museum*, London, 1983.

Linda Parry, *Textiles of the Arts and Crafts Movement*, London, 1988.

Stuart Durant, *The Decorative Designs of CFA Voysey: From the Drawings Collection of The British Architectural Library, The Royal Institute of British Architects*, Cambridge, Lutterworth Press, 1990.

Jill Allibone, *George Devey*, Cambridge, Lutterworth Press, 1991.

Stuart Durant, *CFA Voysey*, London, Academy Editions, 1992.

Wendy Hitchmough, *The Homestead, CFA Voysey*, London, Phaidon Press Ltd, 1994.

INDEX

For Ken

PHAIDON PRESS LTD
Regent's Wharf
All Saints Street
London N1 9PA

First published 1995

© 1995 Phaidon Press Limited

Text © Wendy Hitchmough

ISBN 0 7148 3003 8

A CIP catalogue record for this book is available from the British Library.

Library of Congress Cataloging In Publication Data available.

Printed in Hong Kong.

AUTHOR'S ACKNOWLEDGEMENTS

'To feel the charm of one of Mr. Voysey's houses you must visit the actual building, and you will always find it better than you had hoped.' So wrote Baillie Scott in 1907, and I must begin by thanking all the owners and inhabitants of Voysey houses who so generously let me into their homes and shared their knowledge and enthusiasm with me. I must emphasize too, in fairness to them, that none of Voysey's houses is open to the general public and so anybody hoping to 'visit the actual building' should write a letter first.

Many individuals and organizations have given me practical help, advice and encouragement during the research and writing of this book. Although I cannot name them all here, I am immensely grateful to the librarians, archivists, collectors and other individuals with a specialist or personal understanding of Voysey, who have given me their time and the benefit of their expertise. Special thanks are due to Frances Kelly for her kindness and professional rigour; to Lady Slack for good advice, when it was needed most, and for her tireless help and hospitality; to Helen Watson whose incisive criticisms and suggestions brought discipline as well as clarity to the writing (I hope); and to Joanna Heseltine (née Symonds) whose catalogue of the RIBA's collection of Voysey drawings has been invaluable for its precision and painstaking attention to detail.

I am especially grateful to John Brandon-Jones for his generosity in sharing so much of his personal and professional knowledge of Voysey and his contemporaries with me; and for allowing us to photograph from his collection. His reading of the manuscript, and our meetings and discussions, have meant a great deal to me and they have often caused me to look at my own research in a new light. Peter Davey and Trevor Garnham brought a magnanimity to their reading of the manuscript, which I had no right to expect; their criticisms and recommendations for improvements were given with such enthusiasm and kindness, that the very necessary revisions became a stimulating new challenge rather than the onerous task that they might under less encouraging guidance have become. I must thank, too, my editors David Jenkins and Helen Castle for their steadfast care and attention to detail, and Mark Vernon-Jones who designed the book. I have been extremely fortunate to have worked with Martin Charles. His photographs say things about Voysey's work that words cannot, and I have valued his friendship, his diplomacy and his wit throughout the writing of the book. I must thank Stephen Astley at the Victoria and Albert Museum, Dr Neil Bingham at the RIBA Drawings Collection and Angela Jefkins, who helped research the list of works.

Voysey was a Victorian and his private life was just that. Unlike Lutyens he did not leave a trail of correspondence, which would expose the most personal aspects of his life to historians. The letters to his brother, his grandchildren and to the clients who became his friends show him to have been open-hearted and affectionate, as well as straightforward and direct in expressing his opinions. The sources for building up a picture of Voysey's character are by necessity very varied, and I am immensely grateful to the people who knew him: to his niece Ella Hall, his grandchildren John and Elizabeth Voysey, and again to John Brandon-Jones, for listening to my half-formed impressions, and for their vivid recollections of Voysey's personality.

Finally, I must thank the people closest to me, who tolerated my preoccupation with Voysey for such a long time. Jane Penny, Lucy Crook and my parents were constantly supportive, but most of all I must thank Ken Baker and my children Grey and Matthew.

PICTURE ACKNOWLEDGEMENTS

The publishers wish to thank all individuals, photographers and institutions who have kindly supplied illustrations for this book.

The pictures are numbered according to page and their positions are abbreviated as l = left, r = right, c = centre, b = bottom.

All the photographs in this book are © Martin Charles with the exception of the following: The British Architectural Library / RIBA Drawings Collection, London: 21 (b), 23, 24, 28, 31, 34 (t), 39 (t, b), 50, 51, 55, 60, 70 (t), 82, 83 (t), 86, 90 (t), 95 (t), 118 (t), 119 (t), 131 (l), 140, 172 (r), 180, 182 (t), 184, 192 (tl), 203 (t), 207 (t, b), 211; Christie's Images, London: 144 (t); © Country Life Picture Library: 155 (t), 157, 159; kind permission of the Governors of Dulwich College: 16; © Wendy Hitchmough: 10 (t, b); Ian Jones: 129 (t, b); courtesy of the National Portrait Gallery, London: 3; courtesy of the RCHME © Crown copyright: 123; courtesy of the Board of Trustees of the Victoria & Albert Museum: 4, 21 (t), 142, 144 (bl), 145, 200; Victoria & Albert Museum, London / Bridgeman Art Library, London: 14, 18, 19.

The below are by kind courtesy of a private collection: 2, 8, 11 (t, b), 12, 52, 53, 54, 56 (t, b), 57 (t, b), 58, 61 (cr, br), 62 (t), 63 (t, c, b), 73 (b), 115, 181, 183, 190, 191, 206, 210 (t, b), 220, 221, 220, 221, 222, 223 (t, b); as are the following: 27, 33, 34 (b), 36 (t, b), 37 (t, b), 38 (t, b), 41, 42, 43 (t, b), 47 (b), 59 (l, r), 61 (tl, tr), 62 (b), 65, 67 (t), 69, 73 (t), 74, 81 (t, b), 83 (b), 87, 92, 93, 95 (b), 116, 117 (b), 119 (b), 120, 125, 128 (l, r), 146 (t, b), 147, 149 (t, b), 150 (c, b), 151 (t), 171 (t, b), 172 (l), 174, 175, 176 (t, b), 177 (b), 178, 179 (t, c, b), 182 (b), 185, 192 (tr), 194 (l, r), 195 (l, r), 197 (t, b), 198, 201, 202 (l, r), 203 (b), 204, 205 (t, b), 208, 209, 217, 218 (t, cr, b).

The photographs on pages 126 and 158 are reproduced with the kind permission of Mr and Mrs Warner; and the pictures on pages 70 (b), 71 and 72 were photographed with the kind permission of John De Carle.